WHAT IT'S WORTH

STRENGTHENING THE FINANCIAL FUTURE OF FAMILIES, COMMUNITIES AND THE NATION

Federal Reserve Bank of San Francisco & Corporation for Enterprise Development

FEDERAL RESERVE BANK OF SAN FRANCISCO
101 Market Street
San Francisco, CA 94105

CFED
1200 G Street NW, Suite 400
Washington, DC 20005

Editors
Laura Choi
David Erickson
Kate Griffin
Andrea Levere
Ellen Seidman

ISBN 978-0-692-53170-9

Library of Congress Control Number: 2015951667

Printed in the United States of America

This book is dedicated to **Robert Friedman** whose unwavering belief in the capacity of every person to create his or her economic future — if given access to the necessary tools and resources — has inspired the growth of a field dedicated to expanding economic security and opportunity.

TABLE OF CONTENTS

2 WHY FINANCIAL WELL-BEING MATTERS FOR ALL

The Economy, the Financial Services System and Community

Employment and Business

Education

ACKNOWLEDGEMENTS

What It's Worth is a joint project of the Corporation for Enterprise Development (CFED) and the Federal Reserve Bank of San Francisco. This book would not have been possible without the support of the Citi Foundation, which provided CFED not only with the funding necessary to work on this ambitious endeavor, but also thoughtful engagement on the content and how to leverage it for lasting impact in our collective work.

We would like to thank our authors, each of whom brings a unique perspective to these topics that broadens our understanding of what financial health and well-being means for our nation. The members of our advisory committee—a diverse set of experts with varied views on the subjects we address—deserve special recognition for their guidance. Their early thoughts fundamentally shaped the direction we took with the book, encouraging us to capture both the systems at work and the lives impacted. Special thanks go to Ray Boshara of the Federal Reserve Bank of St. Louis and Jennifer Tescher of the Center for Financial Services Innovation for their leadership and editorial partnership as co-chairs of the advisory committee.

Barbara Ray and her team at HiredPen, Inc. provided first-rate copy-editing and thoughtful nudges to make sure we didn't get lost in our own jargon. Maya Kopytman and Melinda Sekela at C&G Partners, LLC designed a distinctive look for the book that perfectly captures our intent to build bridges across society to address financial health and well-being. Burness was invaluable in helping us to position the book for a wider audience and provide ways for readers to engage deeply with the ideas presented here.

Many others worked hard to bring this book to fruition and helped inform this collection with thoughtful insights: Jennifer Brooks, Jeremie Greer, Leigh Tivol, Doug Ryan, Carl Rist, Ezra Levin, Harold Pettigrew, Kristin Lawton, Sean Luechtefeld, and Merrit Gillard at CFED; and Scott

Turner, Naomi Cytron, and Ian Galloway at the Federal Reserve Bank of San Francisco. Daria Sheehan, Brandee McHale, and Kristen Scheyder at the Citi Foundation were with us from the start, shaping the ideas for what this book can and should be.

We are also grateful to the board of CFED and to John Williams and Adrian Rodriguez of the Federal Reserve Bank of San Francisco for their ongoing engagement and support as we conceived of this book and brought it to life.

This book builds on two earlier volumes: *Investing in What Works for America's Communities*, and *What Counts: Harnessing Data for America's Communities*. Each are part of an important national conversation on addressing poverty and identifying solutions to intractable issues. We are grateful to the Low Income Investment Fund and the Urban Institute for their leadership in these earlier volumes and partnership in moving this work forward.

Thanks, finally, to our readers for engaging in this conversation. We look forward to building these bridges together.

Editors
Laura Choi
David Erickson
Kate Griffin
Andrea Levere
Ellen Seidman

Advisory Committee

Ray Boshara, Co-Chair
Senior Advisor and Director of the Center for Household Financial Stability
Federal Reserve Bank of St. Louis

Jennifer Tescher, Co-Chair
President and CEO
Center for Financial Services Innovation

Nancy Andrews
President and CEO
Low Income Investment Fund

Kerry Anne McGeary
Senior Program Officer
Robert Wood Johnson Foundation

Camille Bussette
Lead Financial Sector Specialist
Consultative Group to Assist the Poor

J. Michael Collins
Associate Professor of Public Affairs and Human Ecology
University of Wisconsin–Madison

Reid Cramer
Director, Asset Building Program
New America

Erin Currier
Director, Financial Security and Mobility
The Pew Charitable Trusts

Xavier de Souza Briggs
Vice President for Economic Opportunity and Markets
Ford Foundation

Lisa Forti
Policy Director
Alameda County Social Services Agency

Jonathan Mintz
President and CEO
Cities for Financial Empowerment Fund

Luis Pastor
President and CEO
Latino Community Credit Union

José Quiñonez
CEO
Mission Asset Fund

Ida Rademacher
Executive Director, Financial Security Program
The Aspen Institute

Janneke Ratcliffe
Assistant Director for Financial Education
Consumer Financial Protection Bureau

Cy Richardson
Senior Vice President, Economics and Housing
National Urban League

Jonathan Zinman
Professor of Economics
Dartmouth College

FOREWORD

Janet Yellen[1]

Board of Governors of the Federal Reserve System

The financial crisis and the Great Recession demonstrated, in a dramatic and unmistakable manner, how extraordinarily vulnerable are the large share of American families with very few assets to fall back on. We have come far from the worst moments of the crisis, and the economy continues to improve. But the effects of the recession are still being felt by many families, particularly those that had very little in savings and other assets beforehand.

To help make this point, I'd like to cite a few numbers from the Federal Reserve's 2013 Survey of Consumer Finances. The Survey is conducted every three years and this new edition provides one of the first good looks at how families in different economic circumstances have fared in the recovery.

For lower-income families, what we find is sobering. The median net worth reported by the bottom fifth of households by income was only $6,400 in 2013. Among this group, representing about 25 million American households, many families had no wealth or had negative net worth. The next fifth of households by income had median net worth of just $27,900. These numbers represent declines from 2010. One reason is that income has continued to fall for these families.

Another likely reason for this decline in net worth is the lingering effects of the housing crisis. Home equity accounts for the lion's share of wealth for most families and many of these families have not yet recovered the wealth they lost in the housing crisis. The housing market is improving and housing will remain an important channel for asset building for lower and middle income families. But one of the lessons of the crisis is

1 This foreword is based on a speech on asset development given by Chair Janet L. Yellen at the "Assets Learning Conference" of the Corporation for Enterprise Development on September 18, 2014.

the importance of diversification and especially of possessing savings and other liquid financial assets to fall back in times of economic distress.

Yet for lower- and middle-income families, financial assets, including 401(k) plans and pensions, are still a very small share of their assets. According to the 2013 survey, the bottom half of families by income held only 8 percent of all financial assets held by households.

A larger lesson from the financial crisis, of course, is how important it is to promote asset-building, including saving for a rainy day, as protection from the ups and downs of the economy. I surely hope that our nation will not face another crisis anytime soon as severe as the one we recently experienced. But for many lower-income families without assets, the definition of a financial crisis is a month or two without a paycheck, or the advent of a sudden illness or some other unexpected expense. Families with assets to draw on are able to deal with these developments as bumps in the road. Families without these assets can end up, very suddenly, off the road. According to the Board's recent Survey of Household Economics and Decisionmaking, an unexpected expense of just $400 would prompt the majority of households to borrow money, sell something, or simply not pay at all.

The Federal Reserve's mission is to promote a healthy economy and strong financial system, and that is why we have promoted and will continue to promote asset-building. One way we do this is through the Community Development programs at each of our 12 Reserve Banks, and through the Federal Reserve Board's Division of Consumer and Community Affairs in Washington. As a research institution, and a convener of stakeholders involved in community development, I believe the Fed can help promote the ideas contained in this book, to encourage families to take the small steps that over time can lead to the accumulation of considerable assets.

■ ■ ■

JANET L. YELLEN *took office as Chair of the Board of Governors of the Federal Reserve System on February 3, 2014, for a four-year term ending February 3, 2018. Dr. Yellen also serves as Chairman of the Federal Open Market Committee, the System's principal monetary policymaking body. Prior to her appointment as Chair, Dr. Yellen served as Vice Chair of the Board of Governors, taking office in October 2010, when she simultaneously* *began a 14-year term as a member of the Board that will expire January 31, 2024. Dr. Yellen is Professor Emeritus at the University of California at Berkeley where she was the Eugene E. and Catherine M. Trefethen Professor of Business and Professor of Economics and has been a faculty member since 1980. Dr. Yellen took leave from Berkeley for five years starting August 1994. She served as a member of the Board of Governors of the Federal Reserve System through February 1997, and then left the Federal Reserve to become chair of the Council of Economic Advisers through August 1999. She also chaired the Economic Policy Committee of the Organization for Economic Cooperation and Development from 1997 to 1999. She also served as President and Chief Executive Officer of the Federal Reserve Bank of San Francisco from 2004 to 2010.*

INTRODUCTION

This book examines the concept of financial health and well-being from many perspectives, bringing together the voices of long-time champions of financial capability and newer voices hailing from a variety of sectors, such as public health, criminal justice, and business. What unites them is the shared recognition that we must do more to help all Americans have control over their financial lives and achieve their financial goals. As represented on the book's cover, financial health and well-being is the bridge to a strong financial future, connecting individuals and families to greater opportunity, creating more vibrant communities, and in turn, strengthening the social and economic fabric of our nation.

In the United States, we have traditionally defined financial status by income or wealth, but experts in policy and practice from a range of fields are expanding our focus to better understand what consumers actually want and need in their financial lives. A consensus is emerging that satisfaction with one's financial life has elements that are both objective (income, wealth, cash flow) and subjective (financial freedom, on track to meet financial goals). And as many of the authors in this book make clear, financial health is deeply tied to the availability of opportunity, which too often depends on factors outside an individual's control, such as race, parental socioeconomic status, and macroeconomic climate.

A NOTE ON TERMINOLOGY

In early 2015, the Consumer Financial Protection Bureau released their initial report on consumer "financial well-being." Their definition, shaped through interviews held with a cross-section of Americans, focuses on financial security and freedom of choice, in the present and the future. Around the same time, the Center for Financial Services Innovation released the findings of its national survey on consumer "financial health," defined as effective management of day-to-day finances, financial resilience and capacity to seize opportunities. In effect, both financial well-being and financial health capture the same objective and subjective elements. In this book, we use the terms financial health and financial well-being interchangeably. As with any emerging field, we do not know which nomenclature will find the greatest audience, and for which purposes. Both express what this book is about and reflect our expanded notion of what matters to households in their financial lives.

A ROADMAP FOR THE BOOK

We have organized the book into four sections and hope that the following roadmap provides useful guidance for readers seeking a place to start:

- Section 1, *Where We Are*, is comprised of three essays that set the stage, describing the current state of Americans' financial lives and efforts to improve financial health and well-being.

- Section 2, *Why Financial Well-Being Matters for All*, delves into the many ways that financial well-being influences social outcomes that matter for every American, from public health and education to economic growth and social stability. The essays are full of new information, practical experience, and ideas for changes in policy and practice.

- Section 3, *Who is Being Affected?*, examines financial health through the lens of demography, exploring issues of race and ethnicity, gender, and age. The authors discuss both the historical origins of demographic disparities and ideas for a more equitable future.

- The final section, *What To Do Next*, contains a summary piece bringing the book's themes together, as well as calls to action to philanthropy, the private sector, community and asset development and the research community, ending with a call for all of us to work together to improve the financial lives of all Americans.

As the quote by Isaac Newton on the inside cover of this book states, "We build too many walls and not enough bridges." We hope that *What It's Worth* contributes to the important national dialogue about economic opportunity and motivates readers to break down the walls of their own silos. We hope you will join us in the search for new partners, new resources, and new ideas that will enable all Americans to secure a strong financial future.

1

WHERE WE ARE

Understanding the Financial Lives of America's Households

HOW THE ROAD TO FINANCIAL SECURITY IS PAVED WITH FINANCIAL CAPABILITY

Andrea Levere and Leigh Tivol
CFED

At CFED (the Corporation for Enterprise Development), we often joke that our parents don't understand what it is we do for a living. "Expanding economic opportunity"—okay, sounds nice, but what does that *mean*?

The truth is, it's complicated. Poverty is complicated. Inequality is complicated. And if we have learned anything over the years, it's that there is no silver bullet, and we have a long way to go to find effective solutions.

And yet we believe that we are on the right track. During the past few decades, the community of people and organizations who care about these issues has grown exponentially. We have learned from experience, and we have not been afraid to try new ideas, even if they have not all worked quite as we imagined. Today, we stand together on the verge of a new era—an era of *financial capability*—that represents a more holistic, sophisticated, cross-sector, and data-driven set of approaches to help people and their families achieve lasting financial well-being. This opening chapter of *What It's Worth* traces the path that has brought CFED and the field to this point, envisions the road ahead, and sets the stage for the thoughtful and provocative ideas, evidence, and opinions voiced by our fellow authors in the chapters that follow.

THE PROBLEM: GROWING FINANCIAL INSECURITY IN AMERICA

Decades ago, few would have anticipated the dramatic increase in the complexity of the American economy, financial systems, and social safety nets, or how that complexity would transform the economic lives of individuals and families. Today, nearly every aspect of American life, from employment to housing to the generational transfer of wealth (and poverty) is tied to financial systems and other institutional structures, such as the workplace. Although these systems and structures provide valuable benefits, including the democratization of credit and technology-driven cost savings in the delivery of products and services, they bring new risks to consumers as well.

The fact is, it's hard to be a consumer of financial services these days. Anyone who visits the website of a major financial institution or drives through a busy street filled with billboards advertising check-cashers and payday lenders can appreciate the pace and extent of change in the financial services marketplace in recent decades. This increasingly complex marketplace demands corresponding savvy to navigate successfully.

Consider that 50 years ago, our parents or grandparents:

- Weren't bombarded by tempting credit offers in the mail. Credit cards weren't born until the 1950s, and not widespread until deregulation in the 1980s. Today, more than 70 percent of Americans have at least one credit card,[1] and the typical borrower carries nearly $10,000 in revolving debt (including debt from credit cards, private label cards and lines of credit).[2]

- Had never heard of an adjustable-rate mortgage. Homeownership rates expanded significantly during the last 100 years (from 46 percent in 1910 to 64 percent in 2013),[3] thanks largely to the post-Depression launch of the 30-year mortgage. The 2000s brought experimentation with the mortgage market—and in some cases, overtly predatory actions—that stripped the wealth of millions, especially households of color and those of lower income. Former FDIC chair Sheila Bair, writing in 2012, observed that as a result of "reckless" mortgage lending practices, "five million families have already lost their homes, an even

---

1 Gallup, "Americans Rely Less on Credit Cards than in Previous Years" (April 25, 2014).

2 CFED, "Assets and Opportunity Scorecard, Average Credit Card Debt" (2014).

3 U.S. Census, Historical Census of Housing Tables – Homeownership (October 31, 2011); CFED, "Assets and Opportunity Scorecard, Homeownership Rate"(2013).

greater number are still at great risk of foreclosure, and nearly a fifth of mortgage holders owe more than their homes are worth."[4]

- **Did not fear that a single unpaid bill might torpedo their credit score.** The use of credit scores as a "screen" has a profound effect on financial security in light of the fact that more than one-half of all consumers currently have subprime scores;[5] tens of millions more are outside the credit mainstream because of "thin" or nonexistent credit files;[6] and millions of consumers do not regularly check their credit scores.[7] Without a good credit score, obtaining access to capital is difficult, expensive, or impossible.

- **Likely had greater access to a mainstream or lower-cost financial institution.** Between 1984 and 2011, more than 15,000 banks exited the industry; of these, about one-half merged with another bank, and one-third consolidated with other charters within their existing bank holding company. Bank branches have been steadily closing. The FDIC reports nearly 5,000 closures between 2009 and 2014.[8] At the same time, high-cost "fringe banking" services have proliferated, particularly in poor communities and communities of color. Although usury is certainly nothing new, its scope and scale (and the devastation left in its wake) have reached new heights in the last few decades. In 2014, the Federal Reserve Bank of St. Louis reported, "Today, there are approximately 20,000 storefront lenders... By comparison, in 2012, there were 14,157 McDonald's restaurants in the United States."[9]

Of course, all of this was happening while two other developments were making people even more dependent on this complex financial system: skyrocketing student loan debt, and the demise of the defined benefit plan/

---

4 Sheila Bair, "Foreword." In *The State of Lending in America and Its Impact on U.S. Households*, edited by Debbie Bocian et al. (Washington, DC: Center for Responsible Lending, 2012).

5 CFED, "Assets and Opportunity Scorecard, Main Findings" (2015).

6 Michael A. Turner, Patrick Walker, and Katrina Dusek, "New to Credit from Alternative Data" (Durham, NC: PERC, March 2009).

7 Anne Kim, "What's Your Number? Credit Scores and Financial Security" (Washington, DC: CFED, 2013).

8 Federal Deposit Insurance Corporation, "Community Banking Study" (Washington, DC: FDIC, December 2012).

9 Federal Reserve Bank of St. Louis, "Payday Loans: Time for Review," *Inside the Vault* (Fall 2014).

pension and subsequent reliance on individual retirement accounts, such as the 401(k).

The steady rise in the cost of public and private higher education, coupled with growth of for-profit educational institutions, has created unprecedented levels of student debt. The Brookings Institution found that in 2000, the average student borrowed only 38 percent of net tuition costs (or about $3,600) to finance his or her tuition. Ten years later, that figure had risen to nearly 50 percent (or $5,500).[10]

With the decline of the defined benefit pension, retirement income became much less a benefit of one's job and much more a personal responsibility. In 1978, Congress passed legislation that enabled Americans to save through tax-sheltered work contributions. The major role of employers was to establish these programs, advertise them to employees, and at times offer a match. Yet many companies failed to set up these programs, and too many employees with the option to save did not sign up. Today, numerous studies estimate that more than one-half of employees, and perhaps as many as two-thirds, have inadequate savings to support themselves in retirement. One analysis suggests that one-third of current workers aged 55 to 64 will have incomes below 200 percent of the federal poverty line once they retire.[11] In his book *The Great Risk Shift*, Yale professor Jacob Hacker documents this trend of public and private institutions passing economic risk to consumers under what he describes as the guise of "personal responsibility."

Mainstream sources of financial stability—long-term job security, the defined-benefit pension, the neighborhood bank—are fast disappearing. These factors have been accelerated by the reality that achieving the American dream has become more elusive for the majority of the nation. A high school education is insufficient to achieve a sound middle-class existence. Our financial relationships and access to financial products increasingly occur online or through an unfamiliar agent on a customer

---

10 Michael Greenstone and Adam Looney. "Rising Student Debt Burdens: Factors Behind the Phenomenon." (Washington, DC: Brookings Institution, the Hamilton Project, July 5, 2013).

11 Teresa Ghilarducci, Joelle Saad-Lessler, and Kate Bahn, "Are U.S. Workers Ready for Retirement? Trends in Plan Sponsorship, Participation, and Preparedness," *Journal of Pension Benefits* (Winter 2015): 25–39.

service phone line. Personal integrity is no longer sufficient collateral to secure a loan or get a job.

In addition, inequities by race, class, and gender are becoming even more apparent in the widening income and wealth gaps between the haves and have-nots (see the essays in this volume by Dedrick Asante-Muhammad, José Quiñonez, Lisa Hasegawa and Jane Duong, Elsie Meeks, and Heidi Hartmann). We witness how the economic frameworks that create opportunity for some systematically deny it to others. Not only is the playing field not level, but the goalposts keep moving farther away. The lack of transparency in many financial products and the extent of predatory practices mean that financial decisions can have an outsized impact on consumers' lives, especially when things go wrong, as they did so dramatically during the Great Recession.

THE SOLUTION: CREATE ECONOMIC HEALTH AT THE HOUSEHOLD LEVEL FOR EVEN THE POOREST AMERICANS

These increasingly risky financial and economic realities have shaped CFED's work over more than three decades. We have sought to expand economic opportunity, reduce financial insecurity, and create wealth. We began in the early 1980s with a focus on promoting self-employment as a route out of poverty for low-income people. Virtually no one believed this was possible until we spent five years tracking American women on welfare who started their own businesses through the Self-Employment Investment Demonstration (SEID). We discovered that:

- Of the 1,316 welfare recipients who participated in SEID, 408 started businesses—a percentage roughly equal to the percentage of business owners in the U.S. economy overall;
- 79 percent of SEID businesses were still operating 2.6 years after starting;
- Six times the number of SEID business owners derived their primary income from their business after participation than before; and
- Reliance on Aid to Families with Dependent Children (cash assistance) and food stamps declined 65 percent and 62 percent, respectively, among business owners participating in SEID.

This experience taught us that low-income people have more capacity than opportunity, and that it was our responsibility to create on-ramps into the economy that provided the structure and incentives that all Americans need and deserve to succeed.

When we launched the American Dream Demonstration in the late 1990s to test the power of Individual Development Accounts (IDAs), which are savings accounts that receive additional dollars from government or philanthropy as a match, few policymakers or practitioners believed that low-income people could save at all. Even more disturbing was the critique that it was "unfair" to ask people who have too little money to begin with to save. What did we discover from this experiment? Not only did low-income people clearly demonstrate that they *could* save, but in fact, the poorest 20 percent of accountholders—with incomes less than 50 percent of the poverty line—saved at a rate more than three times that of the highest-income accountholders. They told us, essentially, that it was the price of hope. Otis, a saver at Capital Area Asset Builders in Washington, DC, summed it up: "When you first get your money, it is easy to spend it on dinner. But once you realize the money is for your future, you start to really save."[12]

This demonstration taught us many new things that influence our work today. Incentives, such as savings matches, matter—but not as much as we thought. Institutional arrangements, from direct deposits to peer counseling, mattered as much or more in helping the savers reach their goals of education, homeownership, or entrepreneurship. When financial education was paired with an account and savings goal, outcomes improved. Each hour of financial education, up to 10 hours, increased average monthly net savings by $1.16, or $139 per year, a substantial sum for families living near or below the poverty line.

Yet while IDA programs were clearly transformative for many, these programs also revealed that not all low-income households were ready to save for a long-term asset. How could we help them get there? After all, if households, particularly those of low and moderate income and households of color, lack access to the information and skills to make

12 CFED, "Downpayments on the American Dream Policy Demonstration (ADD)," *Common Progress Report* (Spring 2001).

sound financial decisions in an increasingly complex environment, they are likely to find achieving economic security elusive at best, and impossible at worst.

KNOWLEDGE IS POWER: THE FAITH IN FINANCIAL EDUCATION

By the 1990s, Americans had latched onto the idea of financial education as a response to these new financial realities. Educators, employers, bankers, and policymakers alike supported financial education programs as a seemingly simple solution to the financial challenges faced by low-income consumers. If people just had more information, the thinking went, they would be able to make wiser financial decisions.

In the 1990s and 2000s, there was enormous growth in financial education programs and initiatives in every sector. Federal financial education commissions and advisory councils sprang up. Hundreds of curricula were developed, including the widely used FDIC *Money Smart* materials, as well as a multitude of teaching and learning materials created by nonprofits and for-profits alike. Foundations invested millions in supporting financial education programming in every corner of the nation. States began to require it in schools. Financial education was, in short, a hot topic.

Banks furthered this trend for several reasons. Many saw it as a good business development tool, a way to get new customers in the door.[13] In addition, banks offering financial education could receive Community Reinvestment Act (CRA) credit by providing services in low- and moderate-income neighborhoods. And financial education also represented a new tool in the arsenal for managing credit risk among borrowers who were increasingly taking on additional debt.

Finally, financial counseling was integrated into federal programs that involved use of credit or other financial products, especially homeownership programs. In addition, IDA programs mandated general financial education and offered additional asset-specific training as incentives to promote homeownership, entrepreneurship, or postsecondary education.

---

13 Federal Deposit Insurance Corporation, *FDIC Money Smart Survey of User Organizations, 2003 to 2004* (Washington, DC: FDIC, 2004).

ENHANCING FINANCIAL EDUCATION WITH WEALTH CREATION STRATEGIES

At the same time, another significant influence was at play: the growing emphasis on helping low-income households build not just income, but wealth. Beginning with Michael Sherraden's seminal 1990 book *Assets and the Poor*, asset building emerged as a strategy for helping families escape poverty. Whereas traditional approaches to poverty alleviation emphasized increasing income, this newer research recognized that income is necessary but insufficient. Assets—a home, savings, an education, or a business—must accompany income to help families move up the economic ladder. Assets create a financial buffer to weather emergencies, promote success in the labor market, inspire long-term thinking and planning, and enhance the economic and psychological well-being of individuals and their families. An entire field of practice, policy, research, product innovation, and philanthropy has developed in the asset-building space over the past 35 years.

At the heart of the asset-building field is a simple premise: Given the right frameworks and incentives, people will save, regardless of income, and move toward asset ownership. From the start, practitioners experimented with and adopted as a best practice the integration of asset-specific and general financial education into their programs, with the added element that the education was tied directly and continually to the promotion of specific behaviors and actions.

One powerful measure of how much the asset-building field has grown in just the last decade is captured by the growth in partners for CFED's *Assets & Opportunity Scorecard*, the nation's most comprehensive benchmarking tool in how well state governments build and protect assets for their residents. When CFED released the first edition of the Scorecard in 2003, we partnered with just five organizations—which was the number of state organizations with a mission of building assets for low-income Americans. The number of partners grew and by 2012, CFED organized a group of advocates, practitioners, policymakers and others—the Assets & Opportunity Network—to connect the growing number of state, regional, and local organizations dedicated to expanding financial capability and opportunity. Today, this Network represents 1,840 members, whose work has connected financial education with building financial security and assets, and redefined how these two efforts worked together.

Yet in the early years of the new century, as the recession loomed and student debt and foreclosures continued to mount, it became clear that neither financial education nor asset building were enough to improve economic stability and well-being for large numbers of families. Michael Sherraden, whose voice carries great weight in the field, acknowledged with Ray Boshara in 2008 that financial education does not necessarily translate to a direct path toward savings and asset accumulation.[14] By that time, others in the field had also begun to question the impact of financial education programs. Many programs included no evaluation of their efforts at all, and for those that did, the evidence of effectiveness was spotty. The Consumer Financial Protection Bureau (CFPB) noted in 2013 that "while some of these programs ... show promising results, overall there is limited systematic evidence to tell us about the most effective ways to improve consumer knowledge and decision making about personal finances."[15]

At the same time, many stakeholders who had long identified as asset-builders were recognizing that for some households, the goal could not be to buy a house, or start a business, or save for retirement—not yet. What these households needed first was a broader array of services: credit repair, a simple bank account, access to public benefits, plus the knowledge and know-how to navigate financial systems.

MORE THAN FAITH: THE RISE OF FINANCIAL CAPABILITY

Experience has taught CFED and the field that we must help people not just learn, but act. We must not only make sure that doors of opportunity are open, but that people walk through them. This understanding was the impetus for the birth of the field we now know as "financial capability." The term itself first gained traction internationally and quickly took root in the United States. The Center for Financial Services Innovation

---

14 Michael Sherraden and Ray Boshara, "Learning from Individual Development Accounts," in *Overcoming the Saving Slump: How to Increase the Effectiveness of Financial Education and Saving Programs*, edited by Annamaria Lusardi (University of Chicago Press, 2008), 264–283.

15 Consumer Financial Protection Bureau, "Feedback from the Financial Education Field" (Washington, DC: CFPB, May 2013).

succinctly describes the difference in both nomenclature and impact in its aptly titled 2009 report, *From Financial Education to Financial Capability: Opportunities for Innovation*, noting: "The shift in language is more than semantics. Financial education is a set of provider outputs; financial capability is a set of consumer outcomes" that make a difference in peoples' lives—for instance, being able to meet monthly expenses, planning for the future, and choosing quality financial products.[16]

As the notion of financial capability began to take hold, many in the emerging field were coming to another critical realization: that despite good products, good services, and the very best of intentions, many low-income households were not using the financial opportunities being offered. With apologies to *Field of Dreams*, we were building it, but they weren't coming.

Practitioners and policymakers began to realize that part of the problem was that we were not listening to the customer. To use an entirely unrelated example: If we were McDonald's and considering creating a new sandwich, there would be an enormous amount of thought put into how to develop, refine, and market that product to the consumer. Focus groups and pilot tests would ensue, and the new product would be designed and polished to within an inch of its life before it ever came close to hitting the streets. In addition, McDonald's would use all the information it had about its customers' behaviors to inform its decisions—their preferences, patterns, and psychologies, and what made them choose to buy (or not buy) one product over another. Yet the financial services field was charging ahead with little more than a notion that the approach should work.

That has begun to change in the past few years, with exciting applications of traditionally for-profit product development tools to financial capability products and services. The notion of human-centered design, which examines the needs, dreams, and behaviors of people who will be affected by a given product or program,[17] is beginning to make a real change in how organizations design financial products and services for low-income individuals and families. Human-centered design has also prepared the

---

16 Josh Sledge, "From Financial Education to Financial Capability: Opportunities for Innovation" (Chicago: Center for Financial Services Innovation, March 2010), 5.

17 IDEO, "Human-Centered Design Toolkit, 2nd Edition" (San Francisco: IDEO, July 2011), 18.

field for the next leap—integrating behavioral science and economics into our work. The field now has a deeper understanding of what promotes or impedes "good" consumer behavior.

After all, at the end of the day, our goal is behavior change, to ensure that people make use of opportunities for financial security to better their financial position. To continue the *Field of Dreams* metaphor, the question becomes: If we build it, how do we make it as easy as possible for them to come and stay? In financial capability terms, this translates to strategies such as opt-out and automatic savings programs; thoughtfully designed incentives and rewards for desirable financial behaviors; and fewer barriers to achieving financial goals. For instance, where a financial education class might have simply offered information on where a person could open a bank account, financial capability programs would bring a banker to the class to open accounts on the spot and help participants set up direct deposit. This makes savings automatic and easy, in addition to providing direct access to a mainstream financial account with lower fees and interest costs than found with alternative financial services providers such as payday lenders or check cashers.

Tax time is when these innovations have been most rigorously tested. Tax season is the moment when low-income families often have the largest amount of cash, thanks to refunds from the Earned Income Tax Credit (EITC) and the Child Tax Credit (CTC). Using core principles such as easy account opening, powerful incentives, and well-timed "prompts" or messaging, the SaveUSA program (sponsored by the New York City Department of Consumer Affairs Office of Financial Empowerment) tested treatment and control groups to see if these factors could encourage more savings at tax time. The results are convincing. Between 9 percent and 23 percent of the control group deposited some or all of their tax refunds. In contrast, 90 percent of the treatment group with access to a well-designed product saved.[18]

Outcomes of similar magnitude have resulted from decisions by companies to switch from an opt-in to opt-out retirement savings program in which an employee must actively say no to an automatic deduction.

---

18 Rachel Black and Elliot Schreur, "Connecting Tax Time to Financial Security" (Washington, DC: New America Foundation, February 2014).

Between 2003 and 2011, the percentage of companies offering opt-out 401(k) programs skyrocketed from 14 percent to 56 percent.[19] An analysis from the National Bureau of Economic Research examined one medium-sized U.S. chemicals company that implemented automatic 401(k) enrollment for new hires and found that the plan participation rate was 35 percentage points higher after three months on the job than for "standard" enrollees, and remained 25 points higher after two years.[20]

HOW FINANCIAL CAPABILITY CHANGED CFED'S STRATEGY TO BUILD WEALTH FOR LOW-INCOME AMERICANS

In many ways, CFED's own experience in grasping the importance of the financial capability concept reflects the evolution of the larger field. In 2010, we realized that we needed a better way to capture the entirety of families' financial needs, not just financial education and asset building. Our Household Financial Security Framework (see Figure 1) was an attempt to build household financial security over time. We began to think about reducing poverty and achieving financial security and empowerment as a dynamic process. Households gain financial management skills, build human capital, increase income, begin to save, leverage saving into assets, and protect gains made along the way. Households can engage this cycle at many places along the continuum; they also iterate and evolve their strategy over time.

The Framework describes the cycle of financial capability from the household perspective. Households need enough income to finance basic consumption and pay down debt with enough left over to save for the future. Once savings have accumulated, they can be invested in assets, which can then help households boost their incomes through increased earning capacity or income-generating dividends or profits. Throughout the cycle, access to insurance and consumer protections helps households protect their gains. This is an ongoing process in which each component contributes to the next, and to the household's overall ability to become financially stable.

---

19 Richard Thaler and Shlomo Benartzi, "Behavioral Economics and the Retirement Savings Crisis," *Capital Ideas* (Summer 2013).

20 John Beshears et al., "The Importance of Default Options for Retirement Saving Outcomes: Evidence from the United States." In *Social Security Policy in a Changing Environment*, edited by Jeffrey Brown, Jeffrey Liebman, and David Wise. (Cambridge, MA: National Bureau of Economic Research, 2009).

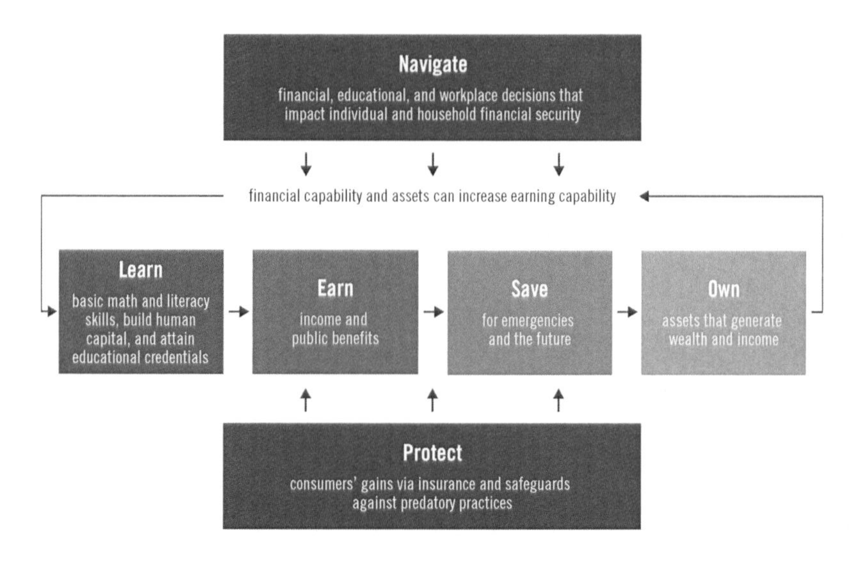

Figure 1: Household Financial Security Framework

The development of the Framework was a turning point in the way we thought about our work. It gave us a way to weave a powerful, cohesive narrative about the many different and interconnected ways that could support the burgeoning asset-building field. It also allowed us to bring new, unexpected partners into our orbit, players who might touch only one part of the financial capability "cycle" but who represented important constituencies or vantage points. Suddenly, we had a tool that allowed a wide range of organizations—health, affordable housing, public safety, community development finance, education, employers—to see the specific ways their work contributed to the financial betterment of families.

We began to see more sectors concluding that financial capability was essential to achieving their own larger goals. For example, at a recent convening hosted by Stewards of Affordable Housing for the Future (SAHF)—an organization composed of many of the most productive affordable housing organizations in the nation—Patricia Belden, President of POAH Communities, said: "If we want to improve the lives of our residents, we need to go beyond traditional property management and work with partners who can help our residents build credit, save for a home or college, or start a business. We want to give our residents the financial tools to help them to make their dreams for the future a reality."

FINANCIAL CAPABILITY GAINS MOMENTUM

The Great Recession accelerated the adoption of financial capability as a concept by leaders in government, the social services sector, academia and the private sector, especially as financial insecurity spread to formerly middle class households. In 2010, President Obama created the first President's Advisory Council on Financial Capability, followed in 2013 by a similar council focused on youth. Also in 2010, Congress passed the Dodd-Frank Wall Street Reform and Consumer Protection Act. Intended as widespread reform in response to the Great Recession, it established what would later become the Consumer Financial Protection Bureau (CFPB). The CFPB seeks to "make markets for consumer financial products and services work for Americans"—a mission accompanied by greater emphasis on building financial capability coupled with enforcement powers when necessary. For the first time, we have a government agency charged with, among other things, ensuring that all Americans become more financially capable.

In less than five years, the design and delivery of financial capability services have been championed and incorporated into core lines of business in the public, nonprofit, and private sectors. With a growing body of research on the subject making the theoretical case for financial capability, and the successful experiences of "early adopters," this new field began to flourish. Yet the job of building financial security for individuals, households, and communities is just beginning.

Four words or phrases describe the trends and practices that are expanding the field's scale and impact today: integration, coaching, credit scores, and product innovation.

Integration

Growing numbers of government agencies, nonprofits, and for-profit businesses (especially employers) are embedding financial capability into their core programs and services. At the federal level, the departments of Treasury, Health and Human Services, Education, and Housing and Urban Development have each launched or begun to explore initiatives to integrate a range of financial capability strategies into their agencies' service delivery programs.

Integration is even farther ahead at the state level. Delaware's Stand By Me partnership, led by the state and the United Way of Delaware, locates financial empowerment centers within public agencies, nonprofits, employers, and educational institutions (see Rita Landgraf's essay in this volume). In Colorado, the Department of Human Services and the Department of Education are planning a two-generation initiative that will embed financial capability services for parents into the state's early childhood programming (see Reggie Bicha and Keri Batchelder's essay in this book).

Cities have gotten into the game as well. In 2006, New York City launched the nation's first municipal Office of Financial Empowerment to build financial capability among low-income families. Today, 14 major cities compose the Cities for Financial Empowerment Coalition, providing financial capability services to millions of people through innovative one-stop centers and community partnerships. As Greg Fischer, mayor of Louisville, KY (one of the Cities for Financial Empowerment) writes in his essay in this book, "We are developing an integrated, community-wide system... Leaders across multiple departments have embraced the goal of improving the financial stability of the residents we serve by promoting financial access, capability, and asset-building strategies."

The nonprofit sector also began to blend financial capability into other services: offering assistance with workforce training and education; helping clients gain access to public benefits, tax credits, and financial aid; and offering financial education, counseling, or coaching, along with access to financial products and services. The Working Families Success Network is an example of this integrated approach and has more than 100 sites across the country. Section 2 of this book highlights examples of integration from multiple sectors, such as Skyline College's on-campus SparkPoint Center, which provides services and resources to help students and community members achieve financial self-sufficiency (see Regina Stanback Stroud's essay). The private sector is also beginning to incorporate financial capability strategies into employee benefits, such as Staples' efforts to leverage financial games and new financial products like "myRA" to increase employee engagement with retirement savings (see Regis Mulot's essay in this volume).

Financial coaching

One-on-one financial coaching is growing rapidly, with powerful results (see the essays in this book by Michael Collins, Michael Rubinger, and Rita Landgraf for more information). Such coaching helps consumers set goals, establish a plan of action, and change behaviors. Meeting people where they are, the main idea behind modern financial coaching, empowers participants and allows them to have ownership over their financial choices and behaviors. Unlike a quick class or workshop, coaching is a long-term relationship, helping people to organize and prioritize their financial needs, supporting them, holding them accountable to their self-determined goals, and monitoring those behaviors over time.

For instance, Destiny, a client with The Financial Clinic in New York City, wanted to pay down her substantial debt, and in the longer term, buy a car to help her more easily commute to her job. Through the coaching relationship, Destiny set a realistic budget, identified opportunities to save, and established an income-based repayment plan for her student loan. By the end of her first year in coaching, Destiny had already paid off a quarter of her debt, increased her credit score by 30 points, and saved $3,000, all while sticking to her budget.[21]

Credit scores

A credit score plays a powerful role in determining everything from accessing credit to renting an apartment to securing a job. Not only must the methods of credit scoring today be made transparent, but we should also leverage the power of "big data" to develop alternative methods of creating meaningful scores. Such alternatives could bring tens of millions of "credit invisibles"—consumers without scores—into the credit system. The Credit Builders Alliance (CBA), for example, is helping nonprofit lenders report loan data to credit reporting agencies. In 2014, CBA released a study with Experian that analyzed outcomes for consumers, including credit invisibles, who opened credit products offered by CBA members. Over two years, 58 percent of these borrowers saw their credit score increase, and more than 20 percent moved to a lower risk category (i.e. from subprime to nonprime credit).[22]

---

21 Financial Clinic, "Annual Report for Fiscal Year 2013" (2013).

22 Credit Builders Alliance, *Analysis of CBA Members: Confirms Value of Credit Building*, August 2014.

Product innovation

The design and distribution of safe, affordable, high-quality financial products and services, ranging from prepaid cards to new methods of credit scoring, are enabling consumers to match products not only to their specific financial needs, but to their desired financial behaviors as well. The FDIC Model Safe Accounts, which bring the underserved consumer into the financial mainstream with safeguards such as the elimination of overdrafts, is one of the most promising trends. In addition, the expansion of employer-based financial education or financial wellness programs and savings products—especially opt-out retirement programs—creates opportunities to reach millions with financial capability products and services. Finally, applying innovations from other sectors—such as leveraging the concept of lottery winnings into prize-linked savings awards as championed by Doorways to Dreams—combine the best in consumer marketing with proven wealth-building approaches.

HOW FINANCIAL CAPABILITY PROMOTES FINANCIAL WELL-BEING

As important as financial capability may be, it is not the end goal. Ultimately, we are aiming to improve the financial situation for families, narrow the gap between rich and poor, and increase the opportunity for all households to be financially *well.* This notion of "financial well-being" is the most recent advance in understanding how to build financial security and opportunity. It builds on what has been learned while offering a new framework that more accurately and effectively assesses the financial condition of a household.

In early 2015, the CFPB released four criteria to describe financial well-being. The list was developed through an extensive research effort with consumers themselves.

To be financially well, a person:[23]

- Feels in control of his or her day-to-day finances;
- Has the capacity to absorb a financial shock;

23 Consumer Financial Protection Bureau, "Financial Well-Being: The Goal of Financial Education" (January 2015).

- Is on track to meet financial goals, whatever those might be; and
- Has the financial freedom to make choices to enjoy life.

For the first time, we have criteria and a set of metrics to use in charting the road ahead (see Jennifer Tescher and Rachel Schneider's essay in this volume for further discussion). Yet we also have the data that show us how far we still have to go. A dwindling set of American households can claim to meet the CFPB's financial well-being criteria today. More than one-third of households have no emergency savings,[24] and 44 percent do not have sufficient liquid assets to survive for three months in a fiscal emergency.[25]

Additional CFPB research has identified key factors of financial well-being, including social and economic environments; available opportunities; and individual personality, attitudes, knowledge, and skills. All of these can affect consumers' behavior in the financial realm, and their ultimate satisfaction (or lack thereof) with their financial situations. Some, particularly individual factors, are within a consumer's control, while others, such as the socioeconomic climate, are not.[26] The charge for practitioners and policymakers, then, is to help individuals make the most of the agency they do have, and to tailor their services and strategies accordingly. It also highlights where this work, which focuses largely on the individual or the household, intersects with place-based strategies of the community development field (see, for example, the essays in this volume by Angela Glover Blackwell and Paul Weech). The possibility of building new bridges between these two fields holds great promise.

In the same way that the subject of calculus weaves together many strands of mathematics, the notion of financial well-being combines many of the interventions that we have described in this essay. It starts with high-quality and culturally appropriate financial information. Financial coaches heighten the value and impact of this information by encouraging self-directed goal-setting and personal accountability. Yet individual effort is not, nor should be, enough. The lessons from behavioral economics,

---

24 NeighborWorks America, "One-in-Three U.S. Adults Has No Emergency Savings Despite Improving Economy." Press release (March 31, 2015).

25 CFED, "Assets and Opportunity Scorecard, Liquid Asset Poverty Rate" (2011).

26 Consumer Financial Protection Bureau, "Financial Well-Being: What It Means and How to Help" (2015).

marketing, and policymaking affirm that the design of products and services, the delivery structures and platforms, and financial incentives and regulatory protections matter just as much as an individual's actions in achieving financial well-being. In many ways, financial well-being captures the ultimate outcome that we've been seeking when we align people, systems, and policies towards a common goal.

"WHAT IT'S WORTH": ADVANCING IDEAS, SHARING EXPERIENCE AND CHANGING POLICY

The field of financial capability is young. But the rapid growth of interest and activity signals that it is addressing a vital need within our economy and society.

This book aims to accomplish three goals:

1. Illustrate the realities of the financial problems and challenges faced by American households today (Section 1);

2. Capture the enormous creativity and innovation underway in different sectors, institutions, and among policymakers to expand the content and delivery of financial capability to serve different markets and needs (Section 2); and

3. Point to next steps in research, policy, and practice across all sectors—public, private, and social—to implement both proven and evolving solutions so we can all live a life of financial well-being.

What It's Worth reflects a diverse range of voices. Authors include public health professionals, policymakers, college presidents, bank regulators, economists, and nonprofit leaders who all agree that our financial lives matter. Although the authors approach the topic grounded in their unique backgrounds and experiences, each articulates why financial health and well-being matters to them and the work they are trying to achieve.

The book affirms that this is a universal issue that affects all of us, although not in the same ways. It is not an "us" versus "them" topic; we all can understand, sometimes in a deeply personal way, the challenges and opportunities met while striving for a sense of financial well-being. It presents solutions both practical and strategic to ensure that both practitioners and policymakers can work in concert to set people on the path to financial well-being. We look forward to collaborating with you on this journey.

The authors express deep appreciation to Christopher Bernal of CFED for his research assistance.

■ ■ ■

ANDREA LEVERE *is the President of the Corporation for Enterprise Development (CFED), where she has worked for over two decades building a movement to move low-income communities out of poverty by building financial capability and assets. She began her career in economic development finance after getting an MBA at the Yale School of Management, and has combined these skills along with a commitment to policy change and community practice to expand economic opportunity for all Americans.*

■ ■ ■

LEIGH TIVOL *has worked in the field of financial capability since long before it had that name. She has helped low-income families save for the future, battled predatory lending, secured funding for affordable housing, delivered technical assistance to community organizations, served in state government – and, since 2006, has been expanding economic opportunity on the staff of CFED. Currently, as Vice President for Strategy & Impact, she works to ensure the strategic and operational effectiveness of CFED's programmatic efforts.*

THE FUTURE OF BUILDING WEALTH

Can Financial Capability Overcome Demographic Destiny?

Ray Boshara

Federal Reserve Bank of St. Louis[1]

Bravo to MacKenzie. When she was born, she chose married, white, well-educated parents who live in an affluent, mostly white neighborhood with great public schools. She chose parents who read to her, signed her up for violin and soccer lessons at an early age, and involved her in church and community activities. She also chose her birth year wisely, making sure that she graduated from college and entered the job market when the economy was rebounding from the Great Recession. Thanks to the wealth and financial savvy of her parents, both now in their early 50s, MacKenzie graduated from a private, four-year selective college debt free, giving her many career options as well as the ability to start saving for a home and retirement.

Because of her great "choices," MacKenzie is likely to accumulate wealth and achieve financial health over her lifetime. She and her parents belong to the roughly one in four Americans households we can call "thrivers."

But too bad for Troy, who, despite being just as bright as MacKenzie, chose non-white parents who never married, and a poor, highly segregated neighborhood with lousy public schools and few options to be involved in music, sports, and civic activities. Troy's young, hard-working, conscientious mother was never able to start college and is too busy—with her two part-time jobs, Troy's siblings, and trying to stay afloat—to read to Troy as much as she would like to. In fact, she's accumulating debts to family members and on credit cards so she can manage the increasingly

1 These are my own views, and not necessarily the views of the Federal Reserve Bank of St. Louis, the Board of Governors, or the Federal Reserve System.

frequent ups and downs in her financial life. She also lacks the know-how and networks to get Troy on a college-bound track, something his school fails to do as well. And Troy unwisely chose to finish high school just as the Great Recession was getting underway, so finding any job, let alone a decent-paying one with benefits, eludes him.

Troy, because of his bad "choices," is not likely to accumulate much wealth or feel financially healthy over his lifetime. He and his family belong to the roughly three in four American households we can call "strugglers."

But are Troy and MacKenzie forever consigned to one of these two groups? Can "executive function," or the things they learn and the choices they do make, help them overcome the circumstances of their births, engage their will and intelligence, and enable them to climb to the top of the economic ladder? Is this not America? How much are Troy and MacKenzie's financial futures determined by the choices they did not make: the economic moment in which they were born, their race or ethnicity, their schools and neighborhoods, and their parents? Indeed, isn't this book about enabling more Americans to make better financial choices and, accordingly, realize better financial health and well-being? If, in short, demography is destiny, can the strategies offered in this book succeed? Although we cannot know for sure, I'm encouraged by recent research that sheds light on the nature of the challenge, promising solutions, and lessons and successes from America's Progressive Era a century ago.

Research from the Federal Reserve Bank of St. Louis's Center for Household Financial Stability,[2] which I direct, suggests that three demographic drivers—one's age or birth year, education, and race-ethnicity—may not in fact be destiny, but they do increasingly matter for building wealth and financial security. Indeed, while we find that families who make or are presented with good financial choices are more likely to build wealth, these three demographic drivers either serve as tailwinds (in the case of thrivers) or headwinds (in the case of strugglers) in families' efforts to make those good choices. Other research has focused on the growing importance of family structure and parental education in predicting economic success.

---

2 See Center for Household Financial Stability, at www.stlouisfed.org/hfs. This research is led by my colleagues William R. Emmons and Bryan Noeth, whose excellent work I rely on throughout this essay.

These new economic realities lead, I think, to three policy implications. First, we must expand our understanding of—and response to—economic vulnerability to go well beyond one's income to include these increasingly powerful demographic predictors of wealth and economic opportunity. Second, we must consider new and more robust investments in children, including integrating asset investments into the fabric of other early-in-life interventions. And third, we must embrace a "two-generation" approach, meaning we must invest in adults as well as children, especially in ways that contribute to their financial stability. Combined, these ideas will not only improve financial health for more families, but, as Jared Bernstein argues in his essay in this volume, contribute to a stronger economy as well.

THRIVERS AND STRUGGLERS: A GROWING ECONOMIC DIVIDE

At the Center for Household Financial Stability, we focus on wealth, or more precisely, family balance sheets, for a few reasons. First, given the role that debt played in harming both families and the economy during and after the Great Recession, we must expand our household-level framework from just assets to the broader family balance sheet.[3] Second, a growing body of research suggests that there are distinct, independent, and positive outcomes associated with balance sheet measures—account ownership, savings, assets, debt, and net worth—that are not necessarily associated with income or other traditional markers of social and economic well-being.[4] And, third, net worth is like a barometer of one's overall financial health, a summary measure of one's financial outcomes over a lifetime (and, indeed, the outcomes of one's predecessors), as well as an embodiment of future opportunities for families and their offspring. Wealth is thus integral to, although not the entirety of, one's financial health or financial well-being.

Given wealth's importance, it is disturbing that the wealth gap has grown dramatically during the last few decades. The Federal Reserve's most

3 Ray Boshara, "From Asset Building to Balance Sheets: A Reflection on the First and Next 20 Years of Federal Assets Policy," *CSD Perspective*, No. 12–24 (June 2012); Ray Boshara, "Ownership and Debt: Minding the Balance Sheet," *Democracy* 26 (Fall 2012).

4 See Center on Assets, Education and Inclusion at the University of Kansas, and Center for Social Development at Washington University in St. Louis, for several papers summarizing asset effects.

recent Survey of Consumer Finances[5] shows a massive shift in wealth away from those we are calling strugglers, who generally are younger, less educated, and non-white, and toward those we are calling thrivers, who generally are middle-aged or older, better educated, and white or Asian.[6] Although thrivers' share of the population has risen 9 percent since 1989, their share of the nation's wealth has grown 23 percent. Stated another way, thrivers used to command less than one-half of the nation's wealth, but now they own about two-thirds, despite accounting for slightly less than one-quarter of the population.

This dramatic shift in wealth in just one generation not only underscores the depth and pace of growing wealth inequality in the United States, but also illustrates how one's age, race, and education appear to matter more than a generation ago in determining who does and does not build wealth. In other words, the returns for having these characteristics—or the penalties for not having them—have grown. MacKenzie and her family's efforts to build wealth are buoyed by these demographic tailwinds, while the lack of them create headwinds that hamper Troy and his family's efforts to financially succeed.

Let us consider each of these characteristics, or drivers, separately. As a reference point, Figure 1 shows large differences in current levels of wealth, as measured by median net worth.

Race, Ethnicity, and Wealth[7]

We can begin with race or ethnicity, where a few facts stand out. First, the wealth gaps are disturbingly large and the rankings have persisted since

5 The Federal Reserve's Survey of Consumer Finances provides the most comprehensive picture of American families' balance sheets and financial behavior over time. Although not longitudinal, it uses information from more than 40,000 families surveyed in one of nine waves between 1989 and 2013. By partitioning the sample in each wave into 48 nonoverlapping groups based on four racial or ethnic groups, four levels of educational attainment, and three age ranges, the Center for Household Financial Stability is able to document profound and persistent differences in financial decision-making, balance-sheet choices, and wealth outcomes across groups. The Center's work shows that each demographic dimension is important in its own right.

6 We fully understand that not all Asians (or, for that matter, "thrivers") are financially well off, just that they are more likely to be well off. See Lisa Hasegawa and Jane Duong's essay in this volume for a more nuanced view of Asian American wealth, and papers from the National Assets Scorecard for Communities of Color (NASCC) project for a more nuanced view of the wealth of blacks.

7 William Emmons and Bryan Noeth, "How Age, Education and Race Separate Thrivers from Strugglers in Today's Economy: Race, Ethnicity, and Wealth" *Demographics of Wealth Series* 1. (St. Louis: Federal Reserve Bank of St. Louis, February 2015).

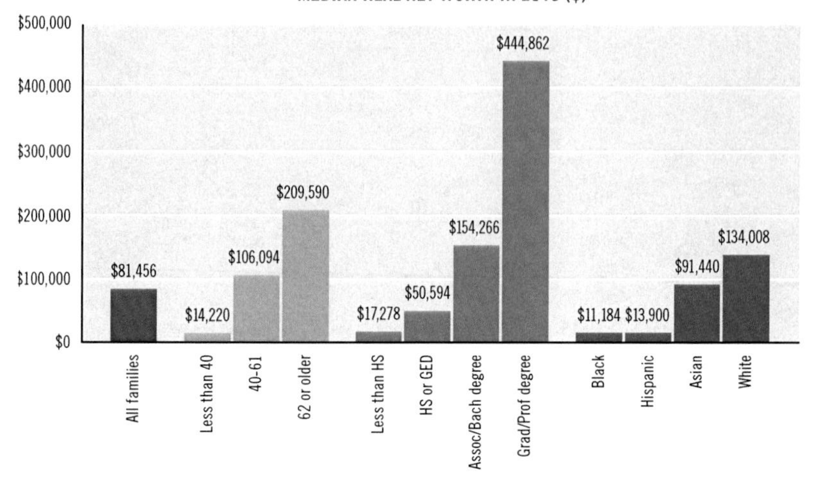

Emmons and Noeth, 2013.
Source: Federal Reserve Board Survey of Consumer Finances

Figure 1: How Age, Education, and Race/Ethnicity are Associated with Wealth

1989. White families rank first, followed by Asian families, Hispanic families, and then black families. With the exception of Asians, the median net worth of all groups in 2013 is about the same as in 1989; the Great Recession wiped out most of the post-1989 gains. However, prior to the recession, whites and especially Asians had seen dramatic increases in their wealth, and since 2010, they have seen their wealth begin to grow again, while the wealth of blacks and Hispanics has continued to decline.

Also, wealth disparities are starker than income disparities. Median wealth for Hispanics and blacks is about 90 percent lower than that of whites. In contrast, median income of Hispanics and blacks is only 40 percent lower. This suggests these two groups may have had few opportunities to "convert" their diminished incomes into wealth, such as through homeownership and retirement plans. And although one would expect age and education to help explain the persistent differences in wealth accumulation across racial and ethnic groups (whites are generally older and better educated than blacks and Hispanics), our research shows that the wealth gap is largely unchanged even among equally educated, similarly-aged whites and nonwhites. Stated more starkly, education does not appear to be an equalizer, at least in terms of wealth. Therefore, other factors must be in play, including early childhood experiences, parental influences, and, of course, deep and historical discrimination against blacks and other minorities.[8]

Education and Wealth[9]

Now let's consider education. Not surprisingly, the association between a family's education and its wealth is very strong and has become stronger with time, leading to large gaps in wealth by level of education. Only families with college degrees or higher have seen their wealth increase since 1989 (even though all groups saw their wealth decline in the Great Recession). Those lacking a high school degree saw their wealth plummet 44 percent between 1989 and 2013, while families with a high school degree saw their wealth decline 36 percent. Meanwhile, families with a two- or four-year degree experienced a 3 percent increase since 1989, while the wealth of those with advanced degrees spiked 45 percent.

Notably, however, the correlation between education and various measures of economic and financial success does not represent causation. That is, the college degree itself may only partially explain differences in wealth: the degree serves as a marker of many other factors also correlated with educational attainment, such as native ability, family background, marriage patterns (i.e., the tendency of college graduates to marry other college graduates), being read to as a child, and the likelihood of receiving gifts or inheritances.

Age and Wealth

Finally, let's look at age or, more precisely, year of birth. Of course older families are expected to have more wealth than younger families, but what we are observing is something deeper, even historical. To our surprise, age is the strongest predictor of balance sheet health, even after accounting for race and education. Americans in their 20s and 30s lost the most wealth in the recession and have been the slowest to recover. The average wealth of older (62 and older) Americans in 2013 was 16.7 percent less than

---

8 See the essays by Dedrick Asante-Muhammad, Lisa Hasegawa and Jane Duong, Elsie Meeks, and Josè Quiñonez in this volume for a fuller examination of the factors driving economic gaps between whites and non-whites.

9 Emmons and Noeth, "How Age, Education and Race Separate Thrivers from Strugglers in Today's Economy: Education and Wealth."

2007.[10] Over the same timeframe, the wealth of middle-age (ages 40–61) families declined 22.6 percent, while younger Americans (under age 40) experienced losses of 24 percent. The wealth of younger adults is concentrated in homeownership, which suffered greatly during the recession. Younger adults also have significant mortgage and consumer debts, few liquid assets, and they faced severe labor market challenges during and following the recession.

But this is not just a recession story; it is also a generational story. Succeeding generations are not as wealthy as previous ones. Our research shows that, holding the key determinants of income and wealth constant, each generation born during the first half of the twentieth century earned more and was wealthier than the generation before. However, among those born during the second half of the century, wealth and income have stagnated at levels below those born in the late 1930s and the 1940s. For example, those born around 1970 will likely have about 40 percent less wealth over their lifetimes than those born around 1940, holding everything else constant, including education, race, and age, and after adjusting for inflation. No doubt sheer luck plays a major role in explaining this—is one, for example, born into a smaller cohort, and does one enter the labor market during a period of strong economic growth? But public policy plays an important role as well: how generous is the safety net when one needs it, and can one pursue higher education without a heavy reliance on student loans?

Others have observed this as well. Research conducted by the Urban Institute finds that Generations X and Y[11] have accumulated less wealth than their parents did at the same age over a quarter-century ago.[12] Similarly, Neil Howe recently observed that the late Baby Boomers were

---

10 Ray Boshara and William Emmons, "After the Fall: Rebuilding Family Balance Sheets, Rebuilding the Economy," *Federal Reserve Bank of St. Louis 2012 Annual Report* (May 2013); William Emmons and Bryan Noeth, "Why Did Young Families Lose So Much Wealth During the Crisis? The Role of Homeownership," *Federal Reserve Bank of St. Louis Review* 95 (1) (January/February 2013), 1–26.

11 Generation X generally includes those born between 1965 and 1984; Generation Y, or "Millennials" are those born after 1984.

12 Eugene Steuerle et al., "Lost Generations? Wealth Building among Young Americans." (Washington, DC: Urban Institute, March 2013).

the last generation to do better economically than their parents.[13] And, as Phil Longman shows in his essay in this volume, today's younger Americans are experiencing a "new normal" of falling living standards and declining levels of upward economic mobility.

Considering all three drivers of the growing wealth gap, a few insights emerge. First, the returns or penalties on one's age or birth year, race and ethnicity, and education appear to have increased dramatically over the last generation. Second, similar investments in the same assets by thrivers and strugglers appear to generate different returns. Whites, for example, may own their homes longer and live in areas with greater appreciation, and they may attend better colleges and rely less on student loans to finance their education. And third, other factors—beyond what correlations and regressions may tell us—appear to be important in understanding growing wealth gaps between thrivers and strugglers over the last generation. Among those other factors are early childhood investments and experiences (which I will return to in the policy section) and family structure, which recent research suggests is potentially important in explaining differences in financial well-being.

FAMILY STRUCTURE AND FINANCIAL WELL-BEING

A growing number of academics on both the political left and right appear to now be coming together around concerns over declining rates of marriage[14] and rising rates of single-parent households, especially among less-educated persons. Their common economic concern: the ability of single parents to make it on one income and get their kids on a track for upward mobility. Jonathan Rauch of the Brookings Institution recently remarked, "There's a growing danger that marriage, with all its advantages for stability, income, and child well-being, will look like a gated community for the baccalaureate class, with ever-shrinking working-class participation. We're not there yet, but that's the trajectory we're on."[15]

---

13 Federal Reserve System, Community Development Research Conference, "Economic Mobility: Research and Ideas on Strengthening Families, Communities, and the Economy," April 2–3, 2015. Conference materials online at www.stlouisfed.org/Community-Development/Economic-Mobility-Conference-2015.

14 For purposes of this discussion, marriage does not include co-habitation; the scholars cited in this section observe that the economic, educational and other outcomes associated with marriage are generally not also associated with co-habitation.

15 Andrew L. Yarrow, "Falling Marriage Rates Reveal Economic Fault Lines," *New York Times*, February 8, 2015, p. ST15.

June Carbone and Naomi Cahn, authors of *Marriage Markets,* report that four out of five couples are married in the top 20 percent of earners, while fewer than one in five couples are married among the bottom 20 percent; they also observe that increasing income inequality influences the markets for marriage.[16]

As shown in Figure 2, the association between marriage and income is substantial, more than just a factor of two people being in a household. The association between marriage and wealth is even more pronounced; other studies have also found that persons with less wealth and more debts, including student debts, are much less likely to marry in the first place.[17] These correlations hold across education; although the associations are especially pronounced among those with college degrees, even high school dropouts appear to enjoy substantial marriage bonuses.

Robert I. Lerman and W. Bradford Wilcox find that the "growth in median income of families with children would be 44 percent higher if the U.S. realized 1980 levels of married parenthood today."[18] They also report that marriage may be as strong a predictor of economic success as education, race and ethnicity, and that growing up with both parents is strongly associated with more education, work, and income.

Robert Putnam in *Our Kids: The American Dream in Crisis* focuses on the implications of this growing class divide for children.[19] He notes that one in three children is being raised by married, college-educated parents, who are investing more time and money in their children than any previous generation. In fact, research by Shelly Lundberg and Robert Pollak finds that marriage is thriving among better-educated couples precisely because it is being used as a commitment device to raise highly

---

16 June Carbone and Naomi Cahn, *Marriage Markets: How Inequality is Remaking the American Family*, (New York: Oxford University Press, 2014).

17 Michael Greenstone and Adam Looney, "The Marriage Gap: The Impact of Economic and Technological Change on Marriage Rates." Blog post. (Washington, DC: Brookings Institution, February 3, 2012); Ron Haskins, "The Myth of the Disappearing Middle Class," *Washington Post*, March 29, 2012.

18 Robert I. Lerman and W. Bradford Wilcox, "For Richer, For Poorer: How Family Structures Economic Success in America," (Washington, DC: American Enterprise Institute, 2014).

19 Robert Putnam, *Our Kids: The American Dream in Crisis*, (New York: Simon & Schuster, 2015).

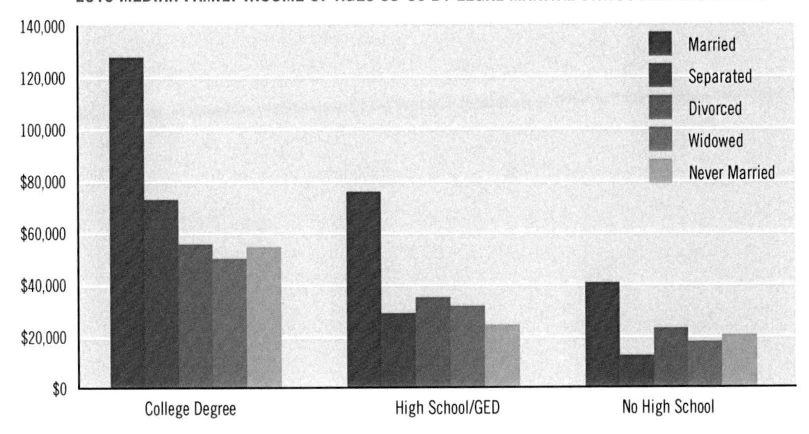

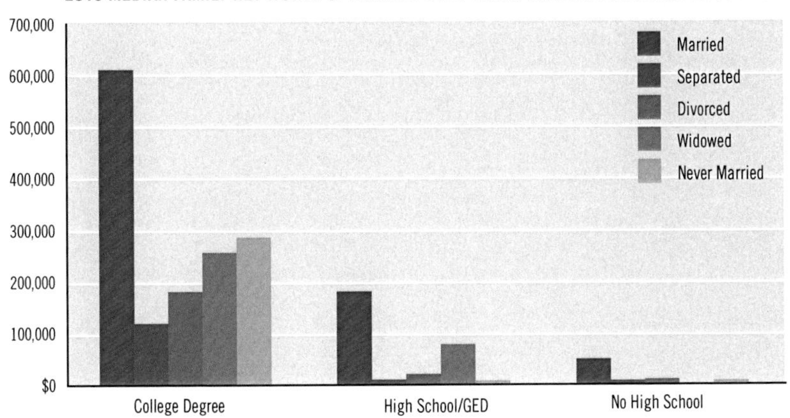

Noeth, 2013.
Source: Federal Reserve Board Survey of Consumer Finances

Figure 2: How Marital Status is Associated with Income and Wealth

successful children.[20] However, Putnam's concern is for the up to two-thirds of kids who, not reaping the myriad benefits of having married, educated parents, are likely to grow up more isolated from strong family and community supports than in previous generations—and thus are not likely to realize either financial security or upward mobility.

20 Shelly Lundberg and Robert A. Pollak, "Cohabitation and the Uneven Retreat from Marriage in the U.S., 1950–2010," NBER Working Paper No. 19413, (2013).

Recent research by Raj Chetty and his colleagues finds that family structure is the strongest of five predictors of upward economic mobility.[21] Specifically, they find that the larger the overall share of single parents in an area, the less likely a child will rise from the bottom income quintile to the top as an adult. Note, though, that it is not single-parenthood per se that causes this outcome; rather, it is living in a community with a large percentage of single parents that is associated with lower rates of upward economic mobility. Scott Winship of the Manhattan Institute, too, remarked that changes in economic mobility rates over the last generation are primarily driven by changes in family structure.[22]

In considering the larger role of family structure on economic success, we must be cautious. Because marriage is associated with economic success, that does not mean marriage causes greater economic success. For example, people who might be financially successful anyway may be more likely to marry. The relationship between marriage and economic outcomes may be strong, but it is complex. Nonetheless, it appears that single parenthood results from, and contributes to, declining economic opportunity in the U.S., and accordingly merits further attention from those concerned about family financial health and well-being.

POLICY IMPLICATIONS AND PROMISING DIRECTIONS

In a world where one's birth year, race or ethnicity, and parents, which no one can control, as well as one's education, which although a choice is influenced by all of the above, appear to increasingly matter for building wealth and financial success, what are the proper policy responses? Recalling the stories and diverging paths of Troy and MacKenzie, this question is particularly poignant for children. Although reversing trends in marriage and single-parenthood appears unlikely and policy responses may prove elusive, there are responses that can directly and substantially help struggling children and families, regardless of their family structure. Three ideas hold particular promise.

21 Raj Chetty, "Improving Opportunities for Economic Mobility in the United States." Testimony before the Budget Committee of the United States Senate, April 1, 2014.

22 Plenary remarks at the Federal Reserve System, Community Development Research Conference, "Economic Mobility: Research and Ideas on Strengthening Families, Communities, and the Economy," April 2–3, 2015.

1. Give greater weight to demographic factors in targeting public resources.

Although income has been the primary benchmark for safety net and tax benefits, our research at the St. Louis Fed suggests that age or birth year, race or ethnicity, and education must now play a greater role in the targeting of scarce public resources. The United States has dedicated massive resources, ruled on issues such as desegregation and voting rights, reduced discrimination in housing and lending practices, built schools and universities, subsidized higher education for disadvantaged students, and otherwise strived and often succeeded in helping less-educated and minority families move forward. College attendance rates have been steadily rising, and minorities now hold more elected offices than ever, for example. However, millions of these families remain economically vulnerable—and, in some ways, are now even more fragile, given growing economic penalties on less educated and non-white families. Therefore, broad, ambitious efforts to invest in less-educated and minority families must not only continue, but be strengthened.

With regard to age, the United States has invested less during the earlier years of life, and it lags in per capita spending on children compared with other advanced nations. In fact, the U.S. social contract has relied on the ability of younger working Americans to finance the safety net of older Americans. However, because that social contract is now threatened, and given the challenges facing younger Americans (as outlined in this and Phil Longman's essay), smarter and more robust investments earlier in life are merited. Could we, for example, consider more of an age-based social contract, where newborns, school-aged youth, and young adults starting their careers and/or families, receive a public benefit to help them build human capital and net worth? These investments could be modeled on the "pay it forward" idea, where public investments in individual families (through, for example, no- or low-cost tuition plans) are paid back later in life directly through earnings or, indirectly, through greater productivity and economic growth.

2. Create ways for families to save when children are young and integrate savings plans into other early interventions.

A growing number of children—up to two-thirds, according to Putnam—may now have a more difficult time getting on a path to economic success. This suggests that policymakers, communities, foundations, and others now have an even greater responsibility to promote a fair shot at upward economic mobility.

Thankfully, a growing body of research suggests that early investments in children can have large and multiplying effects throughout life. Key to overcoming inherited disadvantages is to intervene when investments are likely to have the biggest payoff, which is early in life. Such interventions are likely to generate larger public returns as well.[23]

Our own work shows that factors other than education or age are contributing to the wealth gap between thrivers and strugglers. The factors we identified, using non-Fed, secondary sources of data, include parental influences, native ability, "grit" or determination, neighborhood effects, social networks, and most relevant for this policy discussion, early interventions.[24]

As Putnam and others have documented, factors that influence a child's life well before kindergarten—such as whether a child is read and talked to; has good pre- and post-natal nutrition; lives in a good neighborhood; is cognitively stimulated; has a network of extended family, friends, and institutions; is free of stress, and has good health care may have as much if not more to do with whether a child will eventually achieve social and financial success than, say, the quality of schools or the effectiveness of job-training programs later in life.

The Nobel laureate economist James Heckman documents a much greater return on investments in human capital early in life, including pre-natal investments (see Figure 3).[25] Raj Chetty and his colleagues at Harvard's Equality of Opportunity Project find major differences in rates of upward economic mobility by geographic region; the earlier and longer a child is exposed to a better neighborhood environment, the greater the likelihood of upward mobility.[26]

---

23 Jason Furman, "Smart Social Programs," *New York Times*, May 11, 2015, p. A32.

24 Emmons and Noeth, Febuary 2015, op. cit. For more on grit, see Angela Duckworth et al. "Grit: Perseverance and Passion for Long-Term Goals," *Journal of Personality and Social Psychology*, 92(6): 1087–1101.

25 James Heckman, "Why Early Investment Matters," (Chicago: The Heckman Equation, n.d.).

26 Raj Chetty, "Improving Opportunities for Economic Mobility in the United States." Testimony before the Budget Committee of the United States Senate, April 1, 2014.

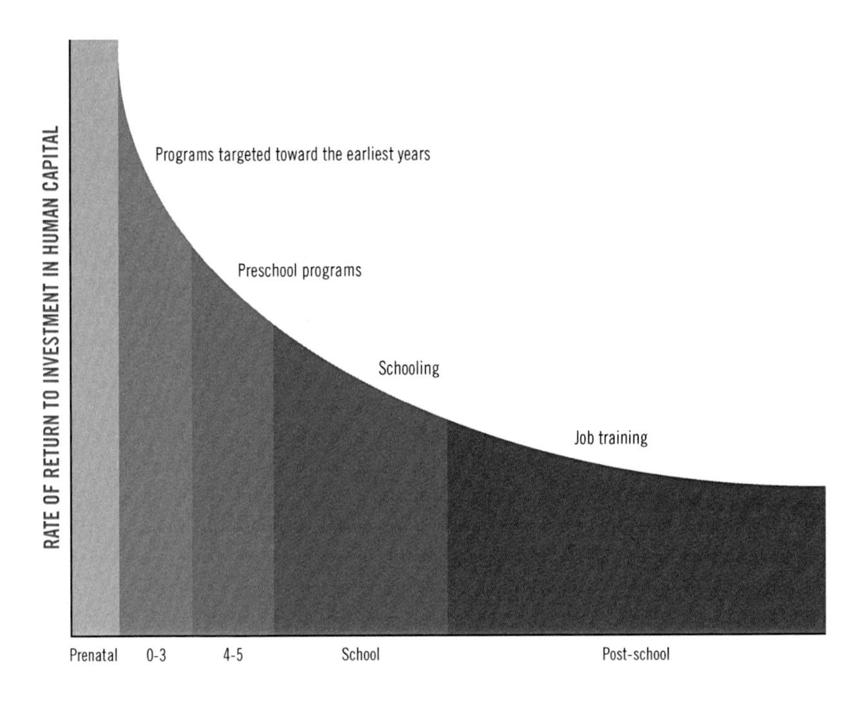

Figure 3: Returns to a Unit Dollar Invested

In the assets field, there is a growing body of evidence that savings accounts and assets early in life lead to better outcomes later in life. The Assets and Education Initiative finds that "early liquid assets (ones the household has when the child is between ages 2 to 10)... work with children's academic ability to influence whether they attend college. The effect is stronger for low-income children than it is for high-income children."[27] Two studies using randomized trials in the SEED OK experiment in Oklahoma show that Child Development Accounts (CDAs)[28] have a positive impact on social development for children around age 4. This effect was greatest in children in disadvantaged groups.[29] A second study

27 William Elliot and Michael Sherraden, "Assets and Educational Achievement: Theory and Evidence," *Economics and Education Review*, 33 (3) (2013): 1–7.

28 CDAs are also referred to as Child Savings Accounts, or CSAs. Many prefer CDAs because it emphasizes the developmental aspects of savings accounts early in life. CDAs/CSAs refer to savings accounts in a child's name that are usually restricted to higher education and are often supported by community organizations, foundations, and state and local governments. See CFED, New America, or the Center for Social Development for specific examples and policy recommendations of how to expand CDAs.

29 Jin Huang et al., "Effects of Child Development Accounts on Early Social-Emotional Development: An Experimental Test," *JAMA Pediatrics* 168 (3) (2013): 265–271.

finds that CDAs increase the psychological well-being of mothers, and again the effect was greatest among disadvantaged groups.[30]

I close this section with two recommendations. First, policies to expand CDAs nationwide should be seriously considered, building on successful state, county-, and city-wide models in Maine, Rhode Island, Nevada, Oklahoma, Indiana, Mississippi, San Francisco, St. Louis, and elsewhere. Every child should automatically receive a funded CDA, ideally at birth or, at the latest, when entering kindergarten. These accounts can then be used to leverage other public, private, charitable, and family investments to build financial capability and to help create a "college-going" culture.

Second, further consideration should be given to strategies that integrate CDAs and similar early asset strategies into the fabric of the other interventions aimed at young children. For example, a CDA might be offered to every mother who enrolls in a prenatal health program, or to every child entering Head Start or any preschool program. Reading programs might offer an education-focused CDA. Pell Grants might be "front loaded" so that income-eligible children at age 5 receive a small portion of their Pell in a CDA, which would then reduce their Pell grant at age 18 accordingly; The College Board has, in fact, advanced a similar idea. It will be difficult, in my view, for stand-alone CDA interventions to reach all economically vulnerable children. Accordingly, integrating early assets and early childhood interventions holds promise for both impact and scale.

3. Help parents and other adults build liquidity and financial assets.

But of course we cannot build family financial health and well-being by investing only in kids and not also their parents and other adults. Accordingly, we should adopt a "two-generation" approach in policies.[31] Struggling families need a range of sound balance sheet investments, including better banking options, credit repair, more college and retirement savings, fewer debts, and paths to sustainable homeownership and small-business opportunities. But one intervention in particular cuts

---

30 Jin Huang, Michael Sherraden, and Jason Purnell, "Impacts of Child Development Accounts on Maternal Depressive Symptoms: Evidence from a Randomized Statewide Policy Experiment," *Social Science and Medicine* 112 (2014): 30–38.

31 See "Helping Parents, Helping Children: Two-Generation Mechanisms," *The Future of Children: Princeton-Brookings* 24 (1) (Spring 2014).

across family balance sheets and promotes both financial stability (a family's first priority)[32] and economic mobility: creating liquidity.

The need for liquidity is well documented, both in this book (see the essay by Jennifer Tescher and Rachel Schneider) and through other research. The Federal Reserve Board's Survey of Household Economics and Decisionmaking (SHED) finds that an unexpected expense of just $400 would prompt nearly one-half of all households to borrow funds, sell something, or simply not pay at all.[33] The SHED also shows that the top savings priority for families is emergency or liquid savings, yet only about one-half of all Americans have such savings. And CFED finds that 44 percent of households are "liquid asset poor."[34]

And it is not just lack of savings that places families at risk; it is also, if not primarily, increasing income and expense volatility. Karen Dynan and colleagues find that the share of households experiencing a 50 percent drop in income in a two-year period rose to approximately 12 percent in the early 2000s, up from 7 percent in the early 1970s.[35] The U.S. Financial Dairies project also finds substantial income and expense volatility (see Jennifer Tescher and Rachel Schneider's essay in this volume). On average, families in the study experienced 2.5 months when income fell more than 25 percent below average, and 2.6 months when income was more than 25 percent above average. This is particularly problematic given that expenses do not conveniently move in tandem. And the JP Morgan Chase Institute, in an analysis of 100,000 of its customers—whose incomes were well into the middle class—reports that a diverse group of consumers has incomes that vary from one month to another by more than 30 percent, and families earning in the bottom 80 percent of households lack

---

32 Anthony Hannagan and Jonathan Morduch, "Income Gains and Month-to-Month Income Volatility: Household Evidence from the US Financial Diaries," Working Paper, (March 16 2015); Erin Currier et al., "The Precarious State of Family Balance Sheets," (Washington, DC: Pew Charitable Trusts, January 2015).

33 Jeff Larrimore et al., "Report on the Economic Well-Being of U.S. Households in 2014." (Washington DC: Federal Reserve Board, May 2015).

34 CFED, "Assets & Opportunity Scorecard."

35 Karen Dynan, Douglas Elmendorf, and Daniel Sichel, "The Evolution of Household Income Volatility," *The B.E. Journal of Economic Analysis & Policy*, 12 (2) (December 2012): 1–42.

sufficient savings to cover volatility in both consumption and income.[36] Clearly volatility has become "a normal part of a lot of folks' lives given the way we're earning today," remarks U.S. Financial Diaries lead researcher Jonathan Morduch. [37]

Many promising policy ideas have emerged to build emergency or flexible savings, including the Obama administration's "*my*RA" proposal, a low-cost, starter savings account created by the U.S. Treasury Department; tax-time savings opportunities, such as the "Refund to Savings" experiment, which uses behavioral savings prompts in TurboTax's federal free edition; employer-sponsored programs, such as AutoSave, which tested the idea of automatic payroll deductions for emergency savings; and products that automatically build liquid savings as families spend or pay down consumer or mortgage debts. Some of the most novel and promising ideas to build liquidity are found in the book, *A Fragile Balance*, edited by J. Michael Collins.

When families have more liquid savings, they can better manage their cash flows and volatility; rely less on friends, family and payday lenders to meet cash shortfalls; have better banking options; and save for education, training, or a small business, as well as a home or apartment in a better neighborhood. A study by Susan Mayer and Christopher Jencks, for example, finds that the ability to borrow $500 in a financial pinch may do as much to reduce material hardship as tripling a family's income.[38] And Putnam conveys research showing that "an increase in family income by $3,000 during a child's first five years of life seems to be associated with the equivalent of 20 SAT points higher on achievement tests and nearly 20 percent higher income later in life."[39]

In my view, then, no intervention better cuts across the health of U.S. family balance sheets, and does more to promote family stability and

---

36 Diana Farrell and Fiona Greig, "Weathering Volatility: Big Data on Financial Ups and Downs of U.S. Individuals." (New York: JP Morgan Chase & Co. Institute, May 2015).

37 As quoted in Nick Timiraos, "Cash Crunch, for Many, is a Monthly Woe," *Wall Street Journal*, May 20, 2015.

38 Susan Mayer and Christopher Jencks, "Poverty and the Distribution of Material Hardship," *Journal of Human Resources* 24 (1) (1989): 88–114.

39 Putnam, *Our Kids*: p. 246.

mobility, than building emergency savings and liquidity. Accordingly, efforts to promote savings and liquidity should be strongly considered.

CONCLUSION

To be most effective, these three policy recommendations must be integrated into other efforts—precisely the topic of this book. The integration of health and wealth efforts, for example, as Jason Purnell describes in this volume, holds great potential. Although no one or two interventions, including the most promising ones, are likely to erase enormous gaps in education, earnings, or wealth, those discussed in this essay and in this book are nonetheless likely to significantly increase the number of struggling Americans who can attain financial health or well-being.

And yet, the questions remain: Are even the most promising interventions at sufficient scale enough to overcome the growing power of demographic headwinds suppressing economic opportunity for millions? Can we really empower more Americans to make sound financial choices and build financial capability when it appears that so many of those "choices" have already been made, especially for children and younger Americans?

It is hard to know, but we have faced a similar challenge before—and realized some remarkable accomplishments. Leading up to the Progressive Era, the roughly 30-year period beginning with the depression of the early 1890s, the U.S. faced a banking crisis and recession, gaping inequality, double-digit unemployment, rapid technological change, an inefficient and expensive health care system, massive consolidation among corporations, a well-organized lobby on behalf of spending on the elderly, and mounting concerns about the environment. Sound familiar?

In response, the Progressives reformed the health care system, created a regulatory regime for Wall Street and the banking sector that prevented any need for massive taxpayer bailouts (including the Federal Reserve Act, one of the most enduring of all Progressive reforms). They stopped predatory lending, instituted the federal, progressive income tax system, installed an ethic of conservation and public service, universalized high school education, seriously reduced the role of money in politics, and left no legacy of public debt.[40]

How did the Progressives accomplish this? Naturally, many factors were in play, including strong national will spanning all political parties. But what drove these reforms was a commitment to protect workers, families, and communities from larger economic, corporate, and political forces. Particularly relevant for our purposes, there was also a commitment to what was then called "thrift"—a musty term today but, in the Progressives' mind, one that meant conserving one's time, health, money, and natural resources. Financially, it meant an aversion to debt and an embrace of what today we would call asset building—accumulating savings and owning assets. To help families achieve thrift, the Progressives forged new initiatives and built new institutions—credit unions and thrifts, money management programs in schools, new consumer laws and regulations, the progressive income tax system, the Federal Reserve system—and applied many techniques that today we would call behavioral economics to ensure those institutions led to savings and property ownership. Though the nation's once-dominant gene of asset-building went recessive as the twentieth century progressed, it is now time for that gene to express itself again.

As Mark Twain is said to have observed, history may not repeat itself, but it often rhymes. For the sake of all families, and especially of Troy's family and millions like theirs, let's hope so.

---

40 Of course, many Progressive Era efforts failed, such as Prohibition, even if it was designed to promote preventive health and financial independence. Many other efforts we would find repulsive today, such as eugenics and other pseudo-sciences that were used to justify deepening repression of blacks and other minority groups. My point in highlighting the accomplishments of the Progressive Era is to show that larger demographic, technological, and economic forces can be overcome with powerful ideas, new policies and institutions, and broad-based political will.

■ ■ ■

***RAY BOSHARA** is senior advisor and director of the Center for Household Financial Stability at the Federal Reserve Bank of St. Louis. Before joining the Fed in April 2011, Boshara was vice president of the New America Foundation, a D.C.-based think tank, and policy director at CFED. He has advised presidential candidates and leading policymakers worldwide, and testified before the U.S. Congress several times. He has written for* The Washington Post, The New York Times, Atlantic Monthly, *among others, and is the co-author (with Phillip Longman) of the 2009 book,* The Next Progressive Era. *Boshara is a graduate of Ohio State University, Yale Divinity School and the John F. Kennedy School of Government at Harvard.*

THE REAL FINANCIAL LIVES OF AMERICANS

Jennifer Tescher and Rachel Schneider
Center for Financial Services Innovation

Millions of Americans continue to struggle financially in the long wake of the Great Recession despite an improving economy. On the surface, many families appear to have the trappings of success—jobs, homes, health insurance, and retirement accounts. Yet a closer look reveals an unsettling level of financial fragility, stress and reduced confidence about the future.

That financial fragility is not simply a result of the recession. Stagnant wages, historic levels of inequality, and technology's role in disrupting labor markets are all trends that grew slowly and quietly but have since caught the country's attention with the spectacular plunge precipitated by the financial crisis. It was easy to miss the growing financial pressure on American families during the last 25 years, in part because consumers were masking their problems with unsustainable levels of debt. It was also easy to miss the growing fragility because of the lack of systematic analysis of the inner workings of households' day-to-day financial systems.

A new body of research offers fresh and powerful insights into the real financial lives of Americans—their needs and aspirations, the choices they face, the networks and resources available to them, and their outlook. The data present a revised diagnosis of the financial pressure that families face and suggest that policymakers and practitioners alike must redefine what financial success means to better align the ways in which they try to advance financial success with consumers' actual expectations and goals. We believe that what Americans want, and what policmakers and practitioners should help them to achieve, is financial health and well-being. Developing a shared definition and metrics for financial health is a crucial first step toward moving the country in this direction, and creating a standard by which to hold policymakers and practitioners accountable for improving the financial lives of Americans.

THE REAL FINANCIAL LIVES OF AMERICANS

Meet Sarah and Sam Johnson. The Johnsons live in Ohio, in a small town near Cincinnati. Sarah is 38, and Sam is 49, and this is a second marriage for both. Sarah works full-time as a human resources assistant and part-time as a secretary. Sam sells electrical equipment, and he also coaches sports and works weekends at a call center. They support their daughter, Amy, age 8, and two grown children from prior marriages. Their son Matthew, age 20, is a full-time student living with them, and their daughter Anne, also 20, lives with them part-time but plans to move.

By their annual income, things look promising for the Johnsons. They have multiple sources of income and earn between $55,000 and $60,000 a year, just above the U.S. median. They own a house and two cars, and they have a 401(k) retirement account and health insurance. They have a bank account and credit cards, and they pay their bills online. They spend money on clothes, entertainment, and celebrating important events in their children's lives.

Yet beneath the surface, the Johnsons are struggling. Despite working multiple jobs and receiving college financial aid, their monthly income is volatile and its timing and frequency is irregular. Their bills' due dates, however, do not fluctuate accordingly. To make matters more complicated, their expenses fluctuate significantly from month to month. With this level of financial uncertainty, the Johnsons have been unable to put aside even a small cushion of savings for unplanned events, like the leaky roof they had, or the income reduction they faced when Sam went on short-term disability while recovering from foot surgery.

How do they cope? Some months they economize by downgrading the amount and quality of the food they buy. Some months they pay their mortgage and car loan instead of the light bill or phone bill. Some months they turn to credit cards, and as a result they have accumulated more than $3,000 in debt across seven cards. When asked to name their greatest financial aspiration, the Johnsons said, "To be able to pay our bills on time."

While Johnson isn't their real name, and some of the details of their story have been changed to protect their identity, their situation is real. They are one of the 235 families that participated in the path-breaking U.S. Financial Diaries project, a joint venture led by Jonathan Morduch of New York University's Financial Access Initiative and Rachel Schneider of the Center for Financial Services Innovation (CFSI). As the U.S. Financial Diaries show, the Johnsons' story is all too common.[1]

The 2015 Consumer Financial Health Survey conducted by CFSI provides a representative snapshot of the struggle American households face:

- 26 percent of Americans say their finances cause them significant stress.
- 43 percent struggle to keep up with bill payments.
- 36 percent are not confident they could come up with $2,000 in the next month for an emergency.
- 30 percent are carrying an unhealthy amount of debt.

Although the struggle cuts across income, age, race and ethnicity, black and Hispanic households of all incomes are struggling more than others:

- 19 percent of black households and 24 percent of Hispanic households are highly satisfied with their present financial condition, compared with 34 percent of white households.
- 35 percent of black households and 40 percent of Hispanic households find themselves always living paycheck-to-paycheck, compared with 29 percent of white households.
- 41 percent of black households and 48 percent of Hispanic households are confident they can meet their short-term saving goals, compared with 54 percent of white households.

In short, according to the Pew Charitable Trusts, American households are "savings limited, income constrained, and debt challenged." Pew's 2015 study, "The Precarious State of Family Balance Sheets," showed that 70 percent of U.S. households face at least one of these three challenges, and more than one-third face two or even all three at the same time.

---

1 For more information on the Diaries and the Johnsons, see www.usfinancialdiaries.org.

NEW DATA, REVISED DIAGNOSIS

We know more about the financial challenges Americans face because of the emergence of several new data sources that are helping paint a more complete, nuanced and complex picture. The Federal Reserve Board's Survey of Household Economic Decisionmaking (SHED) captures a snapshot of the financial and economic well-being of U.S. households, the financial issues they face, and perceived risks to their financial stability. CFSI's Consumer Financial Health Study (CFHS) focuses on consumers' financial behaviors, attitudes, preferences and use of financial services, and uses the data to segment households by their level of financial health. Pew's Financial Security and Mobility project studies how families' balance sheets relate to both short-term financial stability and longer-term economic mobility. The U.S. Financial Diaries (the Diaries) analyzes extremely detailed data on the financial activities of 235 low- and moderate-income households over the course of a year to understand how they manage their daily finances. The inaugural report of the JPMorgan Chase Institute, "Weathering Volatility: Big Data on the Financial Ups and Downs of U.S. Individuals," analyzes proprietary data to determine how customers' income and consumption fluctuated monthly and yearly.

This research differs from other data sets, such as the Federal Reserve's Survey of Consumer Finance (SCF), in a few important ways. The SCF is designed to shed light on what households own and how much they owe in order to analyze trends in net worth. Given that assets are not evenly distributed, the survey oversamples wealthy households, which are most likely to own assets. In contrast, much of the research described above is intended to shed light on an array of household behaviors, decisions, and attitudes that are precursors to net worth—day-to-day cash flow, for instance, or subjective matters such as stress, satisfaction, and confidence. In several of these studies, researchers oversampled households in lower income quartiles to ensure a full picture.

Together, this new body of work creates a different lens on the financial lives of American households. What emerges suggests a set of revised diagnoses of the financial concerns facing Americans and new strategies for treatment.

1. Cash flow is as important an indicator as annual income

The Johnsons' annual tax returns don't tell their whole story. For that, it is necessary to also look at their pay stubs. Their monthly income fluctuates dramatically over time, from about $4,100 to nearly $9,000. The causes are numerous. Sam received only two-thirds of his regular pay while he recovered from his foot surgery. Both Sam's and Sarah's part-time jobs pay irregularly. Sarah's ex-husband pays child support sporadically. Sarah and her son are both attending college, and they both get financial aid, but it arrives in lump sums irregularly during the year.

Income volatility is not a new phenomenon for families, but it is getting more attention lately. Research on the evolution of household income volatility by economists Karen Dynan, Douglas Elmendorf, and Daniel Sichel estimates that American household incomes became 30 percent more volatile between the early 1970s and the late 2000s. Income spikes and dips were commonplace for the families in the U.S. Financial Diaries. Their income had, on average, two and a half spikes and dips—defined as a 25 percent deviation from the norm—for a total of more than five months during the year in which income was materially different from the norm.

Other research has documented this same trend. Pew's Financial Security and Mobility study showed that, in any given two-year period, nearly one-half of households surveyed experience an income gain or drop of more than 25 percent. The Federal Reserve's SHED study found that 21 percent of respondents occasionally experience months with unusually high or low incomes, and 10 percent said that their income varies quite a bit from month to month. Monthly income volatility is more common than annual fluctuations. The JPMorgan Chase Institute "Weathering Volatility" report shows that 84 percent of individuals experienced at least a 5 percent change in their monthly income, compared with 70 percent of individuals who experienced such a change annually. Lower-income households' incomes are particularly volatile. The Diaries found that one-half of households at or below U.S. poverty thresholds had trouble predicting their income during the month, compared to approximately one-fourth of households with incomes greater than twice the poverty threshold.

Complicating matters more, expenses can be as uncertain as income. For the Johnsons, only 20 percent of their monthly expenses are fixed. Over the course of seven months, their monthly expenses varied from $4,660 to $11,000. The $11,000 month included a new, more reliable car for work, a roof repair and clean-up of related water damage. The water damage aggravated their daughter's asthma, so they had to replace the furniture and buy an air purifier.

Invariably, the income and expense shocks do not arrive in tandem, compounding the challenge. For Diaries families, about 60 percent of spending spikes were not accompanied by an income spike in the same month. One-quarter of expense spikes occur when a household's income is below its median income. When families have access to savings or credit, the mismatch between income and spending can be accommodated. But for households without that slack, a mismatch is a source of anxiety and challenge.

2. Income matters, but so do planning and saving

The lack of wage growth in the United States is well documented, and a major challenge. Yet more income does not necessarily translate into financial success. Consider households with incomes over $100,000. According to Pew's Mobility research, 22 percent say they do not feel financially secure, 12 percent have less than $10,000 in non-housing wealth, and 10 percent have no savings.

The CFHS documents similar conditions. One-third of households making more than $100,000 fall into either a coping or vulnerable segment, while two-thirds are healthy.[2] In contrast, approximately one in five households earning less than $30,000 are healthy, as are 39 percent of those earning between $30,000 and $60,000.

Making more money certainly has some effect. For instance, 40 percent of CFHS households earning less than $25,000 a year say they "worry all the time about being able to meet monthly living expenses," compared with 15 percent of households earning more than $100,000. Higher

---

2 The CFHS segmented households into seven categories based on the strength of their day-to-day financial system, their level of financial resilience, and how well positioned they were to pursue financial opportunities. The seven segments were bundled into three groups: healthy, coping, and vulnerable.

income is associated with less financial worry, but more income does not always eliminate worry.

Besides income, what else affects financial health? Planning, saving, and time horizon are most important. A long-term orientation is also key. Households that plan ahead for large, irregular expenses are 10 times more likely to be financially healthy than those that do not. Households with a longer savings time frame (five or more years) are 8 times more likely to be financially healthy than those whose savings time horizon is less than five years. Although households with higher incomes were more likely to be financially healthy, planning is much more predictive of financial health than income.

Against that backdrop, the Johnsons' experience is the norm. It seems likely they would describe themselves as struggling. They work very hard at multiple jobs and earn more than the U.S. median, but none of that mattered when their old car started malfunctioning and their roof sprang a leak.

3. Access to financial services is important but insufficient

A growing awareness of Americans' financial challenges has galvanized financial service providers and policymakers to design strategies to increase access to bank accounts and reduce use of "alternative" products and services like check cashing and payday loans.

However, the CFHS data show that bank account ownership alone is no guarantee of broader financial success. A little more than one-half of survey respondents with a checking or savings account are in the coping or vulnerable groups, in part because nearly one-third have an unhealthy amount of debt. Similarly, a savings account is not synonymous with saving. Approximately one in five savings account holders have less than $1,000 in savings, and slightly more than one-half have no plan for saving regularly.

Consider the Johnsons. They have a checking account, a mortgage, two car loans, seven credit cards, student loans, a retirement savings account, and employer-sponsored health insurance. They also have $3,000 in credit card debt, $8,300 in medical debt, and little savings beyond their retirement accounts. Access to financial services is useful for them, but it is not solving their core financial challenges.

4. Borrowing and saving are opposite sides of the same coin

Borrowing has long been frowned upon, while saving has long been praised. Yet people still choose to borrow, rather than spend their savings. In the CFHS, 39 percent of households say they sometimes leave a balance on their credit cards instead of using savings to pay it off. The SHED survey asked respondents a hypothetical question about how they would allocate an unexpected $1,000 of extra income. On average, respondents said they would spend $227, save $395, and pay down $377 of debt. More than one-fourth of respondents who reported saving some of their income said they were saving to pay down their debt.

Why do people borrow when they have money saved? Sometimes they need more than they have saved. Other times, they do not want to deplete their reserves. They like the idea that they will still have savings in case of an emergency. Some people borrow to repair or build their credit histories. Others use borrowing as a commitment mechanism to continue to build up more savings. In short, the cheapest possible access to funds is not the sole determinant of why people choose to borrow or save, though that is often how traditional economists expect them to make financial decisions.

In fact, both borrowing and saving are simply ways to stretch money by turning a large purchase into a smaller set of more manageable payments. The difference is that saving is free (or sometimes, interest-bearing) and provides the peace of mind that comes with knowing the funds have been socked away for the future, but it requires the self-discipline of accumulating the funds first. In contrast, borrowing allows more immediate gratification and the ability to build a credit history, but comes with a fee and with the potential anxiety of a future obligation. When deciding when to borrow or save, people appear to take both the psychological cost and the financial cost into account.

That is certainly the case for the Johnsons. Sarah says that she would never have been able to save up for the down payment for their house. Coming up with $20,000 would have been too daunting. However, the seller let them accumulate the down payment over 18 months, bundling the payments into their rent while they lived in the house. This converted their savings activity into an obligation like a debt, and gave them access to mortgage credit that would otherwise have been unattainable.

5. Financial progress is complex, unpredictable, and often messy

The financial lives of Americans are often characterized as linear trajectories "up the ladder." When you're young, you accumulate debt, which you pay down as you accumulate wealth over time. But rarely do individuals' lives conform to these neat, stepwise progressions.

Households experience many fluctuations in their wealth, and significant life events can create road bumps in people's financial lives. For instance, nearly one-third of Americans fell below the poverty line between 2009 and 2011, according to a 2014 Census Bureau report, but only a fraction of them stayed there for the entire three-year period. In "Americans' Financial Security; Perception and Reality," Pew reports that six in ten households experienced a financial shock in the prior year, such as a drop in income, a hospital visit, the loss of a spouse or partner, or a major car or home repair. Slightly more than one-half of this group report that the shock made it hard for them to make ends meet. That was particularly true for those making less than $25,000 a year (73 percent), but even for those making more than $100,000 a year, 34 percent felt financial strain.

The Johnsons exemplify the ups and downs families face. Earlier in her life, Sarah had filed for bankruptcy because of credit card debt. By the time she and Sam joined the Diaries study, they had resolved their credit issues enough to qualify for a mortgage and buy their home. After the study, however, Sarah filed for bankruptcy again. This time, it was because she had too many medical expenses.

Practitioners tend to look at household savings balances over time and are disappointed to not see steady growth. During a six-month period, however, the Johnsons' account balance fluctuated between $250 and $8,600. Their experience is typical. Looking at point-in-time savings balances or expecting a constant upward trajectory misses the fact that people are indeed saving. They are just then spending and saving again in short, frequent intervals.

DEFINING THE ULTIMATE OUTCOME

The financial challenges facing Americans are bigger and broader than previously understood. While the FDIC identifies 68 million Americans who are unbanked or underbanked, the CFHS identifies 138 million Americans who are financially challenged. Moreover, families like the Johnsons demonstrate that consumer behavior does not always conform to standard economic theories. Behavior that traditional economists view as "irrational" turns out to be quite rational given people's circumstances and the available choices. When thinking about spending, saving, and borrowing, people are not simply choosing between now and later. The Diaries help us see that "soon"—such as the bill that is due next month—also matters and may influence behavior more than the prospect of putting money away for a distant future. Finally, understanding how households are faring financially is a more complex exercise than was previously appreciated. Though the data help paint a more nuanced picture, they do not suggest the path forward.

Nonprofit practitioners in the asset-building and financial capability fields see these new realities from their positions on the frontlines. As described in the opening essay by Andrea Levere and Leigh Tivol, many have been experimenting with a range of initiatives to address the challenges the Johnsons face, helping consumers build their financial capability through savings, credit building, and coaching. Through trial and error, practitioners have developed valuable insights about how to help consumers behave in ways that lead to better financial outcomes, such as more savings and better credit scores.

Still, the question remains, to what end? There is little clarity about the desired ultimate outcome, beyond the bigger savings balance and improved credit score. For some, the ultimate outcome is alleviating poverty. Yet the data show that the challenge extends beyond the poor, and beyond income. This lack of agreement on optimal outcomes has made it challenging to measure the success of financial capability initiatives. In turn, it is difficult to know which interventions are successful and deserving of greater investment and expansion. This issue plagues not only nonprofit practitioners in the asset-building and financial capability fields, but also private sector providers of financial services and the policymakers who set the ground rules for the marketplace.

But now, with more data in hand, practitioners and financial services providers have a new opportunity to connect their work on the ground to a broader vision for and definition of success that reflects the current realities of Americans' lives. A common goal and a new framework for improving household financial outcomes—one that is broad enough to transcend fields and industries—will enable the complicated universe of government, the private sector and the nonprofit community to work in greater concert, and therefore, to achieve greater impact.

We believe success should be defined as greater consumer financial health and well-being.

A FRAMEWORK FOR FINANCIAL HEALTH

The Consumer Financial Protection Bureau (CFPB), in an effort to create a framework for measuring the success of financial education, has defined financial well-being as "a state of being wherein a person can fully meet current and ongoing financial obligations, can feel secure in their financial future, and is able to make choices that allow enjoyment of life." In "Financial well-being: The goal of financial education," the CFPB goes on to identify four central elements of well-being: 1) control over day-to-day, month-to-month finances; 2) capacity to absorb a financial shock; 3) financial freedom to make choices to enjoy life; and 4) being on track to meet financial goals.

CFSI has been developing a similar success framework for financial health, which we define as when daily financial systems help individuals build resilience and increase opportunity. Table 1 includes the range of indicators we have identified for financial health.

Although the specific language of the CFSI and CFPB definitions differs, the concepts are fundamentally the same. Financial health and well-being is about pursuing dreams and reducing stress. The products and tools individuals use daily and their choices and decisions either help or hinder them in their quest.

A consensus that financial health and well-being is the right path forward is beginning to emerge across government, the private sector, and the nonprofit community. The CFPB has documented growing agreement that financial well-being should be the ultimate measure of success. Financial

DAILY FINANCIAL SYSTEM	▪ Maintains expenses equal to or lower than income ▪ Pays bills on time and avoids late fees ▪ Is able to pay debt obligations ▪ Has an acceptable monthly debt service to income ratio ▪ Is aware of financial situation and status ▪ Plans ahead for large, irregular expenses ▪ Has access to financial services and advice ▪ Is satisfied with current financial condition ▪ Has an acceptable level of financial stress ▪ Is confident in ability to meet short-term goals
BUILD RESILIENCE	▪ Builds savings and achieves short-term savings goals ▪ Owns appropriate insurance policies ▪ Has a diverse safety net, including an emergency fund and access to affordable credit or a social network ▪ Is able to recover from financial problems ▪ Perceives self as in control of financial matters
INCREASE OPPORTUNITY	▪ Saves regularly ▪ Has a retirement plan and saves for retirement ▪ Keeps total indebtedness at a manageable level ▪ Maintains a positive credit profile ▪ Stays on track to meet long-term savings goals ▪ Has the means to improve human capital ▪ Has an acceptable tolerance for risk ▪ Plans ahead for the medium- and long-term ▪ Is confident in ability to meet long-term goals

Table 1. Indicators of "Financial Health"

services firms, both established and new, are experimenting with ways to deliver products and services to help their customers measure, track, and improve their financial health. Leaders in the global financial inclusion community are beginning to explore whether financial health is a useful framework for understanding and measuring success.

Actors beyond the financial services and capability arenas are beginning to recognize the link between their success and the financial success of their customers and stakeholders—as discussed in many of the essays in Part 2 of this book. As Staples' experience demonstrates (see Regis Mulot's essay in this volume), employers across a variety of sectors are introducing financial wellness initiatives to improve productivity and satisfaction. Jason Purnell in his essay shows how the public health community is exploring financial health as a factor in broader health outcomes. Regina Stanback Stroud describes how community colleges are realizing that, to improve college completion rates, they must focus on the financial needs and challenges of their students. Treasury Deputy Secretary Sarah Bloom Raskin reports that the federal government is focusing on rising levels of student debt because it sees the connection between the financial health of Millennials and the health of the broader economy.

Most people have a gut sense of what financial health looks and feels like, but it is a complicated concept to define and measure. Financial health is fluid and dynamic, representing a continuum from poor financial health to good. Achieving and maintaining financial health is a lifelong journey. Even with the new data that now exist, there is still more to know about how families move along the continuum or about the pace of and breaks in their travels. There is also still more to understand about how the experience differs for people of color or for the very poor. Although it is a safe bet that lifecycle plays a part, the data suggest that people may experience financial shifts throughout their lives. To complicate matters further, financial health is not entirely an objective matter. Individuals have different life goals and different personalities. Financial health does not look exactly the same for everyone, nor does the path to achieving it.

Moreover, as the essays by Ray Boshara and authors in Part 3 of this book demonstrate, whether and how individuals achieve financial health depends greatly on the broader environment and institutional structures available to them. Imagine the immigrant who does everything right but cannot qualify for a car loan or a mortgage because she lacks a formal credit file. In this case, the lending institution's practices are blocking the path to financial health.

What is missing is an agreed-upon set of financial health metrics. Building these metrics will require balancing the need for a point-in-time snapshot of families' status with the benefits of a longer term perspective. It will require balancing the value of objective and subjective data, and considering both consumer and institutional needs and opportunities. Yet building the metrics is crucial. With metrics in hand, consumers will be more likely to get the information and insight they need to play their part in improving their own financial health. Nonprofit providers will have the framework they need to ensure their programs are succeeding in helping clients reach the right end goal. Private-sector companies can be challenged to hold themselves accountable for their contributions to the financial health of their employees, their customers, and their stakeholders. Finally, governments can be encouraged to see themselves as having an affirmative responsibility to improve the financial health of their citizens and provide a blueprint for the kinds of policies to enact, especially for American families like the Johnsons who struggle the most.

MORE THAN JUST WORDS: A SHARED VISION ACROSS FIELDS

The first step in designing and applying financial health metrics is to encourage cross-sector information sharing and conversation, which begins in the pages of this book and, hopefully, sparks an even broader dialogue. Different efforts are addressing different strands of the same problem. Developing a shared view about how to define the ultimate goal is critical in ensuring that the whole of the work is greater than the sum of its parts.

Practitioners, providers and policymakers who engage in this dialogue will need to resist the natural temptation to just "get on with it," adopting new semantics before achieving a shared understanding of the ultimate goal. Whether our individual work is anchored in workforce development, community development, asset building or financial capability, we need to complete the hard work of defining the appropriate metrics through which we can each be held accountable. If these metrics are anchored sufficiently in financial health and well-being, they will transcend the specific sector from which we each hail.

Words matter, but the promise of financial health and well-being is more than just new words to describe what we each do. This new paradigm offers a blueprint for how each of our efforts contributes to the overall stability, resilience and upward mobility of American families. Understanding what we each have to offer, in the context of other actors and other fields, is critical. The magnitude of the challenges Americans face, coupled with the questionable future of the economy and our broken political system, demand that we leverage our mutual efforts as much as possible if we are to succeed in moving all Americans toward financial health.

While finding common cause in a clearly defined and measurable outcome is an essential foundation for the work ahead, getting there requires a diversity of approaches and perspectives. The history of the asset-building and financial capability fields demonstrates just how much we are still inventing and learning, and how important it is to keep going, even when we do not know all the answers. Our collective experimentation will be much more powerful if we can all agree that what we are ultimately aiming for is consumer financial health and well-being.

Thea Garon of CFSI provided invaluable assistance in writing this chapter.

■ ■ ■

JENNIFER TESCHER *is the founder, president, and CEO of the Center for Financial Services Innovation. CFSI is the authority on consumer financial health, leading a network of committed financial services innovators to build better consumer products and practices. As an entrepreneur, innovator, and forceful voice for change, Tescher has focused her work and career on the idea that, by aligning consumer and provider success, business can be a force for good in the lives of consumers, communities, and the economy.*

■ ■ ■

RACHEL SCHNEIDER *is a senior vice president at CFSI. Under her leadership, CFSI produces independent, data-driven consumer and industry research and advice. Schneider is also a principle investigator on the U.S. Financial Diaries research study, a project in partnership with the Financial Access Initiative at New York University. The U.S. Financial Diaries collects highly detailed data about more than 200 households, including how they save, spend, borrow and plan their financial lives. She is co-authoring a book with Jonathan Morduch about the U.S. Financial Diaries findings, planned for publication in 2017.*

2

WHY FINANCIAL WELL-BEING MATTERS FOR ALL

THE ECONOMY, THE FINANCIAL SERVICES SYSTEM, AND THE COMMUNITY

FINANCIAL VULNERABILITY IS A PROBLEM
An Economist's View

Jared Bernstein
Center on Budget and Policy Priorities

In this essay, as in this book, "financial health" is taken to encompass both objective and subjective aspects of the economic lives of families, including traditional measures of income and wealth, but also access to opportunity, financial security, and financial resilience, the latter being the ability to bounce back from unexpected setbacks or other economic shocks. A financially healthy, working family putting in substantial hours of work on the job should be able to see living standards rise. Such a family should be able to live in a safe environment and be adequately insured against catastrophe. Their children should be able to achieve their full intellectual potential in school. They should have access to financial services that enable them to save enough to invest in their own and their children's futures.

Not every financially healthy family will be in the top percentiles of the income and wealth scales. There is and always will be a distribution of income in our own and similar economic systems, as well as a distribution of opportunity, educational access, and so on. But "financial health" implies that, conditional on reasonable effort, even those households at the low end of that distribution should have a fair shot at the above aspirations.

Much of the policy analysis around financial health reasonably asks how we improve access to opportunities for middle- and low-income families so they can participate in economic expansions in ways that have generally eluded them in recent decades. My questions, however, are different.

I ask: Do improvements in household financial well-being yield benefits to the health and growth of the U.S. economy, and vice versa? The U.S. economy seems stuck in a deeply damaging cycle of bubbles and busts.

Are there plausible channels through which financially unstable families interact with an under-regulated finance system that are contributing to that unsettling growth cycle? Is it also possible that financially unhealthy families create a drag on future growth by underinvesting in their children's ability to contribute to future productivity?

To telegraph the punchline, there is a growing body of research that convincingly links various aspects of financial health to growth. There is, for example, evidence that inequality, income stagnation, and under-regulated finance interact in ways that have led to bubbles and busts that damage the larger economy. Similarly, underinvesting in children's education and well-being has clear links to diminished health, earnings, and labor supply, all of which have potentially negative growth implications.

FAMILY FINANCIAL HEALTH AND THE BUBBLE AND BUST CYCLE

At least the last two recessions were born of financial bubbles. The 1990s expansion ended when the dot-com bubble burst. The 2000s expansion ended with the bursting of the housing bubble, inflated in no small part by "innovative" finance. The Great Recession that followed was particularly deep and costly, in part because it was driven by debt, and particularly housing debt.

This recent pattern of the U.S. business cycle might be *the economic shampoo cycle*, as in "bubble, bust, repeat." Figure 1 suggests that the financial health of individual households may well play a role in this shampoo cycle, as families with stagnant incomes lack adequate guidance in financial markets, thus making poor choices with negative long-term consequences.

The schematic begins at the top with increased income inequality, which by definition means that less of the economy's income growth is reaching middle- and lower-income households, while wealthy households accumulate both income and wealth. Note, for example, that according to Census data, the real median income of nonelderly households has fallen 11 percent since 2000 (more than $7,000 in real 2013 dollars).[1]

1 Lawrence Mishel and Alyssa Davis, "Modest Income Growth in 2013 Puts Slight Dent in More than a Decade of Income Losses." (September 16, 2014).

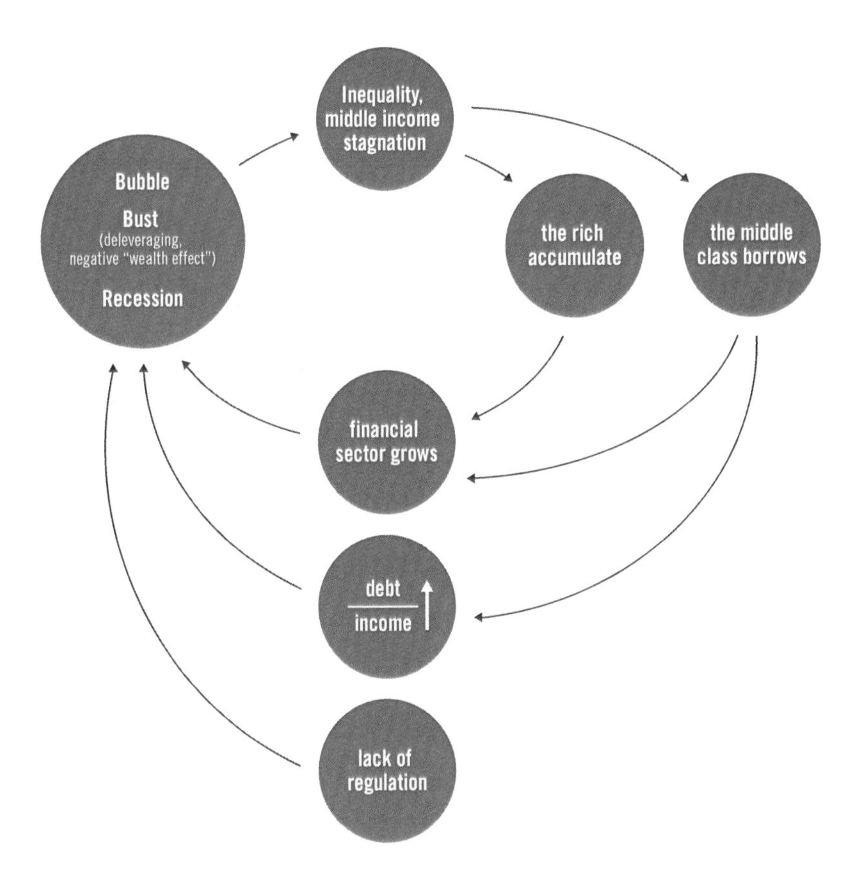

Figure 1

Moving clockwise, this dynamic has two effects. First, given their stagnant/falling incomes and low net worth, low- and moderate-income households turn to credit markets to maintain or improve their living standards. At the same time, wealth accumulates among the top few percent of households, and financial institutions make a large and relatively inexpensive supply of loanable funds available, generating a higher demand for financial intermediation and increasing the size of the financial sector.

At this point, another important dynamic enters the mix, itself a function of high wealth concentration and its disproportionate influence in our politics: the absence of both sufficient financial market oversight and adequate advice or guidance for "low-information" households using credit. This combination of forces is a potent recipe for a dangerous bubble. Financial institutions provide a large supply of loanable funds to a large group of borrowers not supported by much income growth or financial knowledge or guidance. This leads to an increase in the borrowers' debt-to-income ratio. Meanwhile, an under-regulated financial sector grows, leading to a financial bubble inflated by debt.

Add to this volatile mix the fact that the financial system's near-term incentives encourage this cycle. In the most recent iteration of the cycle, the ability of financial institutions to securitize and profitably pass off bundles of loans to other investors helped support reckless mortgage lending based on the assumption of ever-inflating house prices, not a borrower's ability to repay. Leavened by weak oversight and motivated by the ideology that the markets would self-regulate, the sequence inflated a bubble, which burst when home prices could no longer defy gravity. As a result, borrowers aggressively paid down debt, and wealth effects—the extra consumer spending that debt-fueled asset accumulation generated—quickly shifted into reverse, leading to a contraction in overall demand and recession.

It's a logical story, albeit complex. It is certainly reasonable to be skeptical about a chain with this many links, especially since history is replete with bubbles and busts amidst varying degrees of inequality and income stagnation. But there is evidence to support this story of how the Great Recession came to be. For example, there is no question that reckless finance helped to inflate a housing bubble that has been extremely and lastingly costly in terms of growth, jobs, and incomes. There is also good evidence that under-regulated financial practices played an important role in these developments.

A careful analysis of the empirical implications of this cycle finds inequality growing in tandem with the increasing leverage that supported the spending of the bottom 95 percent of households in the run-up to the Great Recession.[2] Then, when the bubble burst and borrowing constraints tightened, spending among this very large group flattened, helping to explain the slow recovery.

---

2 Barry Cynamon and Steven Fazzari, "Inequality, the Great Recession, and Slow Recovery." (October 24, 2014).

With such a complex chain of events, more evidence is warranted; however, these early analyses are convincing that an environment in which a large proportion of U.S. households is not financially healthy plays a role in some bubble/bust scenarios.

FINANCIAL HEALTH AND THE BASIC GROWTH MODEL

The core economic model holds that in the interest of efficient growth, an important role of society is to maximize the quality of inputs, both physical and capital, tasked with creating the outputs we want and need. This basic model makes a number of assumptions about how people and families help to spur growth. For example, at least in advanced economies, it is broadly assumed that education is recognized as an important public good—one that is optimally provided by government. It is assumed that households have some degree of geographic mobility and can respond to market signals that say "don't stay here; go over there for better opportunities." Finally, a lack of opportunity for upward social and economic mobility (that is, persistent poverty) constrains consumption, investments, and savings in ways that could potentially harm growth.

These assumptions in particular explain how financially healthy families contribute to macroeconomic growth and stability. Individuals boost the economy's productivity when they get the education they need to realize their potential, when they efficiently respond to market signals (especially those relating to job opportunities), and when they consume in ways that support growth. This latter channel is particularly relevant in the American case, where consumption is 70 percent of gross domestic product (GDP), compared with 55 percent in Europe and 35 percent in China.

Conversely, financially "unhealthy" families may underconsume, undereducate their children, underinvest (e.g., due to limited access to credit), and be unable to build up the resilience they need to withstand negative shocks.

But is there evidence in support of these assumptions?

Education

Large discrepancies persist between white and minority students, as well as between high-income and low-income children, in academic achievement, dropout rates, test scores, and college completion. In addition, as the gap in income between high- and low-income families has increased, so have the achievement gaps between their children.[3]

More recent research has investigated how these gaps relate to family financial health. Because compared with wealthier parents, parents with fewer economic resources also have fewer key child-rearing resources—money, time, wealth, and ability to responsibly borrow. Children from less financially healthy households have less access to enrichment opportunities such as books, tutoring, computers, sports, and so on. According to consumer spending data, in the mid- 2000s, high-income families spent seven times more than low-income families on enrichment goods for their children. This compares to four times more spending during the more equitable 1970s.[4] Access to quality preschool poses a similar disadvantage to low-income children: 68 percent of 3- and 4-year-old children from families making at least $75,000 a year were enrolled in preschool in 2013 compared with 49 percent from families making less than $40,000.[5]

Family financial health plays a well-documented role at the other end of the educational life-cycle as well: 80 percent of students born into the top income quartile between 1979 and 1982 went on to enroll in college, and 54 percent of these students completed college. In contrast, among students in the bottom income quartile, 29 percent enrolled in college, and only 9 percent eventually earned their degrees.[6] Students who enter college (any postsecondary school) already teetering on the financial edge have difficulty completing school when faced with seemingly minor financial bumps such as car breakdowns or a loss of child care. Furthermore,

---

3 Sean Reardon, "The Widening Academic Achievement Gap Between the Rich and the Poor: New Evidence and Possible Explanations." In *Whither Opportunity? Rising Inequality, Schools, and Children's Life Chances*, edited by Greg Duncan and Richard Murnane (New York: Russell Sage Foundation, 2011). Reardon finds that "the achievement gap between children from high- and low-income families is roughly 30 to 40 percent larger among children born in 2001 than among those born twenty-five years earlier."

4 Greg Duncan and Richard Murnane, "Introduction: The American Dream, Then and Now." In *Whither Opportunity? Rising Inequality, Schools, and Children's Life Chances*, edited by Greg Duncan and Richard Murnane (New York: Russell Sage Foundation, 2011).

5 Author's analysis of Census data (Current Population Survey October 2013 Detailed Tables, Table 3: Nursery and Primary School Enrollment).

6 Timothy Smeeding, "Multiple Barriers to Economic Opportunity in the United States." Paper presented at the "Inequality of Economic Opportunity" Conference at the Federal Reserve Bank of Boston, October 17–18, 2014.

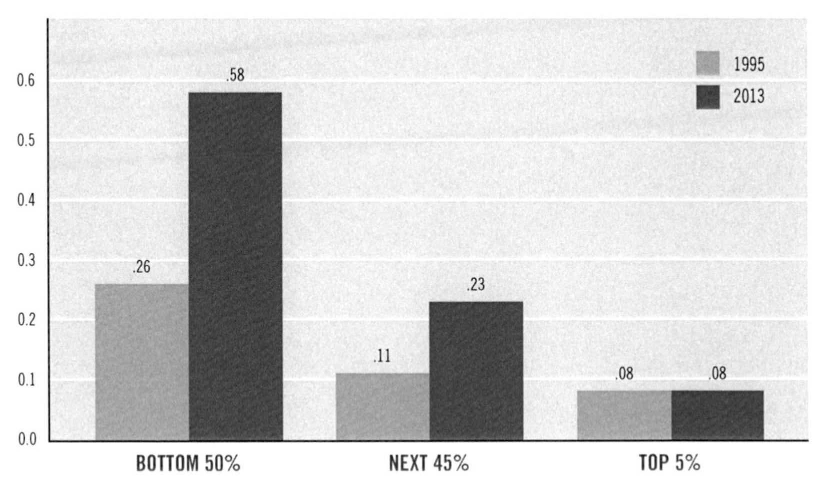

Source: Survey of Consumer Finances

Figure 2: Education Debt Has Increased for Most Americans. Ratio of mean education debt to mean income (for families with education debt) by net worth group.

students from families with less wealth who do go to college are increasingly saddled with debt out of proportion to their families' wealth. Federal Reserve data in Figure 2 reveal that in 2013, the mean debt-to-income ratio was 58 percent for the bottom half of households with education debt. The same ratio for the wealthiest 5 percent of households was under 10 percent.

Both access to borrowing and concerns about their ability to service their debt burdens are deterrents to college attendance for low-income students. These debt dynamics impinge on growth in particular as lower-income students with high levels of debt are less likely to purchase homes, an activity that supports GDP growth.[7]

Strong and compelling evidence, already cited, reveals that poverty and inequality create barriers to educational opportunity, from preschool through college. Moreover, considerable research finds higher education is associated with greater earnings, employment, and less use of public services, all of which boost growth. Regarding macroeconomic growth, Goldin and Katz, for example, find that the direct effect of a more

7 Phil Oliff et al., "Recent Deep State Higher Education Cuts May Harm Students and the Economy for Years to Come." (Washington, DC: Center on Budget and Policy Priorities, March 19, 2013).

educated workforce explains 25 percent of U.S. productivity growth from 1915 to 2005.[8] Careful econometric work has consistently found that an extra year of schooling boosts earnings by around 7 percent, and, as Table 1 reveals, wage, income, and net worth differentials between college and high school graduates are significant, with premiums for net worth ranging from 65 percent to more than 300 percent.

In other words, there is solid empirical evidence that barriers to education exist at all levels of schooling (even K-12, where underfunding in poorer communities leads to worse outcomes), that more education contributes significantly to productivity growth, and that large earnings and wealth differences exist between college and non-college-educated workers. We can thus conclude that education barriers that block children from disadvantaged families from achieving their educational potential are both a symptom of financial ill health and a negative growth factor.

Geographic Mobility and Residential Segregation

Financially healthy families are by definition mobile enough to locate in areas where conditions may be better for their families' overall well-being. However, in recent years, residential segregation by income has significantly increased. Bischoff and Reardon find that the share of families in middle-income neighborhoods fell from 65 percent in 1970 to 42 percent in 2009. The number of families living in either poor or affluent neighborhoods, the two most extreme categories of neighborhood income, increased from 15 percent to 33 percent over these years.[9]

Although these facts are potentially problematic from the perspective of family well-being, does residential segregation contribute to less growth? To the extent that residential segregation affects access to education and is associated with childhood poverty, which leads to lower employment, earnings, and wealth accumulation in adulthood, then negative growth implications are certainly plausible. Reduced geographic mobility could also reduce the efficiency of job matches and thus hurt productivity growth.

---

8 Claudia Goldin and Lawrence Katz, *The Race between Education and Technology* (Cambridge, MA: Harvard University Press, 2008).

9 Kendra Bischoff and Sean Reardon, "Residential Segregation by Income, 1970–2009." (New York: Russell Sage Foundation, October 16, 2013).

	HIGH SCHOOL	COLLEGE	COLLEGE PREMIUM
Hourly Wage	$16.46	$29.55	80%
Weekly Earnings	$668	$1,101	65%
Annual Earnings	$35,309	$62,048	76%
Net Worth (Median)	**$52,500**	**$219,400**	**318%**

Notes: All values for college are bachelor's degree only except net worth, which is for a BA or higher. Weekly earnings are for full-time workers.

Sources: Economic Policy Institute, Bureau of Labor Statistics, U.S. Census Bureau, Federal Reserve Board.[10]

Table 1. Wages, Earnings, and Net Worth by Education Level, 2013

Recent, high-quality empirical research by Chetty and colleagues underscores these points. Their review of the Moving to Opportunity demonstration project found an increase in upward mobility when families with young children moved from high- to lower-poverty neighborhoods. When the children were younger than 13 when they moved to lower-poverty neighborhoods, their college attendance, marriage rates, and earnings rose significantly, by as much as 30 percent. Because earnings feed directly into the size of the economy, such results are associated with more growth relative to a situation where these families remained in high-poverty neighborhoods.[11]

Direct Effects of Financial Ill Health

There are other reasons why families facing financial difficulties because of income, wealth, or credit constraints may lack the ability to optimally consume or invest, thereby reducing growth. They may lose access to credit markets or not save enough for retirement, both of which have

10 Elise Gould, "2014 Continues a 35-year Trend of Broad-Based Wage Stagnation." (Washington, DC: Economic Policy Institute, February 2015); Bureau of Labor Statistics, "Usual Weekly Earnings of Wage and Salary Workers Fourth Quarter 2014." News release (Washington, DC: Bureau of Labor Statistics, January 21, 2015); U.S. Census Bureau, Table P-22, "Educational Attainment—Workers 25 Years Old and Over by Mean Earnings and Sex: 1991 to 2013"; Jesse Bricker et al., "Changes in U.S. Family Finances from 2010 to 2013: Evidence from the Survey of Consumer Finances." (Washington, DC: Board of Governors of the Federal Reserve System, September 2014).

11 The implicit assumption here is that such higher earnings are not "rents" as used in the economic sense (i.e., they are not zero-sum), and thus represent added growth.

potentially negative growth effects. Although for some families, these are only short-term dynamics and thus do not have lasting growth implications, recent research finds that low income that persists through adulthood has generational impacts. It is certainly possible that these disadvantages add up to a constraint on macroeconomic growth. For example, children in families with persistently few economic resources can suffer lasting investment deficits, "environmental" deficits (from exposure to environmental risks such as lead to hearing fewer vocabulary words spoken at home), and high stress levels that impinge on their mobility, their future health, and future earnings. Although this may sound like the same education channel at work, it is likely more than that. The Pew Economic Mobility Project has shown that a child born into the bottom one-fifth of the income distribution who graduates from college still has only a 10 percent chance of making it to the top income quintile as an adult. In contrast, a child in the top quintile who fails to graduate college has a 25 percent chance of staying in the top one-fifth.

Insufficient access to credit that meets a family's needs at an appropriate price can also hurt both family financial health and growth, as it can lead to reliance on overpriced alternatives that may be structured to trap the family in debt. Families stuck outside of the financial mainstream because they are unbanked or have to depend on payday lenders charging usurious rates of interest end up paying an average of $2,400 per year more than financially mainstream families. Whether these fees and rates are a distributional problem or a growth problem (or both) are beyond the data, but to the extent that they hurt the ability of low-income families to save and invest in their futures, it impinges on growth.[12]

Conversely, access to too much credit can also hurt growth, as it fuels the economic shampoo cycle in Figure 1. That cycle gains strength when families take on debt burdens they cannot realistically sustain, at great cost to both their own well-being, and, aggregating across significant numbers of households, to that of the broader economy.

Researchers are actively studying the channels by which financial ill health affects low-income families (see the essay in this book by Jason Purnell).

---

12 Office of the Inspector General, "Providing Non-Bank Financial Services for the Underserved." (Washington, DC: U.S. Postal Service, January 2014).

"Toxic stress"—persistent exposure to stress in daily living—is more common among the poor and leaves lasting damage to parent and child health, cognition, and educational attainment, all of which can negatively impact growth.[13]

Research on various safety net programs, including food stamps, Medicaid, and wage subsidies to low-wage workers finds lasting impacts that could have growth implications. In a quasi-experimental study based on the gradual spread of food stamps, Hoynes and colleagues find that children who received nutritional benefits were 6 percent less likely to experience stunted growth, 5 percent less likely to experience heart disease, 16 percent less likely to experience obesity, and 18 percent more likely to graduate from high school compared with children from similar economic backgrounds who did not receive the benefits. Notably, as adults, women who had received the nutritional benefits were more likely to find work and avoid poverty.

Similarly careful studies have found similar results for Medicaid receipt (lower mortality, higher pay among women, increased college attendance, and greater tax contributions)[14] and wage and income subsidies, including improved test scores for children in families receiving the benefits, along with higher employment and earnings later in life.[15] Other research has found that larger wage subsidies through the Earned Income Tax Credit (EITC) led to reduced incidence of low birth weight and premature births.[16] All of these are clearly pro-growth.

---

13 For example, Aizer, Stroud, and Buka found that children born during times of high maternal stress ended up with "a year less schooling, a verbal IQ score that [was] five points lower and a 48 percent increase in the number of chronic [health] conditions" when compared with siblings who were born during less stressful times. Anna Aizer, Laura Stroud, and Stephen Buka, "Maternal Stress and Child Outcomes: Evidence from Siblings." (Washington, DC: National Bureau of Economic Research, September 2012).

14 Matt Broaddus, "Medicaid-eligible Children Grow Up to Earn More and Pay More in Taxes." (Washington, DC: Center on Budget and Policy Priorities, January 21, 2015).

15 Chuck Marr, Chye-Ching Huang, Arloc Sherman, and Brandon Debot, "EITC and Child Tax Credit Promote Work, Reduce Poverty, and Support Children's Development, Research Finds." (Washington, DC: Center on Budget and Policy Priorities, April 3, 2015).

16 Arloc Sherman, Danilo Trisi, and Sharon Parrot also review all of these results in "Various Supports for Low-Income Families Reduce Poverty and Have Long-Term Positive Effects on Families and Children." (Washington, DC: Center on Budget and Policy Priorities, July 30, 2013).

Although this work is rigorous and convincing at the micro level, no one has linked these benefits to macroeconomic growth, which would be very difficult, given the need to isolate such growth effects in what is today a $17 trillion economy. However, a back-of-the-envelope example may be instructive, as it at least points in the direction of greater employment and thus growth. Duncan and colleagues find that the addition of $3,000 to annual income in early childhood is associated with an added 135 hours of annual work as a young adult.[17] My analysis of children in families filing for the EITC in the early 1990s (who would be young adults today) suggests that this additional income may have led to about 2 million more full-time jobs in recent years. In 2014, that could have boosted the labor force participation rate by almost 1 percentage point, and it should also be noted that faster labor force growth feeds directly into faster GDP growth. Moreover, there is no question that toxic stress, low-birth weight, obesity, diminished cognition, and other conditions related to low income generate real costs to society, and evidence that they are linked to financial ill health is compelling.

Conclusion

As noted, establishing solid empirical links between multifaceted phenomena like family financial health and macroeconomic growth is daunting. Still, numerous channels described above, from financial health to macroeconomic growth, are backed by solid empirical findings, and policy responses are warranted. For example, it is widely recognized that inadequate oversight of what turned out to be a spate of reckless financial practices in the run-up to the Great Recession played a contributing role to that very costly bubble and bust. This inadequate oversight implies the need for policy measures, such as less leverage in systemically important financial institutions and rules that enforce more prudent underwriting. I've also argued, with some evidence, that families' financial ill health, a product in part of growing income inequality, played a role in the economic shampoo cycle that brought on the Great Recession.

We know that on average a person who is blocked from achieving his or her educational potential will earn less, and that, too, will deter growth, particularly if aggregated across millions of disadvantaged households.

---

17 Greg Duncan, Kathleen Zio-Guest, and Ariel Kalil, "Early-Childhood Poverty and Adult Attainment, Behavior, and Health," *Child Development* 81 (1) (2010): 306–325.

Other dimensions of poverty and residential segregation logically have the same effect.

On the other hand, financial bubbles have many causes, as do the factors that promote growth. For example, our economic history reveals bubbles and busts in periods of low inequality and robust middle-income growth. There is still no empirical link between higher inequality, diminished educational opportunity, and labor quality's contribution to productivity growth.

My conclusion, therefore, is that there are good reasons, backed by some empirical evidence, to believe that financially unhealthy families reduce economic growth through the channels articulated above, and vice versa. Given that economic growth is a complex, multifaceted phenomenon, we cannot reliably quantify the magnitude of this relationship. But it is potentially significant, both in terms of financial volatility and squandered human capital. This is a ripe area for further research, especially as data about the long-term effects of the Great Recession become available.

Finally, even if this relationship between financial health and growth were not the case—if family financial health was unrelated to broad economic growth—there are good reasons to intervene on behalf of families and children who suffer the consequences of financial ill health. An advanced society should want to reduce barriers to opportunity based on the simple proposition that all its members should have the chance to pursue and reach their full potential.

■ ■ ■

JARED BERNSTEIN *has been a Senior Fellow at the Center on Budget and Policy Priorities since May 2011. From 2009 to 2011, Bernstein was the Chief Economist to Vice President Joe Biden and a member of President Obama's economics team. In addition to hosting* On The Economy *at jaredbernsteinblog.com, Bernstein has written several books—including* The Reconnection Agenda: Reuniting Growth and Prosperity*—and is a regular contributor to the* Washington Post *and* The New York Times. *He is a commentator on MSNBC and CNBC and tweets often at @econjared.*

WE ARE IN THIS TOGETHER
Bipartisan Solutions to Preserve the American Dream

Phil English
Arent Fox LLP

Jeremie Greer
CFED

Free economies rarely offer equal results or outcomes. Disparities of wealth are inevitable. However, they are only tolerable if the public has confidence that individual freedom can produce economic and social mobility, and that markets can be open to the enterprise of all corners. In the American economy, freedom can only be sustained if the core commitment to equal opportunity is nurtured and sustained. Social stability can only be maintained if the capitalist economy is offering procedural fairness.

—*Franklin Delano Roosevelt*

We come to the public square from two different political backgrounds. Phil was an elected official in a blue-collar Great Lakes city who went to Congress as a Republican. Jeremie leans left and has deep roots in community development. Despite these differences, we come together around the core idea that the shared economic prosperity of the nation depends on the financial well-being of individuals and families and their ability to achieve social mobility.

This idea, which others might simply call the American Dream, is part of our collective identity. It is captured best in the country's founding document, which states that we are all endowed "with certain unalienable rights, that among these are life, liberty and the pursuit of happiness."

This pursuit of happiness presupposes the ability of individuals to have free access to the economy and its rewards.

It is an unfortunate fact that this American Dream has not been equally attainable for all; the complex interplay of race, gender, class and geography creates economic advantage for some, but reinforces long-standing barriers for others. The disparate impact of the Great Recession on communities of color underscores the continued salience of this problem. In addition, social and economic mobility for the working class has become vastly more complicated in a global economy. Yet, we believe that the American Dream—for all of us—is within reach.

Our optimism comes from the recognition that there is more consensus than disagreement on the problems our society faces, namely that opportunity has not been accessible for large segments of our society. As framed above by President Roosevelt, equal opportunity for economic success is a requirement for social stability. We believe that public policy can change the uneven opportunity structure in this country. This essay outlines policy solutions that can gain bipartisan support in Washington and resonate with the American public.

THE FADING AMERICAN DREAM

While the Great Recession destabilized the financial health of millions of U.S. households, we have seen signs of household instability for some time. In particular, stagnant wages stand in the way of economic advancement for many working-class families. Today, the average inflation-adjusted hourly wage of a nongovernmental worker is unchanged since 1979,[1] despite the sustained productivity growth of American business. In short, workers are contributing more to the U.S. economy for less pay. A recent Economic Policy Institute analysis of Bureau of Labor Statistics data found that between 1948 and 1973, hourly wages and productivity were almost aligned, rising 92 percent and 97 percent, respectively. However, between 1973 and 2013, productivity grew a healthy 74 percent while hourly compensation rose a paltry 9 percent.

1 Drew Desiver, "For Most Workers, Real Wages Have Barely Budged for Decades." (Washington, DC: Pew Research Center, October 2014).

Although income helps you get by, assets are what you need to get ahead. Assets, such as savings, investments, a home or small business, allow households to absorb financial shocks, plan for their future, build wealth, and pass that wealth on to future generations. According to CFED's "*Assets & Opportunity Scorecard*," almost one-half of all U.S. households (44 percent) are "liquid asset poor," which means they lack sufficient savings to subsist at the poverty level for three months if they lost their income. This problem is even more severe among women (57 percent), single-parent households (73 percent), and households of color (63 percent) who all experience significantly higher levels of liquid asset poverty. These families do not have a resource base to prepare for emergencies or finance future wealth-building endeavors, such as higher education, a small business, or homeownership. Without assets, families live in a perpetual cycle of "just getting by," where even the notion of building wealth is out of reach.

Although wealth has never been equally distributed in the United States, we are currently experiencing dramatic levels of wealth inequality. According to a Pew analysis of data from the Federal Reserve Board's 2013 Survey of Consumer Finances, the median net worth of the country's wealthiest families was nearly seven times that of middle-income families—the widest wealth gap observed since the Federal Reserve began the triennial survey in 1983.[2] The Great Recession also significantly widened the racial wealth gap. The median net worth of white households is 13 times that of African American households and 10 times that of Hispanic households. This gap is the largest since 1989 for black households and since 2001 for Hispanic households.

To address the triple whammy of income stagnation, liquid asset poverty, and wealth inequality, we must start on common ground. Although the current federal officeholders on both ends of Pennsylvania Avenue display ideological differences, it is clear that there is broad agreement on the need to advance economic mobility. In a recent proposal on expanding opportunity, Republican U.S. Representative Paul Ryan stated that, "Far too many people are stuck on the lower rungs." In his State of the Union address, President Obama asked, "Will we accept an economy where

2 Richard Fry and Rakesh Kochhar, "America's Wealth Gap between Middle-Income and Upper-Income Families Is Widest on Record." (Washington, DC: Pew Research Center, December 2014).

only a few of us do spectacularly well? Or will we commit ourselves to an economy that generates rising incomes and chances for everyone who makes the effort?"

OUR COLLECTIVE FINANCIAL FUTURE DEPENDS ON THE FINANCIAL WELL-BEING OF U.S. HOUSEHOLDS

Today's turbulent marketplace presents an array of structural barriers that cut off access to the critical building blocks of financial well-being. We as a nation must advance public policies that empower families to build wealth and better control their financial lives. Expanding this opportunity will be critical to the financial well-being of U.S. households, and by extension our economy at large.

We must build a twenty-first century policy agenda that supports the capacity of all households to build wealth and financial well-being, and by extension, the economic vitality of the nation (see Jared Bernstein's essay in this book). This policy agenda should be built on a common understanding of the financial building blocks of stable and resilient households:

- Knowledge, experience, and skills to navigate the economy: An individual's ability to navigate the economy depends on both personal (e.g., frugality or diligence) and contextual (e.g., neighborhood quality or intergenerational wealth) factors, and often develops early in life. Understanding how to intervene as early as birth is key to influencing future financial opportunity, as Ray Boshara and Elizabeth Odders-White and Charles Kalish show in their essays in this volume.

- Sustainable and affordable homeownership: Homeownership has long served as a source of household wealth, community stability, and individual mobility, and is central to a dynamic capitalist economy. Creating pathways to affordable and stable mortgage products is a proven strategy to enhance the wealth of U.S. households.

- Access to education: As Sarah Bloom Raskin lays out in her essay in this volume, household finances determine a family's ability to access educational opportunities and, in turn, achieve economic prosperity and mobility. Creating more affordable and accessible pathways to higher education must be a key public policy goal.

- **Liquid Savings:** Households with liquid savings are better positioned to manage unforeseen economic shocks, such as a temporary job loss or medical emergency. Navigating interruptions in income requires building a financial cushion created by liquid savings.

- **Entrepreneurship:** Most new small businesses are financed with personal assets and contribute to dynamism in the national economy and job creation. Expanding capital access and improving the financial health of entrepreneurs are critical paths to economic mobility for many households.

- **Retirement Security:** With major challenges facing public entitlement programs, and the retrenchment of employer-based retirement benefits, personal savings will play a growing and indispensable role in supporting retirees' standard of living. More needs to be done to expand access and use of retirement savings vehicles.

BIPARTISAN SOLUTIONS TO ADVANCE THE FINANCIAL WELL-BEING OF U.S. HOUSEHOLDS

Much of the gridlock in today's political environment has been driven by a lack of political will to rethink and sustain traditional income support programs. However, there has been growing bipartisan interest in asset-based policies that focus on opportunity and mobility by harnessing the capability of American households to build their own economic security and success.

A policy focus that seeks to enhance the economic mobility and wealth-building capacity of U.S. households has several major advantages in the current political environment. First, decades of research have documented that even the poorest Americans can save. Second, this approach is well suited to current public attitudes toward government and its role in individual success. Finally, a faith in the productive capacity of all Americans to contribute to their own success and the broader economy (including students, homeowners, and entrepreneurs) lends this approach broad ideological appeal. Like the Homestead Act and the GI Bill, these policy solutions would empower individuals as societal stakeholders and define a role for government as an arbiter of equal opportunity. Below are five policy ideas that could achieve bipartisan support and lead a twenty-first century social policy agenda.

1. **Provide an opportunity for every child to save and invest in his or her future.** Children's Savings Accounts (CSA) are long-term savings accounts for children that grow over time. Public, private, or philanthropic investments seed the accounts with an initial deposit and augment them with matches and/or other savings incentives. Family, friends, and the children themselves make ongoing contributions to build the savings accounts. CSAs can be provided through 529 college savings plan providers, banks, or credit unions. Research has shown that low-income students with just $500 or less in college savings are three times more likely to enroll in college and four times more likely to graduate.[3] Cities (San Francisco, St. Louis) and states (Nevada, Rhode Island) are paving the way for publicly supported programs that provide every child with an incentivized and earmarked account. The federal government can build on this by passing legislation that would establish universal CSAs for all children born in America.

2. **Support aspiring homebuyers by enhancing their ability to save for a first home.** This objective could be accomplished by expanding support for down-payment savings strategies. One example is Individual Development Accounts (IDA). IDAs have a proven track record of providing working-class families with access to homeownership opportunities. In 1998, Congress created the bipartisan Assets for Independence (AFI) program to help low- and moderate-income families save and invest in higher education, homeownership, or entrepreneurship. Since 1999, AFI programs have served more than 81,000 low-income families nationwide. Expanded investment in savings strategies such as IDAs will provide families the type of support needed to help them realize the dream of homeownership.

3. **Eliminate barriers that provide an explicit disincentive to saving.** Many public benefit programs—including the Supplemental Nutrition Assistance Program, Temporary Assistance for Needy Families, and Supplemental Security Income—limit eligibility to those with few or

3 William Elliott, "Small-Dollar Children's Savings Accounts and College Outcomes." CSD working paper no. 13-05 (Center for Social Development, 2013).

no assets. Asset limits in public benefit programs restrict a family's economic mobility by creating barriers to saving for those who need it the most (see Reggie Bicha and Keri Batchelder's essay in this volume). If a family has assets over a certain threshold, the family must "spend-down" long-term savings in order to receive short-term public assistance. Asset limits discourage families from saving for emergencies, education, homeownership, and retirement, and pose serious obstacles for low-income families or individuals trying to become financially self-sufficient. Since 1996, the federal government has given states some flexibility to raise or waive asset tests for these programs. Congress should reconsider asset limits in public benefits programs, thus freeing low-income families to save the necessary dollars to enhance their financial well-being and leave the public benefit rolls.

4 **Create access to financial products that enhance the financial well-being of micro-entrepreneurs.** Congress and federal agencies can better support microbusiness owners by enhancing access to financial products and services, including savings and credit, which are the building blocks of any successful small business. One approach would be to expand access to the recently established *my*RA program by the U.S. Treasury to the 23 million self-employed Americans so they have access to affordable savings accounts.

5 **Increase access to, and participation in, employer-based retirement accounts.** Retirement savings are an important source of income and financial stability for older adults. Employer-based retirement savings—such as 401(k), 403(b), and IRAs—are the main way retired adults augment Social Security benefits. Unfortunately, many households either do not have access to a plan through their employer or are unable to save the money necessary to ensure a comfortable retirement. To support the retirement needs of U.S. households, the federal government could advance policies that require employers to auto-enroll employees into employer-provided retirement savings plans, and improve the existing federal Saver's Credit—which matches the contributions a low-income tax payer makes to an eligible retirement account—by making it more effective in supporting working-class families.

CONCLUSION

We advocate for an America where financially stable and resilient households are a central building block of the economic vitality of the nation. Inclusive economic growth is an essential ingredient for greater economic opportunity, and it is an indispensable requirement for social justice in a capitalist economy. Further, America is at its best when it resists extremes and seeks to extend the promise of opportunity to all of its citizens. Deep-rooted American principles that promote the dignity of work, asset ownership, and the worth of the individual have united divergent social groups without the deep societal divisions or poisonous ideological conflicts common to other nations. We believe that the policies outlined above, while promoting family economic stability, also lend themselves to a more civil political dialogue. We also each believe through our divergent political perspective that this policy agenda can solve the economic challenges facing families, communities, and the nation.

■ ■ ■

PHIL ENGLISH *is a former U.S. Representative (R-PA) and serves as co-chair of the Government Relations Practice at Arent Fox LLP. As a member of the House Ways & Means Committee, and ranking member of its Select Revenue Subcommittee, English was a strong advocate for rules-based trade, fundamental tax reform, quality health care, and bipartisan reforms for key safety net programs. He has served as member of the U.S. National Commission on U.N.E.S.C.O., and is currently a member of the boards of CFED, the Tax Foundation, and the Information Technology and Innovation Foundation (ITIF). He is honorary chairman of the Coalition for Strategic Tax Reform.*

■ ■ ■

JEREMIE GREER *is the vice president of policy and research at CFED. In this role, Jeremie oversees CFED's government affairs and applied research teams, which are responsible for developing and executing the organization's policy and research agendas and advocacy strategies. Prior to joining CFED, he was a senior policy officer at the Local Initiatives Support Corporation (LISC), where he led LISC policy advocacy on an array of federal issues. He also spent time at the U.S. Government Accountability Office, where he provided nonpartisan federal policy analysis to Congress. He began his career working in the Columbia Heights and Shaw neighborhoods in the District of Columbia, where he provided capacity-building and technical support to small community-based organizations.*

REESTABLISHING TRUST

An Essential First Step for Financial Institutions

Cathie Mahon
National Federation of Community Development Credit Unions

It isn't easy supporting a household on low wages. There is rent to cover, bills to pay and food to get on the table, not to mention transportation, clothing, and child-care and school related expenses. Conventional wisdom suggests that the simple act of budgeting—itemizing regular and anticipated expenses and adjusting them to the steady biweekly paycheck—will help a household to stay "in balance." Combining that budget with a free or low-cost checking account with direct deposit can save hundreds of dollars over the course of a year in check-cashing and bill payment fees, savings that can be reinvested to build a nest egg. Likewise, loans at reasonable rates can enable families to purchase larger items such as cars or appliances and invest in education, homeownership, or entrepreneurial activities.

Community development credit unions and banks, and microfinance institutions play a critical role by providing low-income families with these types of affordable banking and credit services. These vital and growing community development financial institutions (CDFIs) are organized to meet banking or credit gaps and to bring previously disenfranchised individuals and communities into the financial mainstream. During the past 50 years, they have been remarkably successful.

But the communities these institutions serve are changing, and so are their financial services needs. The overwhelming fact of economic life for many families now is the unpredictability of both income and expenses. Recent studies have confirmed what many practitioners have known for some time: steady jobs with a biweekly paycheck are scarce in low- and moderate-income communities. Instead, households rely on unpredictable part-time and seasonal work, patching together income from multiple sources.

For these households, the standard budget-save-borrow strategy simply does not work. Families incur expenses without any certainty of income to cover them. The frequent shortfalls during the month require complex and time-consuming juggling strategies. Outwardly simple, low-cost checking accounts can become pitfalls and traps as overdraft and insufficient funds fees mount. Many households turn to alternative, high-cost, and often predatory financial services to meet their banking needs and access credit to cover shortfalls. Unfortunately, for households with chronic shortfalls, this practice can spiral into uncontrollable debt.

CDFIs, philanthropy, and other allies in the nonprofit sector have begun digging deeper into household finances to better understand this economic reality and better tailor solutions to address this new paradigm. In addition to the U.S. Financial Diaries Project (described more fully in the essay by Jennifer Tescher and Rachel Schneider) and metrics emerging from the financial empowerment field, the Federation explored preferences and behaviors of very low-income households in its 2014 study "From Distrust to Inclusion: Insights into the Financial Lives of Very Low-Income Consumers." Researchers interviewed a diverse group of very low-income consumers to determine in their own words what they use and value most in financial services, and the central challenges they face in accessing and using financial services amid tremendous uncertainty. When asked what would help them become more financially secure, the answer was inevitably, "just one stable, good-paying job." Nevertheless, financial institutions can help, if they focus on their clients' actual financial needs.

The results of both studies challenge conventional wisdom about the financial condition of very low-income people, their demand for products and services, and opportunities to bring these consumers into the financial mainstream. Many of these individuals had already found their way to socially minded financial institutions, although many had not.

Highlights from these interviews include:

- Instability and volatility in income and finances are the norm. The overriding context and dominating factor that emerged from interviews is the profound uncertainty and unpredictability of people's lives due to their work situation and lack of a safety net. Financial gaps and severe shortfalls are the rule, not the exception. The concept of "emergency" or unanticipated expenses does not apply to this market, as shortfalls are a constant. This instability and volatility of income makes traditional credit products with recurring monthly payments fundamentally incompatible with families' cash flows. Without adequate income, there is no capacity or cushion to withstand additional risk.

- Traditional budgets are little help in managing household finances and flows. Inadequate, unpredictable, and wildly fluctuating incomes confound the usefulness of traditional budgeting tools to provide useful guidance. Moreover, the information provided by budgets is insufficient; consumers want actual help with their financial needs, especially in areas they find unfamiliar and intimidating, such as negotiation with credit bureaus and creditors.

- Trust and relationships remain key to achieving greater financial stability. What participants in the Federation study most valued from a financial institution was a trusted relationship, not a particular innovation or product. Although they use products, what they seek and need is guidance and advice. The trust they seek is not simply in the institution but in their own ability to manage the products they use.

- Technology alone is not the answer. People felt there were already many, and often too many, technological options and doubted their ability to sift through the details and implications of each. Similarly, although participants regularly accessed information online about financial matters, they rarely felt comfortable making decisions on their own through web or mobile banking. Financial institutions that can help people solve immediate problems earn trust and patronage. Institutions that push new products, even those that may provide long-term benefits, are viewed with suspicion. This has been mirrored by the experience of community financial institutions that introduce mobile and online technology: they provide the greatest benefits for managing and serving existing members but require considerable effort upfront to get consumers to use them.

The uncertainty and complexity in these consumers' needs for financial products and services reveal how our current approach no longer fits the reality of many consumers. CDFIs, policymakers, and others who seek to deliver the right financial services to support lower-income and underserved communities must go back to the drawing board. To better match clients' realities, product innovations must include flexible or customizable underwriting and repayment plans that fit the volatility of the household cash flow during the year. Real-time advisors integrated into service delivery can build trust and help make financial education and counseling relevant and actionable. Ongoing research should incorporate the voices of emerging populations, such as immigrant communities, to expand the reach and deepen the impact of services and relationships. At the same time, those serving lower-income communities must recognize the importance of scaling up operations to reach more households and communities.

The Federation is working with credit union innovators to design just such strategies. Federation consultants engage with credit union leadership on a social audit, called the Emerging Markets Review, that assesses credit union products, services, and operations to better align with emerging markets or emerging needs within existing markets. Efforts to integrate financial counseling and coaching into credit union operations (rather than as separate or affiliated activities) help build trusted relationships and ensure that counseling can better link customers with the products and services that will yield the greatest financial outcomes for the consumer and institution. Innovative microloans that support immigrants during the legalization process are now being tested to determine whether they are effective vehicles for bringing communities with high concentrations of unbanked and underbanked consumers into safe and productive financial services at a pivotal moment of moving out from the shadows.

These are only a few of the emerging innovations among community financial institutions to advance the financial health of low-income and low-wealth households. The financial realities facing these households have changed dramatically during the past decade, and CDFIs have an important opportunity to evolve in response to these changes. By keeping the consumer at the center, with a firm focus on building and retaining trust, and understanding those we serve, CDFIs can ensure that these innovations continue to proliferate, as well as create a guide for the broader financial sector on how to best serve these households.

■ ■ ■

CATHIE MAHON *is the president and CEO of the National Federation of Community Development Credit Unions. The Federation has a 40-year history of bringing safe and affordable financial products and services to underserved and untapped markets across the country. Mahon previously led the New York City Office of Financial Empowerment under Mayor Bloomberg. She has been a consultant to the Aspen Institute and the Annie E. Casey Foundation, and served as the first director of the Asset Funders Network. She began her career representing Central American immigrants as the coordinator of legal services at the Central American Refugee Center in Los Angeles.*

CONSUMER PROTECTION DRIVES FINANCIAL HEALTH

Raj Date
Fenway Summer LLC

In the wake of the financial crisis, consumer protection regulation has focused principally on preventing financial services organizations from doing affirmative harm. That's an excellent start, but going forward, consumer protection can and should help the industry accomplish its best and highest function: making the lives of American families better and more stable through finance.

FIRST, DO NO HARM

Consumer finance can make life better. Much better. For most American families, and especially for those with low or middle incomes, the right financial products delivered at the right time and at the right price can enable happiness and material comfort in both the short- and long-term. The right insurance can provide both peace of mind and financial protection from life's occasionally tragic twists and turns. The right investments can ensure a comfortable and independent retirement. The right mortgage can help a family put down roots and build wealth for future generations. The right student loan can open the door to a brighter future. The right line of credit can absorb a myriad of minor financial mishaps.

Unfortunately, for too many families, both before and during the financial crisis, consumer finance didn't make life better. It actually made life worse. Families of modest means bought into the American dream of homeownership, but at the cost of obligations they had no real shot of ever paying back. Too many students borrowed ever-larger sums to finance educations with dubious financial value. Millions of Americans living paycheck to paycheck covered small but frequent cash shortfalls with hugely expensive overdraft and payday products.

Given that shabby recent track record, it is no surprise that the most energetic recent legislative and regulatory interventions have focused on alleviating the worst of these outcomes and the most pernicious of the industry's bad practices.

The Credit Card Accountability Responsibility and Disclosure Act of 2009 (the CARD Act), for example, has nearly eliminated the faintly ridiculous practice of allowing cardholders to charge a few dollars over their limits, but then immediately slamming them with a $39 fee for the privilege. Gone as well is the practice of hooking customers at a teaser rate, only to turn around and raise prices.

Dangerous practices in the mortgage market have been curtailed as well. The Dodd-Frank Act and the new Consumer Financial Protection Bureau (CFPB) have eliminated the scandalous "liar loans" that helped inflate a massive housing bubble and trigger a global financial crisis. Critically, lenders are now required to actually inquire into and confirm a borrower's ability to repay a loan.

As important, the CFPB has, for the first time, the authority to extend meaningful federal supervisory jurisdiction over more than just banks. That means that the kind of structural "conduct arbitrage" that has long plagued the industry—wherein the sketchiest and sharpest of practices, when prohibited in closely supervised banks, migrate to federally unsupervised non-bank finance companies—has become much more difficult. To date, the CFPB has extended federal supervision (including examinations) to non-bank payday lenders, non-bank mortgage companies, private student lenders, debt collection firms, automobile financing and credit bureaus. Other nonbank sectors will follow. At the same time, an energized and aggressive CFPB enforcement arm has identified and shut down scam artists and fraudsters. Even if a firm avoids the CFPB's direct supervision, the Bureau's enforcement authority can still root out unfair, deceptive, or abusive practices.

By putting an end to some known harmful practices and making it much harder for new ones to take hold, the current consumer protection regime can help ensure that financial products, like good physicians, "first, do no harm."

ENABLING MARKETS THAT SERVE CONSUMERS

These regulatory changes, including enforcement actions, are giant steps in the right direction. Not only have they helped stamp out the potential for consumer harm, but they have also set the table for a marketplace that can help consumers live better lives.

First, an assertive approach to consumer protection is preventing bad practices from crowding out good practices in the marketplace. Consider the example of the broad repricing of credit card teaser rates, which was relatively common before the CARD Act. Teaser rates created real consequences for consumers given that cardholders would sign up for one rate but soon pay a much higher rate without realizing it. This practice also prevented more transparent products from succeeding. When one lender is marketing a deceptively low teaser rate, and another lender is marketing a more accurate, but higher rate, the consumer will likely opt for the lower rate. That means the honest lender will end up with substantially higher marketing costs, which can be crippling. Even worse, the honest lender can suffer "adverse selection" in credit performance. Those borrowers who choose a higher headline rate are not necessarily savvier about teaser rates. Often, the opposite is true. They don't care about price because they do not intend to pay the lender back anyway. That means higher credit risk, on average, which when combined with higher marketing costs is a business killer.

Consumer protection enables a better market in another way: it builds (or perhaps rebuilds) consumer trust in financial services and institutions. Consider the remarkable rise of prepaid debit cards among the underbanked as a substitute for traditional checking accounts. In no small measure, growth in that market stems from a perceived simplicity and transparency compared to "free checking" products that were fueled by repeat overdraft fees. Customers' trust tends to decline when their main interaction with a product is through penalty fees or other unknown or unclear backend charges. By contrast, many of today's prepaid products are considerably more straightforward, with fewer chances for unexpected fees. With time, and especially as the CFPB takes regulatory steps to ensure its continuation, that reliability and predictability can build trust in a product, in a franchise, and even an industry. That in turn can help families confidently live better and healthier financial lives.

ACCELERATING CONSUMER-FRIENDLY INNOVATION

A renewed and re-energized emphasis on consumer protection is already helping the market function better. But by tailoring the administration of that consumer protection regime we can do even more: we can accelerate and catalyze consumer-friendly innovations in financial services.

Stubborn problems in consumer finance, such as how to provide affordable credit options to customers with limited ("thin") credit files, are stubborn for a reason. The problems are not solvable using traditional products, underwriting techniques, or channels. But technological developments are leading to breakthroughs, such as building up those thin files with more data from nontraditional sources, or lowering distribution costs through seemingly ubiquitous mobile devices. Consider the decision-making advantages of machine learning algorithms set to work on non-traditional "big data" sources; consider the cost and speed advantages of a clearing and settlement system based on open source distributed networks.

The challenge, though, is that these technological innovations frequently fall into interstices in the latticework of consumer protection regulations. The resulting uncertainty can stymie the development of new and better products, and, paradoxically, encourage innovation by only the most cavalier entrepreneurs, who build a product first, and figure out the pesky regulatory issues later.

This is unfortunate but not surprising. Consumer protection regulation is much like other forms of regulation; it was constructed over many years to solve problems that were, at the time, urgent and important. Given the particular American legal penchant for clarity and certainty, it tends to solve those problems with hyper-technical and finely detailed rules. Those rules, in fact, do tend to protect consumers interacting with large, existing businesses that use traditional technologies and business practices. But an approach that eschews general principles in favor of specific rules developed with elaborate administrative rule-making processes is inherently bad at anticipating or responding quickly to technological innovation.

Acknowledging this inherent weakness, we can foster innovation through other, nontraditional regulatory mechanisms. Doing this well will require that regulators embrace three new habits.

1. Engage. Regulators cannot enable innovation if they don't know where the innovations are. Regulatory time and attention, at the CFPB and elsewhere, is quite legitimately concentrated on the largest institutions, the most expansive business lines, and the most pressing problems. But doing so risks missing new solutions to big problems. Like everyone else, regulators have finite resources and it makes sense to focus on big, existing issues rather than looking forward to future possibilities. But by doing that, regulators can fall prey to the same incumbency bias that afflicts most large organizations.

   To combat that quite natural bias, regulators should specifically and affirmatively engage with entrepreneurs, small firms, and investors who might be dramatically smaller than typical regulatory charges.

2. Assert principles early. Even "independent" regulatory agencies are subject to political and media pressures. But it is critical that agency leaders not let those pressures result in a paralyzing risk aversion to innovation and change. An agency need not solve every policy detail relating to a new technology before developing and sharing broad principles about substantive fairness and transparency. To be sure, a regulator who develops points of view in fast-moving and dynamic markets will, with some frequency, get things wrong. But it is only in being willing to be wrong (and humble enough to admit mistake and adjust) that regulators can support entrepreneurs who are trying to do right. That same willingness to assert principles early can also stop, or at least slow down, harmful practices before they spread.

3. Make exceptions. Many federal statutes carry surprisingly broad exemption authority, or provide, as a practical matter, considerable regulatory discretion on how to administer statutory mandates. Regulators should use that discretion to relieve regulatory constraints for low-risk pilot programs. Most new ideas do not work on their first iteration. It is only through rapid testing and tinkering that breakthroughs happen. Freighting new programs with industrial-scale compliance requirements impedes rapid testing and tinkering, and therefore

inhibits breakthroughs. Finding ways to aggressively wield exemption authority, while monitoring for potential risk, is an underdeveloped regulatory skill.

Consumer protection regulation in its more assertive, post-crisis formulation has already righted wrongs. But spurring transformative innovation—the kind that can make breakthrough improvements in families' financial lives and stability—is as important a goal as preventing abuse. It is not enough for consumer finance to do no harm; it should make life better. And smart regulation can help.

■ ■ ■

__RAJ DATE__ is the managing partner of Fenway Summer LLC, a venture investment firm focused exclusively on financial services. Until January 2013, Date served as the first Deputy Director of the U.S. Consumer Financial Protection Bureau. He played several leadership roles at the bureau, including leading the organization as the Special Advisor to the Secretary of the Treasury. Earlier in his career, Date was a managing director at Deutsche Bank Securities and senior vice president for corporate strategy and development at Capital One Financial. He is a graduate of the College of Engineering at University of California, Berkeley and Harvard Law School.

RACE, PLACE, AND FINANCIAL SECURITY

Building Equitable Communities of Opportunity

Angela Glover Blackwell
PolicyLink

I grew up in a completely integrated, entirely African American neighborhood in St. Louis, Missouri. Although that may sound like an oxymoron, it was not uncommon during the 1950s and 1960s. In many cities, racial discrimination meant that most black people lived in neighborhoods where nearly everyone else was black. It also meant those neighborhoods were integrated by income, education, and class. The adults were teachers, lawyers, janitors, nurses, entrepreneurs, shop clerks, ministers, and unemployed. Some families were poor, and many were solidly middle class. Most lived in comfortable homes, paying only a modest share of their income to buy or rent them. Bustling neighborhood stores offered great shopping, beloved community spaces, and afterschool jobs.

We children had aspirations for success. Many of us saw pathways to achieve it, supported by a stable community that had hope, high expectations, role models, and informal job networks. Significant numbers of families were able to send their kids to college.

I tell this story not to romanticize the pre-Civil Rights era but to underscore how community assets form ladders to opportunity, allowing people to move up against formidable odds. My St. Louis neighborhood had many assets that shielded us from the vicious forces of racism and segregation while reinforcing the resolve to strive together toward opportunity. Chief among those assets was financial security. Indeed, it was the foundation for all the other advantages and strengths that contributed to the richness of community that enveloped me.

In the current national discussion about rising income inequality and shrinking economic mobility in America, researchers and policymakers pay little attention to the central role that family financial security plays in creating strong, stable neighborhoods—places with thriving businesses, affordable housing, transportation that connects to jobs, and a tax base to support important amenities and services, starting with good schools. Nor is much said about the flip side of the equation: Strong, stable neighborhoods are critical for building and maintaining family financial security. I define this as access to all the resources that support a good standard of living and make it possible to plan for the future, including quality jobs, affordable homeownership and rentals, and financial institutions that facilitate savings and practice fair lending.

To close our nation's economic gaps, we must eliminate barriers to opportunity, and that takes us straight to the relationship between family financial security and community vitality. Quite simply, strong communities and family financial security go hand in hand. Each strengthens and depends on the other. This calls on us to recognize which people and which places are at greatest risk of insecurity, and why. And it demands that we implement policies that simultaneously empower the most vulnerable populations to become financially secure and transform struggling neighborhoods into communities of opportunity.

WHY RACE AND PLACE MATTER

I recently sat on a panel on economic mobility with two leading scholars. One argued that a person's year of birth determines his or her ability to rise in economic status. The other pointed to the socioeconomic status of a person's parents as the strongest determinant. Armed with data, both men made the case that economic mobility is enhanced or limited by factors outside a person's control. Yet they were silent on two other factors beyond our control, though these have long been shown to shape our lives and our prospects for success: race and place.

Where we live determines whether we have access to high-quality schools, good jobs, banks, healthy food, and reliable, affordable transportation. Although laws prohibit many of the overtly discriminatory policies of my youth, address continues to be a proxy for race. Patterns of racial segregation of decades past overlap almost completely with patterns of poverty and opportunity today. This, too, I saw in my St. Louis neighborhood. My family was the second black family on what had been an all-white block. Two years later, the block was entirely black. By the time I finished college, some 15 years later, the whole neighborhood was suffering from severe disinvestment. Families that could afford to move began to do so, leaving behind a community of concentrated poverty.

More than one-half of Latinos in the United States and 65 percent of African Americans live in neighborhoods that are majority people of color, generally low-income ones. Two-thirds of black children live in high-poverty communities compared with 6 percent of white children.[1] Persistent racial segregation, combined with the concentration of poverty in disinvested urban neighborhoods, older suburbs, and rural communities, has stripped countless communities of wealth, jobs, businesses, and other resources families need to secure their finances now and in the future.

Inequities like this did not occur by happenstance or the force of the free market. Facing limited choices, people of color moved into neighborhoods they could afford, most often ones with limited investment in infrastructure. Such investments continued to disappear as more people of color moved in and white residents fled. This absence of investment was supported by Federal home lending policies, local zoning ordinances, discriminatory banking practices, and real estate covenants through much of the twentieth century which shaped neighborhoods and regions across the country. They blocked African Americans and other targeted groups from obtaining low-cost home loans or even buying or renting a home in many communities, and they encouraged white residents to move to the suburbs.

People of color, African Americans especially, made significant gains in homeownership in the decades after the 1968 passage of the Fair Housing Act (another testament to the power of policy to shape communities and create opportunity) only to have those gains wiped out by the financial collapse beginning in 2007. African American, Latino, and Asian households lost more than half of their wealth compared with a loss of 16 percent for white households during the Great Recession.[2] It was the

---

1 Patrick Sharkey, "Neighborhoods and the Black-White Mobility Gap." (Washington, DC: Pew Charitable Trusts, July 2009).

2 Rakesh Kochhar, Richard Fry, and Paul Taylor. "Wealth Gaps Rise to Record Highs Between Whites, Blacks, Hispanics." (Washington, DC: Pew Research Center, July 2011).

largest loss of wealth for black families in recent history, brought about in no small part by targeted predatory lending.[3]

Since then, white households have recouped their losses and seen their wealth grow, while the wealth of households of color has continued to decline. The wealth of white households was 13 times the median wealth of black households in 2013.[4] Including retirement savings, African Americans hold just $200 in liquid assets, that is, the household savings and equity that can be readily converted into cash in the event of catastrophic illness, unemployment, or another emergency. Latinos hold about $340, compared to $23,000 for white households.[5]

For many families, a home is their most valuable asset and an important toehold to the middle class. Policies that restore access to homeownership for all communities are therefore critical for families and their neighborhoods. Homeownership, however, is not the only way to make families and neighborhoods secure and strong. Nor is it sufficient. Rather, we must build equitable communities of opportunity using a comprehensive approach focused both on vulnerable places and the people who live there.

INVESTING IN COMMUNITIES OF OPPORTUNITY

First, a definition of communities of opportunity. In simplest terms, they are places that have the resources and amenities we all need to thrive. This includes robust businesses, including banks and grocery stores, that contribute to community vitality, health, family financial security, and an ample tax base. It includes a mix of housing that provides high-quality affordable options to families in every economic bracket.

Communities of opportunity have safe, clean streets, sidewalks, and parks that are well serviced and maintained by government. They have high-quality affordable child care, strong early education programs, and great K-12 schools. They have public transportation that connects efficiently to all the places that residents need to go—employment centers, libraries,

---

3 Jacob S. Rugh, Len Albright, and Douglas S. Massey, "Race, Space, and Cumulative Disadvantage: A Case Study of the Subprime Lending Collapse," *Social Problems* 62 (2) (2015): 186-218.

4 Rakesh Kochhar and Richard Fry. "Wealth Inequality Has Widened along Racial, Ethnic Lines Since End of Great Recession." (Washington, DC: Pew Research Center, December 2014).

5 Rebecca Tippett et al., "Beyond Broke: Why Closing the Racial Wealth Gap is a Priority for National Economic Security" (Durham, NH: Center for Global Policy Solutions, Duke University, May 2014).

doctors, museums, community college. Most basically, communities of opportunity provide access to jobs that pay wages that families can live on and that offer opportunities to advance.

Many of the same policies and investments needed to build communities of opportunity also would embed financial security over the life cycle of families. That is because opportunities to build and preserve family wealth and assets exist in many sectors and systems, including some, like the criminal justice system, where finance experts and policymakers never look. Below are four ways to build strong, opportunity-rich communities while supporting low-income people and people of color to become and remain financially secure.

Invest in Good Jobs and New Businesses

A major driver of the racial economic gap is household income. People of color are over-represented among minimum-wage workers. The current federal minimum wage, $7.25 an hour, is lower in real value than in 1956.[6] A full-time minimum-wage worker earns $15,080 a year, $4,000 below the federal poverty line for a family of three.[7] A federal minimum wage of $10.10 would raise wages for 30 million people, 46 percent of them people of color, and result in a $32.6 billion net increase in economic activity.[8] Raising the minimum wage is a must. Increasing it to $15 would be even better.

We also must invest in small businesses. Not only are they an important mechanism to build family wealth, but small businesses also create two out of every three jobs in America.[9] Access to capital often determines an entrepreneur's ability to transform an idea into a lucrative business, yet African American-owned businesses received only 1.7 percent of Small

---

6 "Facts on The Fair Minimum Wage Act of 2012." (Washington D.C., U.S. House of Representatives, Office of Ranking Democratic Member George Miller, June 2012).

7 "What are the annual earnings for a full-time minimum wage worker?" (Davis, CA: Center for Poverty Research at University of California at Davis, 2013).

8 David Cooper and Douglas Hall. "Raising the federal minimum wage to $10.10 would give working families, and the overall economy, a much-needed boost." (Washington, DC: Economic Policy Institute. March 2013).

9 Sarah Treuhaft et al., "America's Tomorrow: Equity Is the Superior Growth Model." (Oakland, CA, PolicyLink, 2011).

Business Administration loans in 2013.[10] Expanded access to financing, entrepreneur training, and programs that link all businesses, especially business owners of color, to larger markets and strategic growth opportunities would spur the creation and expansion of businesses and generate jobs for the people who need them most.

Make Housing Affordable for All

Housing costs consume a disproportionately large share of the income of people of color and low-income people, making it difficult for them to save, invest for the future, or spend money in the community. Affordable rent and mortgages, along with access to transportation, can substantially decrease household costs and increase discretionary income.[11] Investments in affordable housing also preserve, improve, and develop diverse housing options that prevent displacement, a critical consideration as urban economies swiftly evolve to harness the skills, energy, and networks of a young, globally connected workforce. More needs to be done to ensure that homeownership remains a safe investment, especially for vulnerable populations, and that renters have adequate protections against rent increases, displacement, and speculative buying.

One good place to start to improve housing affordability is with the tax code. For example, changing the mortgage interest deduction into a refundable credit would allow low-income homeowners, who generally do not itemize deductions, to take advantage of one of the biggest tax benefits available to the middle class and affluent. Amending the tax code to offer a federal renter's credit also would address long-standing inequities in housing-related policy.

Make Higher Education Affordable and Attainable

Postsecondary training and college degrees are critical for financial security. By 2020, 65 percent of jobs will require some college education.[12] Yet college costs have soared beyond reach for all but the wealthiest

---

10 Ruth Simon and Tom McGinty, "Loan Rebound Misses Black Businesses," *Wall Street Journal*, March 14, 2014.

11 Keith Wardrip et al., "The Role of Affordable Housing in Creating Jobs and Stimulating Local Economic Development: A Review of the Literature." (Washington, DC.: Center for Housing Policy, January 2011).

12 Anthony Carnevale et al., "Recovery. Job Growth and Education Requirements through 2020." (Washington, DC.: Georgetown Public Policy Institute, Georgetown University, June 2013).

families, leaving millions of young adults—disproportionately those of color—saddled with debt that will drain their net wealth and discretionary income for years to come.[13] Policy that plants the early seed of savings for college can have an impact on college completion, future earnings, and long-term financial security. That is why a growing number of states and municipalities have launched efforts like San Francisco's Kindergarten to College program, which deposits $50 into a savings account for each child entering public school and provides an additional $50 for poor students.

Of course, solutions must also target college costs themselves. President Obama's proposal to make community college free for all would mark a big step forward.

Reform the Criminal Justice System

Important as it is to focus on policies that bolster family financial security and community vitality, that is not enough. We also must change policies and practices that strip wealth from low-income communities and communities of color. The staggering numbers of people of color in prisons represents one of the most appalling wealth-stripping mechanisms in our nation's history (see the essay by Vivian Nixon and Susan Sturm in this book). Mandatory sentencing for nonviolent offenders, jail time to penalize lapses in child support, or as Ferguson, MO, brought to light, incarceration as punishment for nonpayment of exorbitant court fines and fees for traffic violations, have funneled millions of people behind bars. States spend billions of dollars to keep them there. Criminal records create lifelong barriers to getting a job, obtaining a loan, attending college, and taking other steps toward self-sufficiency and success. This is disastrous for people with records, their families, and their communities.

"Ban the box" policies, which prohibit questions about criminal records on employment applications, open opportunities for people who have served their time. In addition, reforms aimed at dismantling systems of harsh, disproportionate punishment for youth and adults are critical. In November 2014, California voters overwhelmingly approved Proposition

13 Mark Huelsman, "The Debt Divide The Racial and Class Bias Behind the 'New Normal' of Student Borrowing." (New York: Demos, May 2015).

47, which reclassifies six lower-level nonviolent crimes from felonies to misdemeanors. Other states should use this as a model.

EQUITY IS A SUPERIOR GROWTH MODEL

Building equitable communities of opportunity has reached a new urgency in the face of rapid demographic change. By 2044, the majority of the U.S population will be people of color, the very people who have disproportionately been trapped in disinvested communities and burdened with financial risk and insecurity.

This puts our nation at a crossroads. We can continue to squander the talents and skills of large swaths of our population, or we can invest in the places where low-income people and people of color live, and make sure these communities offer full access to the resources and opportunities it takes to prosper and succeed.

There's really no choice at all, because only one path leads forward. Equity—just and fair inclusion in a society in which all can participate, prosper, and reach their full potential—is more than the moral thing to do. It's an economic imperative for families, communities, regions, and our nation.

■ ■ ■

__ANGELA GLOVER BLACKWELL__, founder and CEO, started PolicyLink in 1999 and continues to drive its mission of advancing economic and social equity. Under Angela's leadership, PolicyLink has become a leading voice in the movement to use public policy to improve access and opportunity for all low-income people and communities of color, particularly in the areas of health, housing, transportation, education, and infrastructure. Prior to founding PolicyLink, Angela served as senior vice president at the Rockefeller Foundation. A lawyer by training, she gained national recognition as founder of the Oakland (CA) Urban Strategies Council. From 1977 to 1987, Angela was a partner at Public Advocates.

STABLE HOUSING, STABLE FAMILIES

Thinking Beyond Homeownership

Rick Lazio
Jones Walker LLP

We face a silent housing crisis in America, and it is becoming worse each year. Nearly 20 million lower-income families spend more than one-half of their monthly income on housing. Another 20 million low-income households also lack access to transit, good schools, and jobs, or are living in concentrated poverty. Most of these families are renters, who have only $565 a month, on average, or $20 a day, to cover food, transportation, medical care, clothing, utilities, childcare, and all the other necessities of life.[1]

The trend is alarming. During the past 50 years, the percentage of those who are cost burdened—defined as paying more than 30 percent of income for housing—has doubled. Households who are extremely rent burdened (defined as paying rent that exceeds half their income) have also been on the rise. Couple the growing rent burden with the extreme financial stress facing households with minimal or negative net worth, and the result is a number of predictable, negative financial outcomes. Healthy, decent, affordable housing is a key determinant of financial security, especially for those living close to the financial waterline.

Take a single mother working two minimum-wage jobs. She would like to build her skills to earn more, but she cannot afford to take time off to get the training she needs. She lives paycheck to paycheck, despite her long hours. To help make ends meet, she looks for the lowest possible rent, but unfortunately, there are few housing options in her price range. The only

1 Joint Center for Housing Studies, "State of the Nation's Housing 2013" (Cambridge, MA: Harvard University, June 2013), p. 31.

apartment she can afford is far from transit and the local schools have a poor reputation. But she can't be too picky—the family has already moved four times in the last seven years. Each time, personal belongings were damaged or left behind and her children had to be pulled out of school.

Every time the kids start over, they feel lost and their confidence drops. As a result, the children do not have the same educational foundation as their peers; they are falling behind and cannot keep up in their classwork. They are unable to focus on their homework or sleep soundly at night because activity around the apartment is chaotic at all hours, and the walls are thin. In the morning, there is not much to eat, so the children arrive at school stressed, tired, and hungry. To the children, school often feels hopeless.

The new apartment is cramped, but the bigger problem is that it is poorly maintained, dark, damp and moldy. The local clinic recently diagnosed the six-year old with asthma. Faced with a difficult choice, the mother decides to pay the heating, electricity, and grocery expenses, which leaves no money for the medication.

For this hypothetical family, it is clear that the lack of decent, healthy, affordable housing is undermining overall financial security. The family is perpetually on the edge of crisis and has little prospect for improving their situation. The mother cannot build her skills to earn more, the children's health problems are likely to escalate (requiring more parental time and expenses), and the lack of classroom attendance (and attention) means that the children are increasingly likely to drop out of school, creating another generation for which financial and housing insecurity is the norm.

That this story is likely familiar in places all over the country suggests that we are on a toxic path that will lead to negative economic outcomes for families, communities, and the nation. This situation also raises important questions about whether housing can be a vehicle to increase financial stability. If secure and stable housing *can* help to create financial well-being, what type of housing is most effective: rental or owner-occupied? And if renting is a valid housing strategy for securing financial well-being, what can we do to bring parity to the financial incentives for renters and owners?

COMPLEX CONNECTIONS: HOUSING SECURITY, HOMEOWNERSHIP, AND RENTING

Housing insecurity—defined by the Department of Health and Human Services as high housing costs in proportion to income, poor housing quality, unstable neighborhoods, overcrowding, or homelessness—affects millions in America. Factors such as race and socioeconomic status play an important role in determining whether an individual or family can establish financial stability and housing security. For example, as of 2013, the median net worth of white households was approximately 13 times higher than that of black households. Between 2010 and 2013, median wealth for black families fell 33.7 percent, while white households experienced an increase in median wealth.[2] Median household net worth of African American renters in 2010 was an appalling $2,100 while Hispanic renters had only $4,500.[3]

Although racial segregation peaked in the 1970s, recent racial tensions amplify the fact that segregation is still very much part of the landscape of American cities. White city dwellers typically live in a neighborhood that is 75 percent white, while black city dwellers, on average, live in a neighborhood that is 35 percent white. Add to this another stark statistic: African Americans with a home mortgage were twice as likely to be affected by the recent foreclosure crisis. This was often because they were sold high-interest, subprime mortgages during the preceding housing bubble. Whatever the cause, the consequences have been disastrous for many African American communities that appeared, at the end of the 1990s, to be on their way to stability. Many factors influence financial stability and housing security, and vice versa. The connections are complex and—as the housing bubble and bust demonstrated—go beyond the simple distinction of whether one owns or rents a home.

America's 42.4 million renting households comprise almost 36 percent of the nation's population.[4] About 65 percent of all renter households are low-income, meaning they earn less than 80 percent of area median

---

2 Rakesh Kochhar and Richard Fry, "Wealth inequality has widened along racial, ethnic lines since end of Great Recession"(Washington, DC: Pew Research Center, December 2014).

3 Joint Center for Housing Studies, "State of the Nation's Housing 2013," p. 14.

4 National Multi Family Housing Council, "Quick Facts: Resident Demographics" (February 2014).

income (which in most areas translates to about $50,000 annually for a family of four).[5] A staggering 11.25 million renter households,[6] including approximately seven in ten renters earning less than $15,000 annually (a fair proxy for full-time, minimum-wage work), spend more than 50 percent of their income on housing.[7]

While more Americans are spending an unsustainable amount of their income on housing, the availability of affordable and suitable rental housing to lower-income households continues to shrink. There are only 65 affordable and available rental units for every 100 "very low-income" renters. This represents a nearly 10 percent decrease in the availability of such homes from just a decade ago.[8]

Given these sobering statistics, is homeownership, rather than renting, a primary key to housing security and stability? Not for every household. Of the 20 million families who suffer from housing insecurity in this nation, 8.9 million are severely cost-burdened *homeowner* families. And there are only 29 affordable and available homes for owner-occupancy for every 100 extremely low-income families (earning 30 percent of area median income) in America, many in places far from the population that needs them.[9]

OWNING VERSUS RENTING A HOME: POLICY MUST SUPPORT BOTH

Whether homeownership or rental is a more effective vehicle to build wealth and financial stability is a hotly debated topic. Federal expenditures on housing tilt heavily toward rewarding ownership. But it is not at all clear that spending federal money this way is the most effective use of resources for families or the country. In fact, the choice between rental and ownership may be a false choice. Depending on the stage of life and

---

5 United States Census Bureau, American Community Survey (ACS) (2012).

6 United States Census Bureau, American Community Survey (ACS) (2013), tables B25003 & B25033.

7 Joint Center for Housing Studies, "State of the Nation's Housing 2013," p. 5 and figure 5.

8 Barry L. Steffen et al, "Worst Case Housing Needs: 2015 Report to Congress." (Washington, DC: Department of Housing and Urban Development,April 2015), Executive Summary.

9 Daniel McCue, "The Burden of High Housing Costs," *Cascade* (Winter 2015). Federal Reserve Bank of Philadelphia.

circumstances of a given household, either choice may be optimal from the standpoint of financial security.

Policies that promote renting and ownership are not zero sum and in fact, effective national rental policies could serve to make homeownership a realistic objective for many families. The availability of affordable rentals is a significant advantage for households that aspire to homeownership, as it provides housing stability while enabling the family to build a financial cushion and save for a down payment. In contrast, households that are spending one-half or more of their income on rent are less likely to be able eventually to buy a home. There is often no money left at the end of the month to save, which in turn is the primary source of a down payment. In addition, a family that is forced to make toxic tradeoffs is a family that is more likely to live in financial crisis. Compromised mental and physical health, job insecurity, and spending on cars and appliances that are near or past their useful life create yet more financial risk. In addition, many families that are rent burdened run into the dual problems of having a poor credit profile while lacking adequate savings for a required down payment.

The fact that our housing policies are so out of balance—for every $1 of federal tax benefit for renters, there are $11 for homeowners—should be a wakeup call that we are failing to prepare millions of aspirational homeowners to achieve their dream. The challenge will only grow worse during the next two decades. An estimated 77 percent of new household formation this decade and an astounding 88 percent of new households in the next decade are expected to be made up of minorities,[10] many of lower wealth; without inspired policy changes, more households will face financial instability and homeownership rates will be pressured.

We must also consider policies that address the physical nature of the housing stock. America looks very different than it did when much of its housing was built. In 1940, only about 7 percent of Americans lived alone. Divorces were less common, men married earlier, and women often stayed with their parents until they were married. Today, social, medical, and economic changes have reshaped the housing landscape. The strongest

10 Laurie Goodman, Rolf Pendall and Jun Zhu, "Headship and Homeownership: What Does the Future Hold?" (Washington, DC: Urban Institute, June 2015).

growth in housing demand will come from minorities, singles, aging Baby Boomers, new immigrants, and Millennials. Can we alter policies so that these renters and homeowners are not paying for more space than they need? This will be particularly relevant for singles and those who are retired and downsizing. Single seniors are living longer, and more than 25 percent of all U.S. households consist of a single individual. Many neither want nor need housing that was built for a traditional family. How might the federal presence in housing finance, both directly and through the guarantees that are issued by the two largest government-sponsored enterprises, Freddie Mac and Fannie Mae, be used to better align the supply of housing with the emerging demand? How can local governments, who have the largest role in land use decisions, best address these issues? Could smaller, less expensive and more efficient housing be a solution to the affordability gap, allowing lower-income singles to spend less and save more?

Benefits of Homeownership

One of the most commonly cited benefits of homeownership is that it generates savings. The vast majority of home mortgages are amortizing; as regular payments reduce the principal balance and interest payments shrink, equity increases at a faster pace, creating a "forced savings" mechanism. The longer one owns a home, the greater the benefit. The process of accumulating the down payment and demonstrating a commitment to savings confers additional financial benefits to homeowners.

Additional benefits relate to the long-term financial returns of homeownership. For example, a homeowner can borrow against (that is, leverage) equity to generate substantial real returns, even when nominal returns on home values are marginal or do not exceed inflation. For many lower-income homeowners, similar leverage is unavailable for other investments and asset classes. Of course, the leverage also creates downside risks that were all too evident in the last major housing correction.

Homeownership has also historically been an effective hedge against inflation. Although some costs of homeownership rise over time, such as maintenance and property taxes, the mortgage payment is generally fixed. Most housing costs thus remain constant for owners, and over time, housing cost relative to income generally declines. In contrast, renters are likely to experience ongoing rent increases. Although these benefits were lost in some of the bad lending of the housing bubble, reforms put in place after the financial crisis favor fixed-rate mortgages with fair terms and underwriting.

In addition, single-family homes over most, but not all, periods of time generate real returns. The creation of new homes historically has not kept pace with population growth, leading to increased prices for existing houses. The Federal Housing Finance Agency found that compound annual growth rates in home prices exceeded inflation by 0.8 percent nationally between 1975 and 2012, although certain U.S. markets such as the South and the Midwest underperformed the east coast and west coast metropolitan areas. In addition to regional variation in home prices, other factors influence the real returns on homeownership, including the timing of the purchase and sale of a home. These often get masked in national figures.

Lastly, homeownership advocates point to the tax advantage of owning a home. Potential tax benefits include the mortgage interest and property tax deductions, and the ability to exclude from income gains from the sale of a house (up to $250,000 for an individual, or $500,000 in the case of a married couple). However, these benefits are extremely skewed toward upper-income homeowners. For example, almost one-half of homeowners do not itemize their tax returns because the value of the mortgage interest and property tax deductions to the homeowner does not exceed the value of the standard deduction. And senior homeowners who have paid off their mortgage receive no benefit from the mortgage interest deduction.

Risks of Homeownership

Although homeownership creates opportunities for financial security, it also presents significant risks. Thus, for many families, it is important to think of homeownership as an *end*—a goal achieved as the result of having several years of housing security and enough time to build savings—and not as the means to that end. In fact, when we think of housing security as the higher goal, we can easily see that homeownership poses a number of financial challenges, especially to already-struggling families. In some cases, homeowning families may find themselves at even greater risk of housing insecurity than families who rent.

Homeowners who put their life savings into their house have concentrated all their wealth in a single asset, with no ability to diversify their investment risk. As a result, the use of debt leverage is a double-edged sword. It can greatly magnify returns, but the reverse is also true; even modest declines in home values can sizably reduce equity, and a serious market correction can wipe it out entirely. Zillow estimated that nearly 15 million homeowners were "underwater"—they owed more on their mortgage than their home was worth—during the height of the recent Great Recession, when nominal prices were down nationally by more than 25 percent.

The unpredictability and difficulty of "timing the market" also creates risk. Lower-income homeowners typically lack the flexibility to buy and sell according to market fluctuations, and they often lack the mobility to move to more housing-favorable neighborhoods or regions of the country. But even if they could, the high transaction costs typically involved, such as a 6 percent real estate broker commission, could preclude them from doing so. Another homeownership risk is the possibility of unexpected major maintenance and repair costs, such as roof replacements or heating system failures. The failure to keep up with routine maintenance costs over time can cumulatively lead to disrepair and adversely affect the home's value.

All of these risks are exacerbated during economic downturns, when jobs are lost, housing demand declines, and house prices plummet simultaneously. If at the same time, the sale of a home is forced by health problems, job loss, or divorce, the timing can translate to financial calamity. During the most recent housing bubble, even minor financial setbacks led to disaster for many borrowers who took out mortgages with variable and increasing payment terms and did not have enough cash on hand to withstand temporary financial challenges, much less long periods of unemployment or underemployment. In contrast, a renter who invested the marginal savings created by renting rather than buying a house could have potentially established the financial liquidity and investment diversity necessary to weather the storm.

MEASURING THE RETURNS

Calculations of expected returns in housing can be complex and depend on important assumptions. Nobel Prize-winning economist Robert Shiller has argued that over the very long run, housing prices in real terms have barely exceeded inflation, making homeownership a weak wealth-building prospect.[11] He notes that investments in diversified public equities and bonds would have provided a significantly higher real return for the investor.

Belsky and Duda studied four market areas between 1982 and 1999 and found that one-half of the owners who purchased and sold homes had negative returns after figuring in closing costs.[12] They concluded that the timing of the purchase and sale of the home relative to the market cycle was as important as the location.

In a 2010 study, Jordan Rappaport of the Federal Reserve Bank of Kansas City compared the wealth-building results of U.S. homeowners and renters for 10-year periods from 1970 through 1999, and found that homeownership was only slightly more effective at building wealth than renting.[13] During the 2000s, homeowners were at a clear financial disadvantage relative to renters.

A conclusion that renting is preferable in the context of building wealth depends on many variables, including the mortgage market, prices of comparable homes for sale, the need to be able to relocate to another market for employment opportunities, and other issues. As was noted earlier, single-family housing as an asset class has had an uneven record, depending on location. Other investments have produced better risk-adjusted returns. However, those who suggest, such as Robert Shiller, that homeowners might have historically built more wealth by investing in equities rather than by buying their home, rest their premise on the renter having fewer outlays than the homeowner and then having the discipline to invest all of those savings in a diversified basket of securities or an index fund. Some recent studies suggest that discipline can be elusive.[14]

---

11 Morgan Housel, "Why your home is not a good investment," *USA TODAY*, May 10, 2014. See also Robert Shiller, "Home Buyers are Optimistic but not Wild-Eyed," *New York Times*, December 13, 2014, Pg. BU7.

12 Eric Belsky and Mark Duda, "Asset Appreciation, Timing of Purchases and Sales, and Returns to Low-Income Homeownership." In *Low-Income Homeownership: Examining the Unexamined Goal*, edited by Eric Belsky and Nicolas Retsinas. (Washington, DC: Brookings Institution, 2002).

13 Jordan Rappaport, "The Effectiveness of Homeownership in Building Household Wealth," *Economic Review* (Kansas City, MO: Federal Reserve Bank of Kansas City, Fourth Quarter 2010). But see Christopher E. Herbert, Daniel T. McCue, and Rocio Sanchez-Moyano, "Is Homeownership Still an Effective Means of Building Wealth for Low-income and Minority Households? (Was it Ever?)," (Cambridge, MA: Harvard University, September 2013).

14 Allison Freeman and Roberto G. Querica, "Low- and Moderate-income Homeownership and Wealth Creation," (Durham, NC : University of North Carolina Center for Community Capital, April 2014).

HOUSING SECURITY SOLUTIONS FOR RENTERS AND HOMEOWNERS

Taking all of these considerations into account, it becomes overwhelmingly clear that neither renting nor homeownership inherently meets the goal of housing security. Rather, it is a combination of many factors, including the price, quality, stability, and location of the home, that determines whether it will enhance a family's economic, physical, and psychological health.

One of the causes of the foreclosure crisis and the broader recession was the lowering of credit barriers for people who were unable to maintain monthly mortgage payments. In response, lending standards have grown tight, and many creditworthy potential homebuyers have been shut out of the market. To begin to reach a better equilibrium, the broader housing community (developers, lenders, owners, etc.) should consider whether new technologies can deliver better tools to help individual homebuyers determine whether renting or owning is the wiser choice given their unique goals, lifestyles, professional choices, and saving habits. Employers use a range of tests when determining which job candidate to hire. We should invest in the technology, statistical models, and basic data already available to provide families with similar tools for making housing choices—tools that go well beyond the often homeownership-biased calculators on many websites today.

Federal and state governments also have a role to play in positively influencing housing and lending markets, and their leadership may be key to stimulating change among commercial lenders, developers, builders, and owners. Today, the federal government alone spends more than $200 billion annually to incentivize housing through appropriations, tax expenditures, and subsidies. The vast majority of these—about 75 percent—are allocated to homeownership, even though homeowners on average have twice the income of renters.

The first step should be to rethink the billions of dollars earmarked for homeownership tax benefits each year. The largest tax subsidy is the mortgage interest deduction (MID), and costs the U.S. Treasury between $70 and $90 billion annually, which exceeds the entire budget for the Department of Housing and Urban Development budget. The MID is available for people who itemize their tax deductions and who have a mortgage balance, but there is no comparable program for renters who save or those who have paid off their mortgage. For such taxpayers, the MID provides no benefit.

Further, for the MID to be worthwhile, it must be more valuable than the standard deduction. Most lower-income families have less expensive homes and smaller mortgage balances; as a result, the MID is no better than the standard deduction. Recent data indicate that more than 80 percent of the MID goes to families earning more than $100,000 annually and one-half of that—fully 42 percent—goes to filers making more than $200,000 each year. Nearly one-half of homeowners who have mortgages, the majority of whom are middle- or lower-income, do not benefit from the MID.[15] It is time to consider addressing this misallocation of tax resources in a way that helps more renters.

Even federal funding programs targeted to housing more generally tend to operate paradoxically. Housing programs are established to benefit people in certain income brackets, communities or target groups, but then these programs proceed to treat all potential borrowers, developers, and homeowners equally. Programs are also typically implemented at the national or state level, ignoring the regional, local, and cultural differences that exist in specific markets.

Many programs also have inappropriate timeframes for implementation. Tax credits for developers are, for example, offered for certain behaviors (such as setting aside a certain number of housing units for low-income tenants), but are accompanied by relatively short income restriction time limits. After the time limits expire, federally funded properties can often be bought and sold at full market value. In fact, more than 2 million rent-restricted units financed by the federal Low Income Housing Tax Credit will be at risk of large rent hikes in the next few years, as their 15-year compliance period expires.

15 Joint Committee on Taxation, "Estimates of Federal Tax Expenditures for Fiscal Years 2014–2018," Prepared for the House Committee on Ways and Means and the Senate Committee on Finance (November 7, 2014), Table 3. Mark P. Keightley, "An Analysis of the Geographic Distribution of the Mortgage Interest Deduction," (Washington, DC: Congressional Research Service, January 30, 2014), Pg. 5.

It is time to reassess and rebalance existing programs and tip them toward those who are most in need, whether this means identifying and assisting certain neighborhoods, cities, states, or economic groups—and directing more of our attention and resources to helping renters and aspirational homeowners. Could some of the incentive disparities between homeownership and renting be addressed by creating more sophisticated options for targeted housing subsidies and government grants? One idea would be to create a tax advantaged account (like an individual retirement account) where the default choice would be a blended and diversified bond and equity fund. This could be used for limited purposes related to housing, such as for a down payment for a home purchase. It could be funded by rebalancing the federal subsidies so that they are targeted to households who want to become homeowners, or renters who need an emergency fund to pay their rent during a crisis.

Could programs be created that encourage developers and owners to offer longer (perhaps five- to seven-year) leases to good tenants at all income levels who commit to staying in a property, given that predictability benefits landlords and tenants alike? Might we develop a sustainable and scalable Rent-To-Own program? Imagine a financial product that uses Federal Housing Administration or state Housing Finance Agency programs for the entity who owns the house while the occupants are renting. The mortgage would be assumable, and the landlord/owner would transfer a portion of the loan to the tenant/homebuyer when they are able to accumulate the necessary 3.5 percent down payment from the carved out rental payments and meet other underwriting criteria. The transfer would come with predictable costs to the buyer, and there would be visibility for both parties to the transaction.

Finally, creating strategies to deal with unforeseen financial emergencies, whether caused by a boiler failure, job loss, or an illness, could make an enormous contribution to reducing financial stress, which often compounds risks to household wealth. Managing those risks for homeowners and renters is one key to financial stability. Is it time to create a public incentive to either private mortgage insurers or employers to offer safe and affordable "rainy day" insurance products to low-income households? The insurer would be eligible for tax credits in return for extending limited and capped insurance against certain financial emergencies, such as housing repairs, a death in the family, or a sudden reduction in income. Getting past such an emergency without wiping out savings, or worse yet, going into a debt spiral, is essential to household stability and wealth accumulation.

CONCLUSION: FOCUSING ON HOUSING SECURITY—NOT TENURE—IS ESSENTIAL

Housing is synergistic. A stable, healthy affordable home helps families organize themselves to be successful and to effectively confront life's inevitable challenges, whether educational, health-related, or financial. Individuals and families who lack that stable foundation are far more likely to fall between the cracks.

We can do so much more to help promote housing security and create financial well-being for all. Certainly, there are many issues and challenges that must be addressed: racial disparities and regional, cultural, and social differences; financial literacy; resistance and inertia among established government entities, lawmakers, and real estate industry participants; well-established tax policies; privacy concerns; and the delicate balance between the needs and goals of renters, landlords, developers, and buyers.

We must, however, overcome these challenges if we wish to see advances in the financial well-being of families and improved economic performance of the country. If we have the will, we will find the way.

■ ■ ■

*Former U.S. Representative **RICK LAZIO** (R-NY) is a partner at the national law firm of Jones Walker. Rick heads the firm's New York office and the National Housing Finance Practice Group, with focus on issues of affordable housing and related housing finance, as well as financial services. He served four terms in the U.S. House of Representatives and was the chairman of the Housing and Community Opportunity Subcommittee of the Financial Services Committee for three of those terms. He was appointed Deputy Majority Whip and Assistant Majority Leader. Rick previously served as president and CEO of the Financial Services Forum and was subsequently named to the executive committee of JPMorgan Chase where he also served as executive vice president and later managing director in the bank's Asset Management division. He is active as a director on numerous civic, philanthropic and public company boards. Rick is a graduate of Vassar College and Washington College of Law.*

STARTING AT HOME

Housing-based Approaches to Financial Stability

Paul Weech
NeighborWorks America

Housing plays a central role in the financial stability, or too often the instability, of America's families and communities. Housing costs are typically the single largest expense in a family's budget and, especially for low-income families, often a significant financial burden. The massive job losses and high levels of underemployment during the Great Recession exacerbated the national housing affordability crisis. Worst case housing needs—defined as very low-income renters paying more than 50 percent of their income for rent, living in substandard housing, or both—have risen to more than 7.7 million households, or 6.7 percent of all households, in 2013.[1] The recession caused many homeowners to lose their homes; others watched their equity disappear and ended up "underwater," owing more than their houses were worth.

Too many Americans are living at the edge, where life's emergencies—the loss of a job, break up of a marriage, major health event, or death of a loved one—can mean financial disaster. The 2015 NeighborWorks survey on financial capability found that 34 percent of adults do not have any emergency savings.[2] This figure increases to 50 percent for African Americans and 42 percent for Hispanics. Studies show that it will take an average of 31 weeks for someone who is unemployed to get a new job, a timeframe that requires more than two times the average amount in reported emergency savings. Across the country, high housing costs remain a barrier to savings.

---

1 Barry Steffen et al., "Worst Case Housing Needs: 2015 Report to Congress" (Washington DC: U.S. Department of Housing and Urban Development, April 2015).

2 NeighborWorks America, *Consumer Finance Survey Results.*

Housing stability itself is a predicate to financial stability. For homeless and very low-income families and individuals, permanent supportive housing, "housing first" models, and subsidized housing provide stable housing situations and provide families and individuals room to work on other financial needs. For many in communities with rapidly rising rents, an amortizing, fixed-rate mortgage option is another form of financial stability that makes budgeting for other life needs relatively easier. For low-income and minority communities, home equity remains an important source of household wealth, and the promise of sustainable homeownership remains an important path to savings and intergenerational wealth transfer.

Nationally, housing markets are showing signs of improvement, but the recovery has been uneven across communities—millions remain underwater on their mortgages and millions more are living in neighborhoods ravaged by blight and abandoned properties. The lack of affordability remains a major challenge in many communities and further harms families struggling to achieve financial well-being.

The nation needs to redouble its efforts to lower housing costs and increase earnings to help lower-income families both afford decent housing and have sufficient resources to meet other basic needs. The nonprofit housing and community development organizations in the NeighborWorks network focus on stabilizing neighborhoods and helping communities and families recover.

REBUILDING RESIDENT FINANCIAL CAPABILITY

Housing and community development nonprofits are combating housing and financial instability by offering an array of services that promote stable housing and stable household budgets. The central services available throughout the NeighborWorks network are homebuyer education, housing counseling, financial capability and coaching services, access to affordable mortgage products, and post-purchase assistance. Homebuyer education helps families prepare for the complexities of the home buying process, from working with a REALTOR© and selecting a lender and the right mortgage product, to analyzing the household budget and understanding the costs of homeownership, including those that are unforeseen. Sometimes the right answer is that now is not a good time to purchase a home.

The housing counselor plays a particularly important role as a trusted advisor—someone who can provide guidance on the paperwork and loan terms on the front end, and can also step in if financial issues arise at any time during the homeownership experience. Although buying an affordable home in the right place with the right financing is not a guarantee of financial success, it remains a proven strategy for wealth-building for a large number of families, especially with the kind of support NeighborWorks organizations provide.

Our network has also expanded the availability of new tools to support family economic stability through a national initiative focused on training nonprofit professionals as financial coaches. The program has shown great results: 57 percent of participants who started with no savings were able to establish a savings habit following coaching, and 48 percent of those who were already saving increased the amount they regularly set aside. The programs vary by area and are often targeted to meet the needs of specific populations. For example, the Her Family program offered by the Primavera Foundation of Tucson, Arizona, helps single mothers and their daughters learn about building a healthy financial future. Mothers work one-on-one with a financial coach and focus on the family budget. Daughters attend peer-led classes where they learn to participate in family budgeting and have the opportunity to open their first savings account.

NeighborWorks supports homeownership as a HUD-approved housing counseling intermediary and through a network of 100 Homeownership Centers around the country. The centers provide a one-stop shop for people seeking to buy a home. Recognizing that the lack of savings for down payments is a significant barrier to homeownership, NeighborWorks administers a down payment assistance program called LIFT that has expanded opportunities for thousands of homebuyers across the country.

By shoring up property values in a community, neighborhood stabilization programs are another strategy for increasing household financial stability. New, more sophisticated approaches to community revitalization are emerging to help stabilize neighborhoods that are at the tipping point between recovery and falling into further disinvestment. These include strategic investments, such as fixing up multiple homes at the same time or demolishing vacant properties, combined with marketing and rebranding efforts to help communities move beyond stabilization and build positive momentum.

For example, despite a variety of amenities, the community of Roseburg, Oregon is often associated with crime and disinvestment. To counter these perceptions, NeighborWorks Umpqua and its partners held a branding design session as part of the Neighborhood Marketing Program, a national effort to create strong neighborhood brands and rebuild market demand. More than 100 community members convened at a local church to share what they liked most about the downtown area. Based on their ideas, the group selected a new name for the district, the Heart of Roseburg, and created a logo. They developed a Facebook page and produced videos in which residents shared personal stories. These activities hold the promise of stabilizing home values, stimulating investment, and attracting more visitors to the Heart of Roseburg.

ADVANCING THE NONPROFIT SECTOR'S ROLE IN FINANCIAL STABILITY: POLICY AND PRACTICE

In the wake of the financial crisis, policy makers and practitioners alike must apply the lessons learned to advance policy and practice. First and foremost, we must focus attention on the sustainability and impact of the nonprofit housing and community development delivery system on which we rely to provide services to people and communities. For example, the sector and the communities we serve will benefit from the increased use of social enterprise models, which apply more business-like principles to achieving the organizations' missions. Social enterprise approaches include charging fees for services; better using and leveraging private capital; taking advantage of economies of scale; adopting new branding and marketing techniques; diversifying revenue sources; and improving operational efficiencies and managing costs. Meanwhile, as we seek to rebuild the path to homeownership for those families who need time to accrue savings and repair credit, policymakers should consider how to expand the availability of hybrid tenure models, such as lease-to-own, community land banking, and shared-equity models—the success of which often depends on the work of a strong nonprofit.

We also must recognize the importance of community stability to family financial stability. To this end, we must continue to promote the development of the "community quarterback" model. The quarterback is the convening organization that articulates the vision, marshals the funding sources, and aligns the work of partners required to execute successful community development.[3] Strong nonprofit institutions that play this central role of coordinating multiple players are critical for restoring low-income neighborhoods. Beyond Housing, a network member working in suburban St. Louis exemplifies the power of this role. Beyond Housing has taken the lead in attracting new development to Pagedale, Missouri, including the community's first grocery store and bank branch. Beyond Housing has also worked to organize the mayors of 24 municipalities to provide support and services designed to help the school district regain its accreditation. Good schools are critical to stabilizing property values and building future financial opportunities for kids.

Finally, we need to pursue strategies to make financial advisors and coaches more readily accessible and affordable to low-income households. Accessibility will improve as we work to embed access to homebuyer education and counseling into the housing finance system. The costs of these services can be shared among all the beneficiaries of a system that produces ownership-ready homebuyers and better performing mortgages. But more is needed. One way to expand the availability of these services is to build strong nonprofits that can cover the costs of financial coaching in the context of other sustainable social enterprise activities. Homewise, a NeighborWorks affiliate in New Mexico, has been at the forefront of this effort. Homewise's vertically integrated business model enables it to provide assistance to potential homebuyers from initial counseling through finding a home, securing a mortgage, and post-purchase guidance. They do so using revenue from the organization's real estate brokerage and mortgage banking.

---

3 See, for example, "Routinizing the Extraordinary," by David Erickson, Ian Galloway, and Naomi Cytron in *Investing in What Works for America's Communities*, edited by Nancy Andrews et al. (San Francisco: Federal Reserve Bank of San Francisco and the Low Income Investment Fund, 2012), p. 377.

The challenge of restoring stability to troubled families and communities is large, but we have the tools to make it happen. NeighborWorks affiliates across the country are helping to lead the way.

■ ■ ■

***PAUL WEECH** is president and CEO of NeighborWorks America. In the two years before joining the organization full-time, he provided policy leadership for both the Housing Partnership Network and the Stewards of Affordable Housing for the Future. He has served as chief of staff at the U.S. Small Business Administration, staff director for the Subcommittee on Housing and Community Development for the U.S. Senate Committee on Banking, Housing and Urban Affairs, and senior analyst for Housing and Credit for the U.S. Senate Committee on Budget. He also worked in various mission-related roles in the National Community Lending Center and the office of corporate strategy at Fannie Mae.*

EMPLOYMENT AND BUSINESS

MAKING WORK PAY
Building Financial Health Improves Employment Outcomes

Michael Rubinger
Local Initiatives Support Corporation

In the world of community development, we have come to understand that revitalizing a neighborhood demands a holistic approach. Affordable housing, community safety and health, economic development, quality education, financial opportunity—each of these forms a mutually reinforcing strand in the well-being of a place and the people who live there. A neighborhood cannot transcend poverty without comprehensive support in all of these areas. The same truth applies for individuals. Supporting people along the path to financial health requires tackling all the facets of financial life. A job, though essential, is not enough.

At the outset of my career, I was assistant commissioner for the New York City Department of Employment and observed dozens of job training and workforce development programs brimming with good ideas and intentions. They placed thousands of New Yorkers in jobs every year. But what these programs could not do, despite offering skills training, on-the-job support, and all manner of follow-through, was to ensure that people kept those jobs and remained steadily employed. We saw clients chronically losing or leaving work, exacerbating the very cycle of debt and poverty we were trying to break. We understood why people became unemployed. If a child got sick or a car broke down, a worker might not have the means to hire a caretaker or repair the car, leaving him or her at risk of missing work and losing pay or being fired. What we didn't know was how to reverse the trend.

During the past 10 years, we at the Local Initiatives Support Corporation (LISC), the nation's largest community development intermediary, have been working to break the cycle of job placement and abandonment. To do so, we have embraced a comprehensive approach, carried out through our Financial Opportunity Centers (FOCs), that recognizes the multi-faceted nature of financial well-being.

REAL RESULTS FOR REAL PEOPLE

Inspired by the Center for Working Families model developed by the Annie E. Casey Foundation, FOCs offer an integrated, or "bundled," set of three essential elements: employment services, financial education and coaching, and access to income supports. The centers' immediate aim is to help clients increase their monthly net income by reducing expenses through budgeting and improvements in credit scores; securing a sustainable job for those who are unemployed or a higher-paying job for those whose wages or hours worked do not meet monthly expenses; and using income-boosting benefits such as food stamps, utility assistance, or children's health insurance. In five years, LISC's seed funding and ongoing technical assistance have enabled FOCs to grow from just four centers in Chicago to more than 75 centers in some 30 cities, and these number continue to grow. Across the country, a wide spectrum of neighborhood-based nonprofits—including workforce agencies, faith-based organizations, housing counseling groups, prisoner re-entry programs, and community colleges—have also incorporated the FOC model into their programming.

For many people, the cycle of negative monthly net income creates a sense of futility around finances and work. But when monthly cash flow moves from negative to positive, sticking with a job and working toward career advancement become part of a larger picture of financial stability. FOC clients feel encouraged and empowered to take on credit, savings, and longer-term career planning. In this way, the core FOC services build on one another.

HOW IT'S DONE: THE FOC PROCESS

We have discovered that financial coaching combined with job training and placement services is particularly effective (for more on financial coaching, see Michael Collins' essay in this book). A recent LISC report analyzing nearly three years of client data from 62 FOCs showed that for half the clients entering the program, their incomes were not enough to cover their expenses.[1] The median initial income was $800 monthly, while median initial expenses were $924. But by the time they completed the program, 76 percent of clients were in a better position. For clients who accessed both financial and employment counseling, average monthly net income grew by $518. For those who took advantage of all three services—financial, employment, and income supports—average net income climbed by $528. Data also indicate that the more intensive the coaching, the more job retention rises. Seventy-four percent of clients who committed substantial time and effort to all three areas of coaching were able to find jobs, and 78 percent retained those jobs for at least six months. Not surprisingly, this group significantly boosted their net income, posting gains that were 2.5 times that of other clients.

It is also important to ensure that clients receive the bundled services in an effective, consistent way. In nearly all centers, clients begin with an orientation of how the FOC works and learn about the three types of counselors—a financial coach, an employment coach, and an income support coach. Many clients want to start with employment services, but our model usually begins with a financial coach. Clients then continue to work with that coach as they move on to employment training. We use financial coaching as the FOC entry point because we understand its importance for long-term financial stability, and experience suggests that clients who receive employment services first may not return for financial coaching.

Making a Plan

At the initial visit, the client and financial coach conduct a thorough review of the client's finances and create a plan for budgeting and building credit. Improving one's credit history and planning for asset building are crucial early steps in managing expenses. Coaches remark that this first meeting is eye-opening for most clients and often the first time they have taken a comprehensive look at their finances. "The first thing I usually hear clients say is 'I don't have money, so I don't need money management,'" says Christopher Vargas, manager of financial services at the Jane Addams Resource Corp FOC in Chicago. "But when they sit down and do

---

1 Sarah Rankin, "Building Sustainable Communities: Integrated Services and Improved Financial Outcomes for Low-Income Households." (Local Initiatives Support Corporation, April 2015).

a self-assessment and reflect on the fact that they do have a financial life, they're amazed. They see that they have some control over their outcomes."

Tackling Credit and Assets

Part of the job of a financial coach is to point out how the client's money management technique may be sapping their income. Low-income people who lack emergency savings or a decent credit score often turn to the few alternatives available to them: payday lenders, check-cashing services, high-interest auto lots, and rent-to-own stores. The fees, deposits, and high interest charges demanded by these providers take a significant bite out of monthly cash flow. In many markets, utilities and cell phone providers also require hefty up-front deposits to establish service for people with poor credit or no credit. Together, the coach and client go over ways to stanch these expenses, build credit, and, ultimately, start saving.

Employment and Other Services

After their initial meeting, the financial coach might refer the client to an income support counselor while also matching him or her with an employment coach who will provide services such as resumé preparation, job-readiness workshops, "soft skills" training, and educational or vocational programs. At some sites, participants also enroll in financial education classes to broaden their knowledge of such topics as budgeting, credit building, banking products, and short- and long-term saving. As clients progress toward their employment goals, they return to the financial coach to update budgets and continue to address assets, debts, and credit.

The Importance of Client Empowerment

The FOC process is client-driven. Resources are made available, but each participant maps out and is responsible for following his or her own path through those options. Accountability and self-reliance, say coaches, can bloom during the financial training phase. "Financial coaching helps remove the barriers to whatever is keeping the client back, with or without money," says Vargas. "That awareness allows them to understand that they have a relationship with their money, that the relationship is a process, and that taking ownership of that process can lead to something stable."

FOC CLIENTS ARE NOT ALONE IN THEIR STRUGGLES

Millions of Americans are like our clients. Dig below the surface of official unemployment rates and it becomes apparent that many jobs do not lead to financial stability. Although job figures as of spring 2015 look encouraging, the "real" unemployment rate, according to the Bureau of Labor Statistics, is nearly 12 percent. This figure includes some 8 million people termed "marginally attached to the labor force" or "discouraged workers," those who were not looking for jobs at the time they were surveyed, in part because they believed they lacked adequate skills. That number is greater than the populations of Massachusetts, Washington, and Arizona combined.

These are the very people that FOCs work with—people deemed "hard-to-employ" by the Department of Labor. They may have limited education, little or no work history, and few, if any, marketable skills. They may be homeless or formerly incarcerated, which can prejudice employers and make entering or re-entering the workforce particularly hard. They are people with low or no credit ratings and, given that businesses often do not employ applicants with poor credit, they may have been barred from jobs as a result.[2] Indeed, few FOC clients have savings accounts or credit cards, and 87 percent are in the bottom one-fifth of the U.S. income distribution.

In their groundbreaking book, *Scarcity: The New Science of Having Less and How It Defines Our Lives*, Sendhil Mullainathan, an economist, and Eldar Shafir, a behaviorist, describe how getting by with less than we need puts us in a kind of cognitive tunnel. It depletes our self-control and makes us more impulsive. This kind of psychological scarcity—a narrowing of mental bandwidth, as the authors say—is at play for many financially strapped people. A person's work habits and ability to make decisions on the job suffer when he or she is distracted by mounting medical bills or a debt collector's harassing calls. Having limited bandwidth can make it very difficult to summon the drive and optimism required to stick with and advance in a job.

A related outcome of crushing financial stress is a shortened "time horizon." When income is not enough to meet monthly expenses, it is

---

2 Carolyn Heinrich and Timothy Smeeding, "Helping the Hard-to-Employ and their Families." (Madison, WI: Institute for Research on Poverty, September 2014).

much harder to think about the long-term benefits of training for and keeping a job or saving and building good credit. Yet developing a longer time horizon—planning for the future, making choices that will result in long-term financial stability—can help an individual pull out of poverty.

Financial coaching targets these key psychological components of bandwidth and an orientation toward the future. The basic act of sitting down to take a realistic look at income, assets, and expenses and creating a budget with an informed, neutral party can be profoundly empowering. It is a crucial start toward exercising control of finances and grasping the impact of one's financial decisions. An FOC client might see on paper how taking a job could boost her income by $1,000 per month, and that giving up cable will cut expenses by $100, thereby lifting net income by $1,100. This kind of perspective on how to arrive at financial well-being can be a major incentive in sticking with employment once a person has landed a job.

A TWO-WAY STREET: EMPLOYMENT AS A SPRINGBOARD FOR FINANCIAL HEALTH AND VICE VERSA

James Skiles, a Chicago man in his early 40s, was overwhelmed by years of financial difficulties and, as he put it, having "no skills, no confidence." In 2013, Skiles was living in a homeless shelter on the north side of Chicago. He was shouldering $7,000 in medical debt and plagued by collection agencies. Delinquent student loans from a vocational school were adding to his pile of stressors and damaging his credit score.

Then Skiles learned about the Jane Addams Resource Corp (JARC), a workforce development center with an FOC integrated into its programming. JARC offered Skiles technical skills training to help him land a full-time, living wage job in manufacturing. Just as important, he received the coaching services he badly needed to build financial stability, all under one roof. Experience has shown that clients are far more likely to take advantage of bundled services when they are seamlessly integrated and co-located with employment programs.

Skiles first enrolled in a "bridge" program to build up his baseline math and reading ability in preparation for JARC's advanced job training. He quickly moved into a technical job-training course and concurrently practiced work-readiness skills through mock interviews, resumé-writing consultations and drafting cover letters. Skiles met regularly with his financial coach to assess and organize his finances. Through this process, he was able to reinstate his student loans and apply for a repayment plan. His medical debt was forgiven. He increased his credit score from 517 to 598, and was accepted into JARC's Twin Accounts program, a low-interest loan that helps clients simultaneously build credit and savings.

Sheryl Morris, director of JARC's FOC, recalls how Skiles went from lamenting that he lacked skills or employment prospects to taking the reins of his financial life. "People come in with so many barriers—not just in terms of education and skills gaps, but in terms of confidence," says Morris. "They lack confidence about their ability to perform on a job, but also as it relates to financial life. We saw that in James. But once he started to see the progress, he became hungry to see more progress. That's what keeps people coming back."

In May 2014, Skiles was hired as a drill press operator by the Howe Corporation, a Chicago-based refrigeration company, at a starting wage of $12 an hour. He has since earned the respect of his supervisors and peers, and a raise. He continues to work with his job developer at JARC, who coaches him through troubleshooting on the job. Lately, Skiles has been trying to boost his productivity at work in the hope of advancing further. And after living in a shelter for 13 months, Skiles recently moved into a place of his own, where he lives with his partner and her son. By drastically reducing the draining interest payments on his debts, curtailing other expenses related to poor credit, and bringing in adequate, full-time income, Skiles has a positive monthly net income for perhaps the first time in his life. Because Skiles' job provides enough income for him to make ends meet, it is not just economically sound—it also feels worthwhile.

As James Skiles discovered, the change in net income for FOC clients who have received bundled services can make a profound difference in both employment and family outcomes. It is impossible to save and build assets without steady income. Getting a job is a first step, but keeping that job and managing expenses are equally important to financial well-being. People who work yet still struggle to make ends meet may often see public assistance as a far more practical and tolerable route to putting food on the table.

This is how LISC's FOCs have proved so transformative. People who are able to see the impact that employment has on their financial health are more likely to stick with and advance in their jobs. And that is at the heart of our mission: helping low-income people build a more confident, productive future—one that lifts their individual prospects and helps them contribute to a stronger, more sustainable community.

■ ■ ■

***MICHAEL RUBINGER**, president and CEO of LISC, has been at the forefront of community development for 40 years. One of LISC's founding staff members in 1980, he took its helm in 1999 and has since led the organization in revitalizing inner-city housing, expanding into neglected rural areas and developing a comprehensive approach to creating safe, healthy neighborhoods known as Building Sustainable Communities. Rubinger has also served as executive vice president of the Pew Charitable Trusts and as New York City's assistant commissioner of employment and training. Prior to that, he worked with the Manpower Demonstration Research Corporation and the Ford Foundation.*

THINKING OUTSIDE THE 401(K)
Employer-Sponsored Financial Health Solutions

Regis Mulot
Staples Inc.

Financial stress can drain employee focus and productivity. A recent report from the Consumer Financial Protection Bureau explored the benefits and opportunities of leveraging employers to improve the financial lives of Americans. Staples, Inc. did not need convincing. We are a Massachusetts-based global office supplier and are committed to offering comprehensive benefits. Recently, Staples invested in innovations to address financial fitness at work. Although improving employee physical and behavioral health has been the focus of human resources and talent management professionals for years, expanding opportunities for financial benefits is relatively new territory. The 401(k) is a core benefit, but Staples sought to provide our more than 50,000 U.S. associates with a more robust financial wellness program.

UNDERSTANDING EMPLOYEES' FINANCIAL FITNESS NEEDS

Staples embarked on a path to offer a comprehensive program to improve the financial well-being of our associates. We found that many associates were not saving for retirement—or saving at all. Through conversations with associates, we found that they lacked confidence in their ability to save long-term and were worried about handling financial emergencies. In addition, associates under age 21 were not yet eligible to participate in Staples' 401(k) program. We wanted to build all associates' confidence in their ability to manage their money and plan for the future, and provide access to the resources that would help them do so. Staples believes that building financial well-being can help associates relieve stress and better manage the inevitable ups and downs of life, while also contributing to improved job performance and reduced turnover. This was the right thing to do for our associates, and the right thing to do for our business. As a result, we set out to change associates' attitudes about participating in workplace savings efforts.

We knew the financial fitness program would have to increase associate financial knowledge and confidence; increase retirement savings by both eliminating the 401(k) engagement gap and identifying a retirement savings product for ineligible associates; and support and encourage emergency savings.

DESIGNING AN INNOVATIVE FINANCIAL FITNESS SOLUTION FOR A DIVERSE WORKPLACE

We needed a comprehensive solution that would provide access to easy-to-understand information and was suited to our associates' needs. In short, we needed a solution that was:

- Sustainable—cost-effective, easy to implement, scalable across the entire company;
- Accessible—easy to use, understand, and obtain;
- Engaging—was fun for associates;
- Impactful—made a difference in associates' lives.

Given our audience, which was younger and less financially astute, we needed to think creatively. Because there were no off-the-shelf solutions, we looked to new partners to help us design a strategy. Innovations from the nonprofit Doorways to Dreams (D2D) Fund and the U.S. Treasury provided the framework for the efforts.

Using Games to Drive 401(k) Enrollment

In 2011, we partnered with D2D Fund to offer their suite of Financial Entertainment games to all associates through an online portal. The portal served as a hub for testing the idea that games could influence financial behavior. As of April 2015, associates logged more than 13,000 sessions and played nearly 17,000 games. Most important, these sessions delivered nearly 900 hours of financial education.

Prior to launching the game portal, Staples and D2D Fund worked together to customize a version of *Bite Club*—an online game that lets players act as the owner of a popular vampire nightclub. For vampires, retirement is eternal, so saving is of "grave" importance.

The Staples-sponsored version prompted employees to take real-world retirement actions at certain points throughout the game. The first prompt requested an email address for associates to opt-in to emails about saving for retirement. The second asked users about their current 401(k) contribution and provided a link to Staples' associate benefits website where they could view and change their account information.

The rollout of the portal site and game coincided with open enrollment for the 401(k). Game tournaments in retail stores and creative marketing messages drove more than 9,600 visits to the game. By framing often dry content in a new way, the approach increased engagement with the topic of retirement. The Financial Entertainment strategy has gained recognition as a best practice in the field and Staples *Bite Club* has received awards from employee benefits groups, including the New England Employee Benefits Council and *Pensions and Investments*.

Encouraging Emergency Savings through Gameplay

This led Staples to further explore using games to drive changes in financial behaviors. The difficulty that many associates experience in saving for retirement and the future reflects a broader financial health concern: many could not save for short-term needs. Like many Americans, Staples' associates were often faced with saving money at the cost of incurring debt to cover weekly expenses. To help address this challenge, we launched a new initiative focused on building emergency savings.

Once again, we partnered with D2D Fund to customize a game. In *FarmBlitz*, players harvest vegetables to pay off loans and grow savings before their debt multiplies like rabbits. Through gameplay, associates learn why maintaining a small amount of emergency savings is important. They also learn about compound interest. In the customized version for Staples, lighthearted anecdotes matched with savings "pro-tips" are woven into the experience and appear between rounds of play. To ensure widespread accessibility, the new version is both online and available as a mobile app for both Apple and Android devices.

In the first six months, the game was downloaded more than 2,000 times. Associates viewed emergency savings pro tips more than 8,000 times in over 3,000 gameplays. As the *FarmBlitz* intervention continues, D2D Fund is tracking changes in associates' reported levels of financial confidence and knowledge.

LEVERAGING FINANCIAL INNOVATIONS TO RETHINK PRODUCT OFFERINGS

Gameplay was making retirement savings more accessible, but for about 15 percent of Staples' U.S. associates, the retirement savings plan itself was not an option. Staples offers 401(k) benefits to part-time associates, but associates under age 21 are not eligible. As a result, more than 7,000 associates were not developing 401(k) saving strategies and lacked a vehicle to begin long-term savings.

Staples partnered with the U.S. Treasury to become the first large company to launch a rollout of the new *myRA* retirement accounts. *myRA* offers the flexibility and low barrier to entry that were needed to supplement the company's 401(k) plans. At Staples, *myRA* accounts are intended to drive engagement among younger associates, increasing the likelihood that they will transition to a traditional 401(k). This was very important to our company as more than half the workforce is under 35. The *myRA* product therefore presents two opportunities to increase the effectiveness of the financial wellness program: it gives all Staples' associates access to a long-term savings vehicle, and it expands engagement with retirement savings to ensure that the accounts have a greater positive impact on employees' financial lives.

myRA fit perfectly as a quick fix for the retirement savings accessibility gap, but we also see exciting potential to do more for associates' financial wellness. Held in government-backed U.S. Treasury securities, savings deposited into *myRA* accounts can be withdrawn penalty-free at any time and remain accessible to account holders if they change jobs, making it an effective vehicle for building short-term emergency savings. In an industry that sees relatively high turnover, it is important that workers have an account that allows them to maintain flexible, risk-free access to their savings wherever they are employed.

This innovative product allows Staples to go beyond immediate wellness in the workplace. By facilitating access to and use of long-term savings products, we aim to help associates become financially fit for life. We hope that the financial wellness program will help associates build confidence and capabilities that can be applied to any career. In addition, it provides the company with the opportunity to foster a lasting relationship with our associates.

Staples has long provided opportunities to associates at all levels and is committed to offering innovative solutions that help our associates plan and reach a secure future. Our comprehensive wellness program is tailored to meet the needs of our associates and encompasses groundbreaking strategies for engaging and linking them to product offerings. As Staples continues to experiment and innovate in this arena, we urge others to join us as we reimagine marketing and associate outreach, reinvent how products are framed, and rethink which products are offered.

■ ■ ■

REGIS MULOT *is executive vice president Global HR at Staples Inc. where he is responsible for Staples' global HR strategies and programs that advance the company's commitment to be the world's largest office products and services company and supporting its 74,000 associates located in 25 countries. Before moving to Staples Headquarters in Framingham, MA, Regis served as the VP, HR for Staples International, based in Amsterdam, Netherlands, where he built an integrated HR team in Europe, Asia, Australia, and Latin America. Regis is also on Staples Foundation as EVP. Regis, a French national, earned his BA in public law at Paris II-Assas University and his master's degree in public administration at Paris IX-Dauphine and Paris XI-Sceaux Universities. Regis is also on the board of NextStep (Cambridge) organization helping young adults with life threatening diseases, and business advisory council chairman of Simmons School of Management (Boston).*

EMPOWERING ENTREPRENEURS, STRENGTHENING COMMUNITIES

Janie Barrera
LiftFund

There's a familiar proverb: "Give a man a fish and you feed him for a day; teach a man to fish and you feed him for a lifetime." As a small business lender, I often add to this saying—help him buy the pond and he will feed his family and community. At LiftFund, providing capital to entrepreneurs is our core business. We believe entrepreneurship is essential to the health and growth of the U.S. economy, and is part of the solution for achieving financial well-being for millions of Americans. As Federal Reserve Chair Janet Yellen has noted, business ownership is one of the building blocks of economic opportunity and is a significant source of household wealth.[1] Although entrepreneurship can build assets, our work begins with building the financial well-being of the individuals we serve. Entrepreneurs often need assistance in strengthening their own finances in order to access the capital necessary for successfully launching, sustaining, and expanding their businesses.

LiftFund began making microloans to entrepreneurs in 1994. The organization—then called Accion Texas—started with a $175,000 loan from four San Antonio banks. Today, we lend across eight states (Texas, Tennessee, Louisiana, Arkansas, Mississippi, Missouri, Alabama, and Kentucky) and in 2014, we lent $26 million to small businesses, with an average loan of $16,400. With that capital, they created nearly 2,000 jobs and retained more than 3,600 jobs, often in struggling communities where a good job matters deeply to all. Throughout our more than 20-year history, we have seen many economic cycles and we've learned to adapt, even managing dramatic growth through the Great Recession, when credit markets dried up and new businesses found it nearly impossible to

1 Janet Yellen, "Perspectives on Inequality and Opportunity from the Survey of Consumer Finances." Speech at the Conference on Economic Opportunity and Inequality, Federal Reserve Bank of Boston, October 17, 2014.

gain access to capital. Today's landscape continues to change. Although financial markets may evolve, the need for capital remains, and entrepreneurs, who are risk-takers at heart, face particular challenges in navigating the path to financial security. LiftFund focuses on both the needs and the enormous strengths of the individuals we serve, supporting deserving entrepreneurs in fulfilling their economic goals.

WE SEE POTENTIAL WHERE OTHERS SEE RISK

The U.S. Small Business Administration defines a start-up as any business in operation for less than two years. By that measure, we provide 52 percent of our loans to start-ups. We also serve a significant proportion of underserved entrepreneurs, including women- and minority-owned businesses. Serving entrepreneurs is risky business, but over time we've refined our approval process and our business support services so that we can grow and thrive along with our borrowers. We provide a wide variety of classes and one-on-one counseling sessions to help our clients learn about credit and assess their readiness for a loan. But that is only the beginning—we also offer continuing education to help business owners maintain and grow their businesses, such as classes on business continuation planning and human resources for small businesses. The approach seems to be working. According to the Bureau of Labor Statistics, businesses have an overall survivability rate of just under 80 percent in the first year.[2] In contrast, according to an Aspen Institute analysis of LiftFund data, the survivability rate of our borrowers is 96 percent.[3] In addition, LiftFund borrowers repay their small business loans at a rate of 97 percent, even though more than 50 percent have a credit score below 650.

Looking beyond a credit score can move people into financial success. Consider our client Ofelia Posas, a Honduran immigrant living in New Orleans who applied for her first loan after only nine months of residency in the United States. Her first loan of $500 helped her start as a Mary Kay consultant and build her credit with her Individual Taxpayer Identification Number, which laid the foundation for greater access to capital. Today, she is on her third loan of $7,000, is a director for Mary Kay in New Orleans and leads a team of 50 consultants.

---

2 Bureau of Labor Statistics, Business Employment Dynamics Establishment Age and Survival Data, Table 7.

3 FIELD at the Aspen Institute, *microTracker*.

Our approach is both personal and rigorous. Our loan officers take a personal interest in our clients and their businesses and often form lifelong relationships in the process. Applicants who may not initially qualify for one of our loans will get a second and sometimes third look to identify other qualities that may be indicative of their repayment potential. Any resulting approvals tend to be based on our staff's experience in serving our target demographics.

Talking about personal and business finance is at the heart of what we do. Whether a client applies for a business loan online or comes into our offices, we provide consultation that prepares the small business owner with a clear understanding of what it means to take on debt. Our goal when visiting with clients is to help them understand where they are financially, both personally and professionally, so they can make good decisions for themselves and their businesses. Our average client has a limited understanding of how a low credit score can affect him or her and his or her business beyond access to credit. That client also often does not know how to repair his or her score. Rather than judging them, we use our consultations as learning opportunities.

We encourage all of our clients, whether or not they receive a LiftFund loan, to be honest with themselves and mindful of their situation. We help them create or assess their business plan in a realistic light while considering other factors that could affect their businesses' survivability, such as competition, economic forecast, or the potentially negative effects of street construction. We provide technical assistance throughout the process, from navigating start-up permitting and business planning to marketing and human resource management to seeking future capital through traditional banks. We work intensively with clients on financial growth, but we've also committed to tracking our own performance and our borrowers' success through our internal risk model of 18,000 borrower files.

OPPORTUNITIES FOR REACHING SCALE

In addition to our core mission of providing credit and services to traditionally underserved entrepreneurs, we are also committed to providing leadership and innovation to the microlending industry, which has yet to grow to scale. We collaborate with other community development finance institutions (CDFIs) directly and through trade organizations, such as the Association for Enterprise Opportunity and Opportunity Finance Network, and constantly push ourselves to serve more clients, both more effectively and efficiently.

To meet the growing demand for our services, we centralized our work and created scalable systems. We have our own online application system and we have developed a risk assessment model using our own portfolio. We have shared our MMS[4] platform, a tailored customer relationship management platform, with other CDFIs to help them streamline their own online application processes. Similar to other CDFIs, our portfolio is diverse and durable. We serve native-born and immigrant entrepreneurs, men and women, veterans, urban and rural businesses, and the full spectrum of racial and ethnic backgrounds. As a result, we have been able to model and test borrower risk and provide a variety of clients with affordable financial products.

On the heels of the Great Recession, we knew we had to do more to serve more start-ups or unscored credit applicants. After considerable research and testing, we launched the Promise Loan in 2012. This financial product relies on a quiz that assesses business acumen, self-reflection, trustworthiness, perseverance, and an understanding of key mathematical concepts. These loans, which cap out at $5,000, are offered to individuals who would not otherwise qualify for one of our traditional microloans. Thanks to the Promise Loan, we have provided more than 1,600 entrepreneurs with capital so they can build assets, shore up their credit, and launch or grow their businesses.

We have taken the Promise Loan premise—efficient and underutilized risk modeling—even further with Automatic Approval, a product that emerged in a rapidly changing lending environment. If an applicant passes our risk model with verification from one to two financial documents, he or she can close on the business loan within two or three business days. Today, we are still modeling both products, and we plan to share the findings and product with our MMS customers.

---

4 LiftFund created the Microloan Management System in 2008, but has since expanded the platform for use with larger loans. The platform is now known simply as MMS.

PARTNERING IS KEY

We know that partners are key to our success. They help us share our story, they provide grants and debt capital so we can carry out our work, they refer clients to us, and they help us scale up our small business lending to assist more entrepreneurs. For example, we connect our entrepreneurs with individual lenders by partnering with the online lending platform Kiva. In addition, we partner with Goldman Sachs to serve established businesses in economically disadvantaged communities, and we partner with the National Association for Latino Community Asset Builders on the emerging Latino Loan Fund, which leverages our money by providing a loan loss reserve. The reserve allows us to take on more risk. Each one of these programs draws on the respective strengths of the partners to better meet the needs of underserved entrepreneurs.

At LiftFund, we never forget that our reason for being is the individuals we serve. This year, I traveled all over our footprint and was reminded that the stories of success, struggle, and gratitude are real. Our loans, coupled with the drive and leadership of our borrowers, are powerful. Elizabeth Govea, owner of Vintage Tile in McAllen, Texas, shared with me that for her business to grow, she needed to build a warehouse and hire employees to gain contract opportunities. She learned about our organization through the local university small business center and was able to work with our lending team to secure a $35,000 loan with a reduced interest rate from LiftFund's partnership with the City of McAllen. Elizabeth's loan was made possible by the Latina Loan Fund, a small business loan fund for Latina entrepreneurs created through a partnership between LiftFund, the Howard Buffett Foundation, and the Eva Longoria Foundation. By helping Elizabeth strengthen her own financial health and ability to take on a loan, we empowered her to extend her business's success to her community. Her story shows the power of connecting to community and building opportunity as a business owner and job creator. Elizabeth, and so many hardworking individuals like her, deserves financial access and we're proud to be part of that success.

■ ■ ■

JANIE BARRERA *is founding president and chief executive officer of LiftFund, where she works to level the financial playing field for entrepreneurs who historically have faced considerable obstacles when seeking the financing they need to start and expand their businesses. She has received recognition for her accomplishments, including the Small Business Administration Financial Services Advocate of the Year and the Minority Enterprise Development Consortium's Corporate Advocate of the Year. She has served on many national, state and local boards, including the Federal Reserve Board's National Consumer Advisory Council. President Barack Obama appointed Barrera to the President's Advisory Council on Financial Capability, and she also was named to the board of directors for the Federal Reserve of Dallas' San Antonio Branch.*

HEALTH AND SOCIAL SERVICES

LOUISVILLE'S "CULTURE OF COMPASSION"
A Model for Community-based Financial Empowerment

Greg Fischer
City of Louisville, Kentucky

In 2015, I began my second term as Mayor of Louisville, Kentucky, by renewing our city's vision, which includes the importance of financial empowerment for all Louisville residents. Our top three goals are to be:

1. A city of compassion. We recognize that we are all interconnected, no matter what part of town we live in or what socioeconomic background we represent. Muhammad Ali, Louisville's beloved native son, reminds us that, "In a competition of love, we all share in the victory."
2. A city of health. We recognize that health (physical, environmental, psychological, and financial) is the foundation for all else. We strive for every neighborhood to be safe and healthy and every family to be financially stable. Our citizens' financial health directly affects the city's ability to reach its fundamental goals related to improving job readiness, education, and the stability of neighborhoods;
3. A city of lifelong learning. We recognize a culture that promotes continual learning and improvement is a culture that succeeds.

This vision is central to our identity as a community, and it continues to guide our work in financial empowerment. We are developing an integrated, community-wide system that considers the needs of our residents holistically in order to provide targeted assistance and resources that will help them achieve financial stability. This work requires that we integrate financial health strategies throughout city government. It necessitates new outside partnerships and depends on connecting our local efforts with national ones.

INTEGRATING FINANCIAL EMPOWERMENT SERVICES IN AGENCIES CITYWIDE

At a time of shrinking federal budgets, coupled with the increasing demand for local governments to measure and justify public investment, Louisville Metro Government has sought innovative and effective solutions to help those in need. Leaders across multiple departments have embraced the goal of improving the financial stability of the residents we serve by promoting financial access, capability, and asset-building strategies. Our KentuckianaWorks one-stop career centers, Metro Parks and Recreation Community Centers, and the Department of Community Services have offered training for staff and clients to raise awareness around financial empowerment services. Our Human Resources Department models financial health by mandating direct deposit for all Metro employees, promoting Bank On Louisville's resources in our employee benefits' materials, and offering ongoing financial education opportunities at work. This integration of financial empowerment strategies, both internally and externally, produces better family outcomes and leads to a more efficient use of city resources in the long-term.

In an effort to increase access and use of our financial empowerment services, we have developed the capacity and confidence of our caseworkers. In 2011, Louisville Metro's Department of Community Services administered a grant from Living Cities, working with a dozen homelessness-prevention service providers to create a model to integrate financial empowerment into service delivery. That model continues to be replicated across other municipal assistance programs, including workforce development, public housing, education, and health care.

To further expand and professionalize the capacity of staff across agencies dedicated to financial empowerment, we launched a Community Financial Empowerment and Training Certification in 2014 with the support of PNC Foundation, the Center for Nonprofit Excellence, and Metro United Way. In the first year, 67 agencies participated, allowing 220 frontline staff to receive training on topics such as money management, behavioral economics, credit, and barriers to financial empowerment.

STRENGTHENING OUR WORK THROUGH LOCAL PARTNERSHIPS

We know we can help more residents achieve financial well-being, particularly those with lower incomes, by working with partners. One of our foundational collaborative efforts in financial empowerment began in 2010 with the Bank On Louisville initiative, which has helped more than 19,000 individuals connect to free or low-cost starter or "second-chance" checking accounts. Bank On Louisville also works in close partnership with the Financial Education Providers Network to increase access to financial education on a range of topics, including budgeting, debt reduction, credit-building, and financial goal-setting. Since 2011, more than 16,500 individuals have participated in these financial educational opportunities.

Other examples of local collaboration include the Family Economic Success (FES) initiative, composed of nearly 20 public, private and nonprofit agencies. FES partners work to empower individuals and families by providing the infrastructure to connect clients seeking financial assistance with the services they need. Organized by Metro Government, this network meets regularly to share referrals, coordinate services, expand resources, and identify gaps in services. FES also functions as the community advisory subcommittee for Bank On Louisville's executive committee.

Our partners, including agencies in city and state government, Legal Aid Society, Goodwill Power of Work, Jefferson County Public Schools, and the Association of Community Ministries, increase our opportunities to serve citizens. Louisville Metro has also partnered with the Louisville Asset Building Coalition to expand free income tax preparation services through the city's nationally recognized Neighborhood Place one-stop service centers and increase the use of valuable tax credits, such as the Earned Income Tax Credit.

Bringing resources to a convenient location provides dividends for many in our city. Each year, Louisville proudly hosts several community-wide events to bolster financial empowerment, such as Financial Fitness Day, which provides access in one location to multiple financial planning tools and strategies. We partner with the Financial Planners Association of Kentuckiana, which brings volunteer financial planners to meet one-on-one with attendees, and we invite organizations such as Apprisen,

Legal Aid, ElderServe, Family Health Centers, and a local Social Security Disability Insurance law firm to participate.

Although connecting to the financial mainstream and building financial capacity are critical to financial empowerment, we know that it takes more than getting a bank account or attending a few beneficial seminars to reach that goal. It also requires additional job training and education. Our city's economic development team, Louisville Forward, focuses on bringing high-paying jobs to our area and ensuring our citizens receive the training needed for those jobs. One example is Code Louisville, a program created to close the skills gap and prepare the region's residents to succeed in high-paying technology jobs. The program offers free training in computer software coding. The program's success resulted in a visit by President Obama in early 2015.

CONNECTING LOCAL WORK TO THE NATIONAL FINANCIAL EMPOWERMENT MOVEMENT

Louisville's commitment to financial empowerment is rooted in our belief that local government can and should prioritize the financial well-being of its residents. We have seen firsthand how a vision, the right partners, and bold, innovative approaches create opportunities to connect our local work with national efforts.

In 2012, Louisville became the 12th member of the Cities for Financial Empowerment (CFE) Coalition, which currently consists of 14 cities that are home to nearly 21 million people. Those cities include Chicago, Hawaii County, Lansing, Los Angeles, Louisville, Miami, Newark, New York City, Philadelphia, Providence, San Antonio, San Francisco, Savannah, and Seattle. Member cities go beyond the traditional view of local government as providing basic benefits and services, to one that proactively works to help residents build assets and become financially empowered.

Multiple forums annually give mayors and administrators invaluable opportunities to teach and learn from one another, which helps us advance innovative financial empowerment initiatives both locally and nationwide. For example, the CFE is taking a leading role in implementing Bank On 2.0, a new effort to create a unified, national approach to delivering safe, affordable banking products and services to low-income and underbanked people through municipal programs across the country. Because of this affiliation, Louisville has learned from peers on how to advance our work in areas such as youth summer employment, best practices for integration strategies, and engagement with national policy.

Louisville Metro Community Services is also part of the Assets & Opportunity Network (A&O Network), a national movement-oriented group of advocates, practitioners, policymakers, and others working to expand the reach and deepen the impact of asset-based strategies, facilitated by CFED. Through the A&O Network, we have opportunities to learn from peers and national experts about innovative approaches and to advance policies that expand economic opportunity. Through the A&O Network's Technical Assistance Fund (which was supported by JPMorgan Chase), Louisville's Community Services Department and Bank On Louisville partnered with the Credit Builders Alliance to develop a new financial education curriculum called Credit As An Asset. This curriculum is designed to: 1) provide residents with new information and tools to build or rebuild a good credit history; 2) help them think about their attitudes, behaviors, and current relationships with credit; and 3) help participants learn to select and use a credit product that fits their needs.

We're also leveraging other national efforts to empower our residents. For example, the National Disability Institutes' National Center on Leadership for the Employment and Economic Advancement of People with Disabilities sought out Louisville to pilot a program that works with service providers in the disability, employment, financial services, workforce, and asset-building arenas to identify opportunities to collaborate and help people with disabilities prepare for a brighter financial future. Another example is the city's participation in the WATER project, in partnership with the Louisville Water Company, in which families indebted to utility companies are offered a restructured payment plan, payment incentives, and a variety of financial empowerment services. The National League of Cities is leading this pilot study along with four other cities. Finally, Louisville was among the cities that worked with the Consumer Financial Protection Bureau in 2013 to develop their toolkit, *Your Money, Your Goals*, which trains social service staff to help clients learn financial decision-making skills and avoid missteps in choosing financial products.

Our city is on an exciting journey toward financial empowerment, among individuals, staff, and community-wide. National recognition for our efforts is a testament to the hard work of our community partners. Together, we have created meaningful, large-scale opportunities to convene organizations and individuals who are developing financial empowerment strategies to improve the lives of all citizens. We are witnessing a cultural shift; it is no longer enough to just help individuals and families through a crisis. We are now helping them to become financially stable for the long-term. By focusing on the financial health and stability of all our residents, we honor Louisville's vision to be a city of health, compassion, and lifelong learning.

■ ■ ■

***GREG FISCHER** was elected Louisville's 50th mayor in 2010 and was sworn in for a second four-year term in January 2015. He is committed to expanding jobs and creating a culture of innovation, entrepreneurship, accessibility, and transparency. Mayor Fischer was named a 2013 "Public Official of the Year" by* Governing Magazine, *the only U.S. mayor to earn the distinction. He is an entrepreneur who started several businesses, including SerVend International and Iceberg Ventures, a private investment firm.*

FINANCIAL HEALTH IS PUBLIC HEALTH

Jason Q. Purnell
Washington University in St. Louis

"If you want to lower my blood pressure, help me pay my electricity bill."

That statement from a resident of Rochester, NY, has remained with me for several years because it so intuitively speaks to the connection between financial health and physical and mental health. When the American Psychological Association released the results of its "Stress in America Survey" in early 2015, money topped the list of worries, ahead of work, family, and health issues. Seventy-two percent of adults worried about money "at least some of the time," and 26 percent worried about their finances "most or all of the time." The connection of financial stress to health is quite explicit in the survey results, with nearly one-third of respondents who say that struggling to get by financially affects their ability to lead a healthy lifestyle, and more than 20 percent who say that they have either considered or have skipped medical visits because they lacked the financial resources. Not surprisingly, adults with lower incomes experience financial stress more acutely, and those who experience high levels of stress related to their finances are more likely to cope by smoking, eating, drinking alcohol, and watching television in excess, all of which increase their risk for chronic conditions like diabetes and heart disease.[1]

It isn't just adults who suffer the consequences of stress when money is tight. Groundbreaking research reviewed in a 2011 report from the American Academy of Pediatrics finds that childhood exposure to poverty and stress has both immediate and long-term effects on development,

1 American Psychological Association, "Stress in America: Paying with Our Health." (Washington, DC: American Psychological Association, February 4, 2015).

behavior, and health.[2] Scientists have identified differences in the structures and functioning of the brains of children in poverty, making them more sensitive to even mildly stressful situations and less likely to be able to learn new information.[3] Children who experience a particularly severe type of stress called "toxic stress" are also at increased risk for negative behavioral and health outcomes as adolescents and adults.

Though commonly thought of as a purely subjective experience of feeling overwhelmed by life's demands, stress is a complex set of physical processes that start in the brain and extend throughout the body's various organs and systems. In the face of mild-to-moderate, isolated and short-lived periods of stress, this response is quite adaptive. It helps us to focus the mental and physical resources necessary to either confront or escape threatening situations. However, when there are multiple sources of severe or inescapable stress, the stress response essentially never turns off, and the body begins to break down. The immune system is compromised, inflammation increases, and the ability to adapt to future stress is disrupted. This is why children who are exposed to abuse, neglect, domestic violence, unstable caregivers, and mentally ill or incarcerated members of their households—all examples of what are called "adverse childhood experiences" by an eponymous study—are at greater risk for social, emotional, and health problems well into adulthood. These children are also more likely to take up risky behaviors as a means of coping in adolescence and adulthood, such as smoking, drug use, overeating, problem gambling, and unsafe sexual practices.[4] This exacerbates the harm that toxic stress placed on their bodies as young children. When these young people become parents, the cycle often continues.

Stress and its related impacts are part of a broader concept in the field of public health called the "social determinants of health." The World Health Organization defines social determinants of health as "the conditions in which people are born, grow, live, work, and age" that

---

2 Jack P. Shonkoff, Andrew S. Garner, and The Committee on Psychosocial Aspects of Child and Family Health, Committee on Early Childhood, Adoption, and Dependent Care, & Section on Developmental and Behavioral Pediatrics, "The Lifelong Effects of Early Childhood Adversity and Toxic Stress," *Pediatrics* 129 (1) (2012): e232–e246.

3 Ibid.

4 Ibid.

are "shaped by the distribution of money, power, and resources at global, national, and local levels." We know that both health behaviors (e.g., smoking, leisure-time physical activity, cancer screening) and health outcomes (i.e., disease, disability, and death) follow a general pattern by which those with incrementally more education, income, and wealth also have incrementally better health. This "socioeconomic gradient in health" not only influences individuals and families, but also the health and vitality of communities and nations.

THE WEALTH (AND HEALTH) OF NATIONS

The United States is the wealthiest country in the world, with a gross domestic product of nearly $17 trillion, between 17 percent and 18 percent of which is spent on health care. Yet our health lags that of other wealthy nations.[5] The poor showing is the result of more limited health care access and affordability; riskier behaviors such as high-calorie diets, drug use, and violence; physical environments that discourage physical activity; higher rates of child poverty; greater income inequality; lower economic mobility; and a weaker social safety net. Our outcomes can't be explained away by our diversity or blamed entirely on the poor. Even white, college-educated, high-income adults with health insurance have worse health outcomes than their similarly situated peers in other nations.

Simply providing more and better health care is unlikely to solve the problem of health disparities. That means that even legislation hailed as the most momentous social policy in at least a generation, the Affordable Care Act (ACA), is not sufficient to the task of alleviating persistent health inequality. Although the ACA gives significant nods to prevention and population health, its central provisions—expanding health insurance coverage to millions of Americans—are not expected to significantly change the outlook for health disparities, if evidence from similar reform

---

5 In fact, a recent report from the Institute of Medicine found that the U.S. fares worse than many advanced economies on a long list of outcomes, including low birth weight and infant mortality; life expectancy at birth; injuries and homicides; teen pregnancy and sexually transmitted disease; HIV/AIDS; obesity; diabetes; heart disease; disability; and chronic lung disease. National Research Council and Institute of Medicine. (2013). *U.S. Health in International Perspective: Shorter Lives, Poorer Health.* Panel on Understanding Cross-National Health Differences Among High-Income Countries, Steven H. Woolf and Laudan Eron, Eds. Committee on Population, Division of Behavioral and Social Sciences and Education, and Board on Population Health and Public Health Practice, Institute of Medicine. Washington, DC: The National Academies Press.

in the State of Massachusetts is any indication.[6] One simple explanation for why this might be the case comes from the United Kingdom, which has had universal access to health care since the 1940s. The landmark Whitehall Studies of British civil servants find a clear link between employment class or rank of civil servants and health. Those in higher-status jobs enjoyed better health and longer lives than those lower down the employment scale. Even in a country with universal health care, health inequality remains.

Under the best of circumstances, the ACA will not achieve universal coverage, and the decision of the Supreme Court to allow individual states to decide whether to expand Medicaid means that many disadvantaged adults will continue to go without insurance coverage. Health care alone is not enough to change disparities, particularly in premature death, because its contribution to the explanation of such deaths is only 10 percent. That is because the contribution of medical care to the overall explanation of premature death in the United States is estimated at only 10 percent. The other 90 percent is a matter of lifestyle behaviors, genetics, social circumstances, and environmental exposures.

Dr. Thomas Frieden, director of the Centers for Disease Control and Prevention, has another way of describing the relative influence of different kinds of interventions on the health of the population. He calls it the "Health Impact Pyramid" (Figure 1).[7]

At the top of the pyramid are interventions that have the smallest total impact on population health. These are familiar counseling and education activities, such as helping patients with diabetes monitor their blood glucose and eat a healthy diet. At the next level are interventions such as medications to control blood pressure and cholesterol, much of what we think of as at the heart of medical care. This set of activities still has a relatively small impact on population health. "Long-lasting protective interventions" have a larger impact, and include immunizations against disease, certain cancer screenings, and smoking cessation programs. The

---

6 Danny McCormick et al., "Effect of Massachusetts Healthcare Reform on Racial and Ethnic Disparities in Admissions to Hospital for Ambulatory Care Sensitive Conditions: Retrospective Analysis of Hospital Episode Statistics," *BMJ* (2015) *350*:h1480; Brian D. Smedley, "Moving beyond Access: Achieving Equity in State Health Care Reform," *Health Affairs* 27 (2) (2008): 447–455.

7 Thomas R. Frieden, "A Framework for Public Health Action: The Health Impact Pyramid," *American Journal of Public Health* 100 (4) (2010): 590–595.

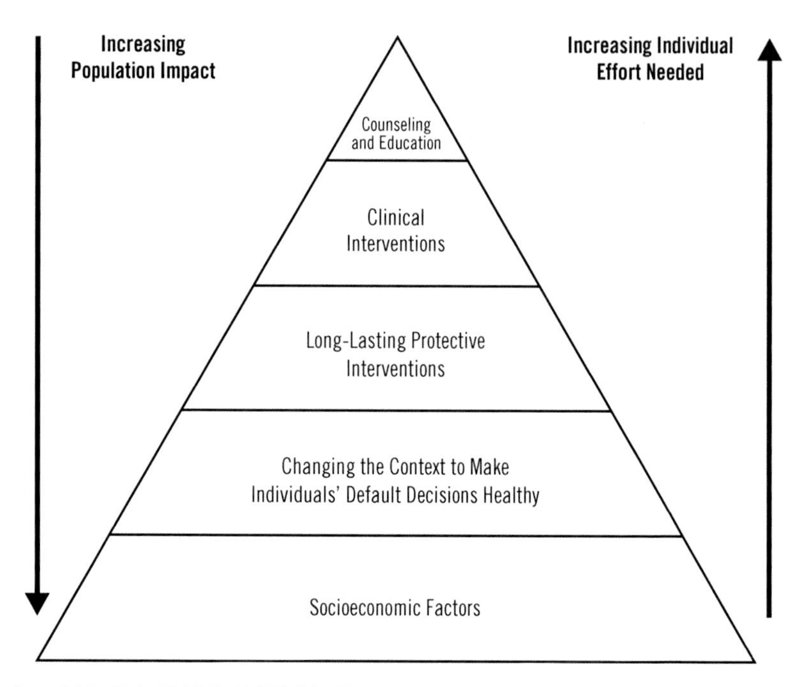

Source: Frieden TR. Am J Public Health 2010;100(4):590-5

Figure 1: The Health Impact Pyramid

bigger impacts come from changes in the environment that make healthy decisions easier, such as adding fluoride to the water supply to prevent cavities or removing lead from paint. These are interventions that protect people from potential threats to health without their having to exert much energy to benefit from them. At the very bottom of the pyramid are social and economic factors such as poverty, education, and adequate housing. These most fundamental resources also have the largest overall impact on health. As Frieden notes, they are also the most politically difficult to address. Indeed, it is at the nexus of culture and politics where the battle for America's financial, physical, and mental health must be fought.

NECESSARY BUT NOT SUFFICIENT

Individualism is a guiding ethic in America, and it provides the lens through which many interpret societal outcomes. Even among those with the most glaring disadvantages, a strong moral sense of personal responsibility for one's lot in life pervades. Nothing delights the American public more than heroic efforts to assume such responsibility in the face of very difficult circumstances. An early 2015 news story featuring a 56-year-old Detroit factory worker who walked more than 20 miles a day to and from work inspired a national outpouring of generosity totaling more than $350,000, including a new car worth $35,000. The flipside of this giddy support for individual heroism is a tendency to very quickly blame individuals or groups who are struggling for their lack of personal responsibility. In a nation in which nearly three-quarters of adults worry about money at least some of the time, where income and wealth inequality are at all-time highs, and where the rate of child poverty is among the highest in the developed world, it is fair to ask whether individual effort can be the total answer to what literally ails, and ultimately kills, Americans.

There is a turn of phrase in science: Conditions can be "necessary but not sufficient" for a particular effect or outcome. For example, water is necessary but not sufficient for ice. No matter how much one may will or wish it to be otherwise, water will not become ice unless it is exposed to a temperature at or below 32 degrees Fahrenheit. In a similar way, individual effort is necessary but not sufficient for what we commonly define as aspects of a successful life: completing education, holding a job, starting and sustaining a family, supporting oneself in retirement and throughout old age. Think of individual effort as the water in this scenario. The average person cannot hope to achieve any of these outcomes without a significant amount of effort, perseverance, and determination—all of which is absolutely necessary, but not sufficient. Young children do not raise themselves nor do they determine their parents' marital status, education levels, or annual incomes. Vaunted though meritocracy may be as an ideal, many people get their first and subsequent jobs through networks of connection rather than laboriously wading through job postings. And a whole host of policies prop up the economic well-being of the relatively well-to-do, from home mortgage deductions to tax-deferred college and retirement savings accounts. Think of these and a multitude of other factors as the freezing temperatures, the context in which the "water" of individual effort is transformed into the "ice" of individual benefit—not merely material benefit, but the very length and quality of life itself.

Despite stacks of studies showing that financial health and physical and mental health are connected and that the conditions in which we live also affect how well and how long we can expect to live, the description above of how individual effort interacts with environment and resources to produce life outcomes remains a tough sell in the current political climate. We are told that the poor and the wealthy alike have gotten what they "deserved" by virtue of their individual successes and failures alone. Even providing health insurance to more Americans is controversial, in part, because it suggests that government is doing what individuals ought to be doing on their own. Either we continue down an unhealthy and ultimately untenable path of ever-increasing health care expenditures for suboptimal and unequal outcomes, or we somehow change the trajectory by changing the way we deliver the message. The latter of these alternatives is the path of a growing number of public health professionals who are convinced by the data supporting the power of the social determinants of health, but also aware that the public and policymakers may not be. In fact, they may not even be aware that the relationships between factors such as household financial status, education, and health are as strong as they are, and that is not their fault. Academics and public health and medical professionals are pretty adept at talking to one another, but their efforts to communicate information clearly and convincingly to the lay public often leave much to be desired.

New models are needed for translating information about the social and economic determinants of health for decision makers from parents to politicians. This was the argument made in a paper in the *Annual Review of Public Health* in early 2015.[8] In it, lead author Dr. Steven Woolf and his team at the Center on Society and Health at Virginia Commonwealth University and my team and I at Washington University in St. Louis offered a framework that includes rigorous research as its basis, but also places emphasis on strategic forms of communication, a thorough understanding of the decision-making context, particularly for policymakers, and thoughtful engagement with key stakeholders. We use as examples of this framework the Education and Health Initiative, a national project led by Dr. Woolf's center, and a local project I lead to improve the health and well-being of African Americans in St. Louis called *For the Sake of All.* Although

8 Steven H. Woolf et al., "Translating Evidence into Population Health Improvement: Strategies and Barriers," *Annual Review of Public Health* 36 (2015): 463–482.

developed separately, each initiative uses the full arsenal of modern communications, from policy briefs and reports to websites, YouTube videos, Twitter feeds, and blog posts to tell the story of how social and economic factors are affecting the health of ordinary individuals. We have some early evidence that the approach is working, or at least that people are talking and thinking in new ways about these issues. The response as measured by web traffic, social media mentions, and local, national, and even international media coverage suggests that this work has hit a nerve. Whether that can translate to changes in policy remains to be seen.

At a recent American Public Health Association meeting to discuss that organization's goal of making America the "healthiest nation in a generation," advanced medical technology was hardly mentioned at all. That was not because any of the speakers (including myself and Dr. Woolf) had a bias against medicine or truly life-saving scientific discoveries made every day. Rather, it was because the speakers recognized the wisdom of that simple statement by the man from Rochester. If we want to help people to live full and healthy lives, we must attend to their *livelihoods*; to the resources that make life possible from the very earliest stages of development to the waning days of old age. We must invest in interventions that address such things as high-quality early childhood development and that provide support for families at all income levels to accumulate and preserve assets. We must redouble our efforts to ensure that all children receive excellent elementary and secondary education and that the most vulnerable children receive the mental and physical health, social, and other services to help them succeed. Those children will also need support in completing postsecondary education and finding jobs with wages that will sustain them and their families, along with a set of benefits such as family and sick leave, retirement savings, and yes, affordable health insurance. And we must not only invest in individuals. We know that poverty, violence, and inadequate resources, services, and amenities affect the health of communities as well. We must find creative ways of making health promotion a central part of community and economic development. In these and many other ways, the inextricable, often stress-laden link between financial well-being and physical and mental health must become the centerpiece of public understanding and public policy. Both our economic health as a nation and the very lives of the American people depend on it.

■ ■ ■

JASON Q. PURNELL *is an assistant professor in the George Warren Brown School of Social Work, faculty scholar in the Institute for Public Health, and faculty director for community engagement in the Center for Social Development at Washington University in St. Louis. Trained in applied psychology and public health, he studies socioeconomic factors contributing to disparities in health behaviors and health outcomes. He leads* For the Sake of All, *an initiative to improve the health and well-being of African Americans in St. Louis through strategic communication of research evidence, community engagement, and policy change.*

TREATING FINANCIAL WELL-BEING AS A PUBLIC HEALTH ISSUE
Lessons from Delaware

Rita Landgraf
Delaware Department of Health and Social Services

Across the country, the following scenario is all too familiar for low- and moderate-income working families.

Mom is a cashier at a local grocery store. It's a good job and she likes the work, but her car is unreliable and she has been late several times during the last few months. She doesn't have enough money in savings for car repairs and she cannot take the bus because she needs to drop off the baby at day care on her way to work. Her supervisor has warned her that if she's late one more time, she'll be fired. If she loses this job, she doesn't know how she'll cover rent and her other living expenses. She's on medication to manage her chronic high blood pressure, and she isn't sleeping well because she's worried about the car, her job, her family, and what might be next. Sometimes, turning the ignition key each morning is almost too much stress to bear.

Financial stress can have a destabilizing effect on health. As such, poverty remains the clearest "upstream" or "social determinant" of health (for more information, see Jason Purnell's essay in this book). To help explain the concept of social determinants, public health officials often use the analogy of fish dying in a river. While it's possible at first to manage the dead fish, eventually as more begin to die, it's better to go upstream and find the root cause of why the fish are dying. Those root causes represent the social determinants of health. Similarly, if we want to improve health outcomes for lower-income people, whose health is typically much worse than higher-income individuals, we need to move "upstream" to address the social and economic factors that influence health, such as education, employment, and financial stability.

According to the Gallup-Healthways Well-Being index, Americans living in poverty are more likely than higher-income Americans to have a variety of chronic health conditions, both psychological and physical. The biggest disparity was in rates of depression. Adults below the poverty line were almost twice as likely to have been diagnosed with depression at some point in their lives than were those with higher incomes (nearly 30 percent vs. 15.8 percent). Similarly, individuals in poverty had higher rates of obesity, asthma, diabetes, high blood pressure, and heart attacks. As Michael Reisch, a professor of social justice at the University of Maryland, put it in his 2013 testimony before a Senate panel, "Poverty is a thief. Poverty not only diminishes a person's life chances, it steals years from one's life."[1] To be clear, it isn't just having more money that extends life. Rather, financial well-being addresses many of the root causes of poor health, including creating a sense of control over one's circumstances and future. Financial empowerment builds our economic security, improves our quality of life, promotes health and well-being, and fosters self-sufficiency.

This connection between financial health and physical health was further cemented for me soon after I became Cabinet Secretary for the Delaware Department of Health and Social Services (DHSS) in 2009. I asked my leadership what the department was doing to foster self-sufficiency. Their answer was both simple and eye-opening: We provide benefits, which can supplement in a crisis, but we do not provide financial sustainability or security. From that stunning admission came the realization that we needed to do more to truly empower people and set them on the path to self-sufficiency. To further physical, emotional, and financial well-being, we must empower individuals to take control of their personal finances.

With the support of Governor Jack Markell, a former Treasurer for the State of Delaware, our team developed a statewide financial empowerment strategy in 2011, which includes:

---

1 Michael Reisch, "Dying Young: Why Your Social and Economic Status May Be a Death Sentence in America." Testimony before the Subcommittee on Primary Health and Aging, Committee on Health, Education, Labor and Pensions, U.S. Senate, November 20, 2013.

- One-on-one financial coaching;
- Alternative financial products to counteract predatory payday loans, pawn brokers, title lenders, rent-to-own stores, and other businesses that profit from a need for quick cash;
- College-bound programs that help students and families navigate the financial roadmap of postsecondary education, including accessing financial aid and managing student loan debt;
- Referrals and collaborative initiatives among nonprofit service providers to support debt consolidation, homeownership and foreclosure counseling, and self-employment; and
- Free, self-help tax preparation online.

Data on Delaware's household financial demographics speak to the need for this intentional focus on financial empowerment. According to the U.S. Census, of the 335,707 households in Delaware in 2013, 42 percent had incomes below $50,000, and 29 percent had incomes below $35,000. Many of these households have traditionally struggled with:

- Monthly expenses that exceed income;
- No savings or safety net;
- Supplementing income with credit;
- Low credit scores;
- High debt for medical expenses, student loans, and credit cards;
- Exploitation by the "fringe" financial sector;
- Lack of access to mainstream financial services and products; and
- Debilitating stress and worry over family finances.

With those statistics in mind, DHSS addressed financial well-being as part of our overall mission: To improve the quality of life for Delaware's citizens by promoting health and well-being; to foster self-sufficiency; and to protect vulnerable populations. To me, they are all intertwined.

Self-sufficiency is intrinsic to health and well-being, and without it, a person is more likely to be vulnerable, which can lead to poor health outcomes and a poor quality of life.

Delaware currently is the only state to have a statewide financial empowerment strategy led by the governor. The program, called $tand By Me ($BM), is headquartered in my department and is a partnership with the United Way of Delaware (UWD). $BM is funded primarily through contributions from local and national foundations, financial institutions, and UWD, with additional state funding to cover five staff positions. $BM's core service is personal financial coaching. This enables each customer to develop a one-on-one relationship with a financial coach, which reduces the fear of dealing with difficult financial issues and encourages personal financial capability (see Michael Collins' essay in this volume for more on financial coaching).

$BM's financial coaching model never dictates, but rather asks each customer to identify his or her own challenges and goals, and come up with a customer-driven action plan. This approach removes barriers of income, race, age, gender, and disability as the customer is empowered to take the lead in developing his or her personalized vision and strategy to achieve financial stability. Because the program is available to all Delawareans, it eliminates the stigma often associated with poverty and encourages individuals to reach out for the support they need.

One of the unique aspects of $BM is that it is designed to be co-located and embedded within organizations that serve the target market, but that do so with very different missions. For example, $BM is offered as an employee benefit in partnership with employers of low-wage workers; as a student resource in community colleges serving nontraditional students; as a service for students and their parents to support college access in partnership with high schools and the Delaware Department of Education; as a service to employees and families in child care in partnership with the Delaware Office of Early Learning and the Department of Services for Children, Youth and Their Families; and as a resource in economically disadvantaged communities in partnership with nonprofit organizations. For example, $BM is embedded within Head Start as both a community service to parents and as an employee benefit to staff. Parents are asked to identify a financial goal as they enroll their children and work with a financial coach who is located onsite at Head Start. This win-win partnership not only enables $BM to reach economically vulnerable families, but it also enables Head Start to respond to federal performance standards to increase the financial stability of the families it serves.

These partnerships mark the beginning of a large-scale change in which financial empowerment becomes a priority for a diverse group of stakeholders representing multiple sectors. $BM customers are working on a variety of financial goals, with many pursuing multiple goals. As of March 2015, 4,272 had attended workshops on financial aid and postsecondary education; 2,385 had created a budget and a plan to improve their daily money management; 1,423 reduced their debt and increased their credit score; 961 were working to obtain consumer-friendly financial services; 743 were working to establish regular monthly savings; and 658 were pursuing improved employment situations.

What started as a philanthropic program now has greater policy implications as a stabilizing force for individuals and families at workplaces, educational institutions, and government agencies. To build security for the future of $BM beyond the current state administration, legislation was passed in 2015 in Delaware's General Assembly to codify the Office of Financial Empowerment within the Department of Health and Social Services. With the passage of this bill, financial empowerment will evolve as a priority for the state of Delaware, from one administration to the next. The office will continue to be led by a director and four staff, supported within the DHSS budget. This team will maintain $BM's public-private partnership with philanthropy and the nonprofit sector to sustain the momentum in support of economic security in Delaware.

Today, $tand By Me provides customized services to people with disabilities, older adults, veterans, people of color, staff and families at child care centers, young people aging out of foster care, dislocated workers, public housing residents, and low-wage workers across a broad spectrum of industries. For these traditionally underserved populations, $BM represents an opportunity to improve economic self-sufficiency and financial well-being—critical upstream factors that contribute to better downstream health. Healthy individuals and healthy families—physically, emotionally, and financially—will lead us to healthier communities. That's the ultimate win for everyone.

■ ■ ■

Since 2009, ***RITA LANDGRAF*** *has served as the cabinet secretary for the Delaware Department of Health and Social Services. For more than 30 years, she has worked on behalf of individuals with disabilities, including as executive director of the Arc of Delaware and NAMI Delaware, and as president of AARP Delaware. In 2015, she was inducted into Delaware Women's Hall of Fame.*

BEYOND FINANCIAL EDUCATION
Supporting Positive Financial Behaviors through Financial Coaching

J. Michael Collins
University of Wisconsin–Madison

Making ends meet can be a real struggle, and in some cases people cannot pay for necessities such as food and shelter. This is not just about lack of income. Two households in the same neighborhood with otherwise similar income and education can display widely different levels of financial "wellness," at least in terms of being able to manage the ups and downs of income and expenses. One family with a limited income might struggle but generally pay bills on time, manage to make bigger purchases when needed, and even have a little money for extras such as entertainment or travel. Another family may struggle much more, frequently miss due dates for bills, be pestered by collectors, and be unable to make larger purchases because they are denied credit. Little about the latter family could be described as healthy.

As others have pointed out in this book, being unable to make ends meet can contribute to general anxiety and harm mental health. It can also have tangible effects on children and families. Financial hardships can also contribute to physical health problems and an overall reduced quality of life. Policies and programs have experimented with a range of approaches during the last several decades to help people become better at personal financial management, with mixed success. Existing approaches show promise, but also shortcomings, including people's initial reluctance to take part and challenges to long-term adherence to new habits. One emerging approach that may help people sustain positive financial practices is financial coaching. Learning from the challenges of past strategies, coaching focuses on people's own goals and motivations, with the ultimate goal of developing greater autonomy and confidence in their ability to manage their finances.

FINANCIAL EDUCATION: NECESSARY BUT NOT SUFFICIENT

During the last two decades, and particularly since the recession in the late 2000s, one widely trumpeted solution for improving financial decision-making is to provide financial education for adults who otherwise have little formal financial education or training. There are dozens of models for financial education in the United States, and many curricula, videos, online learning, and other tools are freely offered in communities. Demand for financial education ought to be robust—a number of surveys and studies show many people lack a basic knowledge of financial products, financial management, and financial planning. Studies also show that limited financial literacy is associated with negative behaviors such as high debt or failing to plan for retirement—that is, people who score poorly on financial knowledge quizzes also tend to show signs of worse financial outcomes.

Yet, the evidence is weak for the positive effect that financial education programs can have on personal financial behavior. For example, in 2014, Daniel Fernandes, John Lynch, and Richard Netemeyer reviewed more than 100 studies to assess the efficacy of financial education interventions.[1] They conclude that very few programs have much of an impact on financial behavior later in life. It appears that educational interventions, particularly those aimed at adults with an established pattern of behavior and habits, are unable to change the kinds of financial decisions that people make.

FOCUSING ON FINANCIAL BEHAVIOR

People learn behavior through a variety of contexts, but social context is particularly important. Parents and extended family shape many people's experiences with finances. People may emulate practices modeled by a parent, for example saving up for a family car or paying bills systematically every Sunday evening. They may also try to avoid the problems a parent or other family member fell into. Other financial behaviors are shaped by relationships—a spouse or partner, but also peers, coworkers, and friends. These can be powerful forces that determine the major financial choices in people's lives.

---

1 Daniel Fernandes, John Lynch, and Richard Netemeyer, "Financial Literacy, Financial Education, and Downstream Financial Behaviors," *Management Science* 60 (8)(2014).

Another factor that strongly influences financial behavior is financial access. The marketplace for loans, savings, insurance, and other financial products and services is central to every financial choice. Access to financial products and services is uneven by location and by market segment, with lower-income areas and households having quite different options than more affluent areas and families. For example, workplace retirement savings accounts make decisions about saving much easier and more convenient than leaving people to find savings products and regularly save on their own. But lower-income workers are much less likely to have a retirement benefit or option provided by their employer. For these workers, the range of available financial products, features, and costs is limited.

Beyond financial access, the regulation of high-cost or predatory financial services also plays a role. A marketplace with clear and effective guard rails to help keep people from getting into trouble can help, but this may be easier said than done. Well-meaning financial regulations can overreach, resulting in too many restrictions, little interest by the private sector in making sound products and services available, and denying people access to financial services from which they can directly benefit.

THE ROLE OF ADVICE

Faced with these factors, how do we get beyond financial education to more effectively help people make better financial decisions? One potential solution is to engage third-party, trusted advisers to help people when faced with financial challenges. Ideally, these objective sources of financial information and advice can help individuals make their own financial decisions—much like a medical professional guides patients to try certain drug treatments or change certain health behaviors. Financial advice might come from a technical expert, such as a tax accountant or a sales professional from a financial firm helping people select from among various products. However, financial advice provided by someone who benefits from the sale of particular financial products or services can create high levels of distrust, as some people will be driven into choices that are in the best interest of the salesperson, not their own. Interestingly, survey data show that people with higher incomes, higher levels of education, and higher levels of measured financial literacy are the most likely to seek out and use financial advice. Financial advice, therefore, is primarily serving as a complement to existing personal financial knowledge and capability, rather than a supplement when someone lacks that knowledge.

CHANGING AND SUSTAINING BEHAVIORS OVER TIME

Even after people develop the capacity to make positive financial choices, they may still struggle. A variety of challenges can get in the way of people's desired course of action, such as failures of self-control or simple forgetfulness. We all face situations where we put off tasks until "tomorrow," sometimes procrastinating indefinitely. Therefore, in some sense, acquiring financial capability is a never-ending task; people need to learn financial information and how to make good financial choices, but they also need the ability to maintain and adapt behaviors over time. Financial counselors, often supported through public programs, can play a role in this regard. Counselors can help solve problems, especially complicated and emotionally charged issues like home foreclosure or credit default. But counseling is ultimately problem-solving mediated by an expert and may not enhance the ability of people to manage their finances in the long run.

Based in part on studies in psychology and behavioral economics, there is some hope that consumers of financial products and services can be guided to make optimal financial choices through nudges, how choices are framed, and reminders. For example, the easiest financial choice is to do nothing. When a financial decision has automatic features, people often choose the default option. For example, if a goal is to use retirement savings accounts more, people could be encouraged to save at a set level of income by their employer through default settings. This will result in more people saving. However, though the approaches are promising, they may not change how someone actively makes financial decisions in his or her life. Take the example of the person who was defaulted into saving for retirement. Their saving was probably not carefully considered or part of an overall plan. They may not have gained much knowledge about retirement savings or financial management; some may not even be able to recall they have a retirement savings account. This is more worrisome when retirement comes and the onus of managing that retirement fund shifts to the saver. People need to take control of their own finances to enhance their ability to manage financial choices.

The Consumer Financial Protection Bureau has defined financial well-being as being able to meet current and ongoing financial obligations, feeling secure about future finances, and having a sense of autonomy about making choices that facilitate lifetime enjoyment. This perspective emphasizes feeling in control of basic financial management decisions, being resilient to setbacks, and being on track with personal financial goals. A sense of personal financial freedom is part of what people perceive as financial well-being. This goes beyond simple education or advisers developing a plan for a client. It involves getting people actively engaged in their own financial management.

ENTER FINANCIAL COACHING

Financial coaching reflects a shift toward engaging people in becoming more active managers of their own finances. It is not about teaching specific personal finance content, but rather helping people to form goals, take actions, and follow through with the behaviors that they themselves deem important. Coaching is not prescriptive. However, coaching techniques share common processes that engage clients in developing patterns of behavior that are sustainable.

Financial coaching applies techniques emerging from research in positive psychology, a branch of psychology focused on improving life experience. Coaching techniques have been used in athletics, health, personnel management, and other settings for decades, and are often embedded into mentoring, counseling, motivational interviewing, or other approaches. More recently, coaching is developing a unique identity related to personal finance, especially in the United States. Typically, financial coaches and clients work on four main issues:

1. Alliance: forming a partnership between the coach and client;
2. Agenda: letting the client decide what is important and define his or her own goals;
3. Awareness: allowing clients to explore their own beliefs and motivation to change behaviors; and
4. Actions: clients act on their plans under the supervision of the coaching relationship.

Coaching should result in greater financial planning, which might include spending or saving plans, reviewing financial documentation or credit reports, and developing action steps to better manage credit or debt. With practice, and the support of and monitoring by the coach, clients are likely to have greater persistence even in the face of challenging behaviors. They are likely to better exert self-control and reduce procrastination. Over time and with some repetition, these steps will begin to focus client attention on problem behaviors and increase the rate of positive behaviors.

The promise of financial coaching is that as people purposefully work toward their financial goals, they increase their self-awareness and self-regulation. People can build a stronger capacity to develop and implement their own solutions as new financial challenges occur. In the long run, people can develop skills and behaviors they can improve independently without needing a coach or counselor, and perhaps even shift the trajectory of their financial decisions.

Ultimately the goal of coaching is greater financial well-being, as measured by reduced stress levels, an increased sense of control, improved ability to absorb a financial shock, and expanded ability to find and evaluate information to make financial decisions. Coaching could engender a greater sense of freedom related to financial decision-making.

Public and nonprofit programs have increasingly been applying coaching techniques to financial capability services, including a funding program from the Consumer Financial Protection Bureau. In part, practitioners have turned to coaching strategies in response to disappointing results in financial education or financial access programs alone in changing behavior. Financial coaching is very much a loosely defined "model" and many components and features are still in development. The intensity of coaching, the length of the coaching relationship, and the extent of supports provided to clients can vary dramatically from a few sessions in a short period to many sessions over many months. Given that coaching involves one-on-one meetings and coaches need to be trained and supported, this is a potentially expensive strategy to improve financial wellness.

In practice, the term "coaching" is sometimes also used to describe programs that are more prescriptive and less client-centered than would be expected in a coaching approach. This is in part due to the technical nature of some personal finance issues, which might require the coach to also be an expert who can instruct and counsel clients on decisions. This balance—between allowing the coaching relationship to evolve organically and more overtly directing the actions of the client—is at the crux of the still-evolving format of financial coaching.

The excitement about financial coaching is grounded in its logic model—that it addresses the issues people seem to struggle with and emphasizes personal growth and autonomy. Although evidence is emerging from health coaching and other settings that point to the benefits of financial coaching for behavior change, solid evidence does not yet exist. However, pilot programs and studies are in progress that can show how coaching influences savings and credit management. Future studies of financial coaching must be carefully designed to test the mechanisms behind various coaching approaches.

Evaluating client-directed goals can be tricky. One person's goal could be to access credit (borrowing more) and another's to pay down debt. Some clients will want to boost savings and others use savings to make a major purchase. Standard measures of financial outcomes may not be sufficient to evaluate coaching models. Instead, measures of financial health and well-being may be more relevant. Reduced stress and anxiety, a greater sense of control and feeling on track to meet long-term financial goals may be the dominant results of coaching experiences. Discussions about the effects of financial coaching can spur a more critical analysis of just what financial capability means, and the extent to which predetermined behaviors such as saving or paying down debt are inadequate to match the wide ranging goals of families.

CONCLUSION

It is tempting to oversimplify household financial management and capability issues. One view is that poverty mechanically results in financial hardships. In this perspective, focusing on building personal financial capability is a distraction—a drop in the bucket given larger socioeconomic challenges. Another view puts responsibility squarely in the hands of individual financial consumers. This approach implies that people are responsible to seek out information about financial decisions on their own and make informed choices. Neither view fully reflects reality. Financial

LORETTA'S COACHING EXPERIENCE

Loretta is a 45-year-old single mother who had struggled with her finances—calls from collectors every few months and little savings cushion to catch her when she had shortfalls. A couple of years ago, she worked with a financial counselor who told her which bills to pay first, and she took a financial education workshop where she made a monthly budget. Neither helped much. A few months ago, she started working with a financial coach based at a local nonprofit organization.

She expected the coach to offer her suggestions or tell her what she was doing wrong. Instead, the coach asked a lot of questions and listened to what she had to say, even before looking at a credit report or financial statement. At first Loretta said her goal was to pay off her debt, but as she talked with her coach, she changed her mind. What she really wanted was to have an emergency savings fund because it would best help her manage the ups and downs of her income and expenses. Her coach checked in with her every couple of weeks, and Loretta reported on her progress. The times she was tempted to spend extra money, she would think of having to tell her coach she missed her goal. Some weeks she had to admit she made little progress, but her coach simply asked her what she would do next week and did not judge her for failing. Loretta gained new confidence and focus on managing her cash flow. In six months she had saved enough to cover a car repair, something that normally would have caused her to miss payments on another bill. Money was still tight for Loretta, but she was feeling like she could manage her finances more independently than before.

well-being is not just a reflection of income or assets; people at a given level of income or net wealth vary in their ability to manage their own finances. But knowledge is not enough. Social context and access to carefully regulated financial products clearly play a role in supporting financial choices and behaviors. Financial coaching suggests a hopeful balance of enhancing personal financial capability with the ultimate goal of enhanced life experience and well-being.

■ ■ ■

*J. **MICHAEL COLLINS** is an associate professor of public affairs and human ecology at the University of Wisconsin—Madison where he serves as faculty director of the Center for Financial Security. He has an MPP from Harvard's Kennedy School of Government and a Ph.D. from Cornell University.*

BREAKING THE CYCLE OF MASS INCARCERATION
A Strategy for Investing in Individuals, Families and Communities

Vivian Nixon
College and Community Fellowship

Susan Sturm
Columbia Law School and Center for Institutional and Social Change

So many people come out with so many good intentions. And every door is slammed on them... When you're told no at the employment line, when you're told no trying to get back to your family, or you're told no because this community is unaccepting of you—you try to figure out where you belong. And for many, sometimes it becomes rough and you resort to that old stuff.

—College and Community Fellowship student

I can't tell you how many formerly incarcerated people or poor people or people of color wouldn't... invest a dollar to get $150 because you have to believe you're going to be here at 65 to want to put away even a dollar for your future.

—Formerly incarcerated leader

During the past four decades, the U.S. prison population has quadrupled, reaching an incarceration rate of nearly one in one-hundred adults. Including those on parole and probation, 7 million people in America were under some form of criminal justice supervision in 2013. The country is experiencing not only mass incarceration but mass criminalization, with nearly 65 million criminal history records on file. The vast majority of these men and women are parents.[1]

Research and experience reveal the consequences of failing to invest in the lives and futures of people and communities affected by the criminal justice system. So many of the people who experience prison have grown up with narratives of low expectations, high risk, and public indifference to the struggles and traumas accompanying poverty. Many in these communities receive attention and resources only when they break the law, and not when and where they need it the most.

Financial well-being, or more importantly its absence, plays a role in this cycle of disinvestment and interaction with the criminal justice system. Affected individuals often live in communities where incarceration is commonplace and quality education is out of reach. Crushing challenges associated with poverty leave little hope for a future that includes a decent job, let alone college and career. Add to that the widespread practices of charging fees and fines, such as for parking tickets, which land people in jail when they are unable to pay. The subsequent stigma of incarceration amplifies barriers to decent employment, financial stability, and safety.

These patterns of disinvestment operate alongside a set of policies that have produced the highest rate of incarceration in the world, creating an unsustainable financial future for these individuals, their communities, and generations to come. Through our work, we have documented how education and social capital can break this cycle, reduce incarceration, and enable people closest to the problem to transform their lives and communities.

---

1 For sources in this paragraph, see: Christy A. Visher and Jeremy Travis, "The Characteristics of Prisoners Returning Home and Effective Reentry Programs and Policies." In *The Oxford Handbook of Sentencing and Corrections*, edited by Joan Petersilia and Kevin R. Reitz (New York: Oxford University Press, 2012); Michelle Natividad Rodriguez and Maurice Emsellem, *65 Million "Need Not Apply": The Case for Reforming Criminal Background Checks*. (New York: National Employment Law Project, March 2011); Hindelang Criminal Justice Research Center, *Sourcebook of Criminal Justice Statistics* (Albany, NY: University at Albany, 2010).

A CYCLE OF POVERTY AND INCARCERATION

Poverty is the largest driving force behind what the Children's Defense Fund calls the "Cradle to Prison Pipeline." Most of the individuals entering the criminal justice system are at a financial disadvantage; about 60 percent of intakes into the state and federal prison systems report annual incomes under $12,000. These low incomes reflect higher rates of unemployment and the unavailability of decent jobs for people who lack a college education.[2] During the past four decades, most of the growth in lifetime risk of imprisonment was concentrated among men who had not been to college. For many of these men, prison has become a normal part of life. According to the National Research Council, among African American men born in the late 1970s and who dropped out of high school, 70 percent have served time in state or federal prison. For white and Latino men in the same cohort, the rates of imprisonment are 28 percent and 20 percent, respectively.[3]

Incarceration sharply curtails the economic prospects of individuals and the communities to which they return. In 2011, nearly 700,000 people were released from either a state or federal prison, and most faced a multitude of challenges on returning to "free" society. Parents with minor children may have accumulated years' worth of child-support arrears or had their parental rights rescinded. With few assets besides the "gate money" provided at release (usually between $50 and $200), those who have been disconnected from friends and family face uncertain housing and homelessness.

Upon release from prison, returning citizens have few opportunities for work that will be satisfying and provide a living wage. The National Research Council reports that up to one-half of former prisoners remain jobless for up to a year after their release. Barriers to employment associated with having a criminal record include restrictions on licenses in certain professions and the loss of personal and professional contacts while incarcerated. People of color with a criminal record have

---

2 Bureau of Justice Statistics, "Profile of Jail Inmates, 2002." (Washington, DC: U.S. Department of Justice, October 2004); National Research Council, *The Growth of Incarceration in the United States: Exploring Causes and Consequences*, edited by Jeremy Travis, Bruce Western, and Steve Redburn (Washington, DC: National Academies Press, 2014), p. 128.

3 National Research Council, *The Growth of Incarceration in the United States.*

a particularly difficult time finding a job, especially one that enables them to invest in their futures, in part because of the stigma that attaches to a record. Blacks without criminal histories experience job callback rates closely matching those of whites with a felony conviction.[4] The National Research Council report suggests that "pervasive contact with the criminal justice system has consequences for racial stratification that extend well beyond individuals behind bars."

Mass incarceration also has a significant impact on U.S. poverty rates. Had it not been for the dramatic rise in incarceration rates between 1980 and 2004, researchers estimate that the poverty rate would have fallen by about 2.8 percentage points, instead of dropping by only 0.3 percentage points.[5] This translates into several million fewer people living in poverty.

SYSTEMS OF DISINVESTMENT HAVE LED TO INCREASED INCARCERATION

Many people affected by the criminal justice system grew up in communities with schools and other public institutions that failed them. As states were dramatically increasing funding for corrections, they were simultaneously cutting or not raising funding for social and government services targeting poverty, such as public assistance, transportation, and education. State spending per prisoner is three times that per public school student, and prison costs exceed spending on higher education in some states.[6] These patterns exemplify the pattern of disinvestment contributing to mass incarceration. Communities of color have borne the brunt of this emphasis on incarceration at the expense of education. Researchers have documented vastly disproportionate incarceration and criminalization of people of color, particularly black men.[7] While people of color make up about 30 percent of the United States' population, they account for more

---

4 Devah Pager, *Marked: Race, Crime, and Finding Work in an Era of Mass Incarceration* (Chicago: University of Chicago Press, 2007); National Research Council, *The Growth of Incarceration in the United States.*

5 Robert Defina and Lance Hannon. "The Impact of Mass Incarceration on Poverty," *Crime and Delinquency*, 59 (2013): 562–586.

6 Children's Defense Fund, "America's Cradle to Prison Pipeline." (Washington, DC: Children's Defense Fund, October 2007).

7 Vivian Nixon, "Opening Remarks." Address at New York Reentry Education Network Pathways of Possibility Conference, City University of New York, Baruch College, New York, NY. February 27, 2013.

than 60 percent of those imprisoned. The Bureau of Justice Statistics estimates that one-third of male African-American children born in 2001 can expect to serve time in prison at some point in their lives, compared to 17.2 percent of Hispanics and 5.9 percent of whites; 5.6 percent of black women born in 2001 are likely to go to prison at some point in their lives, but only 0.9 percent of white women and 2.2 percent of Hispanic women.[8]

At the same time, disinvestment in education, particularly in low-income communities of color, has reduced social mobility and limited access to the social capital needed to revitalize those communities. Incarceration's reach has now grown too big to ignore, with stratification researchers characterizing incarceration as a powerful engine of social inequality.[9]

Mass incarceration has, in the words of Todd Clear in *Imprisoning Communities*, "made disadvantaged communities worse." Patrick Sharkey, in *Stuck in Place*, for example, links the high rates of incarceration with concentrated poverty and marginalization, racial stigmatization, and lack of investment and resources that are fundamental both for the positive development of children and the mobility of adults. The Justice Mapping Center has mapped the concentration of incarceration rates in disadvantaged communities all around the country: millions of dollars per neighborhood are spent to imprison residents of these communities.[10]

WE CAN TURN THIS AROUND: THE TRANSFORMATIVE POTENTIAL OF INVESTING IN INDIVIDUALS, FAMILIES, AND COMMUNITIES

The struggles people face when returning home, including returning to the same context that led to prison, increase the chance that they will give up on the struggle to achieve long-term financial stability through lawful means. But a movement to reverse this tide has emerged. Driven largely by directly affected communities and supported by the contributions of the academic community, this movement links the need for fundamental reform of the criminal justice system with the need for change in the

8 Bureau of Justice Statistics, "Special Report: Prevalence of Imprisonment in the U.S. Population, 1974–2001." (Washington, DC: U.S. Department of Justice, August 2003).

9 Bruce Western, *Punishment and Inequality in America* (New York: Russell Sage Foundation, 2006). p. 198.

10 Spatial Information Design Lab, *Million Dollar Blocks.*

public policies that have underinvested in low-income communities of color and overinvested in the criminal justice system. These advocacy organizations and networks include the Education from the Inside Out Coalition, JustLeadershipUSA, and the New York Reentry Education Network. They are joined by a surprising convergence of public figures across the political spectrum, including Tony-winning composers, political conservatives, and President Obama.

Through this work, we have seen the transformative power of investing in people and communities. By investment, we mean both building financial stability and increasing capacity through education, social capital, and meaningful employment so people can provide adequately for themselves and their families.[11] These forms of investment kindle hope among the formerly incarcerated (many of whom did not believe they even had a future) and enable positive contributions to families and communities. Providing resources, support, and capacity enables people affected by incarceration to invest in their futures and to become actively engaged in the effort to rebuild their communities.

Education is a key component of this investment strategy. Just as lack of educational opportunity increases the likelihood of poverty and incarceration, access to high-quality education plays a critical role in facilitating mobility. One study showed that almost all soon-to-be-released prisoners reported needing more education (94 percent) and job training (82 percent), while the need for a driver's license (83 percent) ranked higher than the need for employment (80 percent).[12] The link between lack of education and recidivism is strong. A bachelor's degree reduces the likelihood of returning to prison to 5.6 percent, in contrast to 66 percent for those without a BA. For those with a master's degree, the recidivism rate drops to less than 1 percent.[13]

Programs such as College and Community Fellowship (CCF) have proved successful in supporting the formerly incarcerated as they move along the

---

11 Susan Sturm and Vivian Nixon, "Home Grown Social Capital: How Higher Education of Formerly Incarcerated Women Facilitates Family and Community Transformation." (Aspen, CO: Aspen Institute, November 2015).

12 Visher and Travis, "The Characteristics of Prisoners Returning Home."

13 College and Community Fellowship, *Statistics*.

path to higher education. CCF supports women affected by the criminal justice system in pursuing a college degree by enveloping them and their families in support services while they complete their degree. CCF was the first reentry-based organization to use postsecondary education as its core strategy for moving women out of marginalized subsistence and into mainstream society. In addition to achieving an extremely low recidivism rate, these programs give people a sense of hope, a belief in the future, and a willingness to invest in themselves, their families, and their communities.

Early in its history, CCF noticed that students needed to build their financial capability to succeed in college and beyond. They found that their students held many misconceptions about financial management and lacked confidence to control their financial lives. These insights triggered a series of efforts to help students address their financial needs.

CCF first introduced a student debt and financial aid counseling program and later added credit counseling services. In 2013, CCF joined The Financial Clinic's New Ground Initiative, a capacity-building initiative that helps New York City reentry programs embed financial development in their services. The New Ground Initiative focuses on improving the lives of formerly incarcerated individuals through a combination of financial development strategies that help build financial security and improve financial mobility. The New Ground Initiative trained all counselors working with students at CCF to integrate "financial development" strategies into their conversations and build financial awareness and training into all services. The Financial Clinic's approach invites all staff to begin with their own personal financial security as a way to build this capacity.

Financial training provides CCF's students with the tools they need to make sound financial choices and build assets. In one year of the New Ground Initiative, CCF pulled credit reports for 100 percent of participants and organized debt for more than 150 participants, including student loan debt. CCF staff worked with program participants to address defaulted student loans, pay down credit card debt, and increase credit scores. CCF also sets goals with 100 percent of participants and works with them to open bank accounts and develop spending and savings plans. By embedding financial development into their existing services, CCF is better able to provide their students with the tools they need to succeed and ensure the sustainability of financial development practices as a central part of CCF's service delivery model.

CCF's work with students also uncovered an important advocacy issue. For-profit colleges were using predatory practices to target individuals with records. Deterring these practices is now part of The Financial Clinic's policy agenda.

As we move into a more progressive bipartisan era of criminal justice policy, we must not relegate those who have been affected by criminal punishment to the economic margins. We must find ways to increase their chances of success by providing reintegration services that offer more than transitional housing, transitional employment, and stopgap medical services. We have the opportunity to embrace a public policy agenda that builds on the successes of programs like CCF.

The climate of public policy reform in the criminal justice sphere has taken on new energy in the past few years. An investment-oriented strategy would build postsecondary education and financial capability services into the design of reforms aimed at reducing incarceration and facilitating successful reintegration. Too often, reentry programs and policies aimed at providing a "second chance" have neglected education, particularly postsecondary education, as a core component of funding, program design, and accountability measures.

Building financial capability should also be a mainstay of criminal justice and educational initiatives. Promising policy directions include President Obama's announcement in July 2015 of an Experimental Sites Initiative, restoring Pell grants for groups of incarcerated students around the country. This initiative was spurred, in part, by the leadership of the Education from the Inside Out Coalition, a national nonpartisan group advocating for access to higher education inside prisons. This kind of investment enables the United States to reduce incarceration and equip individuals, families, and communities with the tool to rebuild their lives and realize their potential.

■ ■ ■

***VIVIAN D. NIXON** is a national criminal justice reform advocate and executive director of College and Community Fellowship, a New York City nonprofit dedicated to eliminating barriers to higher education for people involved with the criminal justice system. She has received multiple honors including the John Jay Medal for Justice, the Ascend Fellowship at the Aspen Institute, the Soros Justice Fellowship, the Petra Foundation Fellowship, the Hudson Link for Higher Education Brian Fischer Award, the Citizens Against Recidivism Mary McLeod Bethune Award, and the Correctional Association of New York Lifting As We Climb Award.*

■ ■ ■

***SUSAN STURM** is the George M. Jaffin Professor of Law and Social Responsibility and the founding director of the Center for Institutional and Social Change at Columbia Law School. Her work focuses on building "the architecture of full participation," making education central for communities affected by the justice system, institutional change, and transformative leadership. She collaborates with a wide variety of higher education and community-based organizations and networks, including the Aspen Ascend Network, Hostos Community College, JustLeadershipUSA, the New York Reentry Education Network, and College and Community Fellowship. She is the principal investigator on Ford Foundation and Aspen Ascend grants aimed at building multigenerational pathways to education for communities affected by incarceration.*

ENDING "WELFARE AS WE KNOW IT"

Redesigning Public Assistance through the Lens of Financial Health and Economic Mobility

Reggie Bicha and Keri Batchelder
Colorado Department of Human Services

In 1996, President Clinton declared the "end of welfare as we know it." The occasion was the signing of the Personal Responsibility and Work Opportunity Reconciliation Act (PRWORA), a response to the bipartisan call for welfare reform. This new law was intended to move people from "welfare to work" by restructuring federal public assistance and replacing the Aid to Families with Dependent Children (AFDC) program with the Temporary Assistance for Needy Families (TANF) program. Initiated in 1935 as part of the New Deal, Aid to Dependent Children (ADC, later changed to AFDC) provided welfare payments to needy children from poor families, but by the 1990s, it failed to provide adequate focus or supports to help people move into employment, and it handcuffed generations of families to poverty. In contrast, TANF imposed greater restrictions on the disbursement of federal assistance, including a new 60-month lifetime limit on TANF benefits and work participation requirements.

But did "ending welfare as we know it" adequately move America and its most vulnerable people forward? If the success of welfare reform is measured solely by the reduction in welfare caseloads, it was, unquestionably, a success (see Figure 1). Millions of Americans moved into the labor market, many for the first time. Childhood poverty rates initially declined. Yet, welfare reform also led to new problems and failed to resolve the economic mobility issues plaguing AFDC. America finds itself, nearly 20 years after welfare reform, with dramatically reduced welfare rolls and an

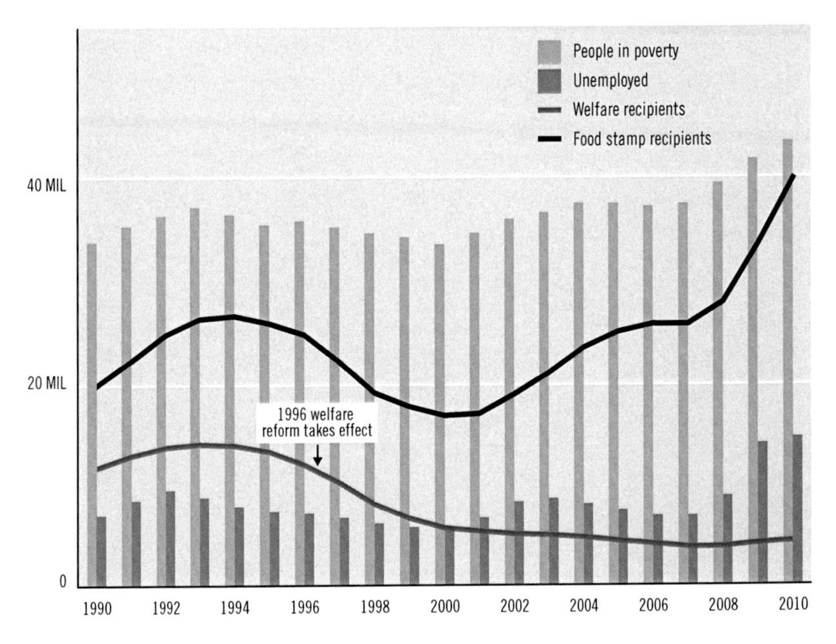

Source: US Dept of Health and Human Services, Dept of Agriculture, Census, Bureau of Labor Statistics

Figure 1: Poverty and welfare in the United States

increasing number of individuals in the workforce, yet significantly more children growing up in poor families.

David Stoesz, a professor of social policy, conveys the predicament. "Welfare reform that offers the welfare-poor an opportunity to become the working poor," he says, "is no real reform at all. The challenge that remains is to devise policies that will accelerate the upward mobility of welfare families so that they can partake in the American dream."[1] To do this, a new call to action is necessary, one that moves people *from welfare to prosperity through work* and asks the question, how must welfare policy be redesigned for the America of today?

REDESIGNING THE SYSTEM

A redesign of PRWORA and TANF requires a different emphasis, one that increases economic mobility and focuses on families' financial health.

1 H. J. Karger and D. Stoesz, *American Social Welfare Policy: A Pluralist Approach* (New York: Pearson Education, 2006).

In defining financial health, the Center for Financial Services Innovation suggests three core elements: day-to-day financial management; resilience to weather ups and downs; and long-term opportunity. These elements must compose the foundation of welfare redesign—a redesign that asks how is public assistance leveraged to build financial health, allowing people to move out of poverty and create opportunity for future generations?

What follows are policy solutions for retooling America's welfare program with a focus on economic mobility. These solutions allow the nation to learn from the experience of the past 20 years; yet, they reflect the reality of America's 21st century economy, the needs of employers, the needs of prospective employees, and the needs of children.

1. Focus on Employment, Earnings, and Retention

The current TANF system is based on an imperfect federal performance measure—the work participation rate—that measures how well states engage families receiving assistance in certain work activities. It does not demonstrate how many individuals receiving TANF become employed or whether they are doing the activities most likely to lead to employment. In fact, states can perform very well on the measure while doing a less than desirable job of getting individuals into the workforce. Federal requirements related to the work participation rate create a disincentive for states to serve "hard-to-employ" individuals who may have any number of barriers to employment, such as health problems, disabilities, criminal records, drug addiction, or limited education. Rather, these requirements encourage states to focus their services on job-ready individuals or individuals who might not need as much assistance.

Some argue that any change to the work participation requirement is a step back from a commitment to the value of work. This is not the case. Moving instead toward measures that hold states and participants accountable to employment goals provides a much stronger commitment to work. States, programs, and participants should be focused on achieving three goals: 1) getting participants a job; 2) ensuring that earnings are sufficient to help participants get ahead, through both wages and number of hours worked; and 3) preparing participants to sustain employment or advance to a better job.

In a redesigned system, employment would be the primary outcome of interest, as employment strongly influences the factors related to financial health, such as the ability to meet basic monthly expenses and the availability of emergency funds. A successful TANF program would engage local employers, fully understand their staffing needs, and help participants develop skills that are in greatest demand. In addition, a premium would be placed on the development of jobs through subsidized employment and career pathway programs. With subsidized employment, public funds are used to create or support temporary employment for an individual who would otherwise be unemployed. Employers are typically expected to attempt to retain the individual once the subsidy is no longer available. Subsidized employment programs have a dual effect on the economy by employing an individual with a meaningful wage and by assisting small and medium-sized businesses to grow. For example, employers who want to expand their workforce but need financial support to take on the risk of an additional expense or a new employee benefit from the employment subsidy. In the career pathways model, TANF participants receive a basic education while also learning the skills needed for a specific job or industry. In this way, the model engages community and technical colleges, training individuals for careers in such fields as health care, early childhood education, and manufacturing.

The late Senator Edward Kennedy asserted on multiple occasions that "if you work 40 hours a week, 52 weeks a year, in the richest nation in the world, you should not have to live in poverty." However, recent analyses demonstrate that wages, especially for low- and moderate-income workers, have stagnated nationally. In many states, a single-parent household with two children would be ineligible for assistance through TANF, even if they are only earning the federal minimum wage ($7.25/hour), working 40 hours a week, every week of the year. Such employed individuals may still need some form of public assistance, such as food assistance or the Earned Income Tax Credit (EITC), to make ends meet. Yet, even with these economic supports added to their earnings, such a family still cannot meet their basic monthly expenses.

What's more, getting a job, even a good paying job, is not enough to move out of poverty if it is temporary or if a worker is unable to succeed in it. Because the current work participation requirement counts activities that may or may not lead to sustained employment, it rewards short-term, unsustainable work for too many participants, such as temporary or seasonal jobs. A new focus on retention and advancement would create incentives for states to support families with services that smooth their transition to permanent employment, such as assistance with child care, transportation, health care, or stress management, all of which can affect a new employee's ability to keep a job. A system that supports participants for a reasonable period after hire could help stabilize an individual in a new job, benefitting both the employee and the employer. Such a focus on retention would reward states that help participants find permanent employment.

2. Expand Access to Job Training, Vocational, and Postsecondary Education

During the 1996 welfare reform debate, Senator Phil Gramm of Texas said the following about work and education:

Work does not mean sitting in a classroom. Work means work... Ask any of my brothers and sisters what 'work' meant on our family's dairy farm. It didn't mean sitting on a stool in the barn, reading a book about how to milk a cow. 'Work' meant milking cows.[2]

Yet it is a false distinction to say that work and education are mutually exclusive. There are many models that combine the concepts of work and education successfully. Cooperative education combines the two by delivering practical work experience with study. Community colleges, with their responsiveness and flexibility to local business, exemplify the idea that work and education are very closely linked.

Following the passage of PRWORA, there was a swift reduction in college enrollment among welfare participants. Nationally, there was an approximately 20 percent decrease in the college enrollment of all welfare recipients over the first two years of TANF.[3] This mass exodus from college jeopardized the ability of these individuals to climb out of poverty, especially in a twenty-first century economy. A 2010 study found that, nationally, fewer than 8 percent of "work-eligible" adult TANF participants were engaged in education or training activities. Although

---

2 *The Family Self-Sufficiency Act*, #473, 104th Congress *Congressional Record* (September 11, 1995).

3 National Urban League Institute for Opportunity & Equality, "Negative Effects of TANF on College Enrollment." Special Research Report (SRR-01-2002). (Washington, DC: June 2002).

these activities do increase the average earnings and overall incomes of families in the short-term, research has demonstrated that only former participants with at least a two-year postsecondary or vocational degree are likely to escape poverty by earnings alone. This research reveals a standard for education and training, attached to the goal of moving out of poverty, that is not supported by the TANF legislation itself.[4] In addition, a study of six states found that 87 percent of former welfare participants who graduated from two- or four-year colleges were still off welfare six years later.[5] Such research underscores the relationship between work and education and provides an illustration of what is possible when adopting a long-term lens focused on eliminating poverty.

The PRWORA sets forth 12 categories of work activities that can count toward the work participation rate, with the parameters for each activity defined by federal rule in the Deficit Reduction Act of 2005. Among these, nine are considered core activities that count toward any hours of participation, and include activities such as employment or on-the-job training. However, three non-core activities—job skills training directly related to employment, education directly related to employment, and satisfactory attendance at secondary school or in a course of study leading to a GED—only count if the individual also participates in core activities for at least 20 hours per week (30 hours for two-parent families).

In a redesigned system, more participants would be able to access education and training activities, along with sufficient time, that would allow them to gain the credentials and skills needed to obtain living wage jobs. Yet, education and training would not be an open-ended activity. Instead, the amount of time an individual spends in such an activity would allow participants to achieve proficiency in a skill, trade, or career that meets the needs of the local labor market and moves them out of poverty.

In Colorado, jobs that have high projected growth rates and openings, and typically offer a living wage, include health care, information technology, construction and extraction, and business and finance. The vast majority of these jobs expect some level of formalized postsecondary

---

4 Betty Reid Mandell, "The End of Welfare as We Knew It," *New Politics* (October 2011).

5 U.S. House of Representatives, Committee on Ways and Means, "Chairman McDermott Announces Hearing on the Role of Education and Training in the TANF Program." Press release, April 15, 2010.

training or education.[6] Nationally, by 2020, 65 percent of all jobs in the economy will require postsecondary education and training beyond high school.[7] It is clear that failing to prepare individuals to meet the needs of the local labor market, in a twenty-first century context, leaves the economy behind as well.

TANF programs would be required to work with postsecondary and vocational education systems to develop career pathways that meet the needs of employers. This necessitates a view of employers as essential to the work of helping vulnerable individuals gain stable, living-wage employment. Furthermore, nontraditional job training opportunities would be expanded and made available for welfare participants to enhance their ability to move into living wage jobs. In this way, the focus of the system moves from compliance and process to income and employment outcomes that truly lead to financial health and economic mobility.

3. Mitigate the Cliff Effect

Currently, working parents who experience wage growth may reach a "cliff," where if they surpass a certain income threshold they lose eligibility for other public assistance, such as child care subsidies, food assistance, health care coverage, and tax credits. The net effect of a 20-cent per hour raise (or $416 per year) can result in the loss of thousands of dollars in work supports. To avoid this cliff, many individuals decline wage increases, overtime, increased hours, or career advancements. The cliff effect has become TANF's new handcuff to poverty.

In this redesigned system, participants who become employed or earn increased wages would transition gradually from government work supports. A tiered benefit approach that allows individuals to improve their earnings and their careers while progressively moving off publicly funded benefits allows for greater economic mobility. The Affordable Care Act moves policy in this direction by providing health care subsidies for working people until they can earn a sufficient income to obtain health insurance without a government subsidy. Child care assistance,

---

6 Colorado State Legislature, "The Colorado Talent Pipeline Report" (January 2, 2015).

7 Anthony P. Carnevale, Nicole Smith, and Jeff Strohl, "Recovery: Job Growth and Education Requirements through 2020" (Washington, DC: Center on Education and the Workforce, Georgetown University, June 2013).

Supplemental Nutrition Assistance Program (SNAP), TANF, and other public benefits should follow a similar course.

4. Emphasize Money Management and Encourage the Accumulation of Wealth

For many people living in poverty, getting a job is the first time they have ever had a steady source of income. Many are not banked, or are underbanked, and have limited knowledge of investments, savings, or money management. In fact, the Office of Inspector General reports that one in four U.S. households lives at least partially outside the financial mainstream, and the average underserved household spends $2,412 each year on interest and fees for alternative financial services.[8] Yet, receiving temporary cash assistance, or getting a job, is not simply about having money; it also requires the ability to manage money. By focusing on financial capability as part of a redesigned system, people can gain confidence in their own ability to plan for their financial future and to weather the next crisis. This will serve as a long-lasting benefit to their health and well-being over time. The TANF system could also create incentives for people to take positive steps toward financial behavior change, such as opening an account and saving in a financial institution, checking a credit report, or establishing a monthly budget.

In this redesigned system, services that build financial capability would be provided alongside cash assistance. Participants would be strongly encouraged to form a relationship with a financial institution by opening a transaction account, receiving their cash assistance through direct deposit, and obtaining a savings account. An incentivized savings program could help people to establish initial savings for a rainy day fund. Credit-building products and counseling services could be integrated to help ensure that credit scores are not getting in the way of job placement, or that poor credit is not inhibiting people from financing a car they need to get to work. Financial coaches who work alongside the other supportive structures (such as job coaches that some agencies deploy; see Michael Rubinger's essay in this volume) help clients with setting and achieving financial goals, which will help to build confidence in changing financial habits over time.

---

8 Office of Inspector General, "Providing Non-Bank Financial Services for the Underserved." Report No. RARC-WP-14-007. (Washington, DC: U.S. Postal Services, January 27, 2014).

5. Remove Asset Limits at the Federal Level

Exaggerated rhetoric surrounding welfare abuses, such as the "welfare queen" accused of enjoying a lavish lifestyle or bank accounts full of cash while receiving public assistance, led politicians to establish and strengthen asset limits. To qualify for public assistance, including TANF cash assistance, individuals or families must have financial resources, or assets, below a set limit, which provides a disincentive to many of the activities suggested in the previous section. Many low-income families are forced to spend down their existing assets to meet these limits and qualify for needed assistance. Asset limits prevent welfare participants from building basic wealth—a dependable car, a home, or savings for a child's education. These are all necessary components for achieving economic independence and moving into the middle class. These very assets can lead the working poor to approach another cliff, similar to the income cliff, which serves as another handcuff to poverty. The current public assistance system forces families into an awful dilemma of choosing between saving money or staying on TANF for its much needed short-term support. While our public assistance system is meant to provide for families when they need it most, asset tests discourage saving and asset accumulation, the very actions that lead to financial health and well-being.

In this redesigned system, federal lawmakers would eliminate asset limits. At present, states can set their own asset limits. Many states, including Colorado, have already removed asset limits, providing a model for federal reform. Removing asset limits allows families to obtain the assistance they need, while helping them to save for the future. Overall, to truly lift families out of poverty and allow them to achieve greater economic mobility, national policy must not be punitive and it must focus on asset building as much as it focuses on income support.

6. Ensure Quality Child Care and Early Learning Opportunities for Working Participants

For parents to enter and stay in paid employment, child care is an essential work support. However, PRWORA eliminated the *guarantee* of child care for welfare participants trying to move into employment, leaving it to individual states to determine whether, and for how long, participants and former participants receive subsidized child care. Many of the jobs that parents obtain require a patchwork of care—part-time, before school, after school, evening, swing shift, and weekends. Parents blend formal care with family, neighbors, and sibling care—arrangements that frequently break down and can be unsafe for children.

Child care without quality is a missed opportunity. More than 50 years of research confirms that children from low-income families with high-quality child care do better on a range of socioeconomic and health outcomes in both childhood and adulthood compared with their counterparts who do not have the same experience. Investments in high-quality child care lead to some of the best returns on investment that exist in the public sector. There is also an opportunity to help children overcome the educational achievement gap that so routinely correlates with living in poverty.

In this redesigned system, working parents eligible for public assistance would have access to and incentives for selecting high-quality child care and early learning opportunities for their children. Colorado House Bill 14-1317, passed in 2014, modifies the state's subsidized child care program, the Colorado Child Care Assistance Program (CCCAP), and aims to provide affordable, high-quality child care for working participants. Colorado HB14-1317 was created with the belief that affordable child care is necessary to support working parents' efforts to find and keep good jobs, advance in their careers and education, and attain financial health and well-being. It further recognized that child care was as much about the child as it was about the working parent, creating statewide supports and incentives to parents and child care providers to expand high-quality access for low-income families. Provisions of the legislation include:

- Eligibility that includes job seekers and those enrolled in postsecondary education or workforce training so that child care concerns do not inhibit efforts to attain a better livelihood;
- An income eligibility structure that allows working families to afford child care despite minor increases in wages, thus lessening the cliff effect that deters families from earning a better wage;
- An allowance for child care beyond a parent's exact hours of work, which encourages consistent, regular care;

- A tiered reimbursement system for child care providers such that those who are rated more highly on the state's quality rating and improvement system receive a higher rate of reimbursement;
- A reduced co-pay for parents who choose a more highly rated child care provider on the state's quality improvement and rating system.

In less than one year, Colorado has increased the percentage of children in CCCAP who receive high-quality care by approximately 10 percent.

CONCLUSION

Welfare policy in the United States needed a change in the 1990s. AFDC, a well-intended policy of a foregone era, became a restraint to economic mobility and paths out of poverty. PRWORA and TANF set out to transform a system that was not working as intended. Although this landmark legislation and program were highly successful at moving Americans off welfare, it failed to create a new path to economic prosperity, especially for America's children. To build this new path to economic prosperity, honest debate and courage from political leaders is required. American families need a public assistance system whose safety net bridges the gap between getting back on one's feet and building the financial foundation necessary for economic security and mobility. We must challenge ourselves to develop a new approach for a new economy, focused on eliminating poverty instead of eliminating welfare enrollment.

At the PRWORA signing ceremony, President Bill Clinton also stated, "This is not the end of welfare reform, this is the beginning." We should continue to evolve our efforts in ways that build the economy, support new strategies related to financial health and well-being, and move Americans out of poverty. Such efforts will set a new direction for helping the poor to overcome poverty through meaningful work and economic mobility, achieving a future where all Americans have the greatest opportunity for life, liberty, and the pursuit of happiness.

■ ■ ■

REGGIE BICHA *was appointed by Gov. John Hickenlooper as executive director of the Colorado Department of Human Services in 2011. Bicha is a social worker, administrator, educator and national leader. He has extensive experience working on child welfare, education, employment, and health issues at the county, state, and national levels. Before moving to Colorado, Bicha served as the inaugural secretary of the Wisconsin Department of Children and Families. In 2012, Bicha was selected for the Ascend Fellowship and in January 2014, Bicha was recognized for his leadership and dedication with the Casey Family Programs "Excellence for Children Award." He and his wife, Becky, have three children and have served as foster parents.*

■ ■ ■

KERI BATCHELDER *is the Two Generation manager for the Colorado Department of Human Services. She has a master's of social work from Colorado State University and a Bachelor of Arts degree in psychology from the University of New Hampshire. Keri has worked in the field of social work for 15 years and has experience in numerous social work/human services disciplines, primarily those in the programmatic area of children, youth, and families. Prior to her current position, she served as the performance analyst for the Office of Community Access and Independence at the Colorado Department of Human Services and with Colorado State University as the assistant director of the Social Work Research Center.*

EDUCATION

PROMOTING FINANCIAL HEALTH THROUGH HIGHER EDUCATION

Sarah Bloom Raskin
U.S. Department of the Treasury

The financial health of every American household is crucial to achieving inclusive growth and prosperity in our country. Indeed, as the recovery from the financial crisis made clear, the American economy is only as resilient as the American households that are its bedrock. Financial health allows households to save, build wealth, and access credit, which not only means they can absorb unexpected fluctuations to their day-to-day incomes and spending needs, but also that they can meet longer-term goals such as buying a home or financing a secure retirement.

Higher education is integrally linked to financial health. As Martha Kanter and Regina Stanback Stroud point out in this volume, members of financially healthy families are better able to take advantage of educational opportunities, and completing an affordable and high-quality higher education program in turn advances the fundamentals of financial health. These higher education outcomes are thus crucial to our nation's growth and prosperity.

With so much at stake, it is not surprising that around kitchen tables everywhere, Americans are discussing a number of essential and complex questions about higher education: How much should taxpayers spend to support higher education? What factors should student borrowers consider when they take on college and graduate school debt? To what extent can tuition rates be lowered without compromising the ultimate value of higher education? This essay provides the context for these discussions.

The financial crisis depleted the assets of many households. From 2007 to 2010, median family wealth fell 38.8 percent as home prices plunged. According to the most recently available comprehensive data, median family wealth fell another 2 percent from 2010 to 2013.[1] Together with unemployment and underemployment, this loss of wealth destroyed many households' financial standing. Many saw their savings decimated, leaving them to start from scratch to rebuild their wealth.

As Ray Boshara establishes at the outset of this book, although the U.S. economy has made progress since the end of the financial crisis, many American households have yet to recover. Too many Americans continue to lack meaningful employment, and for many, wages are little changed. Indeed, Boshara shows that although average household incomes have reached pre-recession levels, the recovery from 2008 to 2012 was driven by the highest two income quintiles while the bottom three quintiles saw little or no income growth. Although the pickup in employment growth since 2013 has improved prospects for households in the lower and middle parts of the income distribution, real median earnings among full-time workers in the second quarter of 2015 were still only about where they were before the recession.

To what extent is higher education able to improve the financial standing of households in the lower and middle part of the income distribution? Research shows that an investment in high-quality, complete, and affordable higher education—that is, higher education that delivers access to meaningful employment and creates the conditions for long-term financial stability and well-being—can boost income and, in turn, be a significant asset-building tool for American households.

Over a lifetime, the average college graduate with a four-year degree in 2013 would earn nearly $275,000 more than someone with a high school diploma alone, after netting out the cost of college and foregone wages while in school.[2] College graduates also experience lower unemployment rates; in 2014, college graduates were approximately 40 percent less likely to be unemployed than individuals with only a high school diploma.[3]

---

1 Federal Reserve Board, "Changes in U.S. Family Finances from 2010 to 2013: Evidence from the Survey of Consumer Finances," (September 2014), p. 12; "Changes in U.S. Family Finances from 2004 to 2007: Evidence from the Survey of Consumer Finances," (February 2009), p. 1.

2 Jaison R. Abel and Richard Deitz, September 2, 2014, "The Value of a College Degree," *Liberty Street Economics*, Federal Reserve Bank of New York.

3 U.S. Bureau of Labor Statistics, *Employment Projections: Earnings and Unemployment Rates by Educational Attainment*, April 2015.

Not only is a high-quality education an important asset for individual households, it can be a collective national asset and a force for societal progress that warrants appropriate governmental investment and stewardship. An educated populace enhances civic engagement, creates less reliance on already strapped social safety net programs, and importantly, builds human capital that propels innovation and economic growth.

Yet significant work remains to enable Americans to prudently invest in their education as an essential financial asset. Like any asset-building investment, investing in a college degree carries risks. Specifically, because of the substantial variation in higher education experiences, in terms of tuition costs, fields studied, types of schools, and completion rates, and because of the particular features of our student loan financing system, in terms of accountability of schools, servicing practices, and dischargability rules in bankruptcy, outcomes vary widely. Students have to consider and understand all these variations and features if they are to make informed decisions about where to obtain post-secondary education and how to pay for it.

The cost of college has risen. Many states have reduced their financial support to colleges and universities at precisely the same time that many households have reduced means to pay for tuition. As a result, students have taken on more debt to finance education. As of 2013, approximately 70 percent of students graduating from public and private nonprofit colleges had student loan debt.[4] At the end of June 2015, the average federal debt per recipient was about $29,000.[5]

In addition, the growth in recent years of for-profit schools of varying quality has raised concerns. For-profit schools have different incentives from traditional nonprofit public and private colleges and universities. One result is that it is now even more difficult to make well-informed enrollment decisions, increasing the likelihood that students will take on significant debt to earn low-quality degrees in fields with limited earning potential. This challenge is exacerbated by the fact that many colleges and universities that benefit from enrolling students who finance their

4 Matthew Reed and Debbie Cochrane, "Student Debt and the Class of 2013" (Washington, DC and Oakland, CA: Institute for College Access and Success, November 2014).

5 Department of Education, Federal Student Aid Portfolio Summary, Fiscal Year 2007- 2015 Q3.

educations with federal and private loans are not held accountable for the outcomes of their students who have taken on debt.

As a result, in some cases individuals never see the financial benefits from higher education—and, in fact, some are worse off after they pay for a degree. Some students obtain degrees that do not improve their wages sufficiently to justify the costs. Others do not complete a degree. Some take on debt they cannot afford, and some default on their loans and, given the current rules of bankruptcy, live with the financial consequences for years and possibly forever.

Recognizing the risks students face—as well as the risks to our economy and society that can emerge if the nation is not adequately building our human capital—at the very least, we should provide better information and guidance to help Americans invest wisely in higher education. Structural reform is certainly necessary. But in the meantime, students should have a better understanding of the varied outcomes from different programs and schools, and how these outcomes influence the way they pay for their education. Is the student likely to graduate? Will a career-path job follow? Will that job support the tuition bill, especially tuition paid through loans? Does the education lead to opportunities to serve in positions, such as teaching in under-resourced communities, that have opportunities for debt forgiveness? These questions are especially pertinent for students from families and communities in which few, if any, members have attained post-secondary education.

Readers of this book can play an important role in helping Americans build greater wealth by promoting awareness of the subtle differences across varying forms of higher education, degrees, and institutions, and by protecting households from foreseeable investment risks. Readers can contribute to discussions regarding policy prescriptions for greater accountability by colleges and universities for the outcomes of their students. We need more discussions about the role of student loan servicers and about obstacles to achieving the fresh start through bankruptcy. In terms of structural reform, these discussions are needed now more than ever in support of a household asset that has the potential to enhance financial well-being for families and, by virtue of the strength of that financial well-being, our country's prosperity.

■ ■ ■

***SARAH BLOOM RASKIN** is Deputy Secretary of the U.S. Department of the Treasury. In addition to directing policies and implementation that sustain U.S. economic recovery and growth, Raskin has brought refreshed focus to the impact of student loan borrowing on our economy and students. Prior to her confirmation at Treasury, Raskin served as a Governor of the Federal Reserve Board. Prior to that, she served as the Commissioner of Financial Regulation for the State of Maryland. Raskin received her B.A. in economics from Amherst College and her J.D. from Harvard Law School.*

A LIFECYCLE APPROACH TO PUTTING HIGHER EDUCATION WITHIN REACH

Martha J. Kanter
New York University

I think by far the most important bill in our whole code is that for the diffusion of knowledge among the people. No other sure foundation can be devised for the preservation of freedom and happiness.

—Thomas Jefferson to George Wythe, 1786

A generation ago, the United States ranked first in the world in the percentage of adults who were college graduates. Our international competitiveness was unmatched, and our universities were the envy of the world. Today the United States is not even among the top 10 nations in terms of college graduates.[1] Our young adults perform at abysmally lower rates in literacy, numeracy, and problem solving than their peers in 21 other countries.[2] This dramatic decline in academic achievement has serious implications for all of us—for the individuals whose education attainment stalls out too early, for their families, and for the nation as a whole.

Georgetown University's Center on Education and the Workforce projects that by 2020, 65 percent of our nation's workforce will need an associate's, undergraduate, or advanced degree to meet the needs of the economy.[3] Yet even as postsecondary education becomes increasingly

1 In the most recent OECD rankings, the United States is #12 in the percentage of adults with undergraduate degrees aged 25–34. Organisation of Economic Cooperation and Development, *2013 Education at a Glance: Country Note* (2013).

2 Madeline Goodman, Anita Sands, and Richard Coley, "America's Skills Challenge: Millennials and the Future." (Princeton, NJ: ETS Center for Research on Human Capital and Education, 2015).

3 Anthony Carnevale, Andrew Hanson, and Artem Gulish, "Failure to Launch: Structural Shift and the New Lost Generation." (Washington, DC: Georgetown University Center on Education and the Workforce, September 2013).

essential for meaningful workforce participation, two powerful trends from the opposite direction are also intensifying: the growing cost of higher education and the growing economic inequality of our society.

Between 1984 and 2007, college tuition and fees increased by 439 percent, far outstripping the 106 percent increase in the general cost of living. By way of comparison, the cost of medical care, the sector showing the second largest increase, grew by "only" 251 percent during that period.[4] Meanwhile, the gap between rich and poor in the United States has also grown substantially during the past decade. The richest 1 percent of Americans received 65 percent of the nation's income growth from 2002 to 2007. Since 2009, that proportion increased to 95 percent, a period when wages have stagnated while stocks and corporate profits have soared.[5]

This general economic disparity is reflected in educational attainment. Approximately 80 percent of high school graduates from high-income families enroll in college, and more than one-half of them attain a college degree. By contrast, only 29 percent of students from low-income families matriculate, and fewer than one in ten go on to graduate.[6] The bottom line is that students from low-income families earn bachelor's degrees at one-eighth the rate—9 percent versus 75 percent—of their more advantaged counterparts by age 24.

All of these trends have been years in the making, but their convergence has serious implications for our country. An economically stable life requires a good job. Good jobs, in turn, increasingly will require postsecondary education—but at the same time, postsecondary education is becoming increasingly out of reach.

The United States was never intended to be a traditional class-bound society where people are born to a certain station in life and remain there all their days. Yet this may become our reality. Already, more than 40

4 National Center for Public Policy and Higher Education, "Measuring Up 2008: The National Report Card on Higher Education." (San Jose, CA: NCPPHE, 2008).

5 Thomas Piketty and Emmanuel Saez, "Top Incomes and the Great Recession: Recent Evolutions and Policy Implications." Paper presented at the 13th Jacques Polak Annual Research Conference, Washington, DC: International Monetary Fund, November 8–9, 2012.

6 Martha Bailey and Susan Dynarski, "Inequality in Postsecondary Attainment." In *Whither Opportunity: Rising Inequality, Schools, and Children's Life Chances*, edited by Greg Duncan and Richard Murnane (New York: Russell Sage Foundation, 2011).

percent of the poorest American children (those in the bottom quintile) remain there into adulthood, as does nearly the same percentage of the children born into the richest quintile.[7]

Other contributors to this volume have noted the ways that higher education both reflects and reinforces the status quo. Regina Stanback Stroud's essay places the role of poverty and its impact on school completion squarely at the center of this discussion. Dedrick Asante-Muhammad writes about this correlation's racial and class overtones—and its implications as the U.S. moves toward becoming a "majority minority" nation.

This vision of our Founding Fathers—of education as the bedrock for the freedom and happiness of the people—requires renewed commitment from every generation. Our urgent task now is to ensure that our nation's young adults, including and indeed especially those from less advantaged families, have the resources to pursue the education they will need to live the twenty-first century version of the "free and happy" life envisioned by our nation's founders 230 years ago.

What America's founders believed as a matter of principle has been amply borne out by scholarly research. Educated people are indeed significantly happier and healthier than uneducated people, and the higher the level of educational attainment, the more significant the differences.[8] Educated people form more stable families. This has been so for at least the past 70 years and, again, the higher the rate of educational attainment, the more significant the difference.[9] Better-educated people participate more fully in civil society and politics.[10] All of these outcomes contribute to the nation's social capital—a term the founders might not have used but that captures the humanizing and civilizing effects they so highly esteemed.

---

7 Pew Charitable Trusts, *Pursuing the American Dream: Economic Mobility Across Generations* (July 2012).

8 Michael Hout, "Social and Economic Returns to College Education in the United States," *Annual Review of Sociology*, 38 (2012): 394.

9 Claude S. Fischer and Michael Hout, *Century of Difference: How America Changed in the Last 100 Years* (New York: Russell Sage Foundation, 2006).

10 See, e.g., Robert Putnam, *Bowling Alone: The Collapse and Revival of American Community* (New York: Simon & Schuster, 2000); Sidney Verba, Kay Schlozman, and Henry Brady, *Voice and Equality: Civic Voluntarism in American Politics* (Cambridge, MA: Cambridge University Press, 1995).

GETTING TO THE STARTING LINE

A critical first step is to help America's families navigate the complex process of financing a college education. Along with the escalating costs of tuition, fees, and living expenses, college today is too often an exercise in confusion for families. Colleges advertise the sticker price for tuition that varies too often from year to year. But the majority of schools use institutional, state, or federal student aid to discount this price. When college costs are advertised, the published prices are often different from the net price after discounts are applied from institutional scholarships, endowments, state aid or federal aid. Families see the sticker price and many turn away thinking it is out of reach, not understanding that the real price may be lower. Furthermore, states can and do vary tuition rates and fees for the public community colleges and universities for which they are responsible. Families, especially those from lower-income, less financially sophisticated communities, become justifiably frustrated about even understanding the actual cost of college, much less figuring out how to pay for it.

The Federal Student Loan Program, intended as a powerful solution to the financial barriers to college, also remains intimidating despite the reforms introduced with the Free Application for Student Aid, a simplified federal loan and grant application form. Subsidized and unsubsidized Stafford loans, PLUS loans, and Perkins loans all have different eligibility conditions and terms, interest rates, and consequences for loan defaults or delinquency. Many students—again, especially those from lower-income families—have trouble decoding the distinctions and may end up burdened with excessive debt.

In addition, many students fail to take full advantage of the available higher education tax benefits including the American Opportunity Tax Credit, the Lifetime Learning Credit, Tuition Tax Deduction Credits, 529 Plans, loan forgiveness options, and interest deductions from student loans. About one in six Americans fails to apply for or use the tax benefits to which they are entitled,[11] leaving money on the table that potentially could make a significant difference in paying for college.

11 As pointed out in an August 2014 letter to U.S. Secretary of Education Arne Duncan from 12 U.S. senators urging the Obama administration to raise awareness about higher education tax credits.

Just raising awareness about tax credits, loan consolidation, and repayment options could ease the burden on overwhelmed families for whom all of these programs remain a mystery. But a broader strategy is required. American families need help navigating the technical aspects of financing a college education, to be sure. But even more, our nation's students, especially those from lower-income segments, need to see college as a realistic option—indeed, as an expectation for success in the twenty-first century.

A LIFECYCLE OF INTERVENTIONS

For more than a generation, numerous studies have documented the success of Children's Savings Accounts, or CSAs, in substantially increasing college enrollment and graduation rates for students from low-income families. While there are various instruments that allow people to save on a tax-advantaged basis for their children's (or other loved one's) higher education,[12] CSAs go one step further as universal (or near-universal) accounts seeded with an initial deposit, augmented by savings matches or other incentives, and used toward asset development after the age of 18, typically for postsecondary educational expenses.

Children with even a small amount of educational savings (e.g. less than $500) are 3 times more likely to enroll in college and 2.5 times more likely to graduate, than a child with no savings.[13] The working hypothesis is that the sheer existence of the CSA creates a college-bound mindset for both the child and his or her family, and that this psychologically powerful image shapes expectations and achievements in positive ways.

More recently, two additional promising new approaches for increasing college access, enrollment, and graduation rates have emerged. First, College Promise Programs (CPP) allow students to complete a certificate, an associate's degree, or the first two years or more of a bachelor's degree at no cost or significantly reduced cost. Early CPP experiences in Tennessee and Chicago inspired the Obama administration to propose a nationwide program to make two years of community college available

---

12 Two common forms of CSAs are Education Savings Accounts (also known as Coverdell accounts), which are limited to individuals whose adjusted gross income is less than $110,00 and state-sponsored 529 accounts (every state offers at least one 529 plan).

13 William Elliott, "Small-Dollar Children's Savings Accounts and Children's College Outcomes," *Children and Youth Services Review*, 35 (3) (2013): 572–585.

to all eligible students debt-free. A subsequent proposal from scholars at the Center for American Progress recommended extending the model to all two- and four-year institutions in willing states. Second, Performance-Based Funding (PBF) incentives are an alternative disbursement model for student aid. Under the traditional model, grants to low-income students are disbursed as lump sums at the beginning of the semester. Using a PBF incentive, student aid can be released in smaller but more frequent payments, like a paycheck designed to increase college retention and persistence rates. Another PBF incentive is bonus payments to students and institutions for achieving good grades and completing their programs of study.

All three of these approaches—CSA, CPP, and PBF models—are innovative yet entirely pragmatic policy efforts to raise the educational levels and outcomes for the nation's students. The challenge now is to put the pieces together—to integrate these policies into a unified whole and then to roll out that lifecycle approach on a large scale.

In the spring of 2012, the U.S. Department of Education announced a call for widespread, scalable CSAs accompanied by financial education strategies to encourage students and families to embrace college-going cultures leading to social, civic, and economic prosperity. This call was based on an understanding that without a comprehensive, holistic approach to building financial capability, families would see college as a pipe dream rather than a real opportunity for them or their children. The department emphasized that the federal government, the states, and other stakeholders could take bolder steps to strengthen college opportunity by consolidating the piecemeal efforts.

The good news is that some of that work to streamline programs is already underway. Scholars and local, state, and federal policymakers are proposing student aid redesign plans that could align existing resources (e.g., the federal Pell grant program, subsidized loans, and income-based repayment options) with the new and existing College Promise program incentives. Adding CSAs to this mix, especially if accompanied by intensive outreach efforts to educate families about their benefits, would increase families' and students' financial capability, set the expectation for college enrollment, and build a nest egg to defray education costs.

If well structured, combining the best-in-breed CSA models, College Promise models, and PBF strategies would provide low-income students the opportunity to afford and complete an undergraduate education while also making college more affordable for the middle class.

PUTTING THE PIECES TOGETHER: A CALL TO ACTION

The time is ripe for putting the pieces together—to convene the nation's most distinguished thought leaders and experts to build on the promising initiatives that are already underway all over the country. This effort would create a model that communities, states, and the federal government could adopt fully or in part to build financial capability and to increase college access, enrollment, and graduation rates. The model would integrate CSA, CPP, and PBF research, incentives, and practical applications into a coherent action plan with intended targets and outcomes.

If the integrated model works, the administrative cost savings could be significant. But more importantly, the "one stop shop" would provide families who currently must pursue multiple and often confusing channels with a single entry point instead. The proposed integrated model must emphasize "skin in the game" for all stakeholders in America's future, including families, education, business, government, philanthropy and nonprofits. And it must be fundamentally premised on practicality and effectiveness. For that reason, the research component is critical (as it is for any evidence-based initiative), particularly around PBF and the Promise programs.

The College Promise models underway are varied, and there has not yet been a meta-analysis that compares them based on student outcomes. PBF was first implemented in Ohio in the 1990s, but was later rescinded by the legislature before a meaningful body of research could be developed. Although, as noted, a solid body of research demonstrates the effect of educational savings on increasing college aspirations and enrollment, a rich avenue for future study will be the effect of CSAs on college performance or post-graduation outcomes, such as employment, life satisfaction, and civic engagement.

To build the evidence base that CSAs make a difference in encouraging a college-going culture, increasing college affordability, and enabling the larger goal of investing in education to produce a more educated society than in centuries past, several College Promise prototypes designed to increase the success of low-income students offer a path forward.

- Arizona Earn to Learn provides eligible students with financial education, one-on-one financial coaching, college readiness training, and ongoing financial literacy support. Students must also save $500 of their own money through an Individual Development Account, a commitment savings product proven to help low-income people build assets. When a student completes the program requirements, he or she receives an 8:1 match of $4,000 in scholarship money per academic year ($2,000 from the federal government's Assets for Independence program and $2,000 from one of the three Arizona state universities).

- City of Chicago Promise provides scholarships for tuition, fees, and books for all students who graduate from the Chicago public schools with at least a 3.0 grade point average and who place into college-level mathematics and English at the City Colleges of Chicago.

- Cuesta College, a community college in California, announced in 2014 that it would waive tuition and fees for the first year for all graduates of a local county high school district. This year, they added the open textbooks initiative to further limit college costs. The *Cuestonian* reported that students taking Professor Nielson's U.S. history class used a textbook from Openstax College, a nonprofit organization sponsored by Rice University dedicated to providing students with free, high-quality textbooks across the nation.

- Denver Scholarship Program offers need-based scholarships to qualified graduates of Denver public schools. The scholarships can be used at four-year colleges and universities, community colleges, or technical schools.

- Kalamazoo Promise pays up to 100 percent of college tuition at state colleges and universities for graduates of the city of Kalamazoo (Michigan) public high schools. Kalamazoo Promise recently announced a partnership with the Michigan Colleges Alliance, a consortium of 15 private liberal arts colleges, under which the members of the Alliance have agreed to absorb the difference in cost between their tuition and that of a public university for qualifying students.

- Tennessee Promise guarantees Tennessee high school graduates with two years at community college or a college of applied technology absolutely free of tuition or fees. After graduating from community college, if students choose to attend a four-year institution, the state's transfer pathways program makes it possible for them to start as a junior. By getting their first two years for free, the cost of a four-year degree is cut in half.
- West Virginia Promise provides eligible high school graduates with up to $4,750 for tuition at state public or private institutions.

To date, there are more than 50 CPPs across the nation. These models are ripe for replication and expansion to further the opportunity for every American to earn a college degree or certificate, ensuring that the nation will have a highly educated workforce and more prosperous communities in the years ahead.

WHAT'S AT STAKE

Our Founding Fathers valued education beyond its material benefits, understanding how indispensable it is for the nation to remain free and self-governing. But those material benefits are not trivial. The average college graduate pays almost twice as much in taxes each year as the average high school graduate, and the average holder of a professional degree pays almost twice as much as the college graduate.[14] College graduates also benefit their local economies. A percentage point increase in the supply of college graduates raises wages for high school graduates by 1.6 percent, and high school drop-outs see wage increases of 1.9 percent.[15] And of course, the benefit to the individuals themselves is dramatic. As Sarah Bloom Raskin points out in her contribution to this volume, one or two years of postsecondary education from a community college or training program can boost a person's lifetime earnings by more than $170,000 compared with a high school diploma alone, and a four-year degree pushes the spread to more than $500,000.[16]

---

14 Exact figures are: $7,100 for the high school graduate; $13,000 for the college graduate; and $25,600 for the professional. The College Board, *Education Pays* (2010).

15 Enrico Moretti, "Estimating the Social Return to Higher Education: Evidence from Longitudinal and Repeated Cross-Sectional Data," *Journal of Econometrics*, 121 (2004): 175–212.

16 Michael Greenstone and Adam Looney, "Where is the Best Place to Invest $102,000—in Stocks, Bonds, or a College Degree?" (Washington, DC: Brookings Institution, June 25, 2011).

The correlation between education and upward economic mobility has never been higher, and stakeholders across the spectrum recognize that reality. The Social Mobility Index (SMI), a joint venture between CollegeNet (a higher education technology company) and Payscale (a compensation data firm) was launched explicitly to rank schools according to how well they prepare disadvantaged students to start careers free of onerous debt. Membership in the Complete College America (CCA) Alliance of States has doubled during the past four years to include 33 states and the District of Columbia. CCA members commit to state- and campus-specific degree completion goals by 2020, with an emphasis on tracking low-income and minority students' progress.

All of these developments are vital because, for the first time in at least 50 years, a majority of public high school students now come from low-income families.[17] Unless we are prepared to write off 40 million children, or to leave their futures to chance, the debate can no longer be about whether to radically expand access to higher education. It can only be about how.

Critical momentum has already been gathering to experiment, find what works, and then build on it to make college a reality for the young people and adults who were left out of the college pipeline.[18] Putting the existing pieces together into a coherent whole is a logical next step to drive down costs, increase access, achieve higher graduation rates, and let us see, once the puzzle is put together, what more needs to be done.

But as with any meaningful change, it will ultimately come down to a question of will. The entire country—politicians, policymakers, experts, the business community, and ordinary taxpaying Americans—must decide whether to sustain higher education as a public good, vital to our economic and civic life at home and to our strength among the nations of the world.

---

17 Steve Suitts, Pamela Barba, and Katherine Dunn, "A New Majority: Low Income Students Now a Majority in the Nation's Public Schools." (Atlanta: Southern Education Foundation, January 2015).

18 The traditional profile of the college student—matriculating straight from high school at age 18 and graduating at age 22—is increasingly a thing of the past. The average age of a college student today is 26, and most are working part- or even full-time while taking classes. See Louis Soares, "Post-Traditional Learners and the Transformation of Postsecondary Education: A Manifesto for College Leaders." (Washington, DC: American Council on Education, 2013).

■ ■ ■

***MARTHA J. KANTER** is Distinguished Visiting Professor of Higher Education and Senior Fellow at New York University. She also directs the College Promise Campaign. She served as Under Secretary of Education from 2009 through 2013. Prior to that, she held numerous roles as an educator and leader, most recently as chancellor of the Foothill-De Anza Community College District, one of the largest community college districts in the nation. She received her undergraduate degree from Brandeis University, a master's from Harvard University, and a doctorate from the University of San Francisco.*

WHEN COLLEGES GET IT RIGHT, STUDENTS SUCCEED

Regina Stanback Stroud
Skyline College

Education is a critical way for people to change the conditions of their lives—and those of future generations. Now, more than ever, colleges should support students in increasing their financial well-being. Why? Because in the United States, one of the biggest factors hindering student success is poverty. Students' access to higher education, their ability to complete degrees and certificates, and for community college students, their likelihood of transferring to a baccalaureate-granting institution can often be predicted by socioeconomic status. The Pell Institute's recent report, "Indicators of Higher Education Equity in the United States," documents how family income has over the past 45 years increasingly been a predictor of bachelor's degree attainment. Yet most education reforms and interventions are designed to address student academic deficiencies, ignoring the major barrier to success that poverty presents.

An example of this mismatch falls close to home in my state, California. On the basis of recommendations from a system wide task force, California recently passed legislation to establish "Student Success and Support Programming" with the goal of improving student outcomes in the state's community colleges. The regulations tie college funding to the implementation of supports to help students commit to attending college full-time, develop student education plans, and provide placement testing early in students' educational careers. These well-intentioned reforms address some dimensions of student success, but they do not address the issue of poverty and its impact on student success, much less codify that acknowledgment in the state's recommendations, regulations, or funding incentives.

This is the kind of missed opportunity that I hope and believe other states and educational institutions will address in the years to come. As the president of Skyline College, a community college just south of San Francisco, I have launched a set of strategies to improve our students' financial well-being. Although San Mateo County is quite affluent, we serve pockets of poverty where some people work four minimum wage jobs to make ends meet. I am driven by the fact that more than 30 percent of the families in the greater Bay Area live below self-sustaining wages. This means more than 650,000 families do not make enough to make ends meet.[1] I am also driven by the fact that faculty members report instances of students coming to class hungry, without shelter, or drinking warm water so they could save their food for their children. I believe that our public institutions should be a vehicle for people to gain access to information that can increase their financial capability—and not one in which staff feel the need to purchase food for hungry students. This experience has persuaded me that strategies to address financial well-being are not just a nice idea; they are an essential component of helping students reach their academic goals.

Although colleges have not typically focused on strengthening the financial capability of their students, such strategies are consistent with the stated missions of many colleges, such as life transformation, upward mobility, preparation for full civic engagement, or participation in and contribution to society at large. It is certainly important to recognize that some financial capability services are not typically colleges' areas of expertise, but those challenges are surmountable if we bring the right partners to the table. At Skyline College, we have demonstrated that strategies that promote financial well-being can successfully be incorporated into the typical operations of an institution of higher education, and that doing so contributes to student success.

THE BUNDLED SERVICES APPROACH

There are many models for integrating financial capability services into diverse delivery channels. As outlined in Michael Rubinger's essay in this volume, one of the best-known is the Annie E. Casey Foundation's

1 United Way of the Bay Area, "Struggling to Make Ends Meet on Minimum Wage." Self-Sufficiency Brief, October 2014.

Center for Working Families (CWF) model. This model bundles three core services in a single, convenient location, including: 1) workforce and career services to promote stable employment and advancement opportunities; 2) income support services to help low-wage workers access public benefits such as the Earned Income Tax Credit; and 3) financial services, including financial coaching and education.

In the San Francisco region, the United Way of the Bay Area (UWBA) has built on the CWF model and opened a dozen one-stop "SparkPoint Centers" that provide core services similar to those in the CWF model. The services are enhanced by partnerships that connect participants to additional services, financial education, and asset-building tools. At Skyline College, we partnered with the UWBA to establish our own SparkPoint Center on campus for students and other members of the community.

MANY SERVICES = MANY PARTNERSHIPS

We quickly recognized that we could not do it all ourselves and expanded partnerships with other organizations that specialize in areas where we needed more expertise. Today, thanks to these collaborations, Skyline College's SparkPoint Center provides a wide range of services, such as:

- Financial coaching: Although any student who receives financial aid must complete financial literacy training, this is usually accomplished by clicking through a presentation on the federal government's student aid website—not what we consider a robust, in-depth financial education opportunity. By comparison, typical SparkPoint Center clients receive individualized financial coaching, financial education, debt reduction assistance and credit repair. The SparkPoint Center collaborated across the college to provide training in financial coaching for financial aid staff and other faculty and staff throughout the college (for more on financial coaching, see Michael Collins' essay in this book). We also hired a counselor to lead the financial coaching component of the SparkPoint Center services.

- Access to affordable financial services: In addition, Skyline College partnered with financial education providers, banks, and credit unions to offer participants broader access to financial information and services, including an opportunity to open bank accounts such as a "new start" account for those who have experienced banking difficulties in the past. Participants can also sign up for a free, prepaid debit card with direct deposit; they can link the card to a high-yield savings account, transfer money between accounts without charge, share money with family or friends, pay bills online, get cash without ATM charges, keep track of their balances, and review transactions.

- Tax preparation: Free tax preparation assistance is available to students through the Volunteer Income Tax Assistance site hosted by the SparkPoint Center and faculty and students of the college's accounting program. In 2014 alone, our SparkPoint Center generated tax returns totaling $357,911 for our students and other community members.
- Employment assistance: Our on-campus career and employment services are enhanced through our partnership with the California Employment Development Department (EDD). We co-located an EDD office at our campus Career Services so community members and students could easily access unemployment benefits and employment services, including resume-writing assistance, job search workshops, interview training, and other supports.

DON'T LEAVE MONEY ON THE TABLE

Colleges can also support students in achieving their educational goals by connecting them to public benefits. In many cases, benefits that would make a difference in low-income students' lives and in their ability to pursue their education go unclaimed. Juggling multiple demands, students often fail to connect with the proper agencies or navigate bureaucratic processes to acquire the benefits to which they are entitled. Many colleges are in a position to facilitate these much-needed connections and are beginning to do so.

Skyline College was one of six community colleges across the United States that participated in the Benefits Access for College Completion (BACC) project, a three-year initiative that investigated innovative ways to connect low-income students to public benefits. Skyline College collaborated with the San Francisco and San Mateo County Human Services Agencies to train Skyline College Sparkpoint Center staff to work with participants navigating the Supplemental Nutrition Assistance

Program (SNAP). The initiative also helped students connect to cash and health insurance benefits through MyBenefitsCalWin.org—a user-friendly portal to the online application for cash assistance (CalWORKs), food assistance (CalFresh), and health insurance (Medi-Cal). Although the BACC project ended in 2014, we have now institutionalized the initiative and continue helping students make these connections to the public benefits they should receive.

IT WORKS

As a shepherd of this strategy, I was confronted with the question of mission creep. Some asked if we were an education institution or a social services agency. It clearly was not enough to articulate the connection between poverty and student success. To continue this initiative beyond a pilot phase, it was important to know that the data substantiated that the approach worked.

One measure of student progress toward earning credentials is persistence, that is, whether a student remains actively enrolled during the academic year. In 2013–14, the college-wide rate for fall-to-spring persistence was just under 55 percent, while 87 percent of SparkPoint participants who used one financial capability service persisted, 90 percent who used two services persisted, and 93 percent of those who used three services remained actively enrolled (Figure 1). Chad Thompson, Skyline College's director of SparkPoint, notes that although we cannot substantiate a causal relationship, "these preliminary data are so promising that we will continue to gather data to better explain the outstanding results we have begun to see among the students we serve."

LEADERSHIP MATTERS

To support the financial well-being of students is to support overall student retention and success. At Skyline College, we believe that the SparkPoint Center is both a physical location and a retention strategy. Any door that a student or community member walks through at Skyline College is likely to lead them to the SparkPoint Center if they can benefit from the services.

And yet it is not simple work to reconceptualize traditional student services, redefine the mission, and change the culture of an institution.

It means disrupting the status quo. It simultaneously takes courage and humility. College leaders are in positions of influence and consequence. We have the opportunity to call on our relationships and credibility with the faculty, staff, community, policymakers, and governing boards to bring the full resources of the college to bear on supporting student success. That means including the issue of poverty as an important barrier to student success. It means including financial well-being strategies in all aspects of the institution, including the planning and budgeting processes, grant writing strategies, educational and facilities master planning, curriculum processes, faculty and staff development, strategic priorities, institutional goal-setting, and accountability systems.

I am proud to have begun this journey at Skyline College and am eager to see my colleagues at other institutions of learning do the same. Together, we can help our students achieve success in college and beyond.

■ ■ ■

REGINA STANBACK STROUD *is the president of Skyline College of the San Mateo County Community College District. She has previously served as a vice president of instruction and a dean of workforce and economic development and is highly regarded for her perspective on student equity and diversity, education/industry collaboratives, community workforce and economic development, and regional and state system policy implications. She holds a doctorate of education in educational leadership from Mills College. She holds a master's degree in human relations from Golden Gate University, a master's degree in educational leadership from Mills College and bachelor's degree in nursing sciences from Howard University.*

WHO IS BEING AFFECTED?

Demographics and Financial Health

WEALTH AND GENERATIONS

Phillip Longman
New America

Writing in 1965, Social Security Commissioner Robert Ball announced that the American economy was on its way to becoming so productive that there was no reason why government could not eliminate all want among the citizenry. "Poverty in the past has been basically the result of the fact that there was not enough to go around," wrote Ball. "By contrast, today it can be taken as a fact that the abolition of want in the United States is no longer a problem of economic capacity."

The next generation was bound to become rich beyond imagination, Bell explained, and so could well afford to pick up the cost of making programs such as Social Security far more generous. "Extremely conservative projections of what has been happening in industry lead to almost unbelievable conclusions," wrote Ball. "If we take not the rate of productivity increases that seems likely to result from the new [automated] approach to problems of production but instead merely the average rate over the past 100 years, our grandchildren will be able to produce in 1 day as much as we do in a 40-hour week."[1]

The American Dream may be a cliché, but faith in its promise has long defined our social contract and ideologies across the political spectrum. During many eras of U.S. history, liberals and progressives like Ball have used the assumed upward mobility of future generations to bolster and legitimize their agendas, arguing in the 1960s, for example, that the cost of the War on Poverty and of new or expanded entitlement programs, such as Medicare, Medicaid, and Social Security, could easily be borne by future taxpayers who would inevitably be many times richer.

The same assumption has been perhaps even more critical to the appeal of conservative ideas throughout American history. In explaining why

1 Robert M. Ball, "Is Poverty Necessary?" *Social Security Bulletin* (August 1965), p. 18.

socialism, communism, and other forms of class-based politics barely got a toehold in the United States, historians typically point to the broad faith most Americans have in their own and their children's ability to rise up the economic ladder. Broad upward mobility across generations diminished the importance of inherited wealth, strengthened faith in the fairness of markets, and, as Richard Nixon proclaimed in his famous "kitchen debate" with Nikita Khrushchev at the height of the Cold War, made it at least superficially plausible to argue that America was a "classless society."

Yet with the benefit of hindsight, we can now see that this underlying premise of the American creed has gradually been turned on its head. Until roughly the 1970s, inequality between generations was large and increasing, but for the happy reason that most members of each new generation far surpassed their parents' material standard of living. Today, inequality between generations is increasing for the opposite reason. Most workers are indeed many times more productive than their counterparts in the past, yet by most measures, they are falling farther and farther behind their parents' generation in economic well-being.

The implications run deep. For younger Americans, the new normal of stagnant or falling living standards compared to the prior generation requires new life strategies, including much shrewder and more deliberative plans for building human capital and lifetime net wealth. At the same time, we need public policies that do not simply assume that each new generation will be richer than the last, but that give individuals and families the specific tools they need to pursue opportunity and upward mobility in the 21st century.

DOWNWARD MOBILITY TAKES HOLD

Defining and measuring the "standard of living" enjoyed by different generations is not straightforward. Among the complicating factors are changes in family structure, the role of women, and the ethnic and racial profile of the population. Other considerations include the true measure of inflation, the amount of financial and unemployment risk borne by individuals in different eras, and changes in educational attainment. Although no single metric is perfect, in combination they tell a dramatic and, by and large, depressing story.

The most straightforward "apples-to-apples" comparison is between the amount of income the typical (median) male with a specific level of education makes today compared with what his counterpart in the previous generation made. According to work done by economists Michael Greenstone of the University of Chicago and Adam Looney of the Brookings Institution, the steepest downward mobility has been among male high school dropouts, who in 2009 earned 66 percent less (adjusted for inflation) than their counterparts did in 1969[2], due to a combination of falling real wages and declining labor force participation rates. The slide for men with only a high school degree, who constitute the majority of men, was a staggering 47 percent. College-educated men did better, but only by falling not as far. For prime-aged male college graduates, real earnings in 2009 were 12 percent below those enjoyed by their counterparts 40 years before. Even among college graduates who worked full-time, real earnings were 2 percent below that of their counterparts in 1969.

These trends were well in place before the coming of the Great Recession. According to work by Jeff Madrick and Nikolaos Papanikolaou, between 1969 and 2005, real earnings for full-time male workers, age 25–34, with only a high school degree, declined from $34,681 to $30,000 (in 2005 dollars).[3] Meanwhile, full-time college-educated male workers of the same age eked out hardly any gains compared with their counterparts in the previous generation, as real wage and salary income for this group increased at an annual growth rate of just 0.1 percent between 1969 and 2005.

A similar comparison between today's working women and their counterparts a generation ago reveals an only slightly less dramatic story. For example, among full-time working women, age 30–45, who lack a high school degree, real wages were 12 percent lower in 2013 than they were for their counterparts in 1990. For the typical woman in this age group who has a high school degree but never graduated from college, wage and salary increases have been hardly measurable from one generation

2 Michael Greenstone and Adam Looney, "Trends: Men in Trouble," *Milken Institute Review* (Third Quarter, 2011): 8–16.

3 Jeff Madrick and Nikolaos Papanikolaou, "The Stagnation of Male Wages," *Policy Note* (New York: Schwarz Center for Economic Policy Analysis, The New School, May 2008), p. 3, Tables 1.1, 1.2.

to the next, rising by just 3 percent between 1990 and 2013. Only college-educated women who worked full-time saw any substantial gains over their counterparts of 1990. This was mostly because of increasing numbers of women moving into managerial jobs rather than to any general increases in wages for the same work.[4]

These trends for men and women converge in the statistics on family income, which especially for the young, had been falling consistently year after year even before the coming of the Great Recession. The median income among families headed by someone under 35 was just $35,500 in 2013. Adjusted for changes in the Consumer Price Index, that is nearly 20 percent below what young families earned in 2001.[5]

LIFETIME INCOME GAINS PEAK EARLIER AND CONTRACT

Another measure to consider is the ever earlier age at which workers' earnings peak. In nearly all previous eras, workers normally saw their income rise in their 20s, 30s, 40s and 50s as they gained education and experience and as wage rates in general grew. Although their earnings might be interrupted by illness or temporary unemployment, most workers generally earned more each successive year until they retired, typically in their 60s. This pattern still held until 2000, after which Americans started seeing their earnings peak and then decline at younger and younger ages even as the standard retirement age went up.

The tipping point came with those born between 1946 and 1950. The median household income of these early-wave Baby Boomers rose steadily during their early working years. Adding to these gains in household income was a sharp increase in the number of working women, as the "two paycheck" family gradually became the middle-class norm. Yet despite this additional income from women, median earnings for these households started declining when their prime wage earners were still in their early 50s—a time of life when members of previous generations were still typically seeing gains in real income from year to year. For these

4 Melissa S. Kearney, Brad Hershbein, and Elisa Jácome, "Profiles of Change: Employment, Earnings, and Occupations from 1990–2013." (Washington, DC: The Hamilton Project, Brookings Institution, April 20, 2015), Figure 1.

5 Federal Reserve Board, "2013 Survey of Consumer Finances." (Washington, DC: Board of Governors of the Federal Reserve System, 2014), Table 1 89-98 01-13.

early Baby Boomers, median houshold income peaked in 2000 at $78,458 at age 50–54 and fell each year thereafter, reaching an inflation-adjusted $50,834 in 2013.[6]

This pattern has grown progressively worse since then. For example, those born between 1953 and 1957 saw their median household income peak at $77,543 in 2002 when they were ages 45–49. For them, household income subsequently fell by 0.5 percent annually during the so-called economic recovery years of 2002 to 2007 and then declined much more during and after the Great Rececssion, falling to $60,100 by 2013. Financially speaking, 50 turned out to be the new 65 for these cohorts, even as they were expected to live longer.[7] And the situation only got worse with younger generations. For example, among persons born between 1962 and 1966, median household income peaked in 2007, when they were still between the ages 41 and 45, and has not yet recovered.

Among today's newest workers, most have already missed out on the rapid increase in earnings that members of previous generations typically enjoyed in their 20s and 30s. This early-career earnings deficit has left them with fewer dollars to save while young, putting them even farther behind their parents in building long-term assets, such as adequate savings for retirement.

MIDDLE-CLASS CHILDREN WHO GROW UP TO BE POOR

Contributing to this downward mobility trend are Americans who were raised in middle-class homes but who have fallen down the economic ladder as adults. According to a study by the Pew Charitable Trusts of children born in the late 1970s, one-third of those raised in middle-class families —defined as families between the 30th and 70th percentiles of the income distribution—have fallen out of the middle class in adulthood. This phenomenon is particularly pronounced among members of minority groups. Among African Americans who were raised in middle-class

6 Robert J. Shapiro, "Income Growth and Decline under Recent U.S. Presidents and the New Challenge to Restore Broad Economic Prosperity," (Washington, DC: Center for Effective Public Management, Brookings Institution, 2015), Table 1.

7 Ibid. See also Table 2.

families, for example, 37 percent were no longer middle class at middle age. For whites, 25 percent were now in the bottom tiers.[8]

How do these rates compare with the number of Americans who move up the income ladder? Recent research by Raj Chetty and others shows that during the last two generations, fewer than one in ten children born to parents in the bottom one-fifth of the income distribution managed to rise to the top one-fifth as adults.[9] This ratio has not changed appreciably since the 1970s. Yet overall income inequality has increased substantially since then, causing the rungs of the income ladder to become farther apart. This in turn makes the consequences of failing to rise up the ladder, or falling down it, harder to bare.

FAMILY BALANCE SHEETS DETERIORATE

Income alone does not define a standard of living. Getting ahead in life also requires accumulating assets such as home equity and savings that exceed one's debts and other liabilities. Without at least some net wealth, it is impossible to finance a first home, pay for a child's college education, enjoy financial security in old age, or leave behind an inheritance.

Until the present era, despite vast disparities and inequalities across different racial, ethnic, and other demographic groups, most American families enjoyed a rising net worth, both within and across generations. Today's older Americans still exemplify this pattern. Americans who were 74 years or older in 2010 had an average net worth that was 149 percent higher than that enjoyed by Americans who were the same age in 1983 (after adjusting for inflation).[10] This pattern has since disappeared, however. The precise tipping point came among people born in 1952. They would become perhaps the first generation in American history to have less real net worth on the threshold of retirement than people born ten years earlier had at the same age. From there, the real net worth of subsequent birth cohorts has generally been stagnant or has declined

8 Gregory Acs, "Downward Mobility from the Middle Class: Waking Up from the American Dream." (Washington, DC: Pew Charitable Trusts, Economic Mobility Project, September 2011), Figure 6, p. 14.

9 Raj Chetty et al., "Is the United States Still a Land of Opportunity? Recent Trends in Intergenerational Mobility." Working paper 19844. (Cambridge, MA: National Bureau of Economic Research, January 2014).

10 C. Eugene Steuerle et al., "Lost Generations? Wealth Building among Young Americans." (Washington, DC: Urban Institute, March 2013), Figure 3.

compared to the lifecycle experience of Americans roughly 10 to 20 years older.[11] For example, after adjusting for inflation, the median net worth of families headed by a person 35–40 years old was 30 percent less in 2010 than it was for their counterparts in 1983.[12]

RETIREMENT LOOMS

Because of the vast upward mobility of the Americans born before the 1950s, and the downward mobility of Americans born later, the economic security of the next generation of elders will, on current course, be much less than that of today's retirees—and their children are even less likely to be able to make up any shortfall. One study by the Pew Charitable Trusts found that the typical retiree couple born between 1936 and 1945 had enough net wealth to replace 100 percent of their pre-retirement income when combined with annuitized assets, such as private pensions and Social Security. In contrast, a typical Gen-X couple (born between 1966 and 1975) is on course to see their income decline by half in retirement.[13]

To make matters worse, this 50 percent decline assumes that both members of such a couple are able to continue working until the previously normal retirement age, which may well not happen. Labor force participation rates for men younger than 65 have been declining sharply, owing to corporate downsizing, low wages, obsolete job skills, rising rates of chronic illness such as diabetes, long-term unemployment, and other factors.[14] Since the 1960s, the share of prime-age men no longer in the workforce has rougly tripled.[15] Taken together, these trends paint a picture of steady declining mobility and shorter and less secure attachment to the workforce for men.

---

11 Ibid.

12 Survey of Consumer Finances 2012, cited by Neil Howe, "Are you Born to be Better Off Than Your Parents?" Forbes.com (July 16, 2014), Figure 4.

13 The Pew Charitable Trusts, "Retirement Security Across Generations: Are Americans Prepared for Their Golden Years?" (Washington, DC: Pew, May 2013), Figure 11.

14 The share of men of prime working age—those 25 to 54 years old—who are in the workforce declined by 5.2 percent between 1992 and 2012. Bureau of Labor Statistics, "Labor Force Projections to 2022: The Labor Force Participation Rate Continues To Fall," *Monthly Labor Review (December 2013),* table: "Civilian Labor Force Participation Rate by Age, Sex, Race, and Ethnicity."

15 Binyamin Appelbaum, "The Vanishing Male Worker: How America Fell Behind," *New York Times*, December 11, 2014.

Adding to the difficulties facing the future elderly is the disappearance of windfall Social Security benefits. In the late 1970s, Social Security paid out benefits to retirees that exceeded the value of their contributions by between $250,000 and $300,000 in today's money.[16] Subsequent birth cohorts have paid a far higher share of their income into the system, but under current law, most members are promised back little more in benefits than they paid in taxes. Social Security payroll taxes remained below 2.5 percent through the 1950s and below 4 percent until the end of the 1960s. But workers born in the 1990s have paid 6.2 percent of their income into the system throughout most of their working lives, and really double that, since most economists agree that the employer contribution in payroll taxes is ultimately born by employees.[17]

Having effectively paid about one out of eight dollars they earned into Social Security, the ability of Americans born during and since the 1960s to save for their own retirement has been correspondingly reduced, even as the Social Security system's rate of return has become progressively less for each new generation. The same diminishing rate of return is found in many private pension plans as well, even as pension coverage itself has also fallen precipitously among today's young and middle-aged workers.

THE MOUNTING COST OF LIVING

The declining cost and increasing quality of digital technologies, as manifested by smart phones and their apps, gives many of today's Americans access to goods and services that were beyond the reach of even the richest people a generation ago. Yet the cost of the goods and services Americans most need to help themselves and their children rise up the economic ladder has grown much faster than family income or general inflation. This is another large factor behind the stark increase in wealth inequality among the generations.

One major example is the inflation in higher education costs. During the last generation, graduating from college has become a near prerequisite to obtaining middle-class status or avoiding losing it. Yet even as paying for higher education became, for that reason, harder for families and

---

16 Sylvester J. Schieber, *The Predictable Surprise* (New York: Oxford University Press, 2012).

17 Social Security Administration, *Social Security & Medicare Tax Rates.*

individuals to avoid, the cost of attending a public or private college escalated 40 percentage points more than the Consumer Price Index between 2005 and 2015.[18]

Compounding the burden, the share of the higher education sector's revenue paid by families and students rose from one-third in 1980 to one-half in 2012, reflecting not just rising tuition, but a sharp decline in needs-based financial aid during the last generation.[19] Closing the gap has been a mountain of debt on household balance sheets. The share of young adults with student loans rose from 26 percent in 2001 to 40 percent in 2013.[20] Total student debt now surpases $1.1 trillion, and sadly, much of this debt is held by people who never finished college, and who have often been victimized by predatory lending practices. Among seniors graduating in 2013, the average borrower owed $28,400 in student loans.[21]

Meanwhile, the dramatic rise of health care costs relative to family incomes has been, and will be, particularly burdensome on younger generations. As recently as the 1960s, health care costs were an incidental expense of most young American families. In 1964, health care spending was just $197 per person per year. This low cost meant that with a mere 78 hours of labor (or by the end of the second work week in January, for those working full-time), the average nonsupervisory worker earned enough to cover the per capita cost of health care, including that of all children and retirees.

By contrast, in 2012, such a worker had to put in 452 hours to cover the average per capita burden of medical expenses, which by then had risen to more than $8,915. Put another way, by 2012, it was nearly March before the typical American working a 40-hour week earned enough to pay the

---

18 Bureau of Labor Statistics data, cited by Annie Lowrey, "Changed Life of the Poor: Better Off, but Far Behind," *New York Times*, April 30, 2014.

19 The Pell Institute and PennAHEAD, "Indicators of Higher Education Equity in the United States, 45 Year Trend Report," (Washington, DC: Pell Institute, 2015), p. 28.

20 Lisa Dettling and Joanne Hsu, "The State of Young Adult's Balance Sheets: Evidence from the Survey of Consumer Finances," (St. Louis, MO: Federal Reserve Bank of St. Louis, May 2014), p. 13.

21 Student Debt and the Class of 2013, Project on Student Debt, November 2014.

health-care sector's growing claim.[22] The total annual cost of health care for a typical family of four—even one covered by a typical employer-sponsored plan—reached $23,215 in 2014, or roughly the equivalent cost of buying a brand new Honda Accord LX every year.[23] The growing burden of health care costs is a major reason why employers are so reluctant to hire and wages remain stagnant.

Although some of the increase in health care costs reflects genuine advances in medicine, most simply reflects rising prices for existing medical services combined with an increasing volume of redundant tests, unnecessary surgeries, and other forms of over-treatment that do not improve health.[24] Peer countries achieve better population health and life expectancy while expending as little as half as much per person on health care services. As such, most of the increasing cost of health care does not reflect improvement to the average Amerian's standard of living.

PREDATORY LENDING AND THE HOUSING BUST

Another factor behind the downward mobility of Americans is the growth of payday loans, subprime mortgage lending, and other wealth destroying consumer finance products. Americans who came of age before the 1970s were largely protected from predatory lending by usury laws, which capped fees and interest costs on loans. But starting in the 1980s, these consumer finance protections largely disappeared. At the same time, financial engineering, including securitization, led to the growth of financial institutions with business models that allowed them to prosper—at least in the short term—by lending money to people who could not afford to repay.

These trends, combined with generally lagging or falling individual and household incomes and rapidly expanding access to credit, often on predatory terms, led to an explosion of borrowing. When this was

22 For health care expenditures, see Centers for Medicare and Medicaid Services, "National Health Expenditures; Aggregate and per Capita Amounts, Annual Percent Change and Percent Distribution, by Type of Expenditure: Selected Calendar Years 1960–2012" (Washington, DC: CMMS, n.d.), Table 1. For hourly earnings, see Bureau of Labor Statistics Employment, "Hours and Earnings from the Current Employment Statistics Survey" (national) (Washington, DC: BLS, 2015).

23 Christopher Girod et al., "2014 Milliman Medical Index" (Seattle: Milliman, Inc., May 2014).

24 See, for example, Atul Gawande, "Overkill", *The New Yorker*, May 11, 2015. Shannon Brownlee, *Overtreated: Why Too Much Medicine is Making Us Sicker and Poorer*, (New York, Bloomsbury, 2010).

followed in turn by a collapse in home prices, the result was devastion to the balance sheets of most Americans under age 50. By 2010, the average family aged 25–49 had a net worth that was 32 percent below that of their counterparts in 1989.[25]

This sequence of events particularly damaged members of Generation X, many of whom took out mortgages on predatory terms at or near the top of the housing bubble. Largely as a result, from 2007 to 2010, Gen-Xers as a whole lost nearly half (45 percent) of their wealth, or an average of about $33,000 subtracted from already low levels. Many were pushed into negative net worth, as their houses became worth less than their mortgage. By contrast, those born during the Great Depression era (between 1926 and 1935) experienced zero loss of net wealth as a group during the Great Recession (2007–2010).[26]

DECLINING ASSETS AND THE SHARING ECONOMY

Most Millennials, whose oldest members are still in their mid-thirties, were too young to be in the market for real estate during the housing bubble and therefore did not directly experience the evaporation of real estate wealth caused by the Great Recession. While they may have dodged that bullet, however, the longer-term trend of declining asset ownership among today's younger Americans has potentially very negative implications for their future net wealth. The rate of homeownership among households headed by a person under age 35 has fallen from 43 percent in 2005 to 35 percent in 2014. To be sure, not every Millennial wants or needs to own a house. But homownership has been the major means by which most ordinary Americans in previous generations built their net wealth and financed their retirements. Moreover, home prices have been recovering since the bottom of the Great Recession, and in many places have escalated sharply. Thus, the continuing decline in the homeownership rate among young households has probably reduced what Millennials' aggregate net wealth would have otherwise been.[27] And if the

25 Lori A. Trawinski, "Assets and Debt across Generations: The Middle Class Balance Sheet 1989–2010." (Washington, DC: AARP Public Policy Institute, January 2013), Table 4.

26 The Pew Charitable Trusts, "Retirement Security across Generations." (Washington, DC: Pew, 2013), Table 1.

27 Current Population Survey/Housing Vacancy Survey, Series H-111, U.S. Census Bureau, Homeownership Rates by Age of Householder: 1994 to Present, Table 19.

typical Millennnial winds up a renter for much, if not all, of his or her life, this will certainly require that the generation acquire some other major means for building assets over a lifetime.

A sharp decline in stock ownership among young adults does not bode well for that possibility. In 2001, 48 percent of persons aged 18 to 31 owned stock; by 2013, this share had dropped to 37 percent.[28] This long-term decline in stock ownership among the young occurred in a period in which stocks, despite volatility, appreciated in value by several-fold. Younger cohorts of Americans are also increasingly less likely to own businesses. On a per capita basis, the rate of new business formation declined by 50 percent between 1977 and 2009, a trend that leaves more businesses failing each year than are started.[29] As Federal Reserve Chair Janet Yellen has pointed out, the declining share of Americans who are business owners diminishes what historically has been "a vital source of opportunity for many households to improve their economic circumstances and position in the wealth distribution."[30]

The trend now seems to be compounding among Millennials, who, despite high aspirations to entrepreneurship, are having a difficult time starting successful businesses. A recent report by the Kauffman Foundation concludes that although Millennials have higher levels of education than previous generations and lifelong exposure to information technology, their shaky finances mean that most "can't afford to become entrepreneurs."[31]

Millennials are also less likely than young adults in the past to own other forms of assets, including cars and many durable consumer items. In some instances this can be positive. If, for example, the growth of services such as Zipcar makes owning a depreciating asset like an automobile unnecessary, this is at least potentially a gain to one's net worth. Being

---

28 Lisa J. Dettling and Joanne W. Hsu, "The State of Young Adults' Balance Sheets: Evidence from the Survey of Consumer Finances," Federal Reserve Bank of St. Louis *Review*, Fourth Quarter 2014 p. 316.

29 Barry C. Lynn and Lina Khan, "The Slow-Motion Collapse of American Entrepreneurship," *Washington Monthly*, July/August 2012; Thomas Edsal, "Has American Business Lost its Mojo?" *New York Times*, April 1, 2015.

30 Janet Yellen, "Perspectives on Inequality and Opportunity from the Survey of Consumer Finances." Speech at the Conference on Economic Opportunity and Inequality at the Federal Reserve Bank of Boston, October 17, 2014.

31 Kaufman Foundation "The Future of Entrepreneurship: Millennials and Boomers Chart the Course for 2020." (Kansas City: Kaufman Foundation, February 2015).

able to "monetize" previously underused assets, such as by renting a spare bedroom through Airbnb, can also have the same positive effects on personal balance sheets.

Yet this "sharing" economy depends on and contributes to the "gig" economy, in which more and more workers are no longer employees, but rather freelancers responsible for the financial security, health, and retirement benefits once provided by employers. The Uber driver, for example, is responsible for purchasing and maintaining the car he or she uses, just as the contract white-collar worker must often finance and maintain his or her own office space, IT systems, career training, and other hard and soft assets necessary for the job. Although difficult to measure, the increasing uncertainty and contingency of today's employment has to be counted as a net negative for most workers' standard of living.

IMPLICATIONS

To be sure, some of the factors behind generational downward mobility are difficult to address through public policy. For example, during the last several generations, the number and share of single-parent families has grown rapidly.[32] Abundant social science research documents that this is both a cause and a consequence of diminishing economic opportunity, yet there is no single policy lever that will reverse the trend.

But many of the major causes of downward mobility do rest squarely within the realm of political economy and public control. One example is the woeful inefficiency of the U.S. health care system. A large body of research now pegs the amount of waste in this burgeoning sector at between 30 and 50 percent of all health care spending. According to the National Academy of Medicine, eliminating this waste would be enough to provide every young person in America (aged 18–24) with the average annual tuition and fees of a four-year institution of higher learning for two years—to take but one example of its tremendous opportunity cost.[33]

---

32 The National Marriage Project, "State of Our Unions," 2012 (Charlottesville, VA: University of Virginia, 2012). As recently as the 1980s, only 13 percent of children born to mothers with only a high school degree were born outside of marriage. By the late 2000s, that figure had risen to 44 percent.

33 Mark Smith, et al., editors, *Best Care at Lower Cost: The Path to Continuously Learning Health Care in America* (Washington, DC: Institute of Medicine, National Academies Press, 2012), pp. 3–11.

The higher education sector is also badly in need of systematic rethinking and overhaul. Individuals need to be cognizant of both the mounting cost of *not* acquiring an education and of the lifelong damage that can result from excessive student debt. At the same time, government and society at large need to attack inflating college costs, which seem to result primarily from growth in administrative spending and a lack of transparency about educational outcomes.[34]

Another priority should be redirecting the vast subsidies the federal government has long expended to help households accumulate financial and tangible assets. These subsidies currently total more than $350 billion a year, with the lion's share going to already wealthy households and individuals. For example, American taxpayers annually spend roughly $70 billion to cover the cost of the home mortgage deduction. Yet 70 percent of this money goes to households in the top 20 percent of the income distribution, while just 8 percent accrues to middle-income households, and almost nothing to the bottom 40 percent. Similar tax breaks nominally meant to encourage saving for college and retirement have similar "Robin-Hood-Reverse" qualities.[35] Much more can and should be done to target resources for asset building for those in, and struggling to reach, the middle class.

Let's not forget another possible policy lever: the money supply. Moderate levels of price and wage inflation have always tended to benefit younger adults disproportionately, because younger households tend to have more debts and fewer assets than older households. Conversely, hard money tends to help older generations, who have fewer debts, less need to worry about unemployment, and more assets to protect from inflation. A big part of the reason that today's 70-somethings did so comparatively well financially over their life was that while they were young, the general wage and price inflation of the 1960s and 1970s eroded the value of their mortgages even as it inflated the value of their homes. Today's young people, being particularly encumbered by debt, would benefit from modest levels of general inflation so long as wages kept pace.

---

34 Paul Campos, "The Real Reason College Tuition Costs So Much," *New York Times*, April 4 2015.

35 Benjamin Harris et al., "Tax Subsidies for Asset Development: An Overview and Distributional Analysis." (Washington DC: Urban Institute and Brookings Institution, 2014).

More generally, we need policies that will allow today's workers to retain more of the value of their increased productivity. In many sectors of the economy, workers do indeed produce as much in one day as their counterparts in the 1960s did in a 40-hour week—just as Robert Ball predicted. Yet the benefits of this increased efficiency have gone overwhelmingly to already established owners of assets, rather than to each new generation of workers.

The reasons behind this shift are varied, but hardly inevitable or unalterable. Since the 1980s, for example, the United States has radically reduced enforcement of anti-trust and fair trade policies. The resulting trend toward concentration in many industries largely explains both the diminishing opportunities for upward mobility through entrepreneurship and the reduced competition among employers for wage employees.[36] Meanwhile, thanks largely to changes in tax law since the early 1980s, major U.S. corporations have used almost all their profits in recent decades to reward their shareholders with dividends and stock buyback schemes, leaving little for investment in productive enterprise or for raising the wages of rank and file workers.[37]

Certainly the potential exists for our children to inherit a far more productive and broadly prosperous society than exists today. Yet for this to occur, it is not enough to focus primarily on individuals or even on the problem of "the 1 percent" growing richer. To turn the negative generational trends around requires that we reverse the deep changes in our political economy that have led to mass inequality across generations.

■ ■ ■

PHILLIP LONGMAN *is the author of numerous books and articles on public policy in realms ranging from demographics to health care and competition policy. He is currently a policy director with New America's Open Markets program, a senior editor at the* Washington Monthly, *and a lecturer at Johns Hopkins University. He lives in Washington, DC, with his wife Sandy and son, Samuel.*

---

36 Barry C. Lynn and Phillip Longman, "Who Broke America's Jobs Machine?" *Washington Monthly*, March/April 2010; Barry C. Lynn, *Cornered: The New Monopoly Capitalism and the Economics of Destruction* (New York: Wiley. 2010).

37 William Lazonick, "Profits without Prosperity," *Harvard Business Review*, September 2014; Dan Carpenter, "What Piketty Missed: The Banks," *Washington Monthly*, March/April 2015.

AFRICAN AMERICAN ECONOMIC INEQUALITY
A Twenty-First Century Challenge

Dedrick Asante-Muhammad
National Association for the Advancement of Colored People[1]

Depressed living standards for Negroes are not simply the consequences of neglect. Nor can they be explained by the myth of the Negro's innate incapacities, or by the more sophisticated rationalization of his acquired infirmities. They are a structural part of the economic system in the United States.

—Dr. Martin Luther King, Jr., 1968

By the middle of the twenty-first century, the United States will be a "majority minority" nation.[2] If we hope to ensure a strong middle class, historically the backbone of the national economy, then the financial health of households of color will become even more urgent than it is today.[3] Closing the persistent "wealth divide" between white households and households of color, already a matter of social justice, must become a priority for broader economic policy. The size of that wealth divide is sobering: the median African American household's net worth is only $7,113, according to the Census Bureau, while the comparable figure for white households is $111,740.[4]

---

1 Dedrick Asante-Muhammad wrote this essay during his tenure as the Senior Director of the Economic Department at the NAACP. He recently left the NAACP to create the Racial Wealth Divide program at CFED.

2 Ruy Teixeira and John Halpin, "Creating an All-In Nation." In *All-In Nation: An America that Works for All*, edited by Vanessa Cárdenas and Sarah Treuhaft (Washington, DC: Center for American Progress and PolicyLink, n.d.), p. 11.

3 Rather than "minority," this essay uses "households of color" and "communities of color" to refer to those ethnic and racial groups who are currently minorities (but are expected no longer to be by the middle of the century). "Black" is used to refer to historical movements or trends (e.g., "Black Freedom") with the terminology by which they were known at that time; otherwise "African American" is used.

4 U.S. Census Bureau, Survey of Income and Program Participation, 2008 Panel, Wave 10, (2013).

As we consider what it is going to take to close the wealth divide, it is useful first to understand and acknowledge the level of resources it took to create it in the first place.

The scale of investment that was required to build the white middle class is underappreciated. According to Ira Katznelson's *When Affirmative Action Was White*: "By 1950, the federal government had spent more on schooling for veterans than on expenditures for the Marshall Plan, which had successfully rebuilt Europe's devastated economic life."[5] Along with funding higher education on that massive scale, the GI bill also financed 40 percent of the mortgages in 1946 and 1947.[6] Yet as Katznelson puts it: "Despite the assistance that black soldiers received, there was no greater instrument for widening an already huge racial gap in postwar America than the GI Bill."[7] It's easy enough to see why. When the GI bill passed, segregation and white supremacy were the law of the land in many states and the de facto reality throughout the nation. So injecting massive resources into that particular status quo had the effect of intensifying a racial economic inequality that endures even today.

THE REALITY OF RACIAL INEQUALITY AND AFRICAN AMERICANS

The Civil Rights movement of the 1950s and 1960s ended the legally sanctioned segregation of the South and challenged de facto segregation across the country. But as in the Reconstruction era following the Civil War, the economic aid and investment necessary for African American communities to develop wealth was denied, leaving racial inequality to endure. Today, as we look back on the term of the first African American president, one would hope that much of the racial inequality between African Americans and white Americans had in fact been overcome. Indeed, this is what most people in the country believed soon after the election of President Obama. According to a 2010 ABC News/Washington Post poll, a little more than 70 percent of white Americans think that African Americans have achieved or will soon achieve racial equality. According to this same poll, African Americans are much more tempered

5 Ira Katznelson, *When Affirmative Action Was White: An Untold History of Racial Inequality in Twentieth-Century America*, (New York: W.W. Norton, 2005), p. 116.

6 Ranajoy Ray Chaudhuri, *The Changing Face of American Banking: Deregulation, Reregulation, and the Global Financial System*, (New York: Palgrave Macmillan, 2014), p. 100.

7 Katznelson, *When Affirmative Action Was White*, p. 121.

in their optimism, but optimistic nonetheless. Although only 11 percent of African Americans believe racial equality has been achieved, almost 40 percent believe it will be soon.[8]

Since the Black-led Freedom movement of the 1950s and 1960s, there has in fact been some progress for African Americans. According to the U.S. Census Bureau, in 2013, 83.4 percent of African Americans received a high school diploma or its equivalent, up from 25.6 percent in 1964.[9] In 1968, the college graduation rate for African Americans was 38 percent that of the white rate.[10] Today it is more than 60 percent that of whites.[11] There has also been progress for the poorest African Americans. Poverty among African Americans has declined from nearly 42 percent in 1966 to about 27 percent in 2012.[12]

Despite gains in educational attainment and declines in the share of African Americans living in poverty, African Americans have gained almost no ground in income disparities. Whether by household or per capita, African Americans do not earn even 60 percent of what white Americans earn, and this gap has barely moved in more than 40 years.[13] And income is only one part of the economic picture. Wealth inequality is another source of great concern for the nation. As noted previously, the median net worth of African American families is less than 10 percent that of white families.[14]

---

8 Taylor Nelson Sofres, ABC News/Washington Post Monthly Poll, January 2010.

9 U.S. Census Bureau, Current Population Survey, 2013 Annual Social and Economic Supplement, "Table 1: Educational Attainment of the Population 18 Years and Over;" U.S. Census Bureau, "Table 1: Years of School Completed by Persons 14 Years Old and Over: March 1964."

10 U.S. Census Bureau, "Table 1: Years of School Completed by Persons 14 Years Old and Over: March 1968."

11 U.S. Census Bureau, Current Population Survey, 2014 Annual Social and Economic Supplement, "Table 1: Educational Attainment of the Population 18 Years and Over."

12 Drew Desilver, "Who's Poor in America? 50 Years into the 'War on Poverty,' a Data Portrait" (Washington, DC: Pew Research Center, January 2014).

13 Tim Sullivan et al., "State of the Dream 2012: The Emerging Majority." (Boston, MA: United for a Fair Economy, January 2012), p. 6–7.

14 U.S. Census Bureau, Survey of Income and Program Participation, 2008 Panel, Wave 10, (2013).

THE REGRESSIVE AMERICAN ECONOMY

Since the Reagan era of the 1980s, the nation's wealth has been increasingly concentrating in the hands of the richest Americans. The U.S. Census Bureau finds that from 1979 to 2008, the real income of the poorest one-fifth of Americans decreased by 4 percent. For the middle one-fifth, real family income increased by 14 percent. For the richest 5 percent, real family income growth has increased more than 70 percent. What this trend has meant for African Americans is that nearly one-third (30 percent) of the African American population saw its income decrease and another 25 percent saw only a small (6 percent) increase—in almost 30 years. Meanwhile, during this same timeframe (1979 to 2008), six in ten whites saw more than a ten percent increase to their incomes, with two-thirds of this group seeing an increase of more than 20 percent.[15]

As with income, assets in America are increasingly concentrated in the hands of the wealthiest. The richest 10 percent of Americans now owns 70 percent of the wealth.[16] The more this wealth concentration intensifies, the less likely the wealth divide between whites and communities of color will ever close.

This racial wealth divide extends to communities of color beyond African Americans. In this post–civil rights era, communities of color in the United States increasingly are recent immigrants.[17] In effect, more and more people of color are being added to a country that is more and more economically segregated. Immigrants of color who come to this country with fewer professional skills or without an elite education become part of the large share of the population that is being left behind by the wealthiest Americans.

---

15 U.S. Census Bureau, Current Population Survey, Annual Social and Economic Supplement, "Table F-3. Mean Income Received by Each Fifth and Top 5 Percent of Families, All Races: 1966 to 2013;" U.S. Census Bureau, Current Population Survey, 2013 Annual Social and Economic Supplement, "Table HINC-05. Percent Distribution of Households, by Selected Characteristics Within Income Quintile and Top 5 Percent in 2012."

16 Jesse Bricker et al., "Changes in U.S. Family Finances from 2010 to 2013: Evidence from the Survey of Consumer Finances." (Washington, DC: Board of Governors of the Federal Reserve System, October 2014).

17 Jeffrey S. Passel, Gretchen Livingston, and D'Vera Cohn, "Explaining Why Minority Births Now Outnumber White Births." (Washington, DC: Pew Research Center, May 2012).

THE NEED FOR RADICAL CHANGE

In the last few years, a series of high-profile events, both tragedies (the killings of unarmed African American youth) and vulgarities (racial and ethnic slurs and stereotypes from NBA owners and presidential candidates) have reminded the American public of the reality that racial inequality and racism are far from a thing of the past. But even before more dramatic events galvanized public awareness around racial inequality generally, there had been a dawning realization that economic inequality was real and growing, and had a racial dimension.

Around the country, city leaders are implementing local initiatives to combat some of the biggest factors driving racial and economic inequality—unemployment, low wages, and expensive housing. A recent example is Ras Baraka, elected mayor of Newark, NJ, in May 2014. Baraka's campaign promise included targeting the chronically unemployed and appointing a "Deputy Mayor for Full Employment." This demonstrates a real focus on the high unemployment that affects most of our urban centers and that disproportionately affects communities of color. It also harkens back to the 1960s civil rights call for full employment.

Seattle was the first big city to raise the minimum wage, from $9.32 an hour to $15 an hour, the highest in the nation. None of the circumstances responsible for the Seattle plan was unique (although the convergence of them was unusual). The plan emerged from the joining of a politically strong mayor, a highly visible worker-organizing campaign, a progressive city council, and a private sector that saw short-term bottom-line costs as only one among many considerations. The phased-in increase in Seattle's minimum wage starts with businesses employing more than 500 workers and then moves on to smaller businesses, which will have five to seven years to put the new minimum wage in place. Crucially, the law is designed so that employers will not cut workers' benefits with the new minimum wages, and wages going forward will be indexed to inflation.

In New York City, the strong economic boom now underway on Wall Street has brought little economic gain to working- and middle-class people. In fact, it has had the opposite effect as affluent professionals, who have benefited from the stock market gains, compete with working-class families, who haven't, for limited space in a geographically small and intensely gentrifying city. In the last decade, median monthly housing costs in New York rose 18.6 percent for renters and nearly 10 percent for homeowners. In the borough of the Bronx, 57 percent of households are rent-burdened, meaning they must spend more than 30 percent of their take-home pay on housing.[18]

In one of the most innovative plans of its kind, New York mayor Bill de Blasio has proposed to use thousands of acres of largely vacant, city-owned public housing land to build as many as 200,000 units of affordable housing to accommodate the city's increasingly strapped working families. Under de Blasio's plan, 50 percent of the units would be sold at below-market rate prices—30 percent of the units to moderate-income households and 20 percent to lower-income residents.[19]

Stable housing and access to steady, living-wage paying work benefits individuals, families, neighborhoods, and communities. Expanding the availability of affordable housing in New York City, raising the minimum wage to a living wage in Seattle, and attacking chronic unemployment in Newark are examples of the types of policies needed to address our challenge of twenty-first century racial economic inequality.

NATIONAL ASSET DEVELOPMENT POLICY

As encouraging as these and other local initiatives may be, the racial economic divide is ultimately a national problem. Just as massive federal investment was necessary to develop the white American middle class economy of the 1950s and 1960s, so too will it be necessary to develop an American economy that finally bridges racial economic inequality. The kind of massive-scale and sustained national policy commitment that is required will depend on strong leadership and broad-based consensus. It should be driven by a comprehensive strategic vision. But existing evidence already suggests several elements that should be included.

Equity Assessment. An equity assessment reviews whether federal funds are being invested in communities that are most in need of federal assistance. A proper assessment should determine where funds go, what jobs

18 U.S. Census Bureau, 2013 American Community Survey, Table B25070, Bronx County, NY.

19 Charles V. Bagli and Mireya Navarro, "Mayor de Blasio's Plan Aims to Spur More Affordable Housing in New York," *New York Times*, May 6, 2015.

are created, and in what communities. This information will help ensure that government funds get to working-class Americans, disenfranchised racial minorities, households with children, and communities experiencing severe economic crisis, all of whom must be at the center of the economic recovery. Equity assessments are already being used in different parts of the United States and Britain. It is important to analyze whether government spending is entrenching economic inequality or bridging it. A regular national equity assessment can develop a clear picture of the policies that advance greater equality and opportunity in this country.

Direct Federal Job Creation. For decades, much of working-class America has had a hard time finding stable employment with wages and benefits that can keep a family in the middle class, even the lower middle class. Former industrial centers have been dealing with high unemployment for years, and African American unemployment, even when at record lows, remains almost twice that of white Americans.[20] A massive federal job program is needed; one that will create jobs for those with the greatest challenges in finding employment and that can lift up marginalized communities. During the most recent recession alone, the federal government spent hundreds of billions of dollars on programs to create temporary work or to stimulate private-sector employment.[21] But the cheapest and most effective means to creating stable working-class employment is to directly create government jobs.

In *Back to Work: A Public Jobs Proposal for Economic Recovery*, the think tank Demos notes that for $46.4 billion, one million jobs could be created through a government program. The report also notes that the creation of those one million jobs would trigger a multiplier effect of about 400,000 jobs beyond the government program. Demos then compares the returns on a two-year $100 billion investment in direct job creation versus investment in benefits and tax cuts, and concludes that direct job creation yields the greater return on investment.[22] To further

20 U.S. Bureau of Labor Statistics, "E-16. Unemployment rates by age, sex, race, and Hispanic or Latino ethnicity."

21 Stephen Wandner and Randall Eberts, "Public workforce programs during the Great Recession." (Washington, DC: U.S. Bureau of Labor Statistics, July 2014).

22 Philip Harvey, "*Back to Work: A Public Jobs Proposal for Economic Recovery*." (New York: Demos, 2011).

increase the return on this federal investment, these jobs should ideally be those that not only hire people from disadvantaged communities but that also are located within and serve those same communities.

Finally, bridging the racial inequality in employment must be an explicit goal of any government jobs program, as should a tracking mechanism to document whether disenfranchised minorities are being hired at a sufficient level. Currently, African Americans make up approximately 23 percent of the unemployed and Latinos approximately 20 percent. Therefore, among those who find employment from the government job program, more than 23 percent should be African Americans and more than 20 percent should be Latinos, in order to bridge racial employment inequality.[23]

No meaningful progress can be made on the larger issue of racial economic inequality until we tackle the foundational issue of racial inequality in employment. The reality is that a public program to close the racial employment gap is necessary because the free market has failed to close it for more than 50 years.

Asset Development Policy. A common response to proposals for investing in asset development is that there are not enough funds available. Yet hundreds of billions of dollars are already routinely invested in wealth development. CFED's "Upside Down: The $400 Billion Federal Asset-Building Budget" highlights how this investment is concentrating wealth among the already-wealthy instead of the asset-poor. "Upside Down" reports that more than one-half of an estimated $400 billion goes to the richest 5 percent of Americans. Effectively, federal investment in wealth development reinforces racial economic inequality among those who have very little wealth.[24]

Part of the solution to racial wealth inequality is simply to ensure that more asset-development investment is directed toward asset-poor communities than to the already-wealthy. CFED proposes a host of reforms, including using refundable tax credits rather than tax breaks to support asset development, placing caps on mortgage interest deductibility,

---

23 Author calculations using Bureau of Labor Statistics data, "Table A-2. Employment status of the civilian population by race, sex, and age."

24 Beadsie Woo, Ida Rademacher, and Jillien Meier, "Upside Down: The $400 Billion Federal Asset-Building Budget." (Washington, DC: Annie E. Casey Foundation and CFED, 2010).

and using direct budget outlays for asset development rather than just tinkering with the tax code (since the people who find it advantageous to itemize their deductions tend to be among the wealthier citizens). In short, a first step in bridging wealth inequality is to stop spending so many federal dollars on asset development for the already-wealthy.

BACK TO THE FUTURE: THE TWENTY-FIRST CENTURY FREEDOM BUDGET

The policy suggestions above are but pieces of what must be a comprehensive plan to rebuild the American middle class—and make it racially inclusive for the first time. In 1967, Black Freedom organizations joined with their allies in civil rights reform to propose a comprehensive Freedom Budget. Economist Leon Keyserling and March on Washington organizer Bayard Rustin created the budget, and Dr. Martin Luther King, Jr., wrote the foreword. The Freedom Budget would have invested $185 billion a year (in contemporary dollars) for 10 years to bridge racial socioeconomic divisions.[25] It involved major investments in public works and infrastructure, training programs that would upgrade skills and education, job creation, and affordable public health services, and it called for a higher minimum wage of $2.00 an hour, or $13.79 in today's dollars.

Dr. King described two phases of the civil rights struggle: "The first phase has been a struggle to treat the Negro with a degree of decency, not of equality... When Negroes looked for the second phase, the realization of equality, they found that many of their white allies had quietly disappeared."[26] The first phase can be described as an attack on southern institutional racism. The second phase was a challenge to the nationwide socioeconomic inequality that helps perpetuate racial inequality to this day. The animating spirit of the Freedom Budget—its remarkable vision at once bold in its scope and pragmatic about what it would take—is as relevant today as it was when it was written nearly 50 years ago. It is that second phase of the civil rights struggle, for meaningful equality—economic equality very much included—for which the Freedom Budget provides a blueprint. And it is that second phase,

25 "Introduction." In *A "Freedom Budget" for All Americans: A Summary* (New York: A. Philip Randolph Institute, 1967).

26 Martin Luther King, Jr., *Where Do We Go From Here?: Chaos or Community?* (New York: Harper & Row, 1967), p. 3.

that long-deferred work, which we must take up today. The increasing diversity of the United States should be something that the country can celebrate—and it will only be so when Americans of color finally achieve the means, economic and otherwise, to pursue the dream of equal economic opportunity and prosperity.

■ ■ ■

***DEDRICK ASANTE-MUHAMMAD** is the former senior director of the NAACP Economic Department. In that role, he oversaw financial and economic education, fair lending, diversity and inclusion, and community economic development program work. Asante-Muhammad's past civil rights experience includes his time at Reverend Al Sharpton's National Action Network, where he first worked as the national crisis coordinator and then as the national field director. His professional work in economic equity began at United for a Fair Economy, where he was the first coordinator of their Racial Wealth Divide Project. Pursuing his work in economic and racial equity, Asante-Muhammad worked at the Institute for Policy Studies in the Inequality and Common Good program.*

LATINOS IN THE FINANCIAL SHADOWS

José A. Quiñonez
Mission Asset Fund

Since the Gold Rush of 1849, California has been the destination of dreamers. Today, San Francisco draws young and energetic entrepreneurs from all over the world. They come with big dreams of starting their own tech companies or building the next big app that will change the world with one (or two) clicks.

Techies are not the only ones with dreams. The people we serve at Mission Asset Fund (MAF)—low-income Latino immigrants across California's Bay Area—have dreams too. They dream of good jobs, of homeownership, of safe neighborhoods with vibrant schools. They dream of providing their families with a better life—the American Dream that still beckons and inspires millions to work hard and overcome seemingly insurmountable obstacles. But these goals often feel out of reach for our clients, who are marginalized by a lack of access to safe, affordable financial products.

Our clients face daunting economic challenges. As low-wage and hourly workers, they struggle to make ends meet. Most live day to day, without the benefit of savings, affordable credit, or other financial tools to manage unexpected expenses, much less a life crisis. They forgo public assistance programs owing to concerns over immigration status or confusion about eligibility. As a result, families in need go without, suffering in the shadows.

These issues are not unique to San Francisco. Across the country, Latinos struggle to secure financial stability and mobility. Despite the highest labor force participation rates in the country (67.2 percent compared with 62.2 percent of whites), Latinos are disproportionately in poverty. In 2013, of the 48.7 million Americans in poverty, 26.8 percent were Latino.[1]

1 Renee Stepler and Anna Brown, "Statistical Portrait of Hispanics in the United States, 1980 – 2013" (Washington, DC: Pew Hispanic Center, May 12, 2015).

Being poor in America is expensive, particularly for those living outside of the financial mainstream. About one in five Latinos (17.9 percent) lack access to the most basic financial services, such as checking accounts, relying instead on high-cost, fringe providers to meet their financial needs.[2] According to the Consumer Financial Protection Bureau, more than 27 percent of Latinos are "credit invisible," meaning that all three major credit bureaus lack credit records for them, or the records are too thin to generate a credit score.[3]

Credit reports are like passports—they are the documents required to enter the financial mainstream. Without them, it is nearly impossible to access safe, responsible loans. Consequently, people who are credit invisible are denied the capital necessary to realize their full economic potential. They cannot get a loan to purchase a car to get to and from work or seed capital to start a small business. A person who lacks a credit history may even be denied the opportunity to rent an apartment or interview for certain jobs.

BUILDING ON WHAT'S GOOD

We launched MAF in 2007 to help low-income immigrants in San Francisco improve their financial security. At the time, an implicit assumption underlying most social policy was that low-income people are poor because they are somehow unsophisticated or otherwise deficient, lazy, or just doing everything wrong. We rejected this "deficit-based model" because it robs people of both agency and dignity.

Instead, we built "strength-based" programs by meeting people where they are, and building on what is good in their lives. Rather than starting from a stereotype, we engaged them to help us understand their financial lives better and identify existing assets and opportunities to expand on. Through those early conversations, we learned that despite few bank accounts or a steady income, many families were nonetheless lending money to one another in small, informal groups. Ten people, for example,

---

2 Susan Burhouse et al., "2013 FDIC National Survey of Unbanked and Underbanked Households" (Washington, DC: FDIC, October 2014), p. 5.

3 Kenneth Brevoort, Philipp Grimm, and Michelle Kamara, "Data Point: Credit Invisibles" (Washington, DC: Consumer Financial Protection Bureau, May 2015).

would form a group and agree to each contribute $100 per month for 10 months. Each month, a different member would receive $1,000 from the group until everyone got a turn.

Peer-to-peer lending like this is common throughout the world. When people do not have access to financial institutions, they often turn to one another for help. These small group loans are called *tandas* and *cundinas* in Mexico, *paluwagan* in the Philippines, and *susus* throughout the Caribbean. Many immigrants in the United States continue this cultural practice, looking to each other to come up with funds for everything from paying rent, to starting a business, to saving income on the upswings. Despite their prevalence, these social loans remain informal and invisible to financial institutions; they are not recorded, nor reported to the credit bureaus. Consequently, they do little to help build or strengthen the formal financial profiles of those who participate.

At MAF, we considered these social loans an example of something that is both beneficial to, and already deeply integrated in, our clients' lives. The loans are critical opportunities for many low-income immigrants, and are assets that can be leveraged to further improve their financial footing. These social loans became the foundation of our emerging "strength-based model." We knew we needed to bring the practice out of the shadows and into the economic mainstream by reporting the repayment histories to the major credit bureaus. The desire to formalize these informal loans led to the creation of MAF's Lending Circles.

Lending Circles transforms the informal group savings and lending practice by requiring participants to open checking accounts and to sign promissory notes, enabling MAF to service loans and report activity to the major credit bureaus. This made the loans visible to the modern banking system. In this way, Lending Circles empowers participants to help one another and opens doors of opportunity by building credit. For individuals without credit scores, Lending Circles helps them establish one. For those with damaged scores, Lending Circles gives them a fighting chance to refinance their debt and rebuild their financial lives. With higher credit scores, participants move away from subprime credit and begin leveraging affordable credit to eliminate high-cost debt, start successful businesses, buy homes, save for college, and build financial stability.

While we have our clients' full attention, we provide financial education to help them navigate the financial marketplace. They build community and financial confidence by gaining experience and knowledge together; they lead, share, and learn from one another. They also take pride in knowing that their loan payments help other participants reach their financial goals, too. They know they are not alone and that their money matters in the lives of other people just like them.

In 2013, the Cesar Chavez Institute (CCI) at San Francisco State University released findings from a two-year evaluation of Lending Circles. On average, program participants' credit scores increased 168 points; those who started without a credit score averaged a score of 600 after completing a Lending Circle. Within 10 months, 69 percent of participants who were credit invisible successfully established a credit score. In contrast, only 13 percent of the control group achieved this result on their own.

In addition to strengthened credit histories, researchers also documented improved financial management by Lending Circle participants, many of whom were using their interest-free loan to refinance high-cost debt, including credit cards, payday loans, and other installment debts. Members in the control group did not have this opportunity to refinance and got further into debt. Lending Circle participants with a credit history reduced their debt by $2,400, while members in the control group with a credit history increased their debt by $2,700.[4]

HIERARCHY OF FINANCIAL NEEDS

The CCI report proved that we were helping clients build credit and reduce debt, opening them to opportunities in the financial marketplace. But did we help them improve their financial lives overall?[5] Did they achieve financial security?

The evaluation did not answer these questions, in large part because we did not have a clear definition of financial security, much less a model for how to measure it. Typically, income or credit scores are considered

4 Belinda Reyes et al., "Building Credit for the Underbanked: Social Lending as a Tool for Credit Improvement" (San Francisco, CA: César E. Chávez Institute, 2013).

5 See Brandee McHale's essay in this book on why asking this question is so important.

proxies for a person's financial status. But these common metrics are inadequate for assessing a person's full financial life. Knowing a person's income alone does not say much about his or her expenses, debts or net worth, especially when income is so volatile.[6] (For a deeper discussion, see the essays by Boshara and Tescher and Schneider in this volume.) Although credit scores predict the probability that a borrower will repay a debt, they tell us little about a borrower's ability to repay. What will it take for a borrower to repay that loan? Will that borrower need a second loan to pay off the first? If so, do they have the ability to repay that initial loan?

We did not have a functional framework to understand the complexities of people's formal financial lives, much less what they do informally. Therefore, the question remained, how could we tell if we were improving our clients' financial security? For answers, we turned to Abraham Maslow.

Maslow's hierarchy of needs explains what people need to realize their true potential. In his seminal work from 1943, Maslow organized human need into five levels, ordered from the most basic (health and well-being) to the most complex (self-actualization), with each level facilitating the satisfaction of the subsequent, higher-order need.[7] Using the same logic, MAF developed the "Hierarchy of Financial Needs" (HFN) to explain what people need to realize their true economic potential (Figure 1).

The HFN identifies financial parallels to physiological needs (*income*), safety (*insurance*), love and belonging (*credit*), esteem (*savings*), and self-actualization (*investments*):

- Income: The most basic financial need is income to cover basic living expenses, such as food, housing, and utilities. Income can take many forms, from wages and dividends to government benefits or even transfers from family or friends. Income is the foundation of financial security.

- Insurance: To protect earnings, people must insure against unforeseen events that create setbacks. This requires taking stock of assets, including cash, belongings, and health, and securing against loss, theft, damage, and illness.

---

6 Diana Farrell and Fiona Gregg, "Weathering Volatility: Big Data on the Financial Ups and Downs of U.S. Individuals" (New York: JPMorgan Chase Institute, May 2015).

7 Abraham Maslow, "A Theory of Human Motivation," *Psychological Review*, 50 (4) (1943): 370–96.

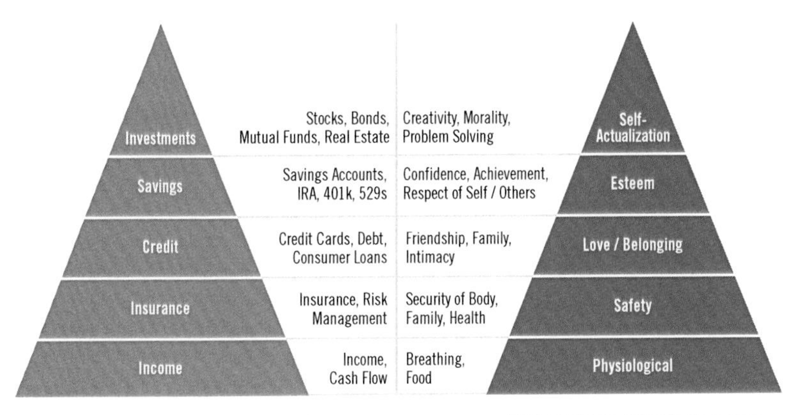

Figure 1: Hierarchy of Financial Needs - © 2015 MAF

- Credit: To acquire assets such as a car, home, or education otherwise unattainable through income alone, people need credit. This requires individuals to have credit histories and credit scores to access, and leverage, low-cost capital.

- Savings: When individuals save, they put away resources for specific goals. The ability to save demonstrates discipline and engenders confidence, a sense of achievement, and respect for oneself and others.

- Investments: The pinnacle of the HFN is when people realize the dynamism of their economic potential. This is the stage where people can invest in ventures that carry risk as well as the potential for return. It represents a turning point because people have investments to generate income, rather than relying solely on earned wages. Through investing, people have the opportunity to attain important life goals such as achieving financial security for their families, retirement, and dignity in old age.

The Hierarchy of Financial Needs is a revolutionary yet simple model that provides clarity regarding what people need to do to realize their true economic potential. For most Americans, financial security starts with a job. People need income to pay for expenses and balance their budgets. They also need to insure against shocks; they need to leverage credit to acquire assets; they need to save for a rainy day; and they need to invest for future returns. Although every individual faces a unique set of circumstances and challenges in managing these needs, the model is applicable across all income and demographic groups. In the same way that Maslow's model applies to all people, we believe HFN applies to everyone as well, providing a clear 360-degree view of people's financial lives.

The question then becomes, *how* do people meet their financial needs? What tools do they use to reach and maintain a sense of financial security? This is where substantial differences emerge across income and demographic groups. High-income individuals manage their financial needs by using financial products in the marketplace, and significantly benefit from tax policies that create incentives to borrow and invest. Indeed, they have entire industries, such as wealth managers and tax advisors, ready to help them manage their wealth.

At MAF, we see low-income Latinos manage their financial needs differently. They combine incomes to meet household budgets and participate in informal practices like hometown associations that pool resources to insure against costs like funerals, or *tandas* to save and borrow from peers. We also see them invest time and energy with family and community to build social capital, the relationships they lean on during difficult times. When they can, they access financial products such as bank accounts to secure their cash or credit cards to leverage resources. When available, they combine public support programs such as the Supplemental Nutrition Assistance Program or the Earned Income Tax Credit to supplement their income to manage their financial obligations.

The way Latinos in the financial shadows manage their financial needs is complicated, to say the least. Instead of dismissing what they do, we are learning from their savvy strategies for mixing and matching informal practices, financial products, and government programs to create a sense of financial security. The nonprofit sector, financial services industry, and policymakers can learn from their innovative strategies.

A PATH FORWARD

We took a page from our clients' playbook by collaborating with our peers—other nonprofits—to achieve what we cannot achieve alone. MAF is building a nationwide network of nonprofit partners to deploy the model broadly. These trusted organizations in ethnically diverse communities have established relationships and a deep understanding of their clients' needs. In 2014, California Governor Brown signed Senate Bill 896, a law that provides exempt status from the state's lender license laws to nonprofit organizations that provide zero-interest, credit-building loans. California now recognizes credit building as a force for good, and calls on nonprofits to innovate in the field and provide meaningful financial services to low-income communities.

In the same way our own work is influenced by our clients, we believe the financial services and nonprofit sectors can also learn from them. It is clear that social relationships are extremely important to low-income consumers, who rely on them in the absence of other assets. Yet today's financial marketplace is transitioning online, away from storefronts and face-to-face interactions. As online banking becomes more mainstream, low-income consumers risk losing access to the tellers and bank representatives who help them navigate a potentially confusing financial system.

Such shifting industry trends create significant opportunities for financial services providers and nonprofits to partner to ensure low-income consumers can access the affordable financial services that are critical to economic security and mobility. Nonprofits can build on their community relationships to serve as trusted financial advisors to communities in need, to help them navigate through the mainstream financial system in the absence of storefronts. Nonprofits have the capacity to provide such services, and the mission to do so. In turn, financial institutions can invest in nonprofits to ensure the organizations have the necessary resources and capacity to effectively serve as financial advisors and to provide many of the needed financial services.

Policy makers can also take a page from our clients' playbook—that of combining benefits to make ends meet. The fact is that low-wage workers are not earning enough income and have to rely on public benefit programs like SNAP or EITC to balance their budgets. Yet many public benefit programs have barriers built in, preventing working poor families from getting assistance. Asset limits, for example, prevent working families from accessing benefits if they have modest savings. Such policies have unintended but significant consequences of keeping people in perpetual financial insecurity. Policymakers should remove eligibility barriers like asset limits, and design programs for success by improving user experience and accessibility.

Although most Americans have a clear and set path to realize their dreams, millions of low-income people are trapped by systemic barriers and pitfalls that diminish their economic potential. The Consumer Financial Protection Bureau is policing the financial marketplace, going after bad actors and eliminating predatory products that trap people in vicious cycles of debt. But helping low-income people improve their financial situation also requires direct and positive interventions to address their diverse and complicated financial needs.

This is not a simple task, nor a one-time, one-year project. For many people, finding their financial footing may well be a multigenerational effort. No one financial product, one federal program, or even an app with one (or two) clicks can bring financial security to Latinos in the financial shadows, much less to all poor Americans. Instead, it will take many solutions, more research, and a deeper understanding of how the financial ecosystem works from the consumer's perspective. Rather than relying on only tech startups or banks to create new products, it will take funding that encourages cross-sector innovations.

It will also take a fundamental paradigm shift in social policy away from a model that engages clients as if they are broken to one that recognizes and uplifts their strengths. We cannot build an inclusive financial system based on distorted views of low-income consumers. Deficit-based programs, products, or policies not only rob people of agency, they also distort our view of what is possible. These distortions constrain our imagination, hampering our ability to build meaningful solutions to people's financial lives.

Techies in San Francisco should not be the only ones to reach their economic potential. The American Dream cannot be reserved for the few. Everyone in America deserves the same right, the same opportunities to see their true selves realized.

This paper benefited greatly from contributions by Dr. Fred Wherry, Tara Robinson, and Loren Berlin.

■ ■ ■

***JOSÉ A. QUIÑONEZ** is the CEO of Mission Asset Fund, a nonprofit organization based in San Francisco. He is also an Ashoka Fellow, the inaugural chair of the CFPB's Consumer Advisory Board, and member of Experian's Consumer Advisory Council. He has a master's of public affairs degree from Princeton University's Woodrow Wilson School.*

THE LAKOTA FUNDS STORY
How Indian Country is Building Financial Capability

Elsie M. Meeks
Lakota Funds

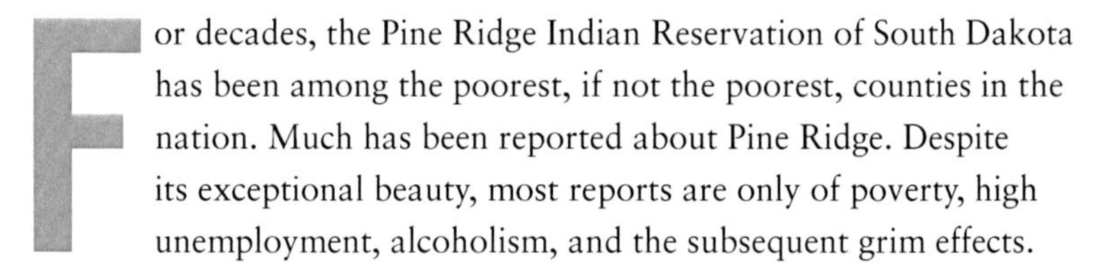

For decades, the Pine Ridge Indian Reservation of South Dakota has been among the poorest, if not the poorest, counties in the nation. Much has been reported about Pine Ridge. Despite its exceptional beauty, most reports are only of poverty, high unemployment, alcoholism, and the subsequent grim effects.

Pine Ridge is not alone in the challenges it faces as a tribal nation. There are 566 tribal nations located across 34 states within the geographic borders of the United States. Each of these tribal nations exercises its own sovereignty and is legally defined as a federally recognized tribal nation. According to the Community Development Financial Institutions (CDFI) Fund's Native American Lending Study, "Economic and social conditions on many Indian Lands and Hawaiian Home Lands place them significantly behind the mainstream U.S. economy."[1] High unemployment and poverty rates along with low homeownership rates contribute to these disparities. In addition, Native people have historically lacked access to financial products and services.

THE DEVELOPMENT AND EARLY CHALLENGES OF LAKOTA FUNDS

Thirty years ago, concerned tribal citizens from across the Reservation decided to take action. There were only a handful of businesses on Pine Ridge and none owned by tribal citizens. Previous economic development consisted of tax credit-financed factories in the 1970s established to provide employment, but by 1985, the credits had expired and the

1 Community Development Financial Institutions Fund, "The Report of the Native American Lending Study." (Washington, DC: U.S. Department of the Treasury, November 2001). As of this writing, the CDFI Fund is updating this research and new figures will be released in 2016.

factories were gone. Tribal citizens believed that a "top down" approach would not work and that the Reservation needed to build the local economy from within. They needed a strategy that would encourage tribal citizens to start businesses and create employment opportunities.

With input from Reservation-wide meetings, citizens began to develop Lakota Funds, the first CDFI on an Indian reservation. The developers believed that loans and technical assistance to tribal citizens would lead to a more robust private-sector economy. Tribal leaders pointed out that Indian Health Service, federally funded schools, Bureau of Indian Affairs, tribal government programs, and other programs received millions of dollars in support, but virtually none of that money stayed and circulated in Pine Ridge. Nearly all of it went to border towns off the Reservation.

Lakota Funds made its first loan in 1986 with capital from a program-related investment from the Ford Foundation and other private investments. This began the program's long and difficult journey. From the beginning, reporting requirements focused only on the number of loans made and the delinquency rate. After 68 loans and six months of lending, the delinquency rate was 85 percent. Lakota Funds needed to adjust its approach so it began to vigorously pursue collections and educate citizens with a lingering "grant mentality" who did not understand that loans needed to be repaid. The Fund managed to improve the delinquency rate, but making quality business loans continued to be a challenge.

After several years of lending, the Fund conducted a survey of borrowers and learned that 75 percent had never had a savings or checking account, 85 percent had never had a loan, and more than 90 percent had never been in business. Still, the Fund slogged on, creating business planning classes and peer lending, but many businesses still failed. Making good business loans in an environment with generational poverty and dependency on the federal government was a challenge. For 10 years, Lakota Funds struggled, learning valuable lessons along the way.

Meanwhile, new policies and practices such as Individual Development Accounts (IDAs) and financial literacy training were developing to help poor people build assets, based on the understanding that increasing income alone was not enough to move and keep people out of poverty. The Community Development Banking Act of 1994 and the 2001 Native

American Lending Study (NALS) led to more tribal interest in starting Native-led CDFIs.

It is a truism of economic development theory that credible institutions are essential to successful development, yet most Native communities lack the nonprofit institutions that are common in urban and rural communities across the country. Like Pine Ridge, many tribes also lack a developed private-sector economy. The situation is more serious when it comes to mainstream financial institutions. According to the NALS, 15 percent of Native communities are more than 100 miles from the nearest ATM or bank, and 86 percent of Native communities lack a single financial institution within their borders. The 2007 National Strategy for Financial Literacy report explicitly identifies Native communities as underserved by financial institutions. Unfortunately, the problem persists today. Although Native CDFIs have increased from two in 2001 to more than 70 currently, many Indian reservations still do not have any financial institutions.[2]

Not only does the lack of financial institutions pose a problem in accessing basic financial services, but it also makes business financing nearly impossible. The NALS found that more than 60 percent of respondents reported that business loans were difficult (37 percent) or impossible (24 percent) to obtain. That rate rose to almost 70 percent with loans of $100,000 or more.

THE TURNING POINT: A SHIFT TO FINANCIAL CAPABILITY

Lakota Funds began to realize that providing capital for loans was not enough. A turning point came in 1999, 13 years after its start. Lakota Funds was at an all-time low. Delinquency was high and operating funds were more difficult to obtain. Staff morale was low because of leadership turnover and lending remained difficult, with seemingly few positive outcomes. The Fund briefly considered closing its doors, and members began to reconsider their original mission to start a private-sector economy.

---

2 A field scan of existing financial capability programs in Indian Country in eight states in the northwest provides more detailed information. See First Nations Development Institute, "Building Assets and Building Lives: Financial Capability in Native Communities." (Longmont, CO: First Nations Development Institute, 2015).

After much discussion, the Fund realized that what it really hoped to accomplish was to provide tools and opportunities for Pine Ridge residents to build personal and financial capability and become financially self-sufficient. Achieving this goal would lead to a nation of people who contributed to an economy instead of being a burden to it. The Fund began to speak about individual wealth creation, an entirely new concept on the Reservation. That focus on wealth creation instead of business development changed the way Lakota Funds did business.

Looking back, this goal should have been apparent. A first step to a successful business is building financial capacity among tribal citizens. Looking forward, the Fund sought out others who were pursuing the same goal. The Fund began coordinating with Tribal colleges and schools to offer financial education, entrepreneurship, and asset-building programs to the students. It also reached out to parents to introduce savings programs. Lakota Funds developed matched savings programs to provide individuals, families, and students with the financial foundation, support, and motivation to achieve their goals. Several years ago, Lakota Funds started the first depository financial institution on the Pine Ridge Reservation—the Lakota Federal Credit Union—a National Credit Union Administration chartered credit union.

Today, Lakota Funds provides credit-builder and business loans, business training, financial management training, and technical assistance. The Fund also promotes postsecondary education among youth, offering "Generations of Wealth," a Child Development Account program since 2011. It is the first matched savings program for grade school children on an Indian reservation. Although preliminary, a 2013 evaluation showed that 90 percent of participating families reported they were more focused on future goals and were connecting economic planning with future opportunities. Among the enrolled children, 78 percent set goals related to college, a specific career path, or improving their prospects by saving more money.

Lakota Funds implemented an IDA in 2001, which includes a matched savings program for adults and a companion program for students entering high school. The student program uses classroom-based financial education and financial literacy apps to encourage teens to save for postsecondary education. Families can open savings accounts at Lakota Federal Credit Union. The program involves monthly meetings with speakers and mentors who can inspire and educate teens about college, financial aid, and career goals.

BUILDING A STRONG FINANCIAL FUTURE IN INDIAN COUNTRY

Real progress in building lasting financial capability in Indian Country requires comprehensive strategies and tools. Several organizations and coalitions advocate for stronger state and federal policies and programs that advance financial capability, including CFED and First Nations Development Institute. The Native Financial Education Coalition (NFEC), a national coalition furthering financial education in Indian Country, has made a number of recommendations that are consistent with lessons learned at Pine Ridge. These include targeted homeownership programs and homeowner education; financial education in school and youth programs such as Native Boys and Girls Clubs; financial education and training through Temporary Assistance for Needy Families and workforce development programs; and Native CDFI development that offers financial education, consumer credit counseling, business planning, credit repair, savings programs, voluntary income-tax assistance, and IDAs.[3]

More broadly, recommendations advocate for stronger partnerships and policies that improve financial access and protection for tribal nations. For example, NFEC recommends enacting consumer protection codes. Financial education can arm tribal citizens with the knowledge and tools to avoid becoming victims of predatory lending practices. Consumer protection codes can provide legal protections within tribal jurisdictions. The Blackfeet Tribe, Grand Traverse Band of Ottawa and Chippewa Indians, Cheyenne River Sioux, and Navajo Nation are examples of tribes who have adopted some type of consumer protection laws. First Nations Development Institute has developed a model consumer protection code that tribes can use as a starting point in their community. Another recommendation is to encourage cross-sector partnerships among tribes, state and local government, and the private sector. South Dakota enacted a law that allows tribal identification cards to be used for opening bank accounts and cashing checks. This helps to expand access to financial

3 For NFEC's full recommendations, see www.ncai.org/initiatives/nativefinancial-ed/NFEC_Factsheet.pdf.

services for tribal citizens who may not have a state driver's license or identification card.[4]

At Pine Ridge, building financial capability among people who lack access to financial institutions is a must, not only to improve individual capacity, but also to ensure that financial programs have a greater chance of success in achieving the goal of wealth creation and a vibrant local economy. One final piece of evidence that these changes have a made a difference: Lakota Funds now has a delinquency rate of less than 5 percent.

■ ■ ■

ELSIE MEEKS *has more than 25 years of experience specializing in Native community development and is the Chairperson of Lakota Funds. In 2009, she was appointed by the Obama Administration to serve as the state director of South Dakota USDA Rural Development, a position she held for over five years. Prior to that, Meeks held president and chief executive officer roles at First Nations Oweesta Corporation, assisted with development and management at Lakota Funds, and was co-owner of Long Creek, LLC and Wanblee Mart. Meeks currently serves on the Board of Directors of the Northwest Area Foundation and was recently elected to serve on the Board of the Federal Home Loan Bank of Des Moines. She has held various local and national board positions over the years and has completed a six-year term on the U.S. Commission on Civil Rights. Meeks is also an enrolled member of the Oglala Lakota Sioux Tribe.*

4 Native Financial Education Coalition, "Supporting the Unique Role of Tribal Government and Community Leaders to Improve Financial Capability." (Washington, DC: NFEC, February 2015).

FINANCIAL INSECURITY IN ASIAN AMERICAN PACIFIC ISLANDER COMMUNITIES

An Untold Story of Racial Wealth Inequality

Lisa Hasegawa and Jane Duong

National Coalition for Asian Pacific American Community Development

In 2010, the Asian American and Pacific Islander (AAPI) community became the fastest growing ethnic group in the country. If this trend continues, the AAPI population will grow to be approximately 9 percent of the U.S. population by 2050 (up from 5 percent).[1] At the same time, the last decade has shone new light on the devastating effects of poverty and economic insecurity on communities of color. Despite common misconceptions, the story is no different for more than 2 million AAPIs living in poverty and the many more that are living on the edges.

Take the Fonua family,[2] Tongan immigrants living in Los Angeles. Since the recession, Mr. Fonua has seen his work hours decline by more than half in the construction industry. His wife has had to relocate to another city to find work as a full-time caregiver. And their youngest daughter has taken two part-time jobs to help pay the family's rent and other bills. She does this while juggling full-time classes on the weekends, working toward her college degree. The family is working hard, but the goals of financial security and economic mobility still feel out of reach.

---

1 U.S. Census Bureau, "National Population Projections 2008."

2 Names have been changed to protect the identity of the family. The Fonuas are clients of Empowering Pacific Islander Communities in Los Angeles, California.

UNDERSTANDING THE SPECTRUM OF AAPI FINANCIAL WELL-BEING

Like the Fonua family, many AAPI groups are struggling day-to-day to pay the bills, let alone save and invest in their future. The population of AAPIs living in poverty has grown by 38 percent since the Great Recession began (27 percent for Asian Americans alone and 60 percent for Native Hawaiians and other Pacific Islanders)—the largest increase among all ethnic groups—significantly higher than the 27 percent increase in the nation's overall poverty population.[3] AAPI concentration in low-wage jobs, particularly those in service industries such as restaurant and retail workers, taxi drivers, and domestic workers, also means fewer opportunities to move beyond poverty.

Opportunities to sustain and build wealth are also limited for many in the AAPI community. Between 2005 and 2009, Asian Americans lost 54 percent of their wealth, compared with a 16 percent decline for whites, much of it due to loss of home equity during the housing crisis.[4] More recent data show that many Asian Americans have been able to regain some wealth since the crisis. However, existing data sources and related analysis fail to provide detail on specific sub-ethnic communities and as a result, AAPI groups that have been relatively more successful vastly obscure the experiences of AAPIs with less income or wealth. Aggregated data also fail to capture any nuance about the varied immigration histories of AAPI communities, which have been major contributing factors in their relative economic success. For example, recent U.S. immigration policy has greatly favored immigration from Asia of highly skilled and highly educated workers. By comparison, many refugees from Southeast Asia and migrants from the Pacific Islands are less likely to have higher education, transferable employment skills, and English language proficiency, which limited their economic prospects.

Financial insecurity persists and wealth-generating opportunities continue to elude many in the AAPI community. Homeownership has been a

---

3 Josh Ishimatsu, "Spotlight: Asian American and Pacific Islander Poverty." (Washington, DC: National Coalition for Asian Pacific American Community Development, June 2013).

4 Rakesh Kochhar, Richard Fry and Paul Taylor, "Wealth Gaps Rise to Record Highs between Whites, Blacks, and Hispanics" (Washington, DC: Pew Research Center, July 2011). Data on Native Hawaiian and Pacific Islander wealth were not available in the report.

primary driver of wealth creation, but access to this important opportunity has been uneven within the AAPI community. For example, in 2013, the homeownership rate was 64.8 percent among Vietnamese households, but 43.7 percent among Hmong households; by comparison, the homeownership rate was 68.8 percent for whites and 45.2 percent for Latinos.[5] Further, Pacific Islanders and many Southeast Asians continue to face major barriers to higher education, such as cost, limited English proficiency, or knowledge of the college preparation and application process, which limit opportunities for these individuals to move into higher paying jobs with better retirement benefits. In addition, the AARP Foundation finds that AAPI seniors are much more likely to be living in poverty and to hold significant housing debt, compared to the general population, further contributing to their household insecurity.[6]

According to an analysis conducted for "Scrimping + Saving," a report of the National Coalition for Asian Pacific American Community Development (CAPACD), 14 percent of low- and moderate-income AAPI respondents had trouble paying bills or needed emergency cash in the last 12 months.[7] Another 23 percent did not know where to turn to raise emergency funds or did not think they could raise them at all. Fully 56 percent of low- and moderate-income AAPI respondents did not know where to turn for financial advice or they turned to potentially unreliable sources such as the internet or family and friends, a risk that is exacerbated for AAPIs with limited English fluency and recent immigration status. The issue of language diversity and proficiency is particularly relevant for the AAPI population, which has the highest proportion of residents who speak a language other than English at home, spanning more than 40 different Asian languages.[8] One in five AAPI households is linguistically isolated, meaning there is no one in the household age 14 or older who speaks English exclusively or "very well," which is on par with Latino

---

5 U.S. Census Bureau, 2013 American Community Survey, 1-Year Estimates Selected Population Profiles, S0201.

6 AARP Foundation, "Are Asian Americans and Pacific Islanders Financially Secure?" (Washington, DC: AARP Foundation, December 2014).

7 Alvina Condon et al., "Scrimping and Saving: A Report on Financial Access, Attitudes, and Behaviors of Low- and Moderate-Income Asian Americans and Pacific Islanders" (Washington, DC: National Coalition for Asian Pacific American Community Development, Spring 2015).

8 Karthick Ramakrishnan and Farah Z. Ahmad, "Language Diversity and English Proficiency." (Washington, DC: Center for American Progress, May 2014).

households.[9] These linguistic challenges create barriers to financial health given their impact on earnings, job quality, access to health care, and the ability to use important social and government services. The different economic prospects across AAPI subpopulations reflect the broader income and wealth stratification within both the AAPI community, and the nation as a whole.

RACE MATTERS: WORKING TOGETHER AS COMMUNITIES OF COLOR

Because AAPI groups are lumped together as one group in data sets, study after study report AAPIs as generally doing the same or better than the general population and in relation to other communities of color. It has led some to claim that race no longer matters and that institutional racism has been dismantled. The reports of National CAPACD and others, and the daily experiences of the network of organizations that make up our national coalition prove otherwise. Including a more nuanced analysis of AAPI data is critical for reasserting that race indeed does still matter and racial discrimination still has major effects on access to opportunity and life outcomes.

AAPI communities face specific challenges in achieving financial security, and their fates are inextricably tied to the experience of African Americans, Latinos, and other communities of color. The Civil Rights movement expanded opportunities for African Americans and brought greater awareness of the need for investments in urban neighborhoods. It also overturned many of the discriminatory policies that stood in the way of economic opportunity for AAPI communities. Segregation and discrimination led to the development of the first Chinatowns in the country, and AAPIs have always lived with and alongside other communities of color. This is particularly true for AAPI households living in poverty. More than 57 percent of Asian Americans and 62 percent of Native Hawaiians and Pacific Islanders live in neighborhoods in which the majority of residents are people of color.[10] Despite mainstream media's attempt to pit AAPI communities against other communities of color, our communities have collectively experienced not just urban disinvestment, but the devastating

9 Ibid.

10 Ishimatsu, "Spotlight: Asian American and Pacific Islander Poverty."

effects of the foreclosure crisis, which have stripped decades of wealth from our communities and further exacerbated the income and wealth divide.

AAPIs must work together alongside other communities of color to invest in promising policies that create systems and infrastructure where all communities are able to thrive. First, federal agencies need to invest in improved data collection systems to more effectively capture the diversity of experiences within the AAPI community. This would include clearer directives from the Office of Management and Budget on the collection of race and ethnicity data. For example, additional data through the Home Mortgage Disclosure Act (HMDA) or small business lending could provide a more accurate picture of which AAPI subgroups are accessing mortgages and small business loans. Where relevant, data collection should include oversampling in specific geographic regions to capture the full complexity of AAPI experiences and avoid the problems arising from samples that are too small for reliable estimations. With this data, we will be able to better quantify and design holistic solutions for improving financial well-being in the AAPI community. In addition, given the lack of English language fluency among many AAPIs, federal policies that support improved language access and enforcement of Title VI regulations are fundamental.[11]

We must continue to strengthen the regulatory framework to ensure that predatory lenders are not allowed to proliferate and strip wealth from communities. In addition, we must work closely with financial institutions to create an inclusive system that allows low-income AAPIs and other communities of color to successfully save and invest in their future. Financial institutions can improve language access in bank branches, create alternative financial products such as peer lending circles, savings groups, credit building tools, or other strategies that embrace the multigenerational nature of many AAPI households, or consider alternative underwriting standards that capture how AAPI households live and run their businesses. For example, Asian Americans For Equality (AAFE), a community-based organization and community development financial institution (CDFI) in New York City has developed a more culturally relevant model for successfully underwriting AAPI-owned small

---

11 Title VI of the Civil Rights Act of 1964 prohibits discrimination on the basis of race, color, and national origin in programs and activities receiving federal financial assistance. National origin discrimination includes, among other things, failing to provide meaningful access to individuals who are limited English proficient.

businesses. The model considers inventory as a financial indicator in addition to business income. Lifting up these types of lessons can help the financial sector develop tools that better meet the demands of a growing AAPI community.

STRENGTHENING COMMUNITY-BASED ORGANIZATIONS TO DELIVER LINGUISTICALLY AND CULTURALLY APPROPRIATE SERVICES

Community-based organizations (CBOs) are a critical component of building financial security for AAPI communities and require greater investment by the public and philanthropic sector. CBOs are at the forefront of innovation and are constantly testing promising solutions that embrace the complexity of how AAPIs live and thrive in American society. These solutions support community members in overcoming barriers, such as language access and education, and honor the cultural experiences of the AAPI community. For example, National CAPACD is currently partnering with eight CBOs across the country to bundle traditional immigrant integration services, such as citizenship and English classes and workforce training, with financial education and coaching.[12] Further, National CAPACD's program partners combined their financial education with Mission Asset Fund's Lending Circle model (see José Quiñonez's essay in this book) to enhance financial capability in low-income AAPI communities. The Lending Circle approach combines the traditional practice of peer lending familiar to AAPI communities and combines it with financial coaching and education. According to data collected, participants saved an average of $535 in six months, and the aggregate repayment rate was 98.4 percent, indicating that almost all participants were able to build their credit because of successful on-time payments.[13]

Similarly, Hawaiian Community Assets successfully developed a financial education curriculum, *Kahua Waiwai*, which incorporates traditional Native Hawaiian cultural concepts to convey financial information. The

---

12 The eight CBOs are Asian Economic Development Agency (AEDA), Asian Services In Action (ASIA), Center for Pan Asian Community Services (CPACS), Chhaya CDC, Chinese American Service League (CASL), Chinese Community Center (CCC), Hawaiian Community Assets (HCA), and Korean Resource Center (KRC).

13 National Coalition for Asian Pacific American Community Development, "The Critical Moments of Immigrant Integration" (Washington, DC: National CAPACD, Spring 2015).

curriculum has been highly successful in engaging both adults and youth in financial conversations and has been a platform for creating innovative financial products such as credit-building and other alternative savings tools. In Queens, New York, Chhaya CDC formed with its peers the Northwestern Queens Financial Education Network to serve the diverse immigrant population in their neighborhood. Its programs offer comprehensive financial education and coaching paired with legal services for community members who may have been victims of financial harm. They also monitor financial trends in the community. Similarly, the Little Tokyo Service Center in Los Angeles has leveraged their expertise in counseling AAPI seniors to provide financial education and coaching that helps seniors avoid predatory lending and protect their assets.

Examples like these reflect the extraordinary opportunity to work in partnership with local practitioners to design solutions that not only benefit individual community members, but also create opportunities to build solutions that cross ethnic lines within neighborhoods and communities. To go even further, we must find new partners representing a broad range of sectors, from housing and health to education and government. Alongside strong regulatory policies and inclusive financial institutions, we can promote a broader system of equity in which AAPI and all other communities are able to participate and thrive.

■ ■ ■

***LISA HASEGAWA** has served as the executive director of the National Coalition for Asian Pacific American Community Development (National CAPACD) for the past 15 years. She has devoted her life to improving the quality of life for low-income AAPI communities by promoting economic vitality, civic and political participation, and racial equity. Prior to joining National CAPACD, Hasegawa was the Community Liaison for the White House Initiative on Asian Americans and Pacific Islanders. Through her leadership with the National Council of Asian Pacific Americans (NCAPA) during the past decade, she has strengthened the overall relevance of AAPIs in housing and economic justice. She currently serves on the boards of the National Low Income Housing Coalition and LISC. Lisa is a fourth generation Japanese American from California, and is a graduate of the University of California, Los Angeles, and the Harvard School of Public Health.*

■ ■ ■

***JANE DUONG** is the director of programs and advocacy for the National CAPACD, where she leads the development and implementation of National CAPACD's housing counseling, asset building, and small business strategies serving low- and moderate-income AAPI communities. Previously, she served as the housing program manager for the Mission Economic Development Agency (MEDA). She graduated from the University of California, Berkeley, and received her Master of Public Administration from New York University's Robert F. Wagner School of Public Service.*

WOMEN AND WEALTH
How to Build It

Heidi I. Hartmann
Institute for Women's Policy Research

Wealth and assets are integral to the economic security of men and women of all ages, races, ethnicities, occupations, and income levels. Although women have made tremendous progress in achieving economic equality with men in all the largest racial and ethnic groups in the United States, they still lag behind men in many aspects of economic advancement. This lag leaves women to experience significantly less financial security and stability across their lifetimes, particularly when they head households on their own. Two periods of vulnerability in women's lives stand out: first, when they are young and often having children without financial support from men, and, second, when they reach old age, after a lifetime of lower earnings, coupled with a greater commitment to caregiving, leaves them with fewer resources to support a longer lifetime.

Historically, marriage was a path to economic security for many women and is still a path to wealth accumulation. But this traditional role of marriage has been weakened by a dramatic increase in women's labor force participation during the last half century, an increase in the average age of marriage, higher rates of non-marriage and single motherhood, the growing financial burdens of care (which fall disproportionately on the shoulders of women), and women's greater longevity compared with men, which tends to leave them single in old age. Moreover, marriage is much less common today among low-income people and among people of color than it is among higher-income or white people. Today's women spend less of their lives in marriage than their mothers did. And since marriage is often transitory and ends in divorce, long-term access to the assets accumulated in marriage is not guaranteed.[1] Although increased education, employment, and earnings mean that many women can successfully support themselves and their children outside marriage, women's economic vulnerabilities are generally greatest when they are single.

WOMEN'S INCOME AND WEALTH

Both income and wealth are sources of financial security. Although we often focus mainly on income, accumulated wealth is of at least equal importance. For example, during the Great Recession, many working-age people used savings, including retirement savings, to tide them over, and they doubled up in housing and stopped saving for retirement. Women used all of these strategies, as well as borrowing against assets, more often than men.[2] Women both earn less than men and have less wealth, and the gender wealth gap is larger than the gender wage gap. Although women earn only 78 percent of what men earn annually at the median, women's wealth is only 32 percent of men's wealth. With less income and less wealth, single women are clearly economically disadvantaged compared with single men.[3]

---

1 The right of women, and especially married women, to hold assets in their own name arrived rather late in the development of capitalism. It began in the United States in the 1840s and 1850s with the passage of Married Women's Property Acts in state after state, but the process was not fully complete until the late 1800s. It was not until the passage of the Equal Credit Opportunity Act in 1974 that single and married women gained the right to hold credit cards in their own names--without "responsible" cosigners. Community property states, with laws based more on continental Europe, tend to be more favorable to women's rights to marital property upon divorce than those more firmly based on English Common law. See Carmen Dianna Deere and Cheryl Doss, "The Gender Asset Gap: What Do We Know and Why Does It Matter," *Feminist Economics* 12 (1–2) (2006): 1–50.

2 In 2010, 45 percent of women and 38 percent of men reported having taken money out of their savings or retirement fund in the past year. Doubling up refers to taking in or moving in with new household members in order to cope financially. Since 2007, 17 percent of women and 11 percent of men reported having doubled up. In 2010, 33 percent of women and 27 percent of men reported having stopped or reduced their contributions to retirement savings over the past year. In addition, 13 percent of women and 12 percent of men said they had borrowed against a retirement plan. Data are from the 2010 IWPR/ Rockefeller Survey of Economic Security. See Jeff Hayes and Heidi Hartmann, "Women and Men Living on the Edge: Economic Insecurity After the Great Recession" (Washington, DC: Institute for Women's Policy Research, 2011).

3 Wage data are based on 2013 medians from the Current Population Survey for full-time, year-round workers ages 16 and over. Wealth data are based on median wealth from the Survey of Consumer Finance in 2013 for single women and men ages 18–64. Data on wealth are for single women and men only and refer to the value of assets net of debts. See Ariane Hegewisch, Emily Ellis, and Heidi Hartmann, "The Gender Wage Gap: 2014; Earnings Differences by Race and Ethnicity." Fact Sheet. (Washington, DC: Institute for Women's Policy Research, 2015); Mariko Lin Chang, "Women and Wealth: Insights for Grant Makers" (Asset Funders Network, 2015).

Native American women and black women experience the highest levels of poverty, 28 percent and 26 percent respectively, while white women and Asian/Pacific Islander women have lower poverty rates, at 12 percent and 13 percent, respectively.[4] Within all major race/ethnic groups, women hold less wealth than men at the median. White men hold nearly twice the wealth of white women, while black men hold about 50 percent more than black women, and Hispanic men own nearly 10 times as much as Hispanic women. Among women, black women have about 1.3 percent of the wealth of single white women, and Hispanic women only about 0.6 percent.[5]

What are the causes of the gender gaps? Because of lower lifetime earnings—caused by both lower wages and more time spent out of the labor force on caregiving—women typically earn less, save less, and have lower wealth than men. Women's poverty rates, based on their incomes, are much higher than men's, not only because of their lower earnings but also because women more often raise children alone than men do. More mouths to feed on an equal income, and even more so on a lower income, translate into a higher poverty rate for women. Although women are poorer than men at every age, they are most disproportionately poor in the childbearing and childrearing years and again at older ages, when they are much more likely to be single.[6]

WOMEN IN THE CHILDREARING YEARS

Two-fifths of births today are to unmarried women. Children contribute to women's poverty and to their inability to acquire wealth while young, thus causing them to miss out on an important stage of wealth accumulation. Among household types, more than two in five (43 percent) single-female-headed households with children live below the poverty line. Compare this with the much lower poverty levels for single-male-headed

---

4 Cynthia Hess, Jessica Milli, Jeff Hayes, and Ariane Hegewisch, "Status of Women in the States 2015." (Washington, DC: Institute for Women's Policy Research, 2015).

5 Chang, "Women and Wealth." Comparing Chang's 2013 analysis with her earlier analysis of the 2004 Survey of Consumer Finances indicates that in constant dollars, minority men and women generally lost huge portions of their income and wealth in the Great Recession; black men lost about 95 percent of their income, and black women more than 90 percent; Hispanic men lost more than half of their 2004 wealth, while Hispanic women increased their median wealth from $0 to $102 by 2013.

6 IWPR analysis of US Census Bureau, "Annual Social and Economic Supplement 2014," *Current Population Survey.*

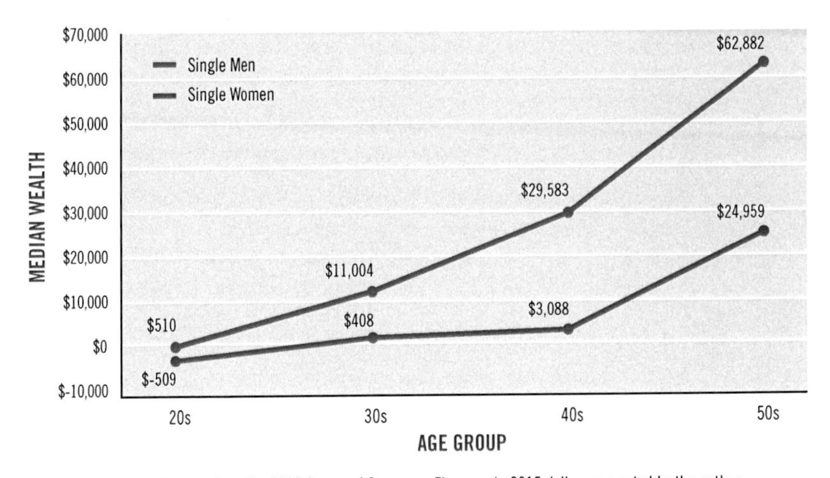

Note: Median wealth data are from the 2013 Survey of Consumer Finances in 2015 dollars converted by the author using the Consumer Price Index for All Urban Consumers, not seasonally adjusted.
Source: Mariko Lin Chang, email communication, July 19, 2015.

Figure 1: Median Wealth by Gender and Age, 2013

households with children (24 percent) and of married couples with children (9 percent).[7]

Figure 1 illustrates how men's wealth often accumulates rapidly when women's does not. It shows what Mariko Lin Chang refers to as the effects of the "wealth escalator," mechanisms that help people build wealth more quickly (including fringe benefits and government policies) and the consequent tendency for wealth to grow with age as the escalator operates.[8] Note that men enter the escalator at a better place than women, with men in their twenties having $510 in wealth in 2013 compared with women's negative wealth of -$509. By their thirties, single men had $11,004 compared with single women's $408. Even by their forties women hold only $3,088 in wealth, while men's wealth is $29,583.

In general, the ratio of women's to men's wealth is most unequal in the earlier age groups; this is significant because wealth that has been held the longest has the most chance to grow. Men are more likely to get early opportunities to save by working for employers who offer pensions or

7 Hess et al., "Status of Women in the States."

8 Mariko Chang, *Shortchanged: Why Women Have Less Wealth and What Can Be Done About It* (New York: Oxford University Press, 2010).

retirement savings plans and are also more likely to receive stock options. Both of these contribute to wealth directly. Women are nearly twice as likely as men to work part-time, and nine times as many women as men reported working part-time because of family care reasons.[9] Working part-time makes it less likely that a worker will receive employment benefits that can help them save, such as paid vacation days, paid family or medical leave, paid sick days, health care insurance, and pensions or employer contributions to retirement saving funds. Because most of these employer benefits are tax-advantaged, the disparity in employer benefits is exacerbated by disparities in tax treatment that favor men.

Among both single and married parents, mothers still do the majority of family work, despite women's increased participation in paid work, and fathers still do the majority of paid work outside the home, even though they have increased their time spent on family work somewhat. The difference in the labor force participation of fathers and mothers of children under age 6 is 27.3 percent nationally; 94.4 percent of fathers are in the labor force but only 67.1 percent of mothers are.[10] Caring for children forces many women to choose between keeping their jobs and caring for their family, as quality child care is unaffordable for many families. Women who are working for pay and raising children on their own have less disposable income available for saving than their male or married counterparts, while those who are not working for pay lose access to employer-provided benefits; neither group is getting on the wealth escalator.

What is needed to help women get on the wealth escalator early and continue to move up? First, raising women's earnings on the job is extremely important. Although young women earn nearly as much as young men when they first start out in the labor market, they fall behind rapidly in the childbearing years (and as we have seen, their wealth accumulation is negative in their twenties). Part of the reason may lie in the continued sex segregation of work, in which many women work in low-paid service jobs, including care work, jobs that are thought to be low paid at least in part because women do them; they also have little

---

9 Hess et al., "Status of Women in the States."

10 Ibid.

wage growth with increased years on the job.[11] Many jobs that women dominate can be done on a part-time basis, allowing women to combine family care with some wage earning, but women often sacrifice access to pensions and paid leave when they work in part-time jobs. A policy change that could help young women in particular is requiring employers to provide the same wages and benefits on a proportional basis to part-time workers as they do to full-time workers, as is required in European Union member countries. Simply put, women need greater access to higher-paying and higher-quality jobs that are also family-friendly. Having access to equal retirement savings opportunities, for example, would help young women get on the wealth escalator early.

Stronger enforcement of Title IX of the Education Amendments of 1972, which applies to all educational programs (not only sports) from elementary school through graduate school, and improved information and counseling would likely help girls and young women prepare for higher-earning fields, and improved family policies on the job would make these higher-paid fields easier to navigate while raising a family. Improved information about earnings can also contribute to pay equity, since when workers know about unequal pay they are in a stronger position to do something about it. Stronger enforcement at the federal level of laws on equal pay (1963), equal employment opportunity (1964), and pregnancy discrimination (1978) is also essential.

Raising city, state, and federal minimum wage laws will also disproportionately help women, since women are more likely to work for the lowest wages. Achieving equal pay with men who are similarly qualified would raise women's pay by thousands of dollars per year and reduce the poverty rate of families with a working woman (and single women) by half.[12] Raising the salary threshold below which workers must receive premium

---

11 Improving the pay, benefits, and working conditions of home care and home health aides would raise the incomes specifically of the many minority women in these jobs, increase their disposable income, and allow them to save more. Higher pay and benefits would also reduce turnover in these jobs and increase the quality of care disabled and older adults receive. Truly valuing caregiving would lift the pay of many occupations such as these. These are occupations that are expected to grow more rapidly than the labor force as a whole since the need for caregiving will expand as the population ages.

12 Heidi Hartmann, Jeffrey Hayes, and Jennifer Clark, "How Equal Pay for Working Women Would Reduce Poverty and Grow the American Economy." (Washington, DC: Institute for Women's Policy Research, 2014).

pay for overtime work would also help women disproportionately.[13] Collective bargaining also increases women's pay and access to retirement benefits.[14]

Beyond increasing pay and benefits, income supports for times when workers cannot work are essential, especially because so many young women give birth when single. Paid leaves for both maternity disability and caregiving of newborns are essential to help increase women's income security.[15] Paid leaves also have the effect of increasing women's job continuity, enabling them to build seniority on the job. Many wealthy countries provide paid leaves of 6–12 months or more, generally through a social insurance system. A fully paid caregiving leave of up to a year is one way to subsidize child care for infants. Beyond that age, the availability of subsidized child care must be increased, as other wealthy countries have been able to do. Indeed, if women's caregiving work were fully compensated—through family caregiving leaves at full pay for sufficient time periods, more child-targeted public assistance (not only subsidized child care but also child allowances typically available in most other wealthy nations), as well as receiving more child support from absent fathers—women would be able to raise children without increasing their likelihood of living in poverty or reducing their ability to build wealth.

In addition, low-income women need to become familiar with ways to enhance their savings during their working years. For example the federal Savers Credit—which should be expanded—helps those with incomes up to $30,000 ($45,000 for heads of households) receive a tax credit for part of the first $2,000 they save for retirement.[16] The Earned Income Tax Credit (EITC) rewards low-income adults, especially those with children, for working, and is another program that increases disposable income

---

13 Heidi Hartmann et al., "How the New Overtime Rule Will Help Women and Families." (Washington, DC: Institute for Women's Policy Research and MomsRising, 2015).

14 Julie Anderson, Ariane Hegewisch, and Jeff Hayes, "The Union Advantage for Women." (Washington, DC: Institute for Women's Policy Research, 2015).

15 A growing number of local and state governments require that employers provide paid sick days, and three states (California, New Jersey, and Rhode Island) require employers to participate in worker-funded social insurance plans that provide paid family leave, albeit only for 4–6 weeks (these three states plus Hawaii and New York also provide social insurance for nonwork-related disabilities up to 26–52 weeks).

16 Internal Revenue Service, "Save Twice with the Saver's Credit," IRS Special Edition Tax Tip 2014–22.

and the ability to save. Because women's earnings are lower than men's and they are more likely to be raising children, disproportionately more women receive EITC benefits.

And as Reggie Bicha and Keri Batchelder and others argue in this volume, federal assistance policy should allow low-income people to build up assets and not have to exhaust them in order to apply for food benefits such as SNAP and WIC or cash welfare assistance, programs that also disproportionately serve women. Those who are forced to exhaust their assets have a harder time climbing out of the situation that resulted in their needing assistance (for example, childbirth, an illness, a lost job). Even owning a modest value automobile, an asset that might be essential for these women to get back on the path toward earning better wages, can disqualify them for these crucial benefits.[17]

WOMEN AT OLDER AGES

Just as young women today do not face the same demographic and labor market conditions their mothers faced at comparable ages, today's older women face different conditions in preparing for retirement than did their mothers. People are living longer and women especially more often face retirement unmarried. The substitution of defined-contribution for defined-benefit pension plans means that even those with access to employer-provided retirement savings plans are responsible for making contributions to the plans and decisions about how to invest the funds. And instead of receiving a predictable amount each month based on how much they earned and how many years they worked for a particular company, older workers' retirement benefits are a function of past savings and investment returns.

Figure 2 shows a marked difference in how men and women's earnings grow with age.[18] Women's earnings are lower than men's at every age and they also stop growing at about age 44, whereas men's earnings

17 It is interesting that other policies that raise the incomes of the poor do not have asset limits. The minimum wage is neither income- nor asset-tested (all workers are eligible for it), while the federal Earned Income Tax Credit (EITC) is only income-tested and has no asset limits.

18 The data shown in Figure 2 are cross-sectional, showing different age groups at one point in time. Similar age earnings profiles are found when using longitudinal data that follow the same workers across time. See Stephen J. Rose and Heidi Hartmann, "Still a Man's Labor Market: The Long-Term Earnings Gap" (Washington, DC: Institute for Women's Policy Research, 2004).

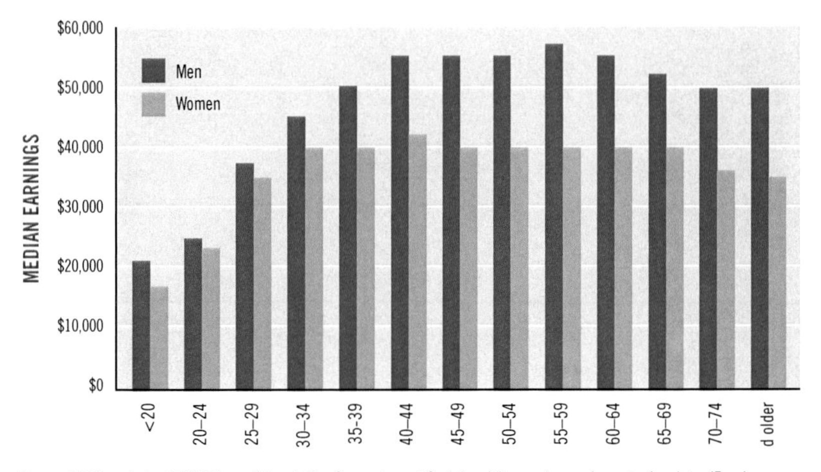

Source: IWPR analysis of 2014 Current Population Survey Annual Social and Economic supplement microdata. (Earnings reported for 2013.) U.S. Census Bureau, "Current Population Survey Annual Social and Economic Supplement."

Figure 2. Median Annual Earnings for Full-time, Year-round Workers by Sex and Age, 2013

for full-time, year-round work continue to grow to age 59. An Institute for Women's Policy Research analysis found that women born in the late 1950s who worked full-time, year-round lost more than $500,000 compared with the earnings of men by age 59.[19]

As we have seen in the discussion of young women, having a job is important, but the quality of the job is often more critical for the wealth building that can make for financial security in the older years.[20] Does the job provide wage gains with seniority on the job, a pension or contributions to retirement accounts, stock options, health insurance, tuition assistance or student loan forgiveness, paid sick days, help with child care and out-of-pocket health care costs, paid sick days, and paid family leave to care for an aging spouse or parent? While the majority of older women who worked full-time likely received basic benefits like health insurance and paid sick days through much of their working lives, many of today's older women, especially those who worked part-time, have had little access to the type of employment-related benefits that would have enabled them to accumulate as much wealth as men their age have been able to do.

19 Hess et al., "Status of Women in the States."

20 Chang, *Shortchanged*.

Like younger women, older women who are also providing caregiving do so at the detriment to their lifetime earnings and retirement savings. According to a 2013 AARP survey of people aged 45 to 74, women are three times more likely than men to quit their jobs due to caregiving.[21] MetLife estimates those who quit will lose nearly $325,000 in earnings and benefits compared with those who are able to continue working.[22]

Although defined-contribution plans tend to be better than defined-benefit plans at accommodating workers who move from job to job or in and out of the labor force, they also leave workers with more uncertainty about their future income and a decreased likelihood of receiving benefits from a former, current, or deceased spouse. This is a feature especially important to women who have ever been married, who have less lifetime earnings but live longer than men on average. Policies that allow automatic enrollment encourage workers to participate in defined-contribution plans since workers have to opt out in order not to participate, but still only 48 percent of the workforce participates in any retirement plan at work. Participation rates are particularly low for part-time workers (19 percent), those in the bottom 25 percent of earnings (18 percent), those working in service occupations (21 percent), and those working in the leisure and hospitality industry (12 percent)—all areas in which women are overrepresented.[23]

Women who work full-time participate in employer-provided retirement plans at a slightly higher rate than male full-time workers (50.6 percent for women versus 46.5 percent for men in 2013).[24] Nevertheless, because of lower earnings and more years in part-time work, when they may not have been eligible to participate, women's accumulations in retirement accounts or their anticipated pension benefits are generally much smaller than men's. Also, when women cash out their pension contributions when they change jobs, they are less likely than men to invest those funds and

21 Rebecca Perron, "Staying Ahead of the Curve 2013: The AARP Work and Career Study." (Washington, DC: AARP, 2014).

22 MetLife, "The MetLife Study of Caregiving Costs to Working Caregivers: Double Jeopardy for Baby Boomers Caring for Their Parents." (Westport, CT: MetLife, 2011).

23 U.S. Department of Labor, "National Compensation Survey" (Washington, DC: Bureau of Labor Statistics, 2014).

24 IWPR analysis of 2014 Current Population Survey Annual Social and Economic supplement microdata, (Participation rate reported for 2013).

more likely to use them to pay for daily expenses.[25] Policy attention must be turned toward new forms of pensions, such as those that simplify small business participation in pension plans. The federal *my*RA, described by Regis Mulot in this volume, is a promising federal initiative.

Even more important would be expansion of Social Security, this country's one truly universal retirement plan. In 2012, women's median Social Security benefits were $12,520 annually, compared with men's of $16,398.[26] Expanding Social Security benefits in ways that especially help women would address their lower benefits. A glaring hole in Social Security is that it fails to acknowledge women's contributions to the economy in the form of caring labor. Providing women with added earnings credits during caregiving years, although they might not have worked for pay then, would help raise women's retirement incomes, just as it does in most of the other Organisation for Economic Co-operation and Development (OECD) countries that already have such benefits. Social Security provides many family benefits that are very valuable to women, such as benefits from husbands' work records, which are often higher than women's own worker benefits. This family-friendliness could be enhanced for married women who have worked most of their lives by raising their benefits if their husbands predecease them. Many public interest groups are calling for increases in Social Security benefits, both those of a more universal nature and those targeted at especially vulnerable populations, including women.[27] Several candidates in the current presidential primary season are also exploring ways to increase benefits, as well as ways to pay for those increased benefits. According to a survey from the National Academy of Social Insurance, three-quarters of Americans think an increase in benefits should be considered, and most

---

25 Lois Shaw and Catherine Hill, "The Gender Gap in Pension Coverage: What Does the Future Hold?" (Washington, DC: Institute for Women's Policy Research, 2002).

26 Social Security Administration, *Fact Sheet: Social Security Is Important to Women.*

27 Maya Rockeymoore and Meizhu Lui, "Plan for a New Future: The Impact of Social Security Reform on People of Color." (Washington, DC: Commission to Modernize Social Security, 2011); Carroll L. Estes, Terry O'Neill, and Heidi Hartmann, "Breaking the Social Security Glass Ceiling: A Proposal to Modernize Women's Benefits." (Washington, DC: National Committee to Preserve Social Security and Medicare Foundation, 2012); National Council of Women's Organizations and Center for Community Change, "Expanding Social Security Benefits for Financially Vulnerable Populations." (Washington, DC: Center for Community Change, 2013).

Americans support the elimination of the cap on taxable earnings, now $118,500.[28]

CONCLUSION

The undervaluation of caring work and women's disproportionate responsibility for it is a central factor affecting women's lower incomes and smaller net worth. The vast majority of both paid and unpaid care workers in the home, as well of care recipients, are women. This caring labor is essential for society, but better ways of relieving women's excess responsibility for it are desperately needed if we want to see greater equity in the wealth attained by men and women and more fulfilling lives for all genders. As Amartya Sen noted in his 1999 book, *Development as Freedom*, we must address the specific barriers women face due to social, institutional, and environmental factors, such as the commonly accepted division of labor between women and men and the many forms of discrimination against women.

If our society hopes to equalize wealth between women and men, two preconditions are necessary. First, women and men must have equal lifetime earnings, and, second, women must not bear the lion's share of the burden of the uncompensated and poorly compensated care work required by our society. Those who do caring labor must be fully compensated through paid leaves, child allowances, and ample subsidies for child care and elder care. The United States is the only economically advanced country in the world that does not have a system of national paid maternity leave; many other well-off countries also provide parental (or caring) leaves to both mothers and fathers. Paid family leave is a vital policy that would keep young adults from falling into financial insecurity when they form families and go a long way toward helping them build a life of financial security for themselves and their children.

Improving the treatment of caring labor would also improve women's financial security during their retirement years. For example, if access to employer-provided retirement plans were increased for part-time workers, then women who work part-time for family care reasons would have access to easier forms of retirement savings. If child care and elder care

28 Jasmine V. Tucker, Virginia P. Reno, and Thomas N. Bethell, "Strengthening Social Security: What Do Americans Want?" (Washington, DC: National Academy of Social Insurance, 2013).

assistance were increased, fewer adult caregivers would have to work part-time; full-time work would not only likely increase their eligibility to participate in employer-provided retirement plans, but also increase their earnings, contributions, and benefits accordingly. Adding a caregiving credit in Social Security would also increase retirement income for women and men who work less or leave the labor market entirely for a period of years in order to provide care to a family member.

From a base of equal lifetime incomes, no discrimination against women, and equalized and fully compensated caregiving burdens, it should be easier to encourage women to build wealth in the same ways as men or to improve upon men's record. Indeed, as we have seen, among full-time workers, women are now participating in employer-offered pension/savings plans at a slightly higher proportion than men. Women seem to have a higher propensity to save, all else equal, perhaps in preparation for an anticipated longer retirement.

In these and other ways, the United States could ensure that women have a more equal chance to build wealth and enjoy an increase in their well-being and financial security. Women's increased well-being would also give their children a better start in life and increase their financial stability throughout childhood, helping them launch more successfully into adulthood. Building wealth for women is truly a two-generation strategy.

■ ■ ■

HEIDI I. HARTMANN *is the president of the Washington-based Institute for Women's Policy Research (IWPR), a scientific research organization that she founded in 1987 to meet the need for women-centered, policy-oriented research. She is an economist with a B.A. from Swarthmore College and M. Phil and Ph.D. degrees from Yale University, all in economics. Hartmann is also a research professor at The George Washington University and a MacArthur Fellow.*

FROM IMPULSE CONTROL TO INTEREST RATES
Building Financial Capability in Children and Youth

Elizabeth Odders-White and Charles Kalish
University of Wisconsin–Madison

Children are fantastic learners. They master spoken language in just a couple of years. They gain control of their bodies and figure out how to navigate the physical environment. Children also learn to negotiate, quarrel, joke, and whine all in the first few years of their lives. However, we rarely let young children get anywhere near money.

Most of us do not see children as competent financial actors until they are well into their teens, if then. Why is this? What is so hard about learning to deal with money and finances? Perhaps most importantly, what do we know about how to help children develop the same competence with finances that they show in so many other areas of their lives? This essay reviews an emerging body of research on how childhood experiences contribute to financial well-being in adulthood.

Financial well-being is a multifaceted concept that transcends both the more traditional understanding of financial literacy and the broader notion of financial capability. According to the Consumer Financial Protection Bureau, *financial well-being* entails having control over one's finances, the capacity to absorb financial shocks, the ability to meet financial goals, and the financial freedom to make choices that allow one to enjoy life.

Certainly as Ray Boshara points out in this volume, factors beyond an individual's control, such as the quality of the neighborhood school, the availability of good jobs, and family wealth, play a significant role in financial outcomes. However, achieving and maintaining financial well-being also depends on a wide range of skills, attitudes, and other personal attributes. That is, someone could have all the advantages of a good school, access to good jobs, and other pluses, but without the necessary skills, financial well-being is unlikely. These internal factors—many of which begin to develop early in life—interact with external factors in complex ways and, together, they drive financial well-being.

So what are the specific internal factors that empower some children to grow into financially capable and satisfied adults while others falter? To answer this question, we reviewed research in developmental psychology, consumer finance, and education.[1] Our review provided insights into both *how* and *when* youth develop the key drivers of adulthood financial well-being.

Early precursors to financial well-being can be grouped into three categories:

- Executive function development: Building the set of cognitive abilities that underlies skills like impulse control and planning; these are particularly critical for very young children ages 3–5.
- Financial socialization: Acquiring financial values, norms, and attitudes; this is key for children ages 6–12.
- Financial knowledge and experience: Establishing skills in navigating financial choices; this is vital for adolescents and young adults ages 13–21.

FRAMING OUR THINKING

In *Thinking Fast and Slow,* Daniel Kahneman shows that we as humans tend to process information and make decisions in two ways: automatically (System 1) and deliberately, based on learned facts (System 2). Each of these approaches is a potential target of interventions. Formal education tends to target System 2, the explicit facts and conscious problem-solving strategies that people employ. System 1 intuitions develop over time as people gain experience. In addition, we know that executive

1 This essay is an adaption of a previously published article by the authors and others entitled, "Foundations of Financial Well-Being: Insights into the Role of Executive Function, Financial Socialization, and Experience-Based Learning in Childhood and Youth," *Journal of Consumer Affairs* 49 (1) (2015): 13–38.

function improves into adulthood, partially driven by neural maturation, but also influenced by experience and practice.

System 1: Automatic and Effortless

System 1 is often characterized by common sense, intuition, rules of thumb, or gut feelings. Psychologists refer to these processes as *heuristics*. Acting on heuristics takes little thought. For example, if faced with two items of the same price, a common heuristic would be to choose the item that offered a larger quantity, thereby getting more "bang for the buck." Buying the same products that most other people are buying is another heuristic. There is significant debate about exactly which heuristics people use and whether they are generally helpful or detrimental.

We tend to associate relying on heuristics with children and immaturity; with age comes more reflection. However, a very influential theory of expertise holds that what really makes someone skilled in a domain is having a good set of heuristics. Adults use heuristics and, critically, we seem to be able to improve our System 1 thinking. Improvement does not tend to happen as a result of formal lessons. Rather, heuristics develop in practice: learning by doing. The common saying that it takes 10,000 hours of practice to become an expert reflects the fact that heuristics are built up with experience, not communicated through instruction.

System 2: Facts and Procedures

System 2 is characterized by explicit knowledge—the facts and procedures people use to solve difficult or unfamiliar problems. In the context of financial well-being, an example would be recalling the formula for compound interest and using it to calculate the return on an investment. Doing an inventory of the pantry, making a list, and planning the shopping trip are also System 2 processes. Most educational interventions, including those related to financial literacy, focus on System 2. We often think of System 2 facts and procedures as being complex and formal and, therefore, more appropriate for older children and adults. However, the characteristic feature of System 2 is not that it is complex and abstract, but rather that it requires deliberate attention and effort. Therefore, even young children can begin to develop System 2 processes.

Regulating Systems: The Role of Executive Function

Control or executive processes determine whether we use System 1 or System 2 in a given situation. Because System 1 is automatic and effortless, it tends to guide our behavior in most circumstances. System 2 requires being careful and paying attention; it takes mental effort. Executive function thus plays the critical role of allowing individuals to switch between the two systems. Resisting a strong temptation, sticking with a plan, or noticing when things aren't working and trying something else are classic executive function processes. Executive function is often associated with System 2, but it is also used to allow System 1 to take control—to turn off the deliberation in System 2.

Our analysis of the development of financial well-being follows a three-part model. Children develop executive function to regulate the way they think and act in financial contexts; they develop habits, attitudes, and norms about financial matters; and they develop formal financial strategies and knowledge. We discuss each of these in detail below.

AGES 3–5: EXECUTIVE FUNCTION AS A BUILDING BLOCK FOR FINANCIAL WELL-BEING

Strong executive function supports positive financial behaviors, including developing a budget, resisting temptation, and delaying gratification, all of which promote financial well-being in adulthood. Executive function develops rapidly during the first five years of life, with genetics, environment, and experience all influencing its trajectory. A child's basic temperament also plays an important role. Some children are more impulsive than others from a very young age. Still, research demonstrates that executive function is a "muscle" that can be strengthened through training and practice. Even more promising, evidence suggests that children with the weakest executive function skills benefit the most from these experiences.[2]

But will strengthening executive function in children make a difference when they are adults? Existing research suggests the answer is yes. One study found that self-control between the ages of 3 and 11 is associated with future savings and investment behavior, home and retirement account ownership, and self-reported money and credit management success (even

---

2 Adele Diamond, "Executive Functions," *Annual Review of Psychology* 64 (1) (2013): 135–68.

after accounting for IQ and socioeconomic status).[3] Early development of executive function skills also facilitates learning more generally, empowering children to develop higher-level financial abilities, such as numeracy and math.

So how can we improve children's executive function skills? Early evidence suggests that approaches that build children's self-efficacy can help. For example, children who are given responsibility for planning, executing, and assessing their own learning have better financial, social, and emotional outcomes in early adulthood.[4] Interventions that become progressively more challenging as children gain skills or mature appear to be most successful.[5] Another important consideration is providing children with frequent opportunities to practice these skills in multiple contexts.

Opportunities to combine executive function and basic financial skills training are particularly intriguing. Programs can develop children's inhibitory control, working memory, and saving skills in concert by teaching strategies for keeping their minds focused on long-term savings goals when faced with an immediate temptation (e.g., asking them to actively visualize the bicycle they are saving for whenever they are tempted by the candy aisle near a checkout counter).[6] Interventions that combine executive function and basic financial skills training may represent an ideal approach to building the early foundations of financial well-being.

AGES 6–12: FINANCIAL SOCIALIZATION

Financial socialization, the process through which individuals develop values and norms about money, begins early. Most children have knowledge and attitudes about their role as consumers before they even start school. As young children enter elementary school, opportunities for true financial socialization emerge.

---

3 Terrie E. Moffitt et al., "A Gradient of Childhood Self-Control Predicts Health, Wealth, and Public Safety," *Proceedings of the National Academy of Sciences* 108 (7) (2011): 2693–98.

4 Lawrence J. Schweinhart and David P. Weikart, "Why Curriculum Matters in Early Childhood Education," *Educational Leadership* 55 (6) (1998): 57–60.

5 Diamond, "Executive Functions."

6 Karen Holden et al., "Financial Literacy Programs Targeted on Pre-School Children: Development and Evaluation" (Madison, WI: Credit Union National Association, 2009).

Financial socialization is not simply learning how to successfully manage economic transactions. It encompasses the development of attitudes, values, and standards that will ultimately either support or hinder financial well-being.[7] For example, healthy attitudes about saving and some level of frugality are necessary for skillful money management. Positive views on budgeting support financial goal-setting and planning, and tempered materialism likely leads to an ability to live within one's means.

Financial socialization happens through many different channels, including school, media, and peers, but it is parents—defined broadly as adults who play a primary role in the raising of children—who exert a particularly strong influence. So what should parents, teachers, and practitioners do to promote positive financial socialization? Not surprisingly, financial socialization generally occurs implicitly (e.g., by modeling behavior) rather than explicitly (via direct instruction). Children become socialized by watching or interacting with their parents in consumer situations, for example. Implicit approaches can be especially important with younger children, who may model financial behaviors they do not understand purely to be more "grown up" or to please their parents.

Explicit instruction also matters, and combining both approaches is important. For example, receiving an allowance as a child does not change savings behaviors as an adult unless it is combined with parental oversight as to how the money is spent and parental teaching about budgeting and the necessity of saving.[8] Another example of explicit financial socialization is providing opportunities for children to manage a savings account, which typically requires parental involvement and can contribute to a child's ability to understand concepts related to saving and investment. Research shows that children whose parents monitored their spending were more likely to perceive themselves as good money managers,[9] and children who discussed financial matters with and learned

7 Sharon M Danes, "Evaluation of the NEFE High School Financial Planning Program® 2003–2004" (Denver: National Endowment for Financial Education, 2004).

8 Alessandro Bucciol and Marcella Veronesi, *Teaching Children to Save and Lifetime Savings: What Is the Best Strategy?* SSRN Scholarly Paper ID 2275929 (Rochester, NY: Social Science Research Network, 2013).

9 Jinhee Kim and Swarn Chatterjee, "Childhood Financial Socialization and Young Adults' Financial Management," *Journal of Financial Counseling and Planning* 24 (1) (2013): 62.

money management from their parents reported healthier financial attitudes when they were college students.[10]

Importantly, research suggests that the financial attitudes children acquire impact their behavior later in life. For example, being raised in a financially prudent household as a child has been linked to engaging in fewer negative financial behaviors such as credit card misuse as a young adult.[11] Similarly, children whose parents oversaw their spending were more likely to own bonds, CDs, or other financial assets as young adults.

Children's attitudes also work in conjunction with executive function. For example, a child who has a strong capacity for self-control may not actually display control if he or she does not think it is important. Similarly, to develop future orientation, children require both the *ability* to focus on the future (executive function skills) and the *motivation* to do so (an attitude that values planning ahead).

Finally, socioeconomic factors may shape parents' socialization practices. For example, if parents lack financial knowledge or experience, they may worry that they cannot effectively teach or model behaviors for their children and could even teach or model detrimental financial behaviors.[12] Children from low-income families may miss out on some important financial socialization experiences because their parents are less likely to participate in the financial system.[13] On the other hand, children growing up with limited means might receive more information than those growing up comfortably buffered from financial worries.

Socialization may best be understood as a matter of fit. The attitudes, values, and norms developed as a child might fit well with the demands of some environments, but serve poorly in other contexts. Because financial

---

10 Bryce L. Jorgensen and Jyoti Savla, "Financial Literacy of Young Adults: The Importance of Parental Socialization," *Family Relations* 59 (4) (2010): 465–78.

11 Jeffery Hibbert, Ivan Beutler, and Todd Martin, "Financial Prudence and Next Generation Financial Strain," *Journal of Financial Counseling and Planning* 15 (2) (2004): 51–59.

12 Margaret S. Sherraden, "Building Blocks of Financial Capability." In *Financial Capability and Asset Building: Research, Education, Policy, and Practice*, edited by Julie. M. Birkenmaier, Margaret. S. Sherraden, and Jami C. Curley. (New York & Oxford: Oxford University Press, 2013).

13 Julia Loumidis and Sue Middleton, "A Cycle of Disadvantage: Financial Exclusion in Early Childhood" (London, UK: Financial Services Authority, 2000).

socialization can take many forms, interventions that adopt a strength-based approach that leverages parents' existing skills are likely to be fruitful. All parents have some abilities to support their children's financial socialization. The challenge for interventions is building on these strengths and expanding children's opportunities.

AGES 13–21: BUILDING FINANCIAL KNOWLEDGE AND EXPERIENCE

As teens, youth become increasingly independent and often begin to control more financial resources. Many will get their first jobs, credit cards, and loans. These new opportunities allow youth to develop the knowledge and skills that underlie financial decision-making in adulthood. Ideally, executive function maturation has laid the cognitive foundation for these skills, and the financial socialization process has established the financial attitudes that encourage these positive behaviors. Furthermore, research suggests that individuals are particularly receptive to financial education when it is relevant and delivered immediately before they face a financial decision.[14] Consequently, the increasing financial independence associated with adolescence and young adulthood presents many valuable opportunities for learning.

As in earlier stages, families can play an important role in helping teens develop conscious (System 2) financial decision-making skills. Some parents begin to involve their children in family finances or open savings or checking accounts for their children, providing guided practice using these accounts. Alternatively, some schools deliver financial education programs, but the evidence regarding the efficacy of these school-based initiatives is mixed. While many studies report an association between participation in financial education and improved financial knowledge, the effects tend to be modest and long-term knowledge retention is usually untested.

Of course, the primary objective of financial education is not to increase knowledge but to promote positive financial behaviors. The apparent benefits of actively using financial services and products imply that experiential learning could offer an effective means of promoting financial well-being. Opportunities for reflection are important to the success of

---

14 Daniel Fernandes, John G. Lynch, Jr., and Richard G. Netemeyer, "Financial Literacy, Financial Education, and Downstream Financial Behaviors," *Management Science* 60 (8) (2014): 1861–83.

experiential programs because the ability to process the experience and to learn from both good and bad choices is critical.[15] Hands-on experiences are also likely to promote feelings of self-efficacy, or confidence in one's ability to manage personal finances. Some researchers recommend that interventions focus not on teaching specific financial facts, but on imparting an understanding of how to acquire the information needed for financial decisions.[16]

The skills that adolescents and young adults acquire by managing their resources and other financial decisions helps to develop the unconscious heuristics that are an important complement to hands-on skills. Repeated practice helps individuals discern when their intuition may fail them and where more conscious, research-based decisions are needed. Habits, as opposed to knowledge, formed during youth are highly influential for adult behavior, and interventions that promote System 1 financial decision-making could have a lasting impact. As such, school-based or other financial curricula that provide opportunities to practice and reinforce positive financial decisions can help young people develop effective habits and heuristics. For example, simulated classroom economies in which students receive paychecks and pay rent offer a natural context in which to build positive habits through repeated cycles of practice and reflection.

CONCLUSION

Although most children and youth do not oversee their household's finances, they are continually apprenticing, acquiring the knowledge, habits, attitudes, and personality traits that will play an instrumental role in their own financial well-being later in life. To ensure more financial well-being in the future, we propose the following strategies:

- Help 3–5-year-olds develop the executive function that undergirds many of the drivers of financial well-being in adulthood, including future orientation, the ability to delay gratification, and the ability to set goals.

- Encourage parents and other adults to guide 6–12-year-olds in learning basic financial skills and establishing healthy financial attitudes and habits.

---

15 For an application to economics education, see James D. Laney, "Experiential Versus Experience-Based Learning and Instruction," *Journal of Educational Research* 86 (4) (1993): 228–36.

16 Fernandes et al., "Financial Literacy."

- Provide hands-on opportunities for 13–21-year-olds to learn financial research skills and heuristics for money management.

Parents and caregivers should be encouraged not only to give their children access to resources to make spending and saving decisions, but to talk with their children about those decisions. Likewise, parents and caregivers could encourage their children to set savings goals and develop other positive financial habits. At school, simple budgeting exercises, role-playing, or computer simulations can help to improve financial decision-making, as do activities that improve critical thinking and research skills. In all cases, research suggests that the key is providing opportunities for practice that are developmentally appropriate and include time for reflection. Through repeated practice that is supported by parents or other adults, children can develop positive financial habits related to skillful money management, goal-setting, and financial research. They can also acquire a crucial sense of self-efficacy, another driver of financial well-being in adulthood.

■ ■ ■

ELIZABETH ODDERS-WHITE *is the Kuechenmeister Bascom professor of business and senior associate dean for academic programs at the Wisconsin School of Business at the University of Wisconsin–Madison. She is also an affiliate of the UW-Madison Center for Financial Security. Her long-standing interest in the development of financial capability among youth has grown to become the primary focus of her research. Odders-White holds a PhD in finance from Northwestern University, a bachelor of science in applied mathematics, and a bachelor of fine arts in vocal performance, both from Tulane University.*

■ ■ ■

CHARLES KALISH *received his PhD in developmental psychology from the University of Michigan in 1993. He has been on the faculty in the Department of Educational Psychology at the University of Wisconsin–Madison since 1993. His research focuses on the development of inductive inference and causal reasoning: How do children predict the future and learn from experience? This work asks how children acquire the set of commonsense beliefs that characterize adult thinking. His research has been supported by research grants from the National Institutes of Health, the National Science Foundation, the Spencer Foundation, and the Institute for Education Sciences. He has consulted with the Credit Union National Association on programs and policies for youth financial education.*

THE UPSIDE OF AGING
Maximizing Wisdom in Financial Decision Making

Ted Beck
National Endowment for Financial Education

Imagine you are at a restaurant with your parents. Your father, as always, handles the bill, but you notice it is taking longer than usual for him to sign the credit card slip. A quick peek at the check reveals that he has drastically undertipped (and it's not just that he is being cheap). Your father has accurately tipped many times before, but this time, he failed to calculate a simple percentage and made an unintentional financial error. Once his back is turned, you quickly drop some cash on the table, but you leave wondering whether there are bigger financial mishaps waiting to happen.

It can be unsettling when you first recognize that a family member is having difficulty with financial tasks where once there was none. But this isn't an isolated occurrence. In just 15 years, one in five Americans will be age 65 or over, and there are currently more Americans over 65 than the entire population of Canada. This demographic shift is already in motion and as we consider the financial health of our nation, it is in our best interest to understand and address the specific financial challenges facing older adults. But what characterizes normal aging, how do inevitable changes in an aging person's cognitive skills affect financial decisions, and most important, what can we do about it?

AGING AND COGNITIVE FUNCTION

As we age, the speed at which we generate, transform, and manipulate new information decreases. This type of mental processing is called *fluid intelligence*, and research has shown that even the healthiest among us has less fluid intelligence as we age.[1] But that is only part of the story. *Crystallized intelligence*—the accumulation of knowledge and experience—increases until about age 60, when it plateaus until about age 80, and eventually drops off. Although fluid intelligence might enable you to more quickly calculate a tip on the fly, your father's crystallized intelligence might help him outperform you when analyzing stock performance and market trends.

There is a lengthy sweet spot where older adults perform comparably to younger adults using different amounts of both intelligences. This is good news because Americans over 65 collectively manage 43 percent of household wealth and 47 percent of stocks and mutual funds.[2] With the increasing transfer of complex financial and health care decisions (such as allocating retirement savings in defined contribution plans) to individuals, it is now more important than ever that financial education, products, and services be intentionally designed to limit the strain of normal cognitive decline and play to older people's strengths—namely that the longer you live, the more you know.

Early Warning Signs of Financial Decline

1. Slowness in completing financial tasks
2. Missing key details in financial documents
3. Problems with everyday arithmetic
4. Decreased understanding of financial concepts
5. Trouble identifying risks in investment opportunities

BREAKING THROUGH THE BARRIER OF DENIAL

As a society we cannot afford to delay the conversation about how normal aging affects financial decision making, especially given a tendency for individuals to develop blind spots to their own cognitive decline. "No one thinks they will end up in a nursing home, and everyone thinks they are

---

1 National Endowment for Financial Education, "Cognitive Capabilities, Decision-Making Ability and Financial Outcomes Across the Lifespan." (New York: Columbia University, 2014).

2 Ye Li et al., "Sound Credit Scores and Financial Decisions Despite Cognitive Aging." *Proceedings of the National Academy of Sciences*, 112 (1) (2015): 65–69.

going to die peacefully in their sleep," says Merrell Bailey, an Orlando-based attorney who serves on our board of trustees at the National Endowment for Financial Education (NEFE). As a specialist in estate planning, Bailey sees families facing end-of-life challenges every day. She says there are three common misconceptions among her clients:

- People think they will be healthier than they will be.
- They think they have more money than they do.
- They think their families will step up and help when needed.

Regardless of one's physical condition, everyone will experience health declines by age 80. A 2014 Consumer Reports survey found that one in four people over age 80 has a hard time just getting out of a chair, and more than one-half report having four or more chronic health conditions.[3] The second misconception is troubling, given the obvious consequences of having a generation of older Americans run out of money when they no longer can work. Although the third misconception potentially presents the biggest challenge, it also is the best opportunity to avert worst-case scenarios.

Many aging adults put off important conversations about their finances despite the desire for their family members to take charge when they become unable. But finding ways to engage family members early on is one of the most significant ways to ensure the overall financial health of aging adults. Not having a plan is a plan. It is important to respect the older adult's independence, emphasizing that discussing contingencies and laying out clear accountabilities is not handing over the keys. It simply enables the family to support the older adult in ways that meet everyone's needs.

THE FINANCIAL CAPABILITY TRIPOD

According to NEFE-funded research from Columbia University, increased financial knowledge positively relates to real-world financial behaviors and can help offset the effects of declining fluid intelligence. But knowledge alone is insufficient to strengthen and secure the financial health of older Americans. The "financial capability tripod" recognizes that the financial challenges facing older adults are complex and that our response

3 Consumer Reports, "Healthy Aging into your 80s and Beyond."

should be similarly multifaceted, encompassing some aspect of all three legs of the tripod. There is no evidence that general crystallized intelligence leads to better financial decision making; just because a person has lived longer does not inherently mean that he or she makes better financial decisions. Effective financial literacy requires understanding financial products, not just experiencing them.

The three legs of the tripod are below.

Leg 1: Financial Education Must Be Delivered Frequently and Regularly through All Stages of Life.

Financial knowledge should be gained through real-world experience, and relevant information should be presented with enough time to guide and inform decision making. Passive, one-off financial education is not as effective as targeted jolts of financial education offered within the context that a person needs it. For example, a person might not need to understand the ins and outs of 401(k) plans until they are electing workplace benefits.

Leg 2: Consumer Protection Must Be Built into Financial Systems and Products, Voluntarily and through Regulation.

With their declining fluid intelligence, seniors might make decisions in the moment, such as signing a contract, that on reflection with their crystallized intelligence are bad decisions. Consumer protections with cooling-off periods provide aging adults with the time they need for further reflection and analysis, and they help mitigate any pressure on older adults' diminished fluid intelligence when they are hustled into signing something quickly. For example, to help safeguard funds prepaid for funerals, Minnesota law requires a funeral director or cemetery operator to place all prepaid funds in a trust account in a bank or other financial institution and allows the customer to request a full refund at any time.

Seniors are also more vulnerable to fraud and scams. We need to help seniors protect themselves, but we must punish bad actors in the industry and diligently prevent abusive practices. This must be carried out by appropriate state authorities and is a priority for regulatory and judicial agencies such as the Consumer Financial Protection Bureau and the Financial Industry Regulatory Authority.

Finally, financial institutions and advisors should use familiar financial terminology so as not to confuse older adults (and to help them tap into their crystallized intelligence). It might seem obvious, but financial institutions can also help by presenting information clearly and in large, legible print.

Leg 3: Smart Defaults Must Be Implemented to Help Consumers Easily Do What They Need to Do.

One of the best ways we can help aging adults is to anticipate what they want to do and help them do it (or at least help them avoid damaging mistakes) by building in "nudges" and defaults. For example, going back to the opening example, many restaurants now include suggested tip amounts on the bill. Automating monthly bill pay is another way to limit potential mistakes and to ensure bills are paid on time, in the proper amounts, to the right creditors.

EMPOWERED FINANCIAL DECISION MAKING (AT ANY AGE)

Empowered financial decision making doesn't just happen. People make the best financial choices when they understand the underlying financial concepts, possess the relevant competencies to weigh the risks and rewards of disparate options, and have the confidence to choose the right option for them on the basis of their lifestyles and values. At the same time, we can prepare younger generations both to assist their elders and fare well as they age by helping them build their own experiential financial knowledge and store of crystallized financial intelligence.

■ ■ ■

__TED BECK__ is the president and CEO of the National Endowment for Financial Education (NEFE), the leading private nonprofit national foundation dedicated to inspiring empowered financial decision making for individuals and families through every stage of life. He was appointed in March of 2014 by President Barack Obama to serve on the President's Advisory Council on Financial Capability for Young Americans. He also serves on the Federal Deposit Insurance Corporation (FDIC) Advisory Committee on Economic Inclusion and as chair of the board of the national Jump$tart Coalition for Personal Financial Literacy.

NEFE 5@50: 5 FINANCIAL STEPS TO TAKE IN YOUR 50s

1 **Come to agreement with your significant other and/or trusted allies or family members.** If you have a spouse or partner, don't assume that you are on the same page. Make sure that there is not only awareness, but agreement about the current and future handling of your money, as well as about who will step in when necessary. If you do not have a significant other, you still have to own your plan and make sure your wishes are known and understood by a trusted ally or family member.

2 **Get your financial house in order.** Consolidate financial resources (bank accounts, retirement assets, investments) and set up automatic payments for regular bills.

3 **Check your paperwork.** A will is important, but a durable power of attorney is perhaps the most important document to have in order. If you become incapacitated without one, often the only way to handle your affairs is to have you named a ward of the court with a court-appointed guardian. And if you designated financial power of attorney in one state, but subsequently moved to another, double check that it is still valid in your new state of residence.

4 **Assign roles.** Communicate clearly within the family who will be responsible for what. Consider delegating financial, medical and social roles to different people based on their strengths. Set a regular time to check in. Continually assess whether retirement and other investment accounts are at the appropriate risk levels and examine credit reports for errors or potential fraud. Also use this time to get a gut check from your inner circle on any offers or sales pitches you might be receiving. One of the early warning signs of financial cognitive decline in normal adults is an overemphasis on potential benefits and a diminished awareness of risk.

5 **Seek professional assistance.** Assemble a trusted team that might include your lawyer, financial professional and, later, a geriatric care manager—particularly if you don't have family members willing or able to step in.

4

WHAT TO DO NEXT

Strengthening the Financial Future

WHAT IT'S WORTH
Building Bridges to Financial Health and Well-being

Ellen Seidman

Although each author in this book states it somewhat differently, each points to the same conclusion: household financial health and well-being is the bridge to a better life, a better community, and a better economy. Our challenge is to make that idea intuitive to policymakers in all parts of society—education, health, housing, justice, the financial markets; to the financial services sector in all its manifestations; and to all those who work with and employ ordinary Americans, particularly those of modest means. For, as Federal Reserve Board Chair Janet Yellen reminds us in her foreword, a large share of Americans are extraordinarily financially vulnerable.

Why does household financial health and well-being matter? Most broadly, Jared Bernstein of the Center for Budget and Policy Priorities and former chief economist to Vice President Biden says in this volume, "there is a growing body of research that convincingly links various aspects of financial health to [economic] growth… [T]here are good reasons, backed by some empirical evidence, to believe that financially unhealthy families reduce economic growth... and vice versa." Likewise, former Congressman Phil English and Jeremie Greer of CFED write that "we advocate for an America where financially stable and resilient households are a central building block to the economic vitality of our nation... [policies that promote] family economic stability also lend themselves to a more civil political dialog." Coming at the issue through a health lens, Jason Purnell of Washington University in St. Louis concludes, "the inextricable, often stress-laden link between financial well-being and physical and mental health must become the centerpiece of public understanding and public policy. Both our economic health as a nation and the very lives of the American people depend on it."

Experience at the ground level links financial health and well-being to success in multiple areas. Rita Landgraf, cabinet secretary of the Delaware Department of Health and Social Services, puts it this way: "financial well-being addresses many of the root causes of poor health, including creating a sense of control over one's circumstances and future. Financial empowerment builds our economic security, improves our quality of life, promotes health and well-being and fosters self-sufficiency." And Regina Stanback Stroud of Skyline College, a Bay Area community college, says "strategies to address financial well-being are not just a nice idea; they are an essential component of helping students reach their academic goals." Reflecting on the criminal justice system, Vivian Nixon of College and Community Fellowship and Susan Sturm of Columbia Law School note that "about 60 percent of intakes into the state and federal prison systems report annual incomes under $12,000," and that "financial well-being, or more important its absence, plays a role in this cycle of... interaction with the criminal justice system."

From the municipal perspective, Louisville Mayor Greg Fischer says, "Our citizens' financial health directly affects the city's ability to reach its fundamental goals related to improving job readiness, education, and the stability of neighborhoods." And Treasury Deputy Secretary Sarah Bloom Raskin completes the circle: "members of financially healthy families are better able to take advantage of educational opportunities, and completing an affordable and high-quality higher education program in turn advances the fundamentals of financial health."

As described by Andrea Levere and Leigh Tivol of CFED, the road to this understanding has been long and winding. It all started with the work of Michael Sherraden, who sets out a future research agenda in this volume. In his seminal 1991 book *Assets and the Poor*, Sherraden established the proposition that when people have assets (wealth), they are more stable along many dimensions.[1] Moreover, assets strengthen the producer (in contrast to the consumer) in all of us, including the poor. Sherraden's work led to the creation of the asset-building field, which generated innovations such as Individual Development Accounts (IDAs), Baby Bonds, and most recently Children's Savings Accounts (CSAs).

---

1 Michael Sheradden, *Assets and the Poor* (Armonk, NY: M.E. Sharpe, 1991).

Even as the asset-building movement was building and innovating, financial services firms (spurred by the Community Reinvestment Act and actions of the federal government such as the creation of the interagency Financial Literacy and Education Commission) and their nonprofit partners were investing heavily in financial education or financial literacy. As Brandee McHale of Citi Foundation notes in her essay, the belief was that if people learned what they could and should do to manage their finances—mainly get a banking account and save before borrowing—they would do so. Unfortunately, as McHale, Levere and Tivol, and Michael Collins of the University of Wisconsin tell us, there is no good evidence that the strategy was effective in changing financial behavior.

In fact, studies late in the 1990s, along with the Federal Reserve's triennial Survey of Consumer Finances and later the FDIC's National Survey of Unbanked and Underbanked Households[2] and the Center for Financial Services Innovation's (CFSI) Underbanked Consumer Study[3] showed that millions of American households remain outside the mainstream financial services system, and millions more who do have accounts at banks or credit unions meet their financial needs through other means. This led to a desire to better understand the context within which people make financial decisions and a focus on "financial capability," the union of knowledge and opportunity to act. "Financial capability" brings together the lessons of behavioral economics about how people make decisions and the asset-building movement's emphasis on having access to the right products and services at the time they are needed. Financial coaching, defined by Collins as "helping people to form goals, take actions and then follow through" to build financial capability and, ultimately, financial health and well-being, is an important part of this strategy.

But understanding and access has not proven to be the full answer. Jennifer Tescher and Rachel Schneider of CFSI note in their essay that often those who seem to have the tools to be financially capable are nevertheless financially insecure and stressed, with highly volatile income and expenses and "spikes and dips" that do not match up. And Ray

2 Susan Burhouse et al., "2013 FDIC National Survey of Unbanked and Underbanked Households," (Washington DC: FDIC, October 2014).

3 Center for Financial Services Innovation, "The CFSI Underbanked Consumer Study Underbanked Consumer Overview and Market Segments Fact Sheet," (Chicago IL: CFSI, June 8, 2008).

Boshara of the Federal Reserve Bank of St. Louis shows just how much race, education, and one's year of birth influence families' financial outcomes. All three essays in the opening section take us beyond assets to the challenges of a family's entire balance sheet (debt as well as assets) and the monthly and yearly variability in household cash flows.[4]

And so we take the next step, asking what are the outcomes we are looking for from asset-building, financial capability, and related work and how do we get them? During the past year, two similar framings of the desired outcomes have taken hold: financial health and financial well-being. In this book, as explained in the introduction, we use the terms interchangeably. According to CFSI, "financial health is achieved when an individual's day-to-day financial system functions well and increases the likelihood of financial resilience and opportunity."[5] The Consumer Financial Protection Bureau (CFPB) defines financial well-being as "a state of being wherein a person can fully meet current and ongoing financial obligations, can feel secure in their financial future, and is able to make choices that allow enjoyment of life."[6] Both terms focus on long-term outcomes, and both recognize that financial health and well-being are not an end state but a continuing life journey, with a definition of success that is in part subjective and is broader than income, credit score, or net assets.

THE CURRENT STATE OF AMERICANS' FINANCIAL HEALTH

Simply put, the state of Americans' financial health is not good. Individual factors such as education and training, experience, personality and age; social factors; the financial system and the economy; and just plain luck, are all at work. Poverty and inequality of both income and wealth are both cause and outcome of the lack of financial health, but they are neither its only cause nor its only consequence.

---

4 See also Karen Dynan, Douglas Elmendorf, and Daniel Sichel, "The Evolution of Household Income Volatility" (Washington, DC: Brookings Institution, 2012); Diana Farrell and Fiona Greig, "Weathering Volatility: Big Data on the Financial Ups and Downs of U.S. Households" (New York: JPMorgan Chase Institute, 2015); Jonathan Morduch and Rachel Schneider, "Spikes and Dips: How Income Uncertainty Affects Households" (New York: U.S. Financial Diaries, 2014).

5 Aliza Gutman et al., "Understanding and Improving Consumer Financial Health in America" (Chicago: Center for Financial Services Innovation, March 2015), p. 1.

6 Consumer Financial Protection Bureau, "Financial Well-Being: The Goal of Financial Education" (Washington, DC: CFPB, January 2015), p. 18.

The Consumer Financial Health Study (CFHS) conducted by CFSI[7] and described by Tescher and Schneider, finds that not only are 57 percent of Americans financially unhealthy, but "26 percent say their finances cause them significant stress, 43 percent struggle to keep up with bill payments and 36 percent are not confident they could come up with $2,000 in the next month if an emergency were to arise." These situations cut across all income groups, but they are especially prevalent among blacks and Hispanics.

How did we get into this situation? Phil Longman's essay describes the long trajectory of intergenerational decline of incomes and wealth in the United States:

Until the present era, despite vast disparities and inequalities across different racial, ethnic, and other demographic groups, most American families enjoyed a rising net worth, both within and across generations.... This pattern has... disappeared, however. The precise tipping point came among people born in 1952. They would become perhaps the first generation in American history to have less real net worth on the threshold of retirement than people born ten years earlier had at the same age. From there, the real net worth of subsequent birth cohorts has generally been stagnant or has declined.

Longman and other authors, such as Martha Kanter of New York University and former undersecretary of education, point to stagnant wages that were well outrun by increases in the cost of health care and education, and accompanied by the demise of the traditional pension system and a decline in the return on contributions to the Social Security system. A changing culture of jobs—including more frequent job changes and the rise of the "gig economy"—have also reduced financial stability. Recent research from the Institute on Assets and Social Policy at Brandeis University also alerts us to the importance of job quality in financial health.[8] And welfare reform, say Reggie Bicha and Keri Batchelder of the Colorado Department of Human Services, in many ways merely offered

---

7 Gutman, "Understanding and Improving Consumer Financial Health."

8 Hannah Thomas et al., "Employment Capital: How Work Builds and Protects Family Wealth and Security" (Waltham, MA: Brandeis University, December 2014). See also Patricia Cohen, "Public-Sector Jobs Vanish, Hitting Blacks Hard," *New York Times*, May 24, 2015, p. A1.

the welfare poor the opportunity to become the working poor, rather than being a road to prosperity through work.

Many of the essays focus attention on the role that race, gender and ethnicity play in financial health. These essays highlight both the fact that households of color and women-headed households have significantly lower incomes and wealth than white and male-headed households and the need to provide far better opportunities to improve the situation. For example, Boshara finds that although the wealth of all ethnic groups took a large hit in the Great Recession, whites and Asians have begun to recover, while blacks and Hispanics have not: their median net worth remains at 1989 levels and is about 90 percent lower than the median wealth of whites (although median incomes are only 40 percent lower).

Noting that the historical pathways to the middle class such as the GI Bill and federally insured homeownership were largely denied to African Americans, Dedrick Asante-Muhammad of the NAACP adds in his essay that the end of legally sanctioned segregation in the 1950s and 1960s was not accompanied by "the economic aid and investment necessary for African American communities to develop wealth." As a result, although poverty among African Americans has declined from nearly 42 percent in 1966 to about 27 percent in 2012, for the past 40 years, African Americans have earned 60 percent of what white Americans earn.

José Quiñonez of Mission Asset Fund, which serves low-income Latino immigrants, says of his clients: "[a]s low-wage and hourly workers, they struggle to make ends meet. Most live day to day, without the benefit of savings, affordable credit, or other financial tools to manage unexpected expenses, much less a life crisis." Eighteen percent of Latinos lack access to basic financial services, and more than one in four is "credit invisible." Lisa Hasegawa and Jane Duong of the National Coalition for Asian Pacific American Community Development reminds us that the Asian American and Pacific Islander (AAPI) community is highly diverse, that poverty is growing faster in that community than in any other ethnic group, and that a high percentage of the population has difficulty paying bills or responding to financial emergencies—and they do not know where to turn for advice.

Elsie Meeks, one of the founders of Lakota Funds on the Pine Ridge Reservation, makes the point that efforts to increase employment in Indian Country have not been accompanied by strategies that build financial capability and a private-sector economy that keeps wealth on the reservation. That 86 percent of Native communities lack a single financial institution, and for 15 percent, the nearest ATM or bank is more than 100 miles away, exacerbates the situation. Heidi Hartmann of the Institute for Women's Policy Research shows the extent to which women face financial challenges. She says that although women have made enormous progress in achieving economic equality, they still earn only 78 percent of what men earn annually and—more alarmingly—women's median wealth is only 32 percent of men's. Ted Beck of the National Endowment for Financial Education reminds us that the ability of even those most capable of successfully managing finances declines with age.

Several of the authors, most notably Angela Glover Blackwell of PolicyLink, former Congressman Rick Lazio, Michael Rubinger of LISC, Paul Weech of NeighborWorks America, Vivian Nixon and Susan Sturm, Asante-Muhammad, and Purnell, relate the current state of Americans' financial health to neighborhood conditions. Purnell picks up on the concept known as "social determinants of health," which emphasizes the importance of environment and neighborhood quality in physical health—connecting it also to financial health.

Glover Blackwell focuses her attention on discrimination and racial inequality. Building on her own story of growing up in a "completely integrated, entirely African American neighborhood in St. Louis" that was quickly challenged by disinvestment as it became a community of color, Glover Blackwell emphasizes the importance of financial health to "communities of opportunity"—"places that have the resources and amenities we all need to thrive." Nixon and Sturm relate the exceptionally high rates of incarceration in some communities to the poverty and paucity of jobs and education in those places—a cycle that is repeated when prisoners are released back into those same neighborhoods without strategies to help them gain financial capability, education, and a job. This focus on the relationship between neighborhood, opportunity and physical, mental, and financial health also runs through much recent research, some of it cited in multiple essays.[9]

Finally, as many of the authors point out, it is impossible to separate the current state of financial health and well-being from the broader economy, including the devastating impact of the Great Recession, and the financial services system. Raj Date, of Fenway Summer and former deputy director of the CFPB, puts it most directly: "Unfortunately, for too many families, both before and during the financial crisis, consumer finance didn't make life better. It actually made life worse." By FDIC estimates, 9.6 million households, disproportionately black, Hispanic, younger and female, do not have bank accounts, and many more also use nonbank financial services. Cathie Mahon of the National Federation of Community Development Credit Unions points out that part of the reason for this may be that even those financial services providers—like community development credit unions—that focus their attention on lower-income and minority households, may be using strategies based on obsolete assumptions, such as the assumption of a steady job with a regular biweekly paycheck.

So, while individual factors are important, taken together our authors point to more systemic issues. As Purnell puts it:

In a nation in which nearly three-quarters of adults worry about money at least some of the time, where income and wealth inequality are at all-time highs, and where the rate of child poverty is among the highest in the developed world, it is fair to ask whether individual effort can be the total answer to what literally ails, and ultimately kills, Americans.

HOW WE CAN MAKE A DIFFERENCE

At its broadest, this book argues that financially healthy Americans are critical to the nation's economic and social well-being, and an essential element in reducing the country's growing wealth inequality. As Tescher

9 See, for example, Raj Chetty et al., "Where is the Land of Opportunity? The Geography of Intergenerational Mobility in the United States," *Quarterly Journal of Economics*, 129 (4) (2014): 1553–1623; Sean Reardon, Lindsay Fox, and Joseph Townsend, "Neighborhood Income Composition by Household Race and Income: 1990–2009," The *ANNALS of the American Academy of Political and Social Science*, 660 (July 2015): 78–97; and Robert D. Putnam, *Our Kids: The American Dream in Crisis* (New York: Simon & Schuster, 2015).

and Schneider point out, we do not yet have agreement on the metrics by which to measure financial health or well-being, but building a common understanding of our goal, from diverse perspectives and experiences, is an important first step.

Many of the essays move from diagnosis to descriptions of current practices that seem to be working to build financial capability and move people toward financial well-being (see, for example, the essays by Landgraf, Nixon and Sturm, Rubinger, Fischer, Quiñonez, Hasegawa and Duong, Barrera and Stroud). Others provide suggestions for future practice (see, for example, Collins, Mahon, Tescher and Schneider, Purnell, Date, Advani, Laura Choi and David Erickson, and McHale). Still others contain recommendations for policy changes. These range from the highly targeted (such as to revise federal tax policy with respect to the Mortgage Interest Deduction—see Lazio and Longman; universal CSAs—see Kanter, Friedman, English and Greer; and helping people make better higher education decisions—see Raskin, Stroud, and Kanter) to broad calls for a National Asset Development Policy (Asante-Muhammad), major changes in income support programs (Bicha and Batchelder, Hartmann), and far more investment in lower-income communities (Lazio, Nixon and Sturm, Glover Blackwell, Weech), and early childhood education (Purnell). The integration and collaboration themes of the first two books in this series—*Investing in What Works for America's Communities*[10] and *What Counts: Harnessing Data for America's Communities*[11]—resonate across all the essays. Choi and Erickson show how financial health and well-being can be the integrating force across disciplines.

Practice Recommendations

Practice recommendations focus on interactions with individuals and families, on governmental and institutional strategies, on financial services delivery and corporate practice in general, on community building, and on research. Among individuals and households, Quiñonez echoes several other essays in urging those working with lower-income, lower-wealth clients to move "away from a model that engages clients as if they are

10 Nancy Andrews et al., *Investing in What Works for America's Communities* (San Francisco CA: Federal Reserve Bank of San Francisco and Low Income Investment Fund, 2012).

11 Naomi Cytron et al., *What Counts: Harnessing Data for America's Communities* (San Francisco CA: Federal Reserve Bank of San Francisco and the Urban Institute, 2014).

broken to one that recognizes and uplifts their strengths." Mission Asset Fund's Hierarchy of Financial Needs does this, using the Lending Circles platform to formalize the informal savings and credit systems already in the community, opening opportunities to build credit scores and enter the financial mainstream. Boshara, Odders-White and Kalish, and Friedman all point to the importance of starting early to teach children, both directly and through practice, the financial knowledge, skills, and intuition they need to be financially healthy adults.

Collins, McHale, Landgraf, and Rubinger all counsel continuing attention to financial coaching, and integrating coaching and financial empowerment strategies within other systems, such as the workplace (Regis Mulot of Staples), workforce development (Rubinger), postsecondary education (Stroud), prisoner reentry (Nixon and Sturm), welfare (Bicha and Batchelder), housing and community development (Weech) or indeed all programs that interact with this population, whether at the municipal (Fischer) or state (Landgraf) level. In particular, Stroud, Nixon and Sturm, Fischer, and Landgraf emphasize that without embedded strategies for building financially healthy individuals and families, other programs—in fields such as health, education, jobs, housing and helping prisoners successfully reenter society—are likely to fail, whether because they fall prey to the stress and lack of hope generated by financial insecurity or simply to the difficulty of managing life on a tight budget. And Elsie Meeks writes that individual wealth-building strategies, such as Individual Development Accounts, were important to helping business-oriented economic development take hold in Indian Country.

In addition to direct work with individuals, governments and institutions can make other changes in practice that can facilitate financial well-being. McHale urges philanthropists to work in partnership, keeping their eye on the ultimate goal: "empowering people to effectively manage their financial lives and to believe they can achieve their American Dream." Bob Friedman, founder of CFED, ends the book with a plea for asset-builders to "link our skills and tools with others... integrating new people and institutions," for people in those other fields to become asset-builders, and "to unleash and harness the voices of the low-income entrepreneurs, homeowners, college students of color, and others who know first-hand the transformative power of financial health and building assets."

Treasury Deputy Secretary Raskin has helped lead the Treasury and other government agencies in providing tools to help prospective students make better choices in the higher education they pursue and in how they pay for it. Noting the complexity of student aid and tax credit programs, Kanter urges us to raise awareness about them, especially among low-income populations. Hasegawa and Duong call for improved data collection systems that will better reveal the significant diversity within the AAPI community. Lazio urges all portions of the housing and housing finance industry to do a better job at helping people make the critical decision whether to own or to rent, using technology well beyond today's online calculators.

In financial services and corporate America more generally there is much to be done. Mahon makes clear that the first job of financial institutions working with lower-income and lower-wealth customers is to build trust. Then, echoing the findings of Tescher and Schneider, Mahon says financial institutions must better match the needs of those customers with flexible or customized underwriting and payment plans that take income volatility into account. Noting that the movement away from branches to online financial services takes away the face-to-face interactions low-income consumers have relied on, Quiñonez challenges the financial services industry to work with nonprofits to restore those critical social relationships. Hasegawa and Duong call on financial institutions to improve language access in bank branches, and to develop and implement lending circles and "other strategies that embrace the multigenerational nature of many AAPI households."

Advani focuses on the opportunities of social entrepreneurs and other double bottom line companies, as well as on business coalitions. The shared value concept suggests businesses can "increase business value by identifying and addressing social problems that intersect with the business." Advani notes that technology creates new opportunities to serve a far broader range consumers profitably, but to do so well, "the ethics and motivations of the management team and especially the founder/owner(s)... become increasingly important." He calls for a business-led coalition to tackle financial insecurity in the U.S.

Barrera, Meeks, Hartmann, and Hasegawa and Duong stress that entrepreneurial business finance is a potentially important source of wealth in lower-income communities, but that it requires financing and support systems that are nurturing, flexible and quick. And, arguing that innovative financial products and services are critical to meeting the challenge of serving consumer financial needs well, Date urges financial services regulators to promote healthy innovation that can enhance consumer well-being by engaging with innovators, putting forth principles that enable innovation to develop under consumer-friendly guidance, and using exception policy to foster positive innovation.

Many of the essays also touch on the essential role of community building in financial health and well-being. Purnell urges those involved with health and with community development to develop far better communications strategies to convince policymakers of the links between community and health. Building on his community focus, Weech urges nonprofits working in the communities to adopt a social enterprise model to increase their sustainability and impact. Choi and Erickson point out that financial health and well-being is often at the root of myriad challenges facing communities and households, and thus can be the organizing principle that helps various sectors align their work. And Hasegawa and Duong provide a wealth of examples about how innovative community-based organizations are integral to building household financial security.

One of the exciting elements of the asset-building movement is that research has been embedded in it from the start. Michael Sherraden and Margaret Sherraden—the field's premier researchers—urge their colleagues to continue this strategy, which directly links research to actionable changes in policy and practice. Researchers should take several important lessons from what has come before: assess impact in the field (not just in theory or the lab); collect and evaluate data that relate to actual financial results; and assess the impact of interventions on multiple dimensions of the well-being of individuals, families, and communities.

Policy Recommendations

Many of the essays call for specific policy changes, especially at the federal level, or broad redirection of federal policy to recognize that poverty is a barrier to success and to refocus both direct and tax expenditures on families and communities in need—especially communities of color. This includes making higher education affordable and attainable (Raskin, Kanter, Glover Blackwell, Stroud), reforming the criminal justice system (Nixon and Sturm, Glover Blackwell), and supporting the ability of workers to retain more of their productive capacity through redirection of trade, tax and antitrust policies (Longman). Hasegawa and Duong remind us that it is essential that Title VI of the Civil Rights Act—prohibiting discrimination on the basis of race, color or national origin in programs receiving federal assistance—be vigorously enforced.

Asante-Muhammad calls for a twenty-first century Freedom Budget, starting with a National Asset Development Policy and including an equity assessment of where federal investments are going; direct federal job creation, as suggested by Demos;[12] and targeting asset development policies to those most in need, as suggested by CFED.[13] Focusing on gender inequality, Hartmann says that "from a base of equal lifetime incomes, no discrimination against women, and equalized and fully compensated caregiving burdens, it should be easier to encourage women to build wealth in the same ways as men or to improve upon men's record."

Building on themes in *What Works* and *What Counts*, Glover Blackwell urges us to "implement policies that simultaneously empower the most vulnerable populations to become financially secure and transform struggling neighborhoods into communities of opportunity." In somewhat different terms, Purnell comes to the same conclusion: we must embed social determinants of health into community and economic development.

Noting that "the correlation between education and upward economic mobility has never been higher," Kanter calls for a unified and integrated life-cycle approach to funding higher education that includes CSAs, College Promise Programs (which reduce or eliminate the costs for the first few years of higher education), and performance-based funding of student aid. Versions of these programs are in existence. The next step should be to "create a model that communities, states, and the federal government could adopt fully or in part to build financial capability

12 See Laura Sullivan et al., "The Racial Wealth Gap: Why Policy Matters." (New York: Demos and Institute for Assets & Social Policy, Brandeis University, March 2015).

13 See Ezra Levine, Jeremie Greer, and Ida Radamacher, "Upside Down to Right-side Up." (Washington, DC: CFED, 2014).

and to increase college access, enrollment, and graduation rates" and to engage in rigorous research about the programs' practicality and effectiveness, especially for low-income and minority students.

Improving federal tax policy to better focus asset-building tax benefits on those who most need them is a theme in several essays. Levere and Tivol, Kanter, Friedman, and English and Greer call for massive expansion of tax-favored CSAs, building on the Campaign for Every Kid's Future, announced at CGI America 2015, to open CSAs for 1.4 million children by 2020. At the other end of the age spectrum, English and Greer, Hartmann, Friedman and others call for both greater access to retirement savings accounts and more flexibility in their use—including support for entrepreneurship. The Treasury's new myRA—whose use at Staples is discussed in Mulot's essay—is a new and exciting option for accomplishing this.

Lazio, Asante-Muhammad, Glover Blackwell and Longman cite the need to reform housing-based tax benefits, especially the mortgage interest deduction, to provide far more of the benefit to those who need the assistance, including renters, and Lazio adds the concept of tax-advantaged housing savings accounts. More broadly with respect to housing policy, Glover Blackwell calls for strategies to make affordable owned and rented housing available to all, and English and Greer call for expansion of housing-oriented IDAs. Lazio recommends extending the time during which income limits would be effective for Low Income Housing Tax Credit projects, providing incentives for longer leases, establishing rent-to-own programs sponsored by the Federal Housing Administration and state Housing Finance Agencies, and creating incentives for insurers to provide affordable insurance to cover housing emergencies such as repairs or temporary loss of income.

Many of the essays emphasize the need to make changes to job, education and income support programs. Asante-Muhammad calls for a direct federal job creation program and Glover Blackwell and others call for a significant increase in the minimum wage. Noting that jobs with critically important benefits such as pensions, paid sick days and help with child care are held disproportionately by men, Hartmann calls for extension of federal and state laws to make these benefits more consistently available to women. Bicha and Batchelder provide an extensive roadmap for reform of income support programs, including eliminating asset limits at the federal level (a recommendation also made by English and Greer, Hartmann, and Quiñonez). Purnell and others urge far more investment in high-quality early childhood education and in education at all levels for the most vulnerable.

CONCLUSION

As with the earlier *What Works* and *What Counts*, creating this book has been a journey that started fairly simply—"let's write a book about the importance of financial capability"—and has become far more complex as authors and editors brought the book to fruition, and as research in our own field evolved to include financial health and well-being. Where the journey, which is ongoing, stands is exemplified by the book's cover: financial capability is an important strategy to reach household financial health and well-being, which is in turn a bridge to much more. Recognizing that the success of a myriad of the nation's social programs and strategies in education, health, workforce development, community development, criminal justice reform, and elsewhere is dependent on financially healthy families, we need to embed effective financial capability strategies into all these systems. That means giving people the information, tools, and opportunity to make financial decisions in real time that are right for them in the short- and long-term. At the same time, we cannot let the financial services sector and other private market players off the hook; they have an obligation to rebuild trust and provide the products and services that facilitate financial health and well-being. Government, too, has a role, in making policy, including tax policy; in implementing programs; and in regulating. Above all else, this book shows that moving toward a more equal society and improving the overall economic health of this country depends on the state of financial health and well-being of every one of us.

■ ■ ■

ELLEN SEIDMAN *works on housing and community development issues. In 2012, she was appointed to the Consumer Advisory Board of the Consumer Financial Protection Bureau. She was a visiting scholar at the Federal Reserve Bank of San Francisco from 2012 through 2014, where she was a co-editor of What Works and What Counts. From 1997 through 2001, she was the director of the Office of Thrift Supervision, and from 1993 to 1997, she was special assistant to the President for Economic Policy. She serves on the boards of several community development financial institutions and is a founder of the Center for Financial Services Innovation. Seidman received her M.B.A. in Finance and Investments from George Washington University, her J.D. from Georgetown University Law Center, and her A.B. from Radcliffe College.*

SO WHAT? KEEPING OUR EYES ON THE PRIZE

Brandee McHale
Citi Foundation

Let's say that you are a philanthropist with a deep commitment to improving the lives of low-income people. You have a healthy budget and a talented staff, and after a strategic planning process worthy of the most rigorous management consultants, you make financial capability a cornerstone of your philanthropic approach. You identify the best thinkers in the field and learn from them. You identify the best practitioners and support their work.

Now let's say that one of your grantees works with a low-income family who has heavy debt, poor credit, and no savings. Through intensive and well-designed interventions, this family improves its credit score, reduces its debt, and opens a savings account. That's good news, and we shouldn't dismiss these gains. But I want to ask a simple, but powerful question: *So what?*

Those metrics don't tell us whether these outcomes are part of a new way of living for that family, or whether they are just a momentary blip in response to a time-bound intervention. They don't tell us whether they have caused, or were caused by, a lasting sense of opportunity and empowerment. In short, these outcomes, positive as they may be, don't automatically mean success as you defined it: improving the long-term well-being of low-income people. Philanthropy, after all, is dedicated to the progress of individuals, families and communities. Metrics are one way to measure success, but they do not define it.

When defining success in the area of financial capability, it's logical to focus on money—it is easy to quantify and can serve as a measurable indicator. But for those of us who work in the field of financial capability and well-being, we must not lose sight of the purpose of our work. I am not suggesting that we toss aside all efforts to measure our work or quantify results. Rather, I am urging that in the process, we keep sight of the equally important question of *so what?*—the question that defines the ultimate purpose of our work and should guide our every action.

First, a bit of background. My institution, the Citi Foundation, has established a long-standing commitment to promoting financial success. When we first began making grants in this space, the Citi Foundation's financial capability strategy stressed classroom-based financial education. Our working hypothesis was that if you taught people how to manage their money, they would be better able to navigate financial choices and challenges, which in turn would improve their financial standing. We felt so strongly about this that we made financial education a core focus area. We invested $68 million over six years to build our own curriculum, train volunteers, and fund community-based organizations to get people into classroom seats so we could educate as many as possible.

Then we noticed that something didn't click.

Imparting information alone wasn't really helping because the core issue in the first place was not solely a lack of information. This is not to say that information is not important; it is a basic building block. But the real trick is translating this knowledge into action and positive financial behaviors. As a general rule, people do not necessarily think their way into a new way of acting. Instead, they act their way into a new way of thinking.

In their white paper, "The Financial Health Check," Antoinette Schoar of MIT and Piyush Tantia with Ideas42, reference a number of studies indicating that the impact of financial education is mixed. Although some studies find evidence that people do learn, others show that financial education has no effect on financial behavior. According to Schoar and Tantia, psychological barriers often prevent people from taking appropriate action. For example, despite good intentions, people may forget to act without a well-structured plan and prompts, and small hurdles or a lack of willpower may discourage them from following through.

What this meant for the Citi Foundation's work, as we discovered, was that financial education was necessary, but by itself, was insufficient for the long-term economic well-being of individuals, families, and communities.

So we modified our tactics to ensure that people have access to more than just information. For example, rather than just being taught the importance of savings, we ensure people can actually open and start managing a savings account while developing savings goals. Over time, we realized, as they watched the balance grow, participants became even more inspired to divert income from consumption to savings until the habit became second nature. We call this approach *financial capability*.

An important part of this effort was recognizing that while households could set a financial goal, staying on track often served as a challenge. As a result, we chose to emphasize financial coaching as a part of our overall financial capability strategy. We were among the early promoters of this coaching approach, which had a powerful impact, giving people the motivation, the hope, and the tools to not only gain control over their short-term financial situation, but to also believe they could manage their money to achieve life goals.

"I learned that I am worth it," as Joanna (pseudonym), a participant in a Citi Foundation-funded coaching program put it. At a graduation ceremony in November 2012, Joanna described for her fellow financial coaching graduates how she had previously survived on payday lenders, emergency loans from increasingly exasperated family members, maxed out credit cards, and overdrawn accounts:

I felt I owed myself that shopping spree because of the stress and the bills . . . At the root of it all, I was afraid to face my ugly financial situation . . . and I had a fear [going into the coaching program] about how I would be perceived. [My coach] made it all bearable; she was gracious the entire year. [I learned that] there are no easy answers, that I must make healthy financial decisions whether I have enough money or not, that paying myself first is actually a benefit to everyone in my family, and that I am worth it—and I am better off for it. I now have a significant amount of savings to put towards a down payment on a home.

When an individual is able to see and believe in a better future, working towards it feels empowering and dignifying, not futile. Dreams no longer seem distant or foreign. Instead those dreams become attainable goals that are within reach and recognizable. That is the essence of the *so what?* And that is what the Citi Foundation strives to achieve.

Since 2010, the Citi Foundation has invested $65 million in the United States to provide people with the tools and guidance to manage their income and expenses more effectively, build savings, reduce debt, build credit, and work toward achieving both short- and longer-term financial goals. In the process, we gathered a lot of data.

In 2014, we saw that more than 63 percent of the participants in our funded financial capability programs had fully achieved a stated savings, debt reduction, or credit score related outcome. We used this data to help bring other funders along with us and adopt a "beyond the classroom" focus.

I am proud that we served as an early adopter of results-focused grantmaking, with real data to guide our work. It was solid data, after all, that signaled more could be done in our efforts around financial education. It was data that allowed us to adjust our strategy to one that has turned out to be so important—for us and, most important of all, for those we aim to serve through our philanthropic investments.

In the classic formulation, we would summarize the lesson we learned as "outputs are not outcomes." Bodies sitting in chairs, or credit hours of financial education delivered, are outputs. Savings accounts opened to prepare for the future or credit scores improved are outcomes. They are more important. But here's the thing: "outcomes" are not ultimately the point either. People like Joanna are.

People's lives are complex and changing. Accordingly, as philanthropists, we need to expand our time horizons and support people in their efforts to adapt, move through their financial lifecycle, and navigate major life events. There is a multi-billion dollar a year industry of financial advisors available to wealthier households. Philanthropy can play an important role leveling the playing field for households with the least ability to weather financial shocks in their lives. One way to do this is to shift our investment horizons from a short-term outlook—namely, how quickly an individual or household resolves a specific financial issue or meets a single one-time financial goal—to a long-term, systems-level view that considers how we inspire people to believe they can reach and reinvent their goals, and just as important, make sure they have the ability to seek out trusted advisors over this lifecycle.

The concept of two Americas is becoming increasingly prevalent, while newspaper headlines assure us that economic indicators are moving in the right direction. But more Americans feel more financially vulnerable than ever, and as asset and income inequality continues to grow, the schism in our society is no longer a risk but an increasing reality. Philanthropists have never been more focused on results, but I wonder whether we are letting our focus with data distract us from the big picture—ensuring that the paths to opportunity and upward mobility still exist.

Whether they focus on income inequality, educational attainment, health outcomes, social development, or the various points where these issues intersect, policymakers and thought leaders recognize the challenge we face. The seeds of change were sown decades ago as middle class wages stagnated and the cost of goods increased more than incomes. Research conducted by the Economic Policy Institute, which has documented hourly wages for nearly three decades, shows that since 1979, the vast majority of American workers has seen their hourly wages stagnate or decline. But you don't need complex economic analysis to know that when expenses exceed income, especially over long periods of time, financial stability erodes.

There is a role for philanthropy in funding interventions that treat the consequences of erosion. When families' margin for financial error shrinks to the vanishing point, the task becomes all the more urgent to build their financial capability. But if we make treating the symptoms the goal—in other words, if we lose sight of the *so what*—philanthropists risk becoming tacit supporters of the status quo.

I doubt any philanthropist would dream of saying, "Our task is to help you better manage your scarcity." But that is exactly what you are saying, if you base grantmaking solely on program performance measures and outcomes. You are accepting that scarcity as a given, and defining "the problem" as the inability of some to manage within the confines presented before them.

Of course, it is futile to imagine that philanthropy alone can undo structural changes brought on by social and economic trends decades in the making. But every philanthropist who is seriously interested in having an impact should look beyond the data and make an effort to understand how to permanently contribute to opportunity and advancement. The role of implementing effective programming, whatever the particular tactical approach, is the job of trusted grantees. The job of staying focused on the *so what?* is, in a perfect world, everyone's responsibility. But it is particularly the duty of philanthropists.

We all care about improving the financial well-being of American families. If we want to help people lead healthier lives, gain and keep good jobs, and obtain affordable and stable housing, then we also need to recognize the critical role that financial stability has in achieving these outcomes. Without supporting strategies that address the financial well-being and empowerment of the people in our communities, it is unlikely that we will ever fully succeed in improving peoples' lives over the long-term.

As many of the contributing authors to this book have noted, financial insecurity is deeply embedded in a variety of social problems. Left unaddressed, the eroding financial security of American households will negatively impact our economy as a whole and threaten our country's future. As philanthropists, we can work across traditional silos and use our investments to inspire families to believe in their own self-efficacy, invest in building social capital that will help them weather financial challenges, and support research and testing that deepens our understanding of how households adapt to socioeconomic challenges and opportunities.

Moreover, we should also be willing to use our philanthropic capital to challenge the status quo by investing in social movements that will bring greater awareness and understanding—both about the impact of financial vulnerability on our society and economy, and about the reasons why our success as a nation depends on reversing this downward economic cycle.

Because financial health is so inextricably intertwined with every other aspect of a person's life, the Citi Foundation is deeply committed to approaching the issue from a holistic perspective. We work hard to break down our own internal funding and wisdom-sharing silos, and we believe in working in partnership with other institutions across sectors, including colleges and universities, municipalities, community development, public health and other agencies. Our vision is to enable these entities to build capacity, pool resources, develop a shared financial capability agenda, and ultimately, reach millions of low-income people. We are open to experimentation to move beyond what feels comfortable or safe, and we engage in an open dialogue with our partners to learn from mistakes as well as successes.

We also believe in sharing those lessons more broadly—to build a body of knowledge and catalyze collaboration with our fellow philanthropists. Adopting a shared narrative among practitioners, policymakers, and funders is important to achieve large-scale impact and create the systems change required to put more American families on the path to long-term financial success.

At the heart of our work is a constant effort to remember that philanthropy by its nature is more of an art than a science, and that it simply is not a business like any other where success can be empirically quantified. There is the old joke among doctors: "Oh, never mind the patient. The patient died on the table, but the operation was a brilliant success." For philanthropists, the equivalent is that the economic divide may not be shrinking, but at least the program data look good.

Philanthropists should value metrics for what they can tell us. At their best and most useful, they can help us correct course by helping us distinguish flawed program design from flawed execution. But they cannot definitively tell us whether we are truly succeeding in empowering people to effectively manage their financial lives and to believe they can achieve their American Dream.

Peter Drucker, the very father of modern business thinking, once famously said that efficiency means doing things right, but *effectiveness* means doing the right things. After working in philanthropy for almost a quarter of a century, I can say that optimism about the future is at the core of every effective intervention I have ever seen.

I believe that the single most important aspect of philanthropy is the ability to inspire people to believe in their own future and eliminate roadblocks that stand in their way. This is not sentimentality, but quite the opposite. Societies where fatalism has taken hold are communities that stop innovating and inventing, a downward spiral from which it can be very difficult ever to escape.

Grantees can guide struggling families along the path to a secure financial future and can monitor their progress. Families need to make that journey themselves; ultimately no one can walk the path for them. *But they have to believe they can get there.* That is the all-important role of philanthropy. If fatalism is contagious, if pessimism is a self-fulfilling prophecy, the good news is that so too is the inspirational power of hope.

Esther Duflo, a researcher from the Massachusetts Institute of Technology's Abdul Latif Jameel Poverty Action Lab, expressed it perfectly. Duflo and her colleagues were responsible for the randomized control trials testing a poverty alleviation methodology in Ethiopia, Ghana, Honduras, India, Pakistan, and Peru. Across these six very different contexts, Duflo and her team found a striking similarity: hope made the difference.

"What we hypothesize, although we cannot directly confirm it using this data, is that this improved mental health is what gave participants the energy to work more, save and invest in their children — we see in the data that children spend more time studying," she said. "A little bit of hope and some reassurance that an individual's objectives are within reach can act as a powerful incentive."[1]

Some will argue that without a single-minded devotion to data and outcomes, it is too easy to "hide behind the mission," to say "well, we can't prove it exactly, but we know we are doing good in the world." I would urge my fellow philanthropists to remember that the risk runs in the opposite direction as well. If you can avoid metrics by hiding behind

1 As quoted in Tina Rosenberg, "Upward Mobility for the World's Destitute," *New York Times*, May 15, 2015.

the mission, you avoid the mission by hiding behind the metrics. You can easily become the boastful doctor focused on the brilliant operation, instead of its impact on the lifeless patient.

The difficult truth is that we may never prove direct causation, much less measure it. The best we can do is to accept the uncertainty inherent in our efforts—easier said than done, to be sure—and pursue our grantmaking with the commonsense wisdom that data can be an excellent servant but a tyrannical master.

■ ■ ■

***BRANDEE MCHALE** is president of the Citi Foundation and director of corporate citizenship at Citi. She oversees the Citi Foundation's global grantmaking strategy and leads Citi's citizenship efforts, including volunteerism and environmental sustainability. She first joined Citi in 1991 and has served in a variety of business management and philanthropy-related leadership roles, including director of operations for Citi Community Capital and as a senior relationship manager in Citi's then Community Relations and Community Reinvestment Act units. Most recently, she has been chief operating officer of the Citi Foundation. From 2004–2007, McHale worked at the Ford Foundation, where she developed a portfolio of investments that supported the efforts of low-income households to achieve financial success and helped to establish a business case for financial inclusion. She is board chair of the Corporation for Enterprise Development (CFED) and also serves on the board of directors of the Local Initiatives Support Corporation (LISC) and Living Cities.*

CLOSING THE FINANCIAL CAPABILITY GAP: A CALL TO ACTION FOR PRIVATE MARKETS

Asheesh Advani
Junior Achievement Worldwide

In recent years, the pace of market-driven innovation in financial services has been breathtaking. Products and services such as prepaid cards, mobile money, payment technologies, and credit score services are making saving, borrowing, and moving money easier than ever. Some of the entrepreneurs driving these innovations have recognized that serving the entire market—lower-income, lower-wealth, and other underserved households included—can be good business when done in a manner that respects the needs and intelligence of these consumers. These innovations can also be pathways into the formal banking system.

To build financial health, access to good products and services must be combined with the knowledge and behavior that enables people to make wise use of financial products. Both financial literacy and capability are essential elements to financial wellness, particularly for new products that use technology to lower the cost of reaching customers. Monitor's 2012 "Bridging the Gap" report detailed this boom in access to finance for the world's poor, and sounded the alarm about the growing financial capability gap: "There is growing consensus that efforts to simply improve financial access without also improving financial capability are inadequate at best, and unsustainable and potentially harmful at worst."[1]

In this essay, I suggest that closing the financial capability gap—empowering individuals who lack the know-how, confidence, and access to the products that will help them achieve financial well-being—is simultaneously an investment opportunity, a value-creating business opportunity,

1 Animatra Deb and Mark Kubzansky, "Bridging the Gap: The Business Case for Financial Capability" (Cambridge, MA: Monitor, March 2012), p. 2.

and a critical collaboration opportunity. I'm calling for private players—whom I'll call "investors," "operators," and "coalitions"—to recognize the opportunity that exists in serving the unbanked and underbanked in America and apply their inventiveness to reach them.

PRIVATE INVESTORS AND THE MOTIVATION OF ENTREPRENEURS

About 15 years ago, I pitched an institutional investor for CircleLending, a peer-to-peer lending venture that was designed to reduce the cost of borrowing for Americans. The feedback was not surprising: this sounds like a nonprofit, not a business. I made the same pitch to an individual "angel" investor and received a completely opposite reaction: what a great idea and a chance to reach an underserved market. After a few months of hearing the same feedback from numerous investors, I decided to focus on raising money from high net worth individuals and raised more than $5 million.

The double bottom line investment was a new idea back then, and more appealing to selected individuals than institutional investors or funds. Today, there is an entire landscape of impact investment funds that raise money to aggregate the complex social and financial motivations of investors and flow funds to ventures like CircleLending.

A 2014 market sizing study by the Center for Financial Services Innovation (CFSI) concluded that in 2013 the financially underserved market in the United States generated approximately $103 billion in fees based on financial product and services volume of $1.3 trillion. Mainstream investors are making plenty of progress funding disruption in payments, banking and financial technologies. But rather than waiting for these innovations to trickle down to unbanked Americans, double bottom line investors are stepping up.

One such impact investment firm is Core Innovation Capital in Los Angeles, founded by Arjan Schütte and built on a decade of work by CFSI defining the nature of the problem of the unbanked and underbanked in America. Core identifies and invests in startup technology companies that are building solutions that address the specific problems that underlie financial insecurity, paying particular attention to the motivations of the founders and management teams of each company. The companies in their portfolio offer a peek into some of the most promising private market responses to the financial capability gap in America today (in the interest of full disclosure, I am an investor in Core). Here are a few:

Problem: *People with limited or damaged credit histories—young adults, immigrants, and people recovering from credit missteps or life events such as divorces—need a way to access affordable credit and improve their credit score.* **Vouch** enables consumers to borrow money at a lower interest rate if they can get their relatives and friends to vouch for them by guaranteeing part of the loan amount. In essence, cosigning meets crowdfunding. **Oportun** (formerly *Progreso Financiero*) offers Hispanic individuals with limited or no credit history loans at responsible and affordable rates and reports results to two of the major credit bureaus. They report that about one-half of their first-time borrowers had no credit score.

Problem: *Low-income people need easy-to-understand sources of financial information to make wise borrowing, credit and saving decisions.* While higher-income Americans can afford advice from a professional advisor, even if it is sometimes conflicted, lower-income Americans often have to make complex financial decisions on their own, relying on advice from friends and the Internet. **NerdWallet** is a consumer friendly website offering information, insight, and consumer-driven advice about personal finance. It has become such a go-to destination for information on consumer finance that general web searches like "best checking account" or "compare car insurance" lead users to the NerdWallet website. In the same way TripAdvisor has changed how we make travel decisions, NerdWallet is changing how we make financial decisions. **SavvyMoney** builds better financial health through credit score improvement. The website offers free ongoing access to a consumer's credit score, explains the factors that affect it, and recommends actions that might strengthen it.

Problem: *Low-income markets are underserved because companies perceive them as unprofitable.* **Banking UP** aims to make full-service banking available for all by offering backend banking and payment services that make products that low-income Americans frequently use more cost effective by using the infrastructure designed for the prepaid card business rather than the banking business. Customers also avoid some fees, such as the convenience fees often charged by traditional prepaid cards. **TIO Networks** is a bill payment processor for some of the largest billers in North America and primarily serves the financially underserved marketplace in the United States, typically at one-tenth the price of Western Union. With a combination of its mobile app and national convenience store network, TIO is easily accessible to consumers and maintains a robust network of common utility providers.

Problem: *Low-income people are typically underinsured.* **Cover Hound** is an insurance marketplace using technology to lower the cost of insurance via comparison shopping and disintermediating the broker.

Impact investors and entrepreneurs will agree that it is hard to build a profitable company dedicated solely to serving the needs of low-income customers. For the company itself to be sustainable, these customers may only be a subset of a larger market, even with first mover advantage or substantial funding. Indeed, impact can sometimes best be served by innovations developed for the mainstream and then adapted to reach a low-income segment. It is unclear whether companies such as Cover Hound or NerdWallet could exist, for example, without serving a broad market of which low-income consumers are one part, albeit an over-represented part relative to the population.

And so, balancing the economics of growing a profitable company with a mission to reach low-income households is a tricky task. For example, new technologies have reduced the cost of delivery of financial products such as money transfer, credit, and investments. These lower costs can translate into lower fees for consumers, higher margin for service providers, or both. It is up to the management team to make the decision of how to divide the savings.

In the absence of perfect regulatory oversight to protect consumers, the ethics and motivations of the management team and especially the founder/owner(s) thus become increasingly important. Historically, private investors have been skeptical of businesses boasting dual motivations of profit and social impact—and for good reason, given that their ability to deliver returns and impact is unproved, if well-intended. But double-bottom line funds and impact investors, like Core Innovation

Capital, are building a new corps of sustainable businesses showing us how it can be done.

OPERATORS CAN CHOOSE TO DELIVER FINANCIAL WELL-BEING, NOT JUST FINANCIAL SERVICES

"Operators" in this essay refer to financial institutions, corporations, and social enterprises with a stake in low-income Americans' financial well-being. I explicitly use the term operators—rather than corporations, businesses, startups, or social enterprises—because I believe that the effectiveness of private markets in serving the needs of low-income Americans comes down to individual people: operators. It takes creative, entrepreneurial, and committed individuals at work within these disparate types of business forms to raise awareness and drive focus. Led by these entrepreneurs and professionals, businesses both large and small can address financial insecurity while generating profits for themselves and their shareholders as a result of their efforts.

Banks as partners in financial well-being

There are significant opportunities for banks to focus on customer financial well-being, regardless of whether there is a regulatory obligation to do so. Branch and call center employees who actively listen to customers, try to understand their needs, and match up bank services with customer goals deepen the relationship. Gallup research found that those customers who said they strongly agree that their bank looks out for their financial well-being on average have more products with their banks, leading to better financial outcomes for the bank.

Banks are well positioned to evaluate and provide the kinds of approaches that can improve customers' financial well-being. The JPMorgan Chase & Co. Institute is publishing analysis of its own account data in an effort to contribute to greater knowledge in the sector about customer habits and motivations. Product-linked financial education is one of the most effective ways of building financial capability because it is action-oriented and affects outcomes via behavior rather than just knowledge. In some cases, one-on-one coaching might be the most effective strategy (see the essays in this volume by Michael Collins, Rita Landgraf, and Michael Rubinger), although delivery of this activity to different audiences is usually outsourced to specialists, both nonprofits and for-profits. Whether through better use of "big data" or through individualized interactions, banks can help customers meet their goals and build confidence.

Social enterprises spark new solutions

Social enterprises, such as the businesses I described from the Core Innovation Capital portfolio, are companies that have seized on one particular problem, or an aspect of financial insecurity, and have built a business around solving it.

For example, social enterprises are starting to show us compelling ways to deliver services such as financial education, traditionally the realm of grant-funded, mandatory group courses. A business called PayPerks has developed a platform that rewards individuals who complete education modules online and demonstrate desired credit card use behavior. The PayPerks platform enables payors (financial institutions, government, and employers) to customize and offer education and rewards programs to payees to help them better understand and make use of financial products. The platform is offered in both English and Spanish and can be extended into other languages, as well as web- and mobile-optimized, to maximize access for underserved consumers.

Small operators like PayPerks and the Core portfolio companies are nimble enough to evolve and test new business practices that may be replicable. The peer-to-peer lending social enterprise I founded, CircleLending, allowed people to restructure their personal loans and mortgages without penalty. We also adapted our platform to accommodate something mortgage companies could not, or would not: mortgage payments that could be delayed, reduced, or deferred until the end of the loan to help borrowers stay in their homes. As an innovative niche operator, we were able to avoid the more rigid lending practices of the broader mortgage industry, showing that by helping borrowers weather a financial crisis and stay in their homes, you could keep a loan on track and not trigger a default or bankruptcy.

Corporate scale and resources are critical

As exciting as the work of impact investors and social enterprises is, it is large corporations that have the greatest potential to bring about the scale of change required to move the needle on financial insecurity nationwide.

In the last 30 years, corporations have grown tremendously in their reach, resources, and role in modern economies. With this ascendency has come a drive externally from civil society organizations and government, and internally from leadership, to recognize the potential environmental and social impacts of the business. A 2010 study of Fortune 500 firms found that 90 percent embrace corporate social responsibility (CSR) as essential in their organizational goals.[2] From its origins in philanthropy and community engagement, CSR has matured into a sophisticated industry of sustainability frameworks and impact measurement and is attracting the brightest minds as a career track.

In addition to the established field of CSR is the newer concept of "shared value." Although CSR relies on the charitable instincts of the corporation and its employees, shared value is a management strategy. The shared value framework guides corporate leaders to seek ways to increase business value by identifying and addressing social problems that intersect with the business. Defined in a *Harvard Business Review* article in 2011 by Michael Porter and Mark Kramer, the concept pushes business leaders to think beyond simply mitigating the risks of their impact on society to integrating social and economic progress into the core of the business in ways that are profitable over the long term. As I previously mentioned, at a time when many banks are seeking ways to stay relevant, investing in products and services that create financial well-being for customers lends itself to a profitable shared value strategy.

At first glance, changing the product strategy or modifying the mission statement of a large corporation seems like a tall order. However, it happens all the time. Early in my career, I worked as a consultant at Monitor Group, a firm cofounded by Michael Porter. I witnessed first-hand how a new CEO or a merger/acquisition transaction would cause companies to recast their product priorities, brand values, and corporate missions. Even in the absence of a new leader or a transaction, a shift in product strategy toward shared values can happen incrementally. I recall working with a client in the financial services industry to help senior executives rethink assumptions about their strategy using a "ladder of inference," consulting-speak for a framework that enables change by

---

2 David Grayson and Jane Nelson, *Corporate Responsibility Coalitions: The Past, Present, and Future of Alliances for Sustainable Capitalism* (Stanford, CA: Stanford Business Books, 2013), p. 12.

questioning first principles, such as the corporate mission. Firms such as FSG continue to work on these types of projects with a clearer focus on shared value strategies.

Today, even in the absence of a strategic realignment of product strategies around financial wellness, companies are addressing financial security in multiple distinct ways, including through: 1) their salary policies and benefit programs, 2) their giving and employee volunteering programs, and 3) participation in coalitions engaged in a coordinated effort to address the issue.

As Regis Mulot detailed earlier in this book, Staples is one example of a corporation that has led the way in investing in employee financial well-being. As Mulot noted, they used gameplay in conjunction with 401(k) enrollment periods to increase financial literacy and engagement with retirement savings. To do this, they partnered with D2D Fund, a leading nonprofit in savings innovations that reach low- and moderate-income families. Staples also offers an alternative savings product to employees ineligible for their 401(k) plan. Through a partnership with the U.S. Treasury, they became the first large company to launch a rollout of the new *my*RA retirement accounts.

In my current role as CEO of Junior Achievement (JA) Worldwide, I get to see firsthand a diverse group of corporations providing funding and volunteers for school-based financial literacy interventions across America. JA is a global organization that reaches school-aged kids with hands-on programs designed to build self-efficacy, particularly with regard to financial skills and behaviors at a young age that prepare them for the workforce. Junior Achievement reaches more than 10 percent of middle school students in the United States and helps them learn about finance using immersive experiences such as *JA Finance Park* and *JA BizTown*. Kids role-play as adults, serving as bank officers and homeowners in a "town" condensed into a building the size of a soccer field or in a virtual environment. Both financial and nonfinancial companies provide much of the funding and (importantly) the experienced volunteers to interact with the kids in Finance Parks and Biz Towns across the country. With more than 400,000 corporate volunteers per year from hundreds of corporations, JA now reaches more than 10 million young people annually with programs in over 100 countries.

As I witness the effectiveness of these corporate partnerships, I can see no reason why JA kids should not be experiencing follow-up programming as they get older (in college and thereafter) in concert with other nonprofits and for-profits. Many of the corporate funders for JA's programs also fund the organizations that serve college-aged youth. To draw a parallel from the process of learning mathematics, it makes no sense for adults to be taught algebra if they have not learned about addition and subtraction. Teaching adults about the amortization schedule for mortgage payments, changing tax incentives for low-income households, or even the costs and risks associated with different insurance products requires an understanding of the basic building blocks of financial literacy.

It seems to me that there is great opportunity to tackle financial insecurity by forming business-led coalitions that can achieve greater coordination and clearer goals. More on that next.

SETTING THE STAGE FOR A BUSINESS COALITION ON FINANCIAL WELL-BEING

As the essay by Andrea Levere and Leigh Tivol explains, we have not made sufficient progress in addressing the issue of financial insecurity in our country despite many years of effort. The pace of product complexity is greater than the pace of consumer financial understanding, particularly among low-income and underbanked populations. To bring about significantly better outcomes in financial literacy, capability, and wellness, companies can collaborate to tackle the issue.

Fortunately, there is a precedent for collective business action. During the last 40 years, CEOs formed the first business coalitions in response to specific crises such as the AIDS crisis, climate change, and cyberterrorism. Although there are a variety of players in the corporate responsibility space, including nongovernmental organizations, consulting groups, and think tanks, I am specifically referring to membership-based organizations that are business-led and business-funded.

Business coalitions today take on a wide variety of different roles to tackle specific problems, including developing codes of conduct, designing self-regulation, and leveraging resources. At least 70 countries have meaningful business coalitions today, and there are several international coalitions. The Corporate Leaders Group on Climate Change is one such coalition that has led the way in setting an impact agenda, targets, and campaigns for collaboration among disparate nonprofits and companies.

Private markets respond well to clear targets, and business coalitions offer a safe space for leaders to rethink strategies and purpose. Business coalitions can achieve impact in three areas:

- Clarifying the scope of the social issue to be addressed;
- Sharing ways to embed new lines of business and responsible mission statements in core business activities; and
- Achieving scale by reaching out to more companies in new geographies.

A recent FSG report, "Banking on Shared Value: How Banks Profit by Rethinking Their Purpose" offers an example of banks working together. A consortium of investment banks—Bank of America, Merrill Lynch, Citigroup, JPMorgan Chase & Co., Goldman Sachs, Morgan Stanley, and Deutsche Bank— collaborated on the "Green Bond Principles" to protect the integrity of the banks' growing business in this area.

Yet today, no business-led coalition exists to tackle financial insecurity in the United States. As a result, leading nonprofits have stepped forward to spur interest and collaboration among organizations. CFED has been an effective catalyst for companies and nonprofits in the asset-building field. This book—drawing from the expertise of thought leaders in public, nonprofit and private organizations—is a result of that work and aims to advance the dialogue on what financial wellness looks like. CFSI, also featured in this book, hosts platforms for peer learning, including the Innovators Roundtable and the Underbanked Solutions Exchange. The Aspen Institute's Initiative on Financial Security seeks reforms to the tax code to provide incentives to increasing savings, and Aspen's Business and Society program promotes values-based business leadership.

What would it take, I wonder, to get a coalition of U.S. corporations to address financial capability or financial health in this same way? What would their response look like? Is the issue too political or can it be understood as a business opportunity? In my view, recasting the objective as an improvement in financial wellness rather than income redistribution paves the way for private markets to provide solutions.

Financial insecurity is not an intractable problem. Technology and business innovations are creating opportunity for millions of people to access financial products and services previously out of reach. The task of closing the financial capability gap with effective financial education, access to products, and real-time, individualized attention is complex. But I am hopeful that private markets—as investors, operators, and coalitions—will step up and play a more significant role in building financial health and well-being in the years ahead. We can do better so this chapter reads differently in the next edition of this book.

■ ■ ■

__ASHEESH ADVANI__ is the President and CEO of Junior Achievement (JA) Worldwide, one of the largest youth services organizations in the world with over 100 million alumni. He is an accomplished entrepreneur, having served as CEO of Covestor (acquired by Interactive Brokers) and CircleLending (acquired by Virgin Group). Advani has served on the board of CFED since 2009 and is currently Vice-Chair. He began his career as a consultant at the Monitor Group and the World Bank. He is a graduate of the Wharton School at the University of Pennsylvania and St. Antony's College, Oxford University, where he was a Commonwealth Scholar.

TOWARD PRODUCTIVE RESEARCH AGENDAS IN FINANCIAL INCLUSION, SECURITY, AND DEVELOPMENT

Michael Sherraden and Margaret Sherraden
Washington University in St. Louis

In this essay, we focus on key themes in research and knowledge building which have the potential to inform and improve research on financial inclusion, security, and development. In doing so, we use current examples in our own work on asset building, child accounts, and financial capability. This is the work we know best, and perhaps the examples are more meaningful and informative as a result. The implications of each theme extend broadly to other topics in financial well-being, and indeed to other topics in applied social research.

Our intent and hope is that these observations will spur interest in and engagement toward better research. Above all, we would like to see research agendas in applied social sciences—in the current case, in financial inclusion, security, and development—reach beyond simple data-based "evaluations" so that researchers can specify theory toward more coherent understanding and ask productive research questions that, when answered, may lead to positive changes in the real world.[1]

To be sure, these are tall expectations, but our experience over the years is that more rigorous applied social science is within reach, and that the resulting knowledge can indeed make positive contributions, with real effects on policy and practice. In that spirit, we hope this chapter

1 Here we focus on applied social science research, particularly focused on interventions. We acknowledge the importance of other data collection and analysis efforts to help us better understand the current state of household financial management in context—efforts such as the U.S. Financial Diaries project, the J.P. Morgan Chase & Co. Institute's report on their own customer data, the Center for Financial Services Innovation financial health study, and the Assets & Opportunity Scorecard. However, we focus specifically on applied social research in this essay.

may nudge both scholars and practitioners to be more thoughtful and productive in their research agendas going forward.

THINKING ABOUT APPLIED SOCIAL RESEARCH

We begin with several general themes in thinking about applied social research. Together, these themes express a very clear approach, with direct implications for designing research agendas. Though a bit on the idealistic side—with inevitable compromises necessary—these themes can serve as a rudder in charting a productive applied social research agenda.[2]

Build knowledge in actual circumstances

For this key point, we turn to the philosophy of Pragmatism, which emphasizes the value of empirical experience. Although somewhat of an oversimplification, Pragmatism defines truth as something that happens in the world. This very applied philosophy was seeded in the late nineteenth century, and flowered in the Progressive Era of the early twentieth century. William James, John Dewey, and Jane Addams are often identified as Pragmatists.[3] And the social sciences, especially the applied social sciences, are sometimes interpreted as congenial applications of Pragmatist philosophy.

On this view, knowledge about the effects of social action is never divorced from experience, and instead is worked out in application. This perspective provides useful footing and an important guidepost for building and applying social knowledge. The overall implication is that assessing innovations can never depend solely on reasoning, nor can it depend on tangential but disconnected data, but must instead rest on the results of actual tests. This is a high standard for evidence, yet ultimately the correct one. One would not want to buy a new model of car that had never been driven.

Consider the individual in his or her social context

In the mid-twentieth century, both academic sociology and the field of social work evolved conceptual statements that considered the individual

---

2 This section is summarized from a more extended presentation by Michael Sherraden entitled *Social Innovation: Vision, Knowledge, and Action* (Oxford University Press, in progress).

3 For example, William James, "Philosophical Conceptions and Practical Results," paper delivered at Philosophical Union of the University of California at Berkeley, printed in the *University Chronicle* 1 (4) (1898).

in his or her social context as the crux of explaining human action. One of the great contributions during that period was from Robert Merton, who, with an eye toward being useful, identified theories "of the middle range" as particularly relevant for understanding social interactions.[4] Not long after, William Schwartz, William Gordon, and Harriett Bartlett in social work defined "person in environment" as a key to defining social work professional practice.[5] Both of these conceptual statements consider the individual in his or her social context as the crux of explaining action.

The "middle range" lies between theories that rely solely on the biology and psychology of individuals (e.g., personality explanations of behavior), and theories that address only social structures (e.g., privilege and power explanations of social class). Both the social context and the individual contribute to action; that is, both the institutions and the individual "behave." Indeed, sometimes institutions do most of the behaving; for example, we have often pointed out that 401(k) plans are highly institutionalized—once an individual is signed up, saving patterns are automatic and result very little from individual behaviors.

Social institutions can and should be specified and tested as specific constructs (e.g., in the above example automatic features would be an important construct), with the goal of explaining patterns of action not by individuals, but in large samples or full populations. Such tests are particularly productive for informing programs and policies—and this must be a main goal of applied social research. Scholars who plow these fertile fields of the "middle range" include social psychologists, institutional economists, institutional sociologists, some behavioral economists, and a majority of social work and public health scholars.

Ask questions well

Over several decades, we have aimed to teach our doctoral students and other younger scholars how to ask better questions. The essential steps are (1) systematically specify theory, which (2) sets the stage for clearly stated hypotheses, that (3) can be represented by a practical intervention, (i.e., the hypotheses are subject to test in the real world), with (4) such tests

---

4 Robert Merton, *Social Theory and Social Structure* (New York: Free Press, 1968).

5 For example, William E. Gordon, "A Critique of the Working Definition," *Social Work* 7 (4) (1962): 3–13.

yielding applied knowledge, that (5) documents efficacy and efficiency (or lack of these) of the intervention being tested. In this way, theory is used not as a brilliant person's idea, nor as a forgone conclusion, nor as a kind of decoration before data are presentation, but instead as a method for rigorous, efficient, and productive inquiry by applied scholars.

Of course, this is just a description of deduction in applied social science. Deduction is a powerful tool—perhaps the single most important contribution of the Enlightenment—though many applied social scholars do not frame and conduct their research in this way. Engaging in scientific deduction is certainly not the only path to knowledge, but it has proved a very efficient and productive method of building knowledge. Therefore, applied scholars should have very good reasons before deciding not to use it.

Above all, intervention research should not be a fishing expedition, looking for anything that shows up in the net as an outcome. A disciplined focus on deduction—theory specification and testing hypotheses—is the way to avoid this.

Focus on solutions

A great deal of applied social research is designed to identify problems and causes of problems, or both. In most of this work is an implicit assumption that if we understand what causes a problem, we will know what to do about it. But this is sometimes not the case. Sometimes the causes of a problem are fixed or intractable (e.g., educational level of parents, racism), and sometimes the causes of problems do not matter in forming a solution. Overall, problem-oriented research is overdone.

More applied social research should be about identifying solutions, even, in some circumstances, when we do not know what causes the problems. Solution-oriented research directly informs interventions that can make a difference. In solution-focused research, we can identify two main types: (1) explanations of the solution (not the problem), and (2) effects of a solution that is put in place. The first type yields knowledge that informs programs and policies, and the second type provides the rationale for the intervention. At present, most applied social research does neither. If applied social science is to reach its potential, a rebalancing is necessary. A focus on empirical tests of purposeful action is consistent with the Pragmatism theme discussed above.

GUIDING CONCEPTS IN FINANCIAL WELL-BEING

We turn next to key themes in the nature and definition of financial well-being, focusing on three areas in particular: financial capability, inclusion, and life course perspective. In fundamental ways, these three concepts are the foundation for effective financial products, programs, and policies. These are what we are all trying to achieve, so it is helpful to keep such core concepts in mind when selecting research questions. When research choices build upon core themes, knowledge accumulates more effectively.

Financial capability

Financial capability combines people's *ability to act* and their *opportunity to act* in their best financial interests.[6] Reflecting a person-in-environment perspective, financial capability is the interaction of individual knowledge and skills, behavior, and institutional structures that creates positive financial functioning. In other words, creating financial capability is not simply a matter of changing individual behavior, but of also changing institutions that play a role in shaping financial opportunities.[7] Informed by capability theory of Amartya Sen in *Development as Freedom*[8] and Martha Nussbaum in *Women and Human Development*,[9] this view of financial capability refutes the assumption that financial vulnerability is a result of individual behavior alone and instead points to the interaction between individuals and social institutions that shape financial well-being. In other words, it differs from common usage that focuses on individual attributes, such as knowledge and skills, attitude, habit, motivation, confidence, self-efficacy, and behavior.[10] Although some of these attributes suggest contextual variables, many current conceptualizations and measures do not

---

6 This definition of financial capability was first presented by Elizabeth Johnson and Margaret S. Sherraden and is expanded upon in Margaret S. Sherraden, "Introduction." *In Financial Capability and Asset Building: Research, Education, Policy, and Practice*, edited by Julie Birkenmaier, Margaret S. Sherraden, and Jami Curley (New York & Oxford: Oxford University Press, 2013).

7 For example, Michael Sherraden and Michael S. Barr, "Institutions and Inclusion in Saving Policy. In *Building Assets, Building Credit: Bridges and Barriers to Financial Services in Low-Income Communities*, edited by Nicolas Retsinas and Eric Belsky (Washington, DC: Brookings Institution Press, 2005).

8 Amartya Sen, *Development as Freedom* (New York: Anchor Books, 1999).

9 Martha Nussbaum, *Women and Human Development: The Capabilities Approach* (Cambridge: Cambridge University Press, 2000).

10 For example, Mike Dixon, "Rethinking Financial Capability: Lessons from Economic Psychology and Behavioural Finance." (London: IPPR, June 2006); Annamaria Lusardi, "Americans' Financial Capability." (Financial Crisis Inquiry Commission, 2010).

specify and measure institutional variables alongside individual behaviors. This contextualized definition of financial capability follows from the "middle range" and "person in environment" discussions above.

Inclusion of the whole population

It is relatively easy to use the word "inclusion," but much harder to achieve it in the real world. As indicated in the discussion of financial capability, access to quality financial services matters, and depending how access is structured, this could (or could not) lead to inclusion of the whole population in effective financial services. As our most successful example, by far the largest inclusive social policy in the United States is Social Security retirement, which achieves wide (though still not fully inclusive) coverage because it is mandatory and institutionalized in employment practice.

Working in a different area of social policy, the Center for Social Development (CSD) at Washington University in St. Louis is demonstrating in the SEED for Oklahoma Kids (SEED OK) experiment that full inclusion in Child Development Accounts (CDAs)—sometimes in this volume called Children's Savings Accounts—can be designed and sustainably put into place.[11] Inclusion in this case means *all children* in a population. Demonstrating full inclusion matters because it sets the stage for universal policy, and this research evidence matters. Results from SEED OK have directly informed CDA policy in the state of Maine that now also reaches all children with automatic accounts opened at birth.[12] Full inclusion is made possible by using the state college savings (529) plan as a platform. SEED OK is an explicit and purposeful test of a fully inclusive policy. This is not the same as undertaking research on many child account projects and hoping that more of them may someday add up to something like inclusion. Instead, *inclusive policy is the primary research question* in SEED OK.

11 Yunju Nam et al., "Do Child Development Accounts Promote Account Holding, Saving, and Asset Accumulation for Children's Future? Evidence from a Statewide Randomized Experiment," *Journal of Policy Analysis and Management*, 32 (1) (2013): 6–33.

12 Margaret Clancy and Michael Sherraden, "Automatic Deposits for All at Birth: Maine's Harold Alfond College Challenge." CSD Policy Report 14–05. (St. Louis: Washington University, Center for Social Development, 2014).

At CSD, we are aiming for a CDA policy model that can one day bring in all children in the nation—meaning every newborn. A nationwide 529 plan, or something like it, will be able to support such an inclusive policy. This is possible because government(s) can require that a 529 financial provider automatically open accounts for all children. In other words, there can be a positive public role in CDAs, even while assets are managed in the private sector. At the end of the day, a public role will be necessary for full inclusion in CDAs.

This example of applied research on inclusive policy is relevant for other types of financial services as well. Other potential candidates are tests of inclusive transaction accounts, tests of inclusive emergency savings accounts, and as a likely delivery system, tests of universal financial access via cellphone. We have little doubt that more such tests of inclusive financial delivery will occur in the not-too-distant future—internet technology now makes them very possible, perhaps inevitable. Indeed, we can imagine a world where inclusive finance becomes as efficient, easy, and safe as plumbing and clean water running to all homes. But for this to occur, purposeful research on financial inclusion must be in the forefront.

Lifelong process

Developing financial capability and assets is a lifelong process.[13] The life course offers a framework for studying financial well-being "at the nexus of social pathways, developmental trajectories, and social change."[14] The life course perspective underscores the reality that although individual choices and decisions matter a great deal, these decisions are shaped by and interact with other factors, such as the timing of events in people's lifetimes, the circumstances and actions of the people around them, and the historical times and the place when and where people live.[15]

---

13 Nancy Morrow-Howell and Margaret Sherraden, editors, *Financial Capability and Asset Holding in Later Life* (New York & Oxford: Oxford University Press, 2015). Content of this section on life course is drawn principally from this book.

14 Glen Elder, Jr., Monica Johnson, and Robert Crosnoe, "The Emergence and Development of Life Course Theory." In *Handbook of the Life Course*, edited by Jeylan Mortimer and Michael Shanahan (New York: Kluwer Academic/ Plenum, 2003).

15 Glen Elder, Jr. and Janet Giele, "Life Course Studies: An Evolving Field." In *The Craft of Life Course Research*, edited by Glen Elder, Jr. and Janet Giele (New York: Guilford, 2009).

Timing, especially when people experience advantage or disadvantage, may shape the next stage in life in important ways, often with persistent effects over the life span. For example, the age when a person gets a job with retirement savings benefits has significant implications for total savings the person has in retirement. *Linked lives* draws attention to how others affect people's well-being. For instance, a woman may withdraw from paid work to care for a sick spouse or an older relative. *Historical time and place* affects access to opportunities and constraints in socio-economic, cultural, historical, and geographical conditions. As Elder and colleagues write, "when times change lives change." Periods of war, economic recession, technological shifts, and cultural transformations affect entire age cohorts in different ways.[16] For example, in financial services we see cohort effects in lower homeownership rates for the "millennial" generation following the Great Recession. Moreover, these effects are compounded for populations of color. Understanding these historical and sociological differences in financial circumstances is a very important research agenda.

TESTING FINANCIAL INNOVATIONS IN THE FIELD

We now turn to some "nuts and bolts" issues in applied social research. These topics arise only in actual research in the field (recall the Pragmatism theme above). Unfortunately, these field research topics are seldom addressed as research methods in scholarly articles, but they are fundamental.[17]

Assessing delivery in the field

Well-designed intervention studies can rigorously document effects on accounts, savings, and asset building, as well as the well-being of families and children. However, effective intervention research rests on several types of knowledge that research methods texts rarely address. In effect, putting the intervention in place in the field—sometimes called the "fidelity" of the treatment—can never be taken for granted. In this discussion, we

16 Karl Mayer, "The Sociology of the Life Course and Lifespan Psychology: Diverging or Converging Pathways?" In *Understanding Human Development: Dialogues with Lifespan Psychology*, edited by Ursula Staudinger and Ulman Lindenberger, (Dordrecht, The Netherlands: Kluwer Academic, 2003).

17 This section is based on CSD research briefs in development by Michael Sherraden and Margaret Clancy. We have realized in discussions of child accounts that a number of nuts and bolts issues in design, delivery, data availability and quality, and measures of outcomes may benefit from clarification. This section is not at all "academic," but rather is very practical, illustrating on-going issues.

sometimes use the example of child account research, though similar lessons apply broadly to other innovations in financial services and policies.

The financial product. As indicated above, the purposes and characteristics of the financial instrument are important to document.

- Primary purpose. What is the primary purpose of the financial product? To take the child account example, is the main purpose financial experience, education, and savings behavior, or is the primary purpose long-term asset building for development goals? Different financial instruments by design serve different purposes. Indeed, a standard recommendation of financial planners is to have both a liquid savings account and a long-term asset-building account. To avoid confusing apples with oranges, it is important to state the primary purpose upfront.

- Does the primary purpose include full inclusion? If so, how is inclusion defined? In the case of child accounts, does this mean all children? Or as in some "universal" child accounts, does this mean only a public school population? If so, we might ask what happens with children who are in parochial or other private school, those who are home schooled, and those who are in institutional care?

- Characteristics. Describe the financial product and its characteristics. In what ways do these characteristics reflect the primary purpose, or not? Characteristics may include universal or targeted, automatic versus sign up (or "opt out" vs. "opt in"), initial deposit or not, types of subsidies if any, and how subsidies are distributed.

Delivery and administration. As the proverb notes, "There's many a slip 'twixt the cup and the lip." We know this to be true—alas, inevitable in the human condition—yet for convenience we often do not assess the slippage. We typically assume that the "intervention" is being "delivered" as designed. Some things to pay attention to include the following:

- Vehicle of delivery. What is the delivery system for the financial product, (i.e., how is the customer engaging with the product and who is in charge of that experience?)? Describe the purpose, auspice, applications, footprint of the delivery system, and details on traffic and use.

- Business fit. Is financial services the primary "business" of the organization? Is the organization involved in financial services, but this account is not a main focus? Especially, to what extent is offering the account "sustainable" based on revenue patterns for the business? For example, is a provider undertaking a boutique project for Community Reinvestment Act compliance or other purposes, or can this be a product that goes to scale and is sustained indefinitely?
- Tasks and responsibilities. What account administration tasks are performed by the sponsoring organization? What tasks are outsourced? For example, is there a third-party record keeper? How is all this working in practice?
- Efficacy of delivery. To what extent is the product delivered consistent with the original design and purpose?
- Data systems. Is there a reliable centralized data system for tracking performance?
- Potential for expansion. Is the provider likely to expand accounts to other settings or groups? If so, describe the likely expansion. If not, explain the situation.

Policy platform. As indicated above, many different local applications of a financial innovation will not necessarily add up to a comprehensive policy. Policy structure matters if full inclusion is to be achieved.

- Policy. To what extent is the financial product and delivery built on an underlying policy structure (i.e., defined and supported by local, state, or federal legislation)?
- Replication. Does a policy platform facilitate implementation of accounts to other geographical locations? What is the evidence that this is occurring, or not?

Fees, investment options, and expected growth of assets. Particularly in long-term asset building, net return (total earnings and gains, minus fees) matters. Topics to assess include the following:

- Fees. What are the separate and total fees associated with the accounts? Are any of the operational costs subsidized by a public funder or other party? Explain in detail.

- Investment options. What investment options are available in the accounts?

- Expected growth of assets over time. What is the range of anticipated growth of assets in the accounts over time?

Assessing actual financial results

Of course, real experience can (and often does) differ from intent and design. To make actual assessments, it is fundamental to have trusted and accurate data on what is occurring in the accounts.

Quality of data sources. Data quality is fundamental, yet this topic is undervalued in social science reporting.

- Data sources on account holding and amounts. What are the data sources on account holding and savings? Is there a systematic database? Are program sponsors entering data? How complete and accurate are the data?

- Reporting. What is the basis of prior reporting of program results? Did objective researchers clean, analyze, and present the data? Are systematic published reports available? And if not, why?

Data on Accounts, Savings, and Asset Accumulation. If long-term financial capability and asset building is the goal, important financial results include account holding, saving patterns, and asset accumulation. It is also important to ask how results differ by subgroup.[18]

- Data on account holding. What is the number of accounts? How does this compare with the target population for this initiative? How does it compare with the full population in this age group?

- Data on savings patterns and performance. What are the patterns of depositing in and withdrawing from the accounts?

---

18 For example, Sondra Beverly et al., "Can Child Development Accounts be Inclusive? Early Evidence from a Statewide Experiment," *Children and Youth Services Review*, 53 (C) (2015): 92–104.

- Data on asset accumulation over time. What is the asset accumulation (deposits minus withdrawals, plus earnings, minus fees) in the accounts over time? How do these results change over time?

Assessing financial security and development

The effect on individuals, families, and communities is the ultimate test of a financial innovation. For example, depending on purpose and design, child accounts may have effects beyond saving and asset accumulation. Indeed, some are specifically designed to achieve other important goals. Types of data sources and research studies, and their quality, are always important considerations.

Types of well-being outcomes. It is possible to assess a wide range of potential outcomes. Below we offer key categories of hypothesized effects of CDAs, based on theory and prior research. Certainly these are not the only categories of potential effects in financial innovation, but they are among the most important.

- Attitudes and outlooks of parents. Do child accounts cause parents to think differently about their child's future, especially their expectations for the child's educational attainment? Do parents in any way show attitudinal or mental health effects related to the accounts?

- Parent–child interactions. Do child accounts affect how parents interact with their children?

- Development of children. Do child accounts affect social–emotional and cognitive development of children?

- Primary schooling of children. Do child accounts affect school attendance, behaviors, and academic performance?

- Attitudes and outlooks of children. Do child accounts affect how children see their future, especially their expectations for educational attainment?

- Secondary schooling of children. Do child accounts affect high school attendance, behaviors, and performance? Especially, do child accounts affect high school graduation?

- Postsecondary schooling. Do child accounts affect college (or other postsecondary) enrollment, progress, and especially attainment of an educational credential?
- Financial capability of children and families. Do child accounts affect financial knowledge and skills of children and families? Are child accounts related to types and quality of other financial relationships?
- Long-term financial well-being. Do child accounts affect long-term asset building, avoidance of debt problems, and other measures of financial well-being?

This is a long list of potential outcomes, all based on our work with CDAs—and this list may also have broad applicability for research in financial innovation. What can we say about such a list? Foremost, it is important in policy and practice that an intervention, inasmuch as possible, has multiple positive effects. The notion of an intervention as solving a single problem is needlessly restrictive, and is another weakness of the problem-oriented approach. A far better idea is an intervention that creates multiple positive outcomes—a concept we have previously called a "strong intervention" or "strong policy." At the same time, however, a single intervention cannot do all things, and happy talk must be avoided. The standard for testing effects should be *reasonable hypotheses given theory and empirical data*. For any financial innovation, careful thought should be given to this range of reasonable outcomes, and research methods should aim to document whether or not they occur.

USING FIELD DEMONSTRATION AND APPLIED RESEARCH TO INFORM FINANCIAL PRODUCTS, PROGRAMS, AND POLICIES

Effective demonstration coupled with intervention research matters. The work in CDAs exemplifies this. Following the first proposal for lifelong asset building starting as early as birth,[19] CFED, CSD, New America Foundation, and other partners implemented a major child account demonstration in SEED.[20] Continuing this work, CSD is now testing fully

19 Michael Sherraden, *Assets and the Poor: A New American Welfare Policy* (Armonk, NY: M. E. Sharpe, 1991).

20 See *Lessons from SEED: A National Demonstration of Child Development Accounts*, edited by Michael Sherraden and Julia Stevens (St. Louis: Washington University, Center for Social Development, 2010).

inclusive CDAs with rigorous experimental methods in SEED OK. As a result of all this, and other demonstration and research activity, today the United States has reached a period of increased understanding and heightened interest in child accounts.

Little of this has occurred by chance. The strategy of purposeful demonstration, as Bob Friedman points out in his essay, in itself informs policy and practice by making the concept of child accounts real in the world. These concrete examples, with real people, generate media attention and serve to educate ordinary people, opinion leaders, policymakers, and others. At the same time, the knowledge gained in research has informed policy development in several states that have recently enacted and implemented CDAs.[21] On this promising foundation, step by step, the United States can now move toward an inclusive and progressive CDA policy.

Further demonstration and research—models and learning—will be required. Researchers must always ask: What is most effective? What strategies can become fully inclusive, progressive, lifelong, and sustainable? As applied researchers continue to ask these important questions, knowledge will continue to spur policy and practice.

Every topic taken up in this volume has its particular history regarding development of concept and research. Content may be very different, yet the important themes and research considerations are largely the same. We hope this chapter has illuminated some of these themes.

As a closing thought, if productive research questions are asked, then research results will find an interested audience—a "social market." This is a very different strategy than asking research questions and then later asking who will be interested in the results. As a simple guideline to avoid potential irrelevance, applied social researchers should ask themselves the following question before finalizing a research topic and plan: If the proposed research supports my hypotheses, what will happen in application? As applied researchers, we should have a clear and reasonably confident answer to this question to justify the time and expense of

21 For recent research and policy impacts see Sondra Beverly, Margaret Clancy, and Michael Sherraden, "The Early Positive Impacts of Child Development Accounts." CSD Research Brief 15–08. (St. Louis: Washington University, Center for Social Development, 2015).

conducting high-quality applied social science. This is once again a high bar, yet when we achieve it, research can contribute to positive change.

■ ■ ■

MICHAEL SHERRADEN *is the George Warren Brown Distinguished University Professor and founding director of the Center for Social Development at Washington University in St. Louis. He is the author or editor of several books on asset building:* Assets and the Poor *(1991),* Inclusion in the American Dream *(2005),* Can the Poor Save? *(2007),* Saving in Low-Income Families *(2008), and* Asset Building Innovations and Strategies in Asia *(2014). He has been a Fulbright Scholar, has held distinguished professorships at universities in the United States and abroad, and has advised heads of state and policy leaders in many countries. In 2010, he was listed by* Time Magazine *as one of the 100 most influential people in the world. He is currently working on a book on* Social Innovation.

■ ■ ■

MARGARET S. SHERRADEN *is Founder's Professor at the School of Social Work at the University of Missouri-St. Louis, and Research Professor at the Center for Social Development at Washington University in St. Louis. Her most recent books are* Financial Capability: Research, Education, Policy, and Practice *(2013) edited with Julie Birkenmaier and Jami Curley, and* Financial Capability and Asset Holding in Later Life: A Life Course Perspective *(2015), edited with Nancy Morrow-Howell. With Julie Birkenmaier and J. Michael Collins, she is currently writing a text for practitioners working with financially vulnerable populations. She is a former Fulbright Scholar and recipient of her university's highest teaching award.*

TOWARD A NEW BUSINESS MODEL

Strengthening Families Helps to Strengthen Communities and the Nation

Laura Choi and David Erickson

Federal Reserve Bank of San Francisco[1]

The fight against poverty and hunger must be fought constantly and on many fronts, especially in its causes.

—Pope Francis, in an address to a joint meeting of Congress September 24, 2015

We are often asked a "resource allocation" question on the best way to serve low-income people and communities given limited money. Which is the most important intervention? Education? Health? Jobs? Public Safety? Asset building? Yet all of these answers are wrong because the question is wrong. As the quote by Pope Francis and so many of the essays in this book make clear, a thriving community or family needs all of these things.

Perhaps a single solution is appealing because it reflects what we think we are capable of doing individually. Like the proverbial drunkard's search, in which a man looks for his lost keys under the lamppost rather than where he actually dropped them, "because that's where the light is," we tend to seek a solution wherever our own light happens to be shining. Yet we know that complex problems require more. To be most effective, we must continue to leverage our respective expertise, but also proactively

1 The views expressed are those of the authors and do not necessarily represent those of the Federal Reserve Bank of San Francisco or the Federal Reserve System.

work with others to find and connect solutions that exist outside of our own field of vision. We also need to better coordinate and share our collective perspectives, competencies, and strategies. That is a tall order, but not an impossible one. To do otherwise wastes time, energy, money, and patience.

What we have learned through the process of bringing this book to fruition is that financial health and well-being are preconditions for nearly all the long-term outcomes that collectively allow people and places to thrive, which is, after all, the goal of community development (for a deeper dive into the concepts of financial health and well-being, see the essays by Andrea Levere and Leigh Tivol, and Jennifer Tescher and Rachel Schneider). Financial health and well-being underpin educational attainment (as described by Regina Stanback Stroud, Martha Kanter, and Sarah Bloom Raskin), good health (see the essays by Jason Purnell and Rita Landgraf), stable employment (see essays by Michael Rubinger, Regis Mulot, and Janie Barrera), and community vitality (see essays by Angela Glover Blackwell and Paul Weech). Yet, despite its significance for the success of so many community development interventions, the concept of household financial well-being is not widely adopted or even understood within the traditional community development field, let alone the many other fields that we hope will embrace it. This book is thus a clarion call for better integration at two levels. First, the asset development and community development fields must become more seamlessly integrated, enabling financial capability strategies to be incorporated into community development activities, such as affordable housing, small business, and workforce development. Second, the community and asset development field as a whole must better integrate with complementary sectors that serve the same population, such as public health, education, and public safety. We propose that financial well-being provides a useful starting point for integration at both levels.

THE FUTURE OF COMMUNITY AND ASSET DEVELOPMENT

This book, along with its predecessors, *Investing in What Works for America's Communities* and *What Counts: Harnessing Data for America's Communities*, examines the lessons of the community and asset development fields and lifts up the innovations. Together, these books and the collective voices they represent are building a unified narrative, asserting that the future of community and asset development must:

1. Adopt a "complex adaptive systems" approach: Communities are complex, as are the underlying factors that contribute to financial insecurity. In a community, everything is connected to everything else and interacts in ways that we cannot predict or control. According to Ronald Heifetz of Harvard's Kennedy School, two types of problems confront leaders: technical problems and adaptive challenges. With technical problems, the problem is often clear and there is a known expert who can provide a solution with some certainty of success. Putting a person on the moon is hard, but we know the parameters of the millions of calculations that are necessary to make it happen, and we have evidence of success, which can be replicated. Adaptive challenges like poverty, on the other hand, present problems that are often not well understood and require innovation, learning, and evolving strategies. No single expert holds a solution; rather, multiple stakeholders must be part of the discovery process, and change must occur in numerous places and across organizational boundaries. The community and asset development field must see its work as part of a larger, complex adaptive system; we are one of many fields seeking to make social change for the benefit of low-income people and places.

2. Integrate across sectors: In many ways, we have treated financial insecurity as a technical problem and have responded by creating a set of technical solutions, such as financial education classes or newly accessible financial services. Both of these are important interventions, yet as Levere and Tivol point out in their essay, these solutions did not fundamentally change the economic prospects of low-income individuals at scale, in part because the solutions did not meet people's complex financial needs. But we are evolving toward a more integrated approach that matches the problem's complexity. Strategies to build financial capability are now being integrated across multiple levels of state and local government (see essays by Landgraf, Reggie Bicha and Keri Batchelder, and Greg Fischer), nonprofits (see essays by Rubinger, Weech, and José Quiñonez), and the private sector (see essays by Mulot and Asheesh Advani). The work is also cutting across disciplines, recognizing the influence of financial well-being on multiple issues such as

housing, health, education, and employment. The interrelated nature of these outcomes demands the integration of strategy—isolated strategies have limited reach at best.

3 Strategies must address both people and place: For decades, community developers wrestled with the question of whether interventions should focus on people or place, and we now understand that this is a false distinction. The essay by Ray Boshara and those in Section 3 vividly demonstrate that personal characteristics and experiences, such as race, year of birth, or parental education, are critical drivers of financial opportunity. Yet, people are a product of their place, just as the place is a product of its people—it is impossible to untangle the two. As former Federal Reserve Governor Elizabeth Duke once said, "The debate is over and both sides won."[2] Margery Austin Turner of the Urban Institute argues for a "place-conscious" approach that "addresses the interconnections between family assets and challenges, conditions in the places [families] live, and access to opportunities in the larger city or region."[3] The field must continue to move toward an ecosystem approach that recognizes individual behaviors and their motivations within the context of place. We must help people learn to make good financial decisions, but we must also work on improving the conditions that enable them to make good choices, which is not just about financial services, but also employment, housing, transit, as well as the basic physical conditions that contribute to public safety and good health. For too long, asset building and financial capability has been squarely considered a people-based strategy; the essays in this volume by Glover Blackwell, Weech, Purnell, Rick Lazio, and others demonstrate that financial well-being is inherently about both people and place.

4 Be guided by data: Perhaps one of the most exciting breakthroughs highlighted in this book is the evolving conceptualization of financial health and well-being as a definable, measurable outcome that ties to many other important outcomes. As Tescher and Schneider articulate in their essay, "A common goal and a new framework for improving

---

2 Elizabeth Duke, "Foreword." In *Investing in What Works for America's Communities*, edited by Nancy Andrews et al. (San Francisco: Federal Reserve Bank of San Francisco and the Low Income Investment Fund, 2012).

3 Margery Austin Turner, "A Place-Conscious Approach Can Strengthen Integrated Strategies in Poor Neighborhoods." (Washington, DC: Brookings, August 2015).

household financial outcomes—one that is broad enough to transcend fields and industries—will enable the complicated universe of government, the private sector, and the nonprofit community to work in greater concert, and therefore, to achieve greater impact. We believe success should be defined as greater consumer financial health and well-being." Much work remains to develop consensus around the specific set of metrics by which to measure financial health and well-being, but setting and defining a goal is a critical first step. It allows us to begin to align efforts in joint action across sectors. This more comprehensive and holistic understanding of financial well-being is both objective and subjective and relies on compiling data from multiple sources to track multiple trends, including data from individuals themselves. New data from sources such as the Federal Reserve Survey of Household Economic Decisionmaking, the JPMorgan Chase Institute, CFSI's Consumer Health study, and the U.S. Financial Diaries enable us to better understand how people actually conduct their finances, while CFED's measure of liquid asset poverty demonstrates the widespread nature of financial insecurity. In addition, the integration of financial data into other data sets such as health and criminal justice provides a better understanding of the relationships between these outcomes and financial well-being. The community and asset development field should stay engaged in the discussion as we collectively build our understanding of financial well-being metrics and data for action. We also must do a better job of using the data to tell the compelling story that household financial well-being fundamentally matters for the success of almost all social innovation outcomes. Finally, we need the data to show the people we serve that they are making progress toward their goals.

5 DEVELOP NEW FUNDING STRATEGIES: We believe that any efforts to end poverty using the strategies we have outlined require a fundamental shift in how we finance social policy and practice. Community and asset developers must continue to seek innovations that result in the development of flexible financing that can cross organizational and sectoral boundaries and enable integrated approaches. We must also figure out how to capture the value and return on investment of improved financial well-being and its contribution to longer-term outcomes such as better health, less involvement in the criminal justice

system, and increased educational attainment, as the essays by Purnell, Stroud, and Vivian Nixon and Susan Sturm make clear.

In addition to working toward more flexible use of funding streams, outcomes-based funding holds the promise of better aligning expenditures and outcomes. Recently, some funders have begun withholding funding until after desired outcomes are produced, protecting themselves from program failure risk and encouraging program adaptation to keep pace with changing circumstances on the ground. "Pay for Success" contracts (alternatively known as Social Impact Bonds) are linking evidence-based nonprofits with government end payers and investors in a unique outcomes-based public-private partnership model. Other forms of outcomes-based financing include prize-based philanthropy and expanded pay-for-performance approaches in Medicare through the Affordable Care Act. Early efforts suggest that meaningful outcomes-based payment strategies are within reach. Although conceptually straightforward, a sector-wide shift toward outcomes-based payments will require, at a minimum: 1) government procurement reform; 2) robust program evaluation capacity; and 3) a financing solution to supply nonprofits with the working capital they need until they can be paid for improving outcomes.

THE DIFFICULTY OF OPERATIONALIZING THIS APPROACH

This vision for the future of community and asset development is necessarily ambitious but incredibly difficult to operationalize. A number of efforts that reflect these principles are blossoming across the country, such as Partners in Progress, Promise Neighborhoods, Purpose Built Communities, The Integration Initiative, and the Working Cities Challenge. Although most of these efforts do not view their work through the lens of financial well-being, they represent the types of integrated, cross-sectoral, and data-driven initiatives we envision for the future. Many of the practitioners engaged in this type of work have been forthcoming about the many challenges they face in operationalizing such complex approaches. Some of the most obstinate barriers include the difficulty of coordinating data systems and aligning metrics, as well as the existence of rigid funding silos, which makes it difficult to pay for integrated approaches. Both of these challenges are compounded by the difficulty of connecting near-term interventions with desired long-term outcomes. For example, there has been great interest in aligning the work of community development and public health to address the social determinants of health (see Purnell's essay), but it has been difficult to connect the impact of a short-term project, such as an affordable housing development, with the trajectory of population health, which unfolds over decades. Therefore, although the concept of integration makes intuitive sense over the long term, practitioners are struggling to figure out what the near-term steps should be.

FINANCIAL WELL-BEING AS A WAY STATION FOR MULTIPLE OUTCOMES

We believe that this daunting approach can be made more manageable by breaking it down into its component parts. That is the breakthrough we see in this book. No matter what your long-term goal may be, whether it is boosting high school graduation rates, improving health, promoting more viable families, or developing better workers for twenty-first century jobs, it requires families and communities to reach some threshold of financial well-being.

This makes household financial well-being an important intermediate step and useful organizing principle that allows different sectors to begin aligning their work. By starting to collectively recognize that financial well-being is often at the root of the myriad challenges other sectors work to solve over the long term, we can begin unifying around a common understanding of the next step forward. The beauty of household financial well-being as a conceptual framework is that it is both a stop on the road and a predictor of future success for so many other important outcomes. Put differently, the road that gets to those important outcomes runs through a way station of household financial well-being.

Starting with integration at the level of household financial well-being also has the advantage of allowing us to experiment with new business models, to learn how to act in concert with others, to measure our progress in a meaningful way, and, finally, to find ways to finance these efforts that solve the "wrong pocket problem," where the investors in one sector create value for another. As Eric Ries argues in *The Lean Startup*, innovation requires the ability to rapidly create prototypes and test and learn in real-time. This, too, is one of the benefits of the financial well-being framework, in that the field can rapidly test new approaches, such as innovations in financial coaching or integrated services, and hope to see near-term results in factors that influence financial well-being, such as credit scores or emergency savings.

We understand that social change takes time, yet we often lose hope when promising programs fail to deliver on their results. If you want to see dramatic improvements in the life chances of low-income people, you must be committed for the long haul. In some instances, it may take more than one generation to make a positive and permanent change. In a world of collective action and an understanding of poverty as a complex adaptive system, it can be overwhelming to know where to start. But household financial well-being is no doubt a starting point and building block for other goals.

TOWARD A NEW BUSINESS MODEL

Focusing on household financial well-being can help us break out of our silos—asset development, community development, health, education, public safety—and reach across sectors to achieve a common goal. We know we have to shift from outputs—the number of bank accounts opened or Head Start slots filled—and focus on outcomes—the numbers of lives improved. Breakthroughs in what is often referred to as "design thinking" are helping us think more holistically about the needs of the family, not our individual programs or products. As the former director of the Domestic Policy Council Melody Barnes said at our first Healthy Communities meeting in 2010, you do not wake up and have a "jobs" day, and the next day is a "transportation" day, and the next an "education" day; every day is an "everything" day. And learning how to provide the interventions a family needs, when they need it, to get on their feet and generate the hope for a better future, as Brandee McHale reminds us in her essay, is the outcome we want.

And of course, as we are successful in one stage of intervention, we must evolve and adapt to deploy new types of interventions in later stages. Once a family undergoes successful credit repair and builds sufficient liquid assets to weather financial unpredictability, it might be time to think about saving for a down payment on a house and developing their children's future-orientation by building college savings (as discussed in essays by Robert Friedman, Martha Kanter, and others in this book). Similarly, the neighborhood on the rebound may no longer need intense community policing, new bus lines, and a school turnaround, but as conditions improve, it must be on guard for new problems such as gentrification and displacement. This requires new partners, new tools, and new approaches.

CONCLUSION

These insights are teaching us how to tackle the next frontier of community and asset development—cross-sector, place-conscious, data-driven and coordinated interventions to empower families and communities to restore hope and a chance at a better future. One way to think about this evolution is to compare it to developments in economic history. There is no doubt that after the invention of agriculture, the Industrial Revolution is the most consequential change in human development. But it was many years before those who were undergoing it even realized it was happening; the term "industrial revolution" was not coined until 150 years after the invention of the steam engine.[4] That is an important lesson in itself—revolutions are hard to see when you are in the middle of them.

But in fact, there were two industrial revolutions. The first took place around 1740-1780 and primarily focused on textiles. It was relatively small in scale and almost every aspect of it required building new ways of doing things, or new systems. For example, the first factory in the United States was built by Samuel Slater in Pawtucket, Rhode Island. It used the power generated from a water wheel to produce cloth and clothing. But it was unclear how the labor would be organized, there was no way to raise money by selling stock, and there were few legal examples for how to organize the firm or protect workers. All of these processes had to be invented, along with new ways to ship raw materials and finished products, market and sell products, insure the process from calamity, and the like.

The Second Industrial Revolution took place in the late nineteenth century and reorganized economic life on a massive scale. It was dominated by steel, ship building, locomotives, chemicals, pharmaceuticals, consumer goods, and later automobiles. The scale dwarfed the First Industrial

---

4 Anna Bezanson, "The Early Use of the Term Industrial Revolution," *The Quarterly Journal of Economics*, 36 (2) (1922): 343-349.

Revolution, but the structure followed the early model closely. In other words, the financial, legal, and organizational systems that were developed for textiles provided the framework for the massive expansion of a new way of managing resources and the economy. The result was the most substantial gain in the standard of living the world had ever seen.

We want to build an "anti-poverty industry" that matches the scale and reach of the Second Industrial Revolution. But to get there, we need a First Industrial Revolution to establish the framework. Achieving widespread household financial well-being might be just that.

What is the way forward then? Begin by asking yourself whether a financially healthy client will be more likely to achieve the primary goals you're interested in. Then flip the question: what can I do to improve the financial well-being of the people I serve in order to achieve better outcomes in the things I care about? Who else is serving the same population, and how does financial well-being cut across our work? These are the foundations of finding meaningful partners—articulating and building shared interests—it is what allows cross-sector work to take shape. The challenge then is for communities to start this intentional linking and raise up champions of financial well-being from different sectors, such as leaders in philanthropy, health, education, and the public and private sectors. In the near term, we hope to see more efforts that build on the cutting-edge practice of complex initiatives, like Partners in Progress or Promise Neighborhoods, bringing together cross-sector leaders to build the financial health of a place and share lessons along the way.

In their book *Built to Last*, Jim Collins and Jerry Porras introduced the concept of the "Big Hairy Audacious Goal," or BHAG, which encourages organizations to define visionary 10-to-30 year goals to progress toward an envisioned future. The authors explain that "A true BHAG is clear and compelling, serves as a unifying focal point of effort, and acts as a clear catalyst for team spirit."[5] We believe that *achieving financial well-being for all* is an important BHAG for the entire community and asset development field, and an important intermediate threshold for the achievement of the longer-term BHAGs of other sectors, like health, criminal justice,

5 Jim Collins and Jerry Porras, *Built to Last: Successful Habits of Visionary Companies* (New York: Harper Business, 1994).

and education. Indeed, this work is big, hairy, and audacious, but reversing the current trends of widening inequality and financial insecurity require no less. We must continue to break down our silos and collectively lift up new data, new partners, and new insights to guide our way. After all, we are in the midst of a revolution.

■ ■ ■

LAURA CHOI *is senior research associate in Community Development at the Federal Reserve Bank of San Francisco, where she examines policy and practice related to the expansion of economic opportunity for lower-income individuals and communities. Her work focuses on issues of household financial stability, cross-sector community development, and regional trends in the Federal Reserve's 12th District. Prior to joining the Fed in 2008, Laura was project manager at Riverside Housing Development Corporation and spent a number of years in management consulting. She holds a BA in economics and a Master of Public Policy degree, both from the University of California, Berkeley.*

■ ■ ■

DAVID J. ERICKSON *is director of the Center for Community Development Investment at the Federal Reserve Bank of San Francisco and edits the* Community Development Investment Review. *Erickson has a PhD in history from the University of California, Berkeley and an undergraduate degree from Dartmouth College. His book on the history of community development,* The Housing Policy Revolution: Networks and Neighborhoods, *was published by the Urban Institute Press. He also co-edited* Investing in What Works for America's Communities *and* What Counts: Harnessing Data for America's Communities.

BUILDING THE OPPORTUNITY ECONOMY

Robert Friedman
CFED

[The objective of government is] to elevate the condition of men—to lift artificial weights from all shoulders—to clear the paths of laudable pursuit for all—to afford all, an unfettered start, and a fair chance, in the race of life.

—Abraham Lincoln

We start with the recognition of the capacity and productive potential of low-income and economically-marginalized people: they are all potential creators of wealth, whether as skilled workers, entrepreneurs, home owners, savers or investors. All of us have weaknesses and needs, but the truth is that meaningful development relies more on building on the strengths of people than on remedying their perceived deficiencies.

Since I founded the organization 36 years ago, CFED has undertaken, with support from many national foundations, a series of large national demonstrations informed by that asset-based thinking.[1] These have involved dozens of community groups and state and federal policy partners, and they have included rigorous evaluation research. The essential lesson is that given a reasonable opportunity, low-income people will save, go to college, start businesses, buy and keep homes, and build their families' economic futures, as well as those of their communities and the country as a whole.

Our earlier work was the outgrowth of two asset-building fields that emerged in the 1980s. They were parallel and largely separate, but, in

1 Examples are the Self Employment Investment Demonstration (SEID, 1986–90), the American Dream Demonstration (ADD, individual development accounts, 1992–1998), the Saving for Education, Entrepreneurship and Downpayments (SEED, including SEED OK, child savings accounts, 2002–present), and I'M HOME (manufactured housing, 2005–present).

a larger sense, joined at the hip. The first was spawned in the women's self-employment field and later encapsulated and impelled by Michael Sherraden's revolutionary *Assets and the Poor*. The second was the Asset-Building Community Development field inspired by John McKnight and his colleagues, built on the theories of Ivan Illich and Paolo Frieri, which insists on treating low-income and marginalized people as assets. Going forward, we should recognize the sisterhood of these two understandings of asset-building.

In the mid-1980s, CFED was charged with studying what worked in economic development. We entered that inquiry suspecting that some strategies—self-employment, training, business lending—might prove superior to others. Instead, we ended up concluding that *all* the strategies worked if they built the confidence, competence, connections, and capital of families.

These earlier foundational concepts have been incorporated in our current understanding of financial well-being and capability. As Andrea Levere and Leigh Tivol note in their introductory essay, the CFPB defines financial well-being as:

- Feeling in control of one's day-to-day finances;
- Having the capacity to absorb a financial shock;
- Being on track to meet financial goals; and
- Having the financial freedom to make choices to enjoy life.

These evolving concepts and lessons are helping us reimagine our work as well. What makes an individual or family financially capable and healthy is very similar to what makes a broader movement successful. In other words, we turned the microscope on ourselves and found that our ability to execute on what our clients needed required new ideas, new partners, and new resources. It requires a new coalition working together for a common cause.

We must integrate financial well-being into social services, housing, education, health, and workforce development programs—helping those fields understand the importance of their clients' financial well-being to the success of their programs. As we build these new relationships and business models, we are reminded of what we learned long ago: multiple strategies are successful if we instill confidence, build competence, extend connections, and add capital.

If we are successful in this broader movement, we will be doing more than helping people climb out of poverty. We will generate economic growth for the nation—building an "opportunity economy." We offer nothing less than opening the doors of this economy to all who would enter—as entrepreneurs, skilled workers, students, homeowners, and creators of wealth. Providing a realistic opportunity for every American to amass a few hundred or thousand dollars each year in liquid assets—if matched by their own work, dreams, saving, and effort—would be transformative. To do this work successfully, along with our partners from other sectors, would give individuals and families a much better chance to succeed and contribute. It would empower and embolden millions of low- and middle-income people and families to re-enter and revitalize the American economy.

If it were successful, this movement could redeem Abraham Lincoln's vision of government; it would create the opportunity economy, where everyone has a chance to play and to contribute his or her vision, talents, and dreams. And in that economy, everyone is better off.

CHALLENGES TO THE OPPORTUNITY ECONOMY

In all the rising talk about inequality, the extent and impact of *wealth* inequality is underappreciated. As the essays by Ray Boshara and Phil Longman (among many others) document, wealth inequality is larger and growing even faster than income inequality. The result, as research discussed by Jennifer Tescher and Rachel Schneider shows, is increasing financial stress and ill-health. Liquid asset poverty—the lack of assets to withstand even a short period without income—extends well beyond the poor, approaching half the population. As Phil English and Jeremie Greer demonstrate in this volume, this is an issue that is affecting a growing share of the American population, creating hardship and limiting opportunity in Red States and Blue States alike, a fact that explains why it draws concern across the political spectrum.

Nevertheless, that asset poverty extends so broadly should not blind us to the fact that its severity, its history, and its dynamics vary across the population. Although a majority of the population suffers liquid asset poverty, it is concentrated. Nearly two-thirds of African Americans, Latinos, and Native Americans experience liquid asset poverty, as do specific subgroups within the Asian American and Pacific Islander community to a lesser, but swiftly growing degree. Although each of these communities of color own just a few cents for every dollar owned by their white fellow citizens—a result of very different histories and structures—each may respond to different solutions. Asset poverty is similarly extreme among younger and older Americans, people with disabilities, ex-offenders, and foster children. Each group deserves its own attention and remedies, even as we build common understanding and solutions.

At a fundamental level, reducing wealth inequality and increasing economic mobility is about money. Especially among the asset-poor majority in this country, the price of entry to the economic mainstream is at least a few hundred to a few thousand dollars. Certainly, respecting the demands of history and justice and beginning to close the racial wealth gap will require developing significant asset bases among excluded and marginalized communities. The essays in Section 3 of this book show just how large that gap is. But if the practice and research of the last 25 years demonstrates anything, it is the power of even a few hundred dollars in disposable assets to unleash the dreams, energy, plans, and investment of families.

HOW DO WE GET THERE?

Julian Bond, a close associate of Dr. Martin Luther King, Jr., used to tell audiences not to confuse the Civil Rights movement with the triumphs like the 1963 March on Washington with its hundreds of thousands. He said that was rare. What built the movement was night after night of meetings in cold church basements with 20 or 30 committed people trying to find how they could contribute to change. It was small acts by ordinary people that added up to a stronger movement. It was a river that was fed by many streams.

Our movement must be fed by many streams, too. It is tempting to try to simplify our path forward by cleaving to one or the other of these streams of innovation and learning in the asset-building and antipoverty fields. But the truth is that the growth of the field has been defined by the interaction of these streams, often turbulent and messy, but essential and procreative. As we move forward, tackling the challenges and opportunities of scale, this interaction will be essential. It will be incumbent on leaders and laborers in the field to remain attuned to the inspirations, challenges, and lessons of the other tributaries. I will highlight thoughts on some of those interrelated strategies below.

One of the streams is savings. And here we have had great successes, such as the Individual Development Account (IDA). This asset-building tool, developed by Michael Sherraden, is elegant, powerful, and (deceptively) simple. It combines financial education with a concrete tool—a savings account—and then layers on another strategy of providing a financial incentive—a match to whatever the individual saves—to create the habit to save and build wealth.

Savings, of course, is much more than just a rainy day fund. It is a change in mindset. Liquid savings have proved to be a key gateway to each of these asset pathways, raising expectations, preparedness, and confidence even while providing the wherewithal to invest in each of these paths.

Children's savings accounts (CSAs), incentivized savings accounts starting as early as birth, which, almost alone among the college finance tools, build not only a college fund but also college expectations, preparedness, and family engagement, must be a critical part of the mix of solutions. The recently launched Campaign for Every Kid's Future seeks to make sure every child in America can be automatically enrolled in a CSA, setting expectations and aspirations that will have reverberations for generations.

Retirement savings rank among the most developed and subsidized class of assets, and a focus of current concern given the ballooning elderly population, most of whom lack adequate retirement savings. For many people, achieving retirement security requires a lifetime of effort, beginning with an early focus on emergency and education savings, and transitioning to entrepreneurship and homeownership in mid-life.

Whatever the power of IDAs and savings accounts, helping families maximize their potential raises a larger challenge and opportunity, which in turn demands a larger palette. Thinking beyond savings often leads to more expansive ideas such as the "household financial balance sheet" and the "Household Financial Security Framework," which embraced and rationalized the growth of the field, extending from financial education to earning, saving, and investing in key assets.

Perhaps the most important key asset is homeownership. Most household wealth, for example, derives historically from homeownership, bolstered by policies such as the creation of the 30-year fixed-rate mortgage by the Federal Housing Administration. This policy opened a powerful asset path for white Americans, even while—as Dedrick Asante-Muhammad points out in his essay—closing it off for many communities of color.

Home equity took a huge hit during the Great Recession, especially in communities of color, who lost up to one-half of their recent gains, plunging many families into debt and homes into foreclosure, and causing asset advocates and the larger community to question the preeminence, even the wisdom of homeownership as an asset-building path. Instead, I believe we must restore this historic source of economic mobility, underwriting as it does educational attainment, social stability and entrepreneurship. At the same time, as Rick Lazio argues persuasively in this volume, we must also devise better tools and policies that make it far easier for renters to build credit, savings, and equity.

Of course, savings and assets are necessary but insufficient pieces of an adequate answer; we must also make higher education more accessible and affordable. Education, especially postsecondary education, is generally recognized as the surest path to a living wage and economic mobility. But as Martha Kanter and Sarah Bloom Raskin suggest in their essays, the student debt crisis and the distressingly low college attendance and graduation rates, especially among low-wealth Americans and communities of color, demand an almost wholesale rethinking and remaking of how we finance postsecondary education and help students choose what is best for them. This includes, as an essential starting block of economic citizenship, CSAs. These progressive, universal accounts feature opt-out automatic enrollment, which catalyzes lifelong savings and lays an early foundation for financial capability where, as former IRS Commissioner Fred Goldberg explains, "everyone has a number and everyone plays."

Entrepreneurship is another key strategy for expanding the opportunity economy. Consider that business assets are second only to home equity as a contributor to household wealth. And entrepreneurship is the key to job creation and employment, as Chair Yellen points out in her foreword. Although most new businesses are financed with personal savings and the savings of friends, family, and associates, none of the current savings account systems—IRAs, 401(k)s, 403(b)s, 529 Plans, *my*RAs— explicitly allows accounts to be invested in entrepreneurship.

We must also remove the many barriers that keep low-income people from fully using their potential in the opportunity economy. One overlooked but critical barrier is citizenship, which generates substantial earnings, mobility, and vitality returns. Another is connecting the 54 million Americans with disabilities to the labor market through innovative new programs and technology. Today, people with disabilities, who compose one-fifth of the population, have a shockingly high unemployment rate of 73 percent.

CONTEXT MATTERS: MAKING THE FINANCIALLY SMART CHOICE THE EASY CHOICE

Many of the biggest innovations in financial capability during the last several years involve low-cost solutions, including opt-out automatic enrollment retirement systems, increased financial access through "Bank On" programs, behavioral economics-informed financial products and services, regulation of predatory lending, and integration of financial capability services within nonprofit and public social service, housing and education programs.

So too, we have learned that quite modest financial incentives can leverage significant changes. Where we once sought the multi-thousand dollar matches of IDAs, we now focus on $50 incentives for CSAs. Where we once sought 1:1 and 2:1 match rates, we now frequently think of 50 percent match rates and less.

We have made great progress in asset policy at all levels; viewed over time, the *Assets and Opportunity Scorecard* demonstrates steady gains in assets policies among states across the spectrum. But cheap policy is not necessarily cost-effective policy. Asset gaps are huge, and we will not even build adequate starting blocks on the cheap. IDAs are among the more expensive asset-building strategies, but the truly transformational nature of the outsized returns—homeless to homeowner, poor kid to college graduate, low-paid employee to independent entrepreneur—are well documented in rigorous evaluations.

HOW DO WE FUND THE OPPORTUNITY ECONOMY?

Where will the money come from to afford this investment in unleashing the productive capacity of tens of millions of Americans on the fringes of the economy? There are two great sources: our existing asset-building tax subsidies and the common assets of the American people.

The United States has a large existing tax policy to encourage asset building—more than half a billion dollars in annual income tax expenditures is devoted to subsidizing homeownership, retirement savings, higher education, business investments, and other types of assets. This subsidy averages out to approximately $1,600 for every man, woman, and child in the country annually.[2] However, as several essays in this book point out, 90 percent of Americans cannot take advantage of their share of this national investment. The system is regressive, wasteful, and counterproductive. Yet the opportunity inherent in this system is tremendous. Without spending any new funds—in fact, even slashing the existing asset tax budget substantially to fund deficit reduction or other needs—we could deliver $1,000 annual savings incentives to every man, woman, and child in this country. In doing so, we could expand the ranks of homeowners, college students, skilled workers, and entrepreneurs by tens of millions per year, generating widely shared growth, jobs, mobility, and economic well-being.

There are also significant assets we hold in common as citizens that could help fund policies and programs that build the movement toward an opportunity economy. Last year, for example, the Alaska Permanent Fund sent checks of more than $1,900 to every Alaskan citizen, their share of proceeds on the sale of the oil endowment of the state. Peter Barnes, in his book *With Liberty and Dividends for All*, argues for establishing similar

---

2 This is my calculation based on information in: Ezra Levin, Jeremie Greer, and Ida Rademacher, "From Upside Down to Right Side Up: Redeploying $540 Billion In Federal Spending To Help All Families Save, Invest, And Build Wealth." (Washington, DC: CFED, 2014).

state and national trusts, recognizing, monetizing, and democratically distributing income from assets that are best construed as belonging not to the public sector or private interests, but to all people in common. These include the carbon-absorbing capacity of the atmosphere, the liquidity of financial markets, and the like. He details how such a national trust could soon provide annual checks of $1,000 to $5,000 to every person in the country, providing a badly needed alternative source of income to stagnant wages, while also curbing greenhouse gas emissions and accomplishing other public purposes.

Although we have made inroads into building household financial well-being with relatively inexpensive programs and policies, meeting a goal of broad-based and equitable financial health cannot be done on the cheap. But what we get in return is more college graduates, fewer people relying on the social safety net, and more productive workers. This is an investment in our future that will yield many dividends. These large changes will take time in coming, however, which is all the more reason to place them squarely on the public agenda now, as the Tax Alliance for Economic Mobility has done.

CONCLUSION

It would be understandable if we in the asset-building field stuck to our knitting, focusing on incremental improvements in our tools, policies, and products. But, as Brandee McHale argues in this book, we cheat the necessity and opportunity of this agenda if we do not raise our sights. We must proceed with confidence in the untapped productive capacity of economically marginalized Americans, and indeed, the leaders in many other sectors, whose good work is represented by the essays in this book.

To build our field, to convert America's annual investment in inequality into an investment in the productive capacity of the American people, to do so with confidence, requires that we expand greatly the ranks of those who understand that building a path to financial health for all is not only a necessity for the well-being of each household, but also a necessary condition to the success of our economy and the systems that underpin it. As Ben Jealous, former President of the NAACP, said, "There are people who would care, if only they knew."

The asset-building and financial capability fields have grown greatly over the last three decades. Now, with economic inequality and mobility at the top of the national agenda across partisan lines, it is time to link our skills and tools with others. That means integrating new people and institutions. The housing, education, business, health, and social service fields are already beginning to see the importance of programs that build financial well-being. If every one of the tens of thousands of practitioners, researchers, policymakers, business leaders, social workers, and health care professionals reach out to a few colleagues, millions more people will become part of the movement toward financial health and well-being. Our success depends on them. And increasingly, they see their success depends on us.

This outreach will require, too, that we communicate better, clearer and more broadly. We must find language that communicates the basic concepts and importance of asset building, financial health and well-being to everyone, including representatives in the statehouses across the country and in Washington, DC. This will require that we unleash and harness the voices of the low-income entrepreneurs, homeowners, college students of color, and others who know first-hand the transformative power of financial health and building assets. Of course, we must harness the power of technology in all of this, too, not only in communications, but in product and market development as well.

This may all sound overwhelming. But it is very doable. Perhaps Gloria Steinem maps the path forward most clearly in her address on the eve of receiving the Presidential Medal of Freedom:

How do we move forward? It's not rocket science. We need to worry less about doing what is most important, and more about doing whatever we can. Those of us who are used to power need to learn to listen as much as we talk, and those with less power need to learn to talk as much as we listen. The truth is that we can't know which act in the present will make the most difference in the future, but we can behave as if everything we do matters.

[T]he end doesn't justify the means; the means are the ends. If we want dancing and laughter and friendship and kindness in the future, we must have dancing and laughter and friendship and kindness along the way.

At my age, in this still hierarchical time, people often ask me if I'm "passing the torch." I explain that I'm keeping my torch, thank you very much—and I'm using it to light the torches of others.

Because only if each of us has a torch will there be enough light.

Today we share our torch light. Today we lift artificial weights from all shoulders. Today we lock arm-in-arm with our partners in the health, education, community development, and other sectors to execute on a shared agenda. Today we strengthen a movement that builds opportunity for all. And, in turn, we will all benefit from a deeper shared prosperity.

■ ■ ■

ROBERT E. (BOB) FRIEDMAN *has helped lead the development of the assets and economic opportunity field for nearly four decades, pioneering self-employment, entrepreneurship, homeownership, education, savings practice, policy, market and research pathways. Bob founded and still works for CFED (Corporation for Enterprise Development) as General Counsel and Chair Emeritus, where he spearheaded major policy and practice initiatives like the Self Employment Investment Demonstration (SEID), American Dream Demonstration (ADD), and the Saving for Education, Entrepreneurship, and Downpayment (SEED) Policy and Practice Initiative. He helped found and Chair the Association for Enterprise Opportunity (AEO). He serves on the boards of Ecotrust, the Rosenberg Foundation, the San Francisco Foundation, the Friedman Family Foundation, and Child and Youth Finance International. He is a former board member of the Family Independence Initiative, EARN, Levi Strauss & Co. and the Levi Strauss Foundation. He is a graduate of Harvard College and Yale Law School, and a recipient of the Presidential Award for Microenterprise Excellence and the Council on Foundations Award for Philanthropic Innovation.*